PRIVATE EQUITY
AT WORK

PRIVATE EQUITY AT WORK

WHEN WALL STREET MANAGES MAIN STREET

Eileen Appelbaum and Rosemary Batt

Russell Sage Foundation · New York

The Russell Sage Foundation

The Russell Sage Foundation, one of the oldest of America's general purpose foundations, was established in 1907 by Mrs. Margaret Olivia Sage for "the improvement of social and living conditions in the United States." The Foundation seeks to fulfill this mandate by fostering the development and dissemination of knowledge about the country's political, social, and economic problems. While the Foundation endeavors to assure the accuracy and objectivity of each book it publishes, the conclusions and interpretations in Russell Sage Foundation publications are those of the authors and not of the Foundation, its Trustees, or its staff. Publication by Russell Sage, therefore, does not imply Foundation endorsement.

Library of Congress Cataloging-in-Publication Data

Appelbaum, Eileen, 1940–
 Private equity at work : when Wall Street manages Main Street / Eileen Appelbaum and Rosemary Batt.
     pages cm
 Includes bibliographical references and index.
 ISBN 978-0-87154-039-3 (pbk. : alk. paper) — ISBN 978-1-61044-818-5 (ebook)
 1. Private equity—United States. 2. Business enterprises—United States—Finance.
 3. Industrial management—United States. I. Batt, Rosemary L. II. Title.
 HG4751.A67 2014
 332'.04150973—dc23

2013041408

RUSSELL SAGE FOUNDATION
112 East 64th Street, New York, New York 10065
10 9 8 7 6 5 4 3 2 1

For Gene and Ron

═ Contents ═

List of Illustrations

About the Authors

Eileen Appelbaum is senior economist at the Center for Economic and Policy Research and visiting professor in the Department of Management, Leicester University.

Rosemary Batt is the Alice Hanson Cook Professor of Women and Work at the ILR School, Cornell University, and editor of the *ILRReview*.

=== Acknowledgements ===

We are grateful to all of the people who gave generously of their time and provided us with information for the book, including the partners at private equity firms, lawyers, pension fund managers and other private equity investors, union researchers and leaders, industry analysts, and others with specific knowledge of the issues we address. We are particularly grateful for the financial and intellectual support of Eric Wanner, former President of the Russell Sage Foundation, and Gail Pesyna, Vice President for Human Resources and Program Management, Alfred P. Sloan Foundation. Special thanks go to Todd Dickey and Jae Eun Lee at Cornell University, to Daniel Alvarado, Marie-Eve Augier, Mark Azic, Will Kimball, and Milla Sanes at CEPR, and to Peter Fogel at PitchBook for their able research assistance. We also thank Dean Baker, Ron Blackwell, Peter Cappelli, Ian Clark, Ellen Dannin, Stephen Diamond, and Arne Kalleberg for their valuable comments and feedback.

═ Chapter 1 ═

Private Equity:
Investors as Managers

Aidells Sausage Company was founded by Bruce Aidell in 1983. A microbiologist and foodie, he developed an artisanal line of chicken sausage products that were widely popular in the San Francisco Bay Area. In 2007 private equity firm Encore Consumer Capital bought the company, provided financial management and operational and marketing expertise, and dramatically expanded its market reach. The company had grown from 140 to 350 employees by 2010, when it was sold to Sara Lee.

Mervyn's Department Store chain was another well-known and popular brand serving the Bay Area and other cities throughout California when it was acquired by a private equity consortium led by Sun Capital Partners: in 2004 its 257 stores and 30,000 employees were acquired in a leveraged buyout worth $1.2 billion. The private equity firms paid $400 million of their own and their investors' cash and debt-financed $800 million using the company's assets as collateral. They soon sold off the property assets, retiring the debt backed by those assets and paying themselves back. The stores were required to lease back the property that housed their operations and pay inflated rents on facilities they had previously owned. The consortium then had the department store chain take on $400 million in additional debt and used the funds to pay dividends to its private equity owners. The store managers were required to make across-the-board job cuts and were unable to maintain long-term relations with vendors. Several rounds of top management left. Mervyn's filed for bankruptcy in 2008: the department store chain had a $64 million loss that year—less than the $80 million increase in rent payments following the buyout by private equity. Over the four years of private equity ownership, 30,000 people lost their jobs.

Private equity firms have emerged in the last three decades as part of a group of new financial actors—or "intermediaries"—that raise large pools of capital from wealthy individuals and institutions for investment funds.

1

These funds undertake risky investments that promise to deliver higher-than-average returns. Private equity funds buy out companies using high levels of debt—referred to as "leverage"—that is loaded onto the acquired companies. The use of debt to take over ownership of mature operating companies in leveraged buyouts and actively manage them are the characteristics that distinguish private equity funds from venture capital or hedge funds. Venture capital and hedge funds are also investment funds that mobilize private pools of capital, but their business models differ substantially from that of private equity.

Why Do We Focus on Private Equity?

We undertook an examination of private equity (PE) in this book because it is the financial intermediary that has the most direct effect on the management of mainstream businesses in the U.S. economy. In 2013, 2,797 private equity firms were headquartered in the United States, with investments in 17,744 U.S. companies, according to the Private Equity Growth Capital Council (PEGCC), the industry's association and chief lobbying group. Since 2000, PE-owned companies have employed some 7.5 million people. Roughly 35 percent of PE investments come from U.S. pension funds, especially public pension funds. Thus, the actions of private equity partners affect not only the employees in the companies they own and the suppliers with whom they do business, but also the retirement income of millions of working and retired Americans.

PE-owned companies are similar to publicly held companies in several ways. Both are under pressure to maximize short-term shareholder value and have an array of financial and organizational strategies to do this. But there are also fundamental differences between them that lead to differences in managerial risk-taking and in stakeholder outcomes. The financial structure and light legal regulation of private equity firms allow them to much more aggressively pursue shareholder value at the expense of others with a stake in the company—its suppliers, employees, customers, and creditors.

A key difference between publicly traded companies and those owned by private equity lies in the way partners in private equity firms are rewarded. In the leveraged buyouts undertaken by PE funds, about 70 percent is funded by debt and the remaining 30 percent by equity, which comes almost entirely from the funds' outside investors. The general partner (GP) in the PE fund, who is a partner in the private equity firm that sponsored the fund, makes the decisions about which companies to acquire for the fund's portfolio, how much debt to use, and how to manage the companies. General partners invest 1 to 2 percent of the equity in the PE fund but receive 20 percent of the returns once the fund achieves a "hurdle"—usually an 8 percent rate of return. The structure of these deals allows the

GPs to take high risks using other people's money. Their goal is to sell the portfolio company in three to five years at a higher price than they paid to acquire it. The downside of the extensive use of debt is that it increases the risk that the portfolio company will experience financial distress. On the upside, however, debt magnifies the returns to the private equity fund. The general partner, who has put up 2 percent or less of the equity, has little at stake if debt drives the acquired company into bankruptcy, but much to gain from a successful exit from the investment. This is a classic case of what economists call "moral hazard." The general partner who makes the decision to load the portfolio company with debt that it is obligated to repay bears very little of the potential costs associated with those risks.

Several other differences are worth highlighting. First, the companies that private equity firms take private are lightly regulated by the Securities and Exchange Commission (SEC) and thus are lightly subject to the same requirements for transparency and accountability as public companies. The general partners can require the portfolio companies to pay them personally, collecting "advisory fees" and "management fees" that can run into millions of dollars annually; no CEO of a publicly traded company can make any such requirement of the company's divisions or subsidiaries. The GPs can also use other financial engineering strategies that would be unacceptable for public corporations to undertake owing to their adverse reputational consequences and shareholder opposition. Second, investors in private equity funds turn over full decision-making power to the general partner of the fund and make a capital commitment for the life of the fund, typically ten years. As a result, PE general partners are not subject to the kind of immediate shareholder pressure or public scrutiny that public companies face. Shareholders in public companies are typically more risk-averse and can pull out their money at any time.

This difference in transparency and shareholder accountability allows private equity to take on substantially more debt than public companies. Private equity turns on its head the capital structure of the typical public corporation: the capital structure of a company acquired by a private equity fund is often 70 percent debt and 30 percent equity, whereas the structure of a publicly traded company is typically 30 percent debt and 70 percent equity. High debt is a high-risk strategy that, when successful, enables outsized returns for the private equity fund; but it also increases the likelihood of financial distress and bankruptcy for portfolio companies, especially in economic downturns. The empirical evidence we review shows that private equity–owned companies historically have had twice the bankruptcy rates of publicly traded companies, and these rates were particularly high after the economic recession of 2007 hit.

Third, the law treats PE firms and their funds as *investors,* even though they behave as *managers* of the companies they buy and sell and as *employers* of the people who work in those companies. PE funds both own and

Table 1.1   Differences Between Private Equity–Owned and Public Corporations

Dimension	Private Equity	Public Corporations
Risk-taking	High	Low
"Moral hazard"	High	Lower
Capital structure	70 percent debt, 30 percent equity	30 percent debt, 70 percent equity
Use of junk bonds	Considerable	Low
Asset sales for profits	Higher	Lower
Dividend recapitalizations	Frequent	Rare
Fees	Key part of earnings	No advisory fees
Taxes	Capital gains rate	Corporate rate
Legal oversight	Low	High
Transparency	Low	Higher
Accountability	Low	Higher

Source: Authors' compilation.

take control of companies, appoint boards of directors, hire and fire top executives, and set the direction of business strategy and employment policies. The general partners and their legal team often negotiate directly with unions in collective bargaining or demand concessions in wages and benefits as a condition of taking over the company. Unlike public companies, however, they are not held legally or publicly accountable for many of the outcomes of their decisions, a pattern we document throughout the book. When something goes wrong in a private equity–owned company, the negative reputational effect typically falls on the company itself, as the private equity owner is behind the scenes with little visibility.

The fundamental differences between private equity–owned and public corporations are summarized in table 1.1. When private equity firms take over companies, moral hazard problems often ensue because the general partners in these firms, in a position to make greater use of other people's money than their own, engage in high-risk behaviors. These include financial engineering strategies such as the substantial use of debt, junk bonds, and other high-risk financial tools; asset sales for profit; and dividend recapitalizations. They also charge large fees not available to public corporations, are taxed at the lower capital gains rate rather than the corporate tax rate, and face little legal oversight—leading to low transparency and accountability.

In sum, the private equity business model represents a test of the notion that pursuing shareholder value aggressively is a good thing by putting the shareholders even more in charge. The argument is that leaving executives in charge of decisions about how companies should be run is problematic because managers have interests that are independent of those of the owners. What happens when decision-making is taken out of the hands of executives and investors take charge of business strategy and operations to a greater extent, as the proponents of the private equity business model propose? The results matter because they inform the broader debate about the consequences of advancing shareholder interests and power even further.

Private equity's controversial business model has ridden at least three waves of major public debate. In the 1980s, leveraged buyouts (LBOs) were viewed as a panacea that solved the problems of the waste inherent in diversified conglomerates and the misalignment of investor and manager interests—a panacea that ended in scandal, disappointing returns, and disgrace by the end of the decade. LBOs seemed to disappear until their reincarnation as private equity in the early 2000s. Suddenly, in the boom years of 2005 through 2007, the media was awash with stories of brilliant financial management and dramatic returns to investors while labor unions took aim at private equity's destruction of jobs and accused the industry of asset stripping and vulture capitalism. With the onset of financial crisis in 2007, public concern shifted to systemic risk and banks that were "too big to fail," and private equity again became a small side show. That changed in 2012 when Mitt Romney became the Republican presidential candidate. His record as a founder and leader of the private equity firm Bain Capital became a centerpiece of debate when credible investigations revealed a series of bankruptcies and job losses in companies bought out by Bain.

In each round of debate, advocates and critics have presented polarized views of private equity's contributions to, or destruction of, the American economy. The Private Equity Growth Capital Council highlights case studies and sponsors research to show how private equity has turned around distressed companies, provided operational expertise, and infused small-cap and mid-cap businesses with the sophisticated management and resources they need to expand to new levels of development. Investigative journalists, trade unions, community advocates, and bankruptcy courts have countered with evidence of healthy companies that fell into distress and bankruptcy when private equity owners loaded them with debt, stripped their assets, and privileged short-term cost-cutting over long-term growth.

How can a single type of investment fund using the same business model yield such polar opposite results? What is private equity, and how does it make money? How much does it influence the U.S. economy, and why does it matter?

This book provides an accessible roadmap to private equity at work. We sort out the evidence on what private equity does, how it makes money, and how it affects the companies it buys, the suppliers and employees it hires, and the creditors and investors it draws on. The book addresses public debates about the role of private equity in the U.S. economy. It informs research in the fields of management and organizations, human resource studies, and labor and employment relations, where the impact of capital markets and ownership structures on companies is of great interest but studies of specific actors is thin. It provides research-based recommendations for public policy changes that could reduce the excessive use of financial engineering strategies and encourage wider use of strategies that improve operations and thus lead to more beneficial outcomes for the wide range of stakeholders involved—the PE-owned companies, their creditors, employees, vendors, and pension funds, and the limited partners who invest in private equity funds.

The Organization of the Book and Findings

In chapter 2, we begin by placing private equity in context and linking its emergence to the deregulation of financial markets, labor markets, and industries and to the rise of agency theory and the shareholder value model of the corporation. Those changes helped reduce the importance of the "managerial business model"—in which returns are generated through productive activities overseen by professional managers—and facilitated the emergence of the financial business model in which companies are viewed as assets to be bought and sold for the sole purpose of maximizing profit. We trace the history of the private equity business model, which took shape in the leveraged buyout movement of the 1980s, reemerged in the late 1990s, and expanded dramatically in the mid-2000s.

This new model of ownership and control poses a challenge to the conventional understanding of the nature of work and employment relations in modern capitalist economies. Most research on management, organizations, and employment relations draws on a concept of the corporation as it operated under "managerial capitalism." This model assumes that management strategies and control of labor and the production process are the keys to creating and extracting value in nonfinancial corporations. In a financial business model, by contrast, value creation and extraction occur through a wider variety of financial and operational mechanisms inside and outside of companies that affect workers in their roles not only as producers but as customers, taxpayers, and community members. This financial business model, as exemplified by private equity, requires a reexamination of assumptions about the nature of the corporation and the capital accumulation process and an exploration of how and why these changes alter the management of productive enterprises.

In chapter 3, we turn to a detailed description of the private equity business model and how PE firms and their investors make money. We present the classic or "generic" model, while recognizing that PE firms do

Figure 1.1   The Structure of Private Equity: Firms, Funds, and Portfolio Companies

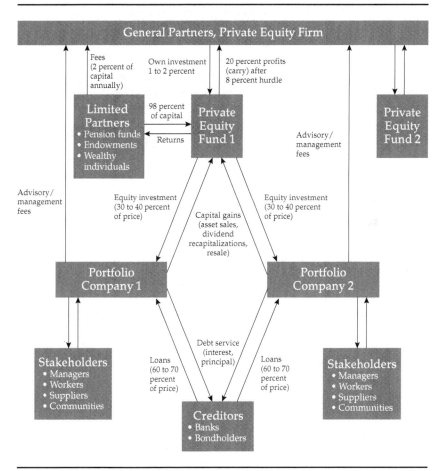

Source: Adapted from Watt 2008.

vary somewhat in their strategies and incentive structures. It is particularly important to recognize that the PE model is multilayered, operating at the level of the private equity *firm,* the *funds* that it sponsors, and the portfolio *companies* that the funds buy (see figure 1.1). At the firm level, private equity is typically structured as a limited liability partnership that in its operations resembles a diversified conglomerate but with centralized control of legally separate portfolio companies; this structure reduces the legal liability of the firm and its funds for the companies in the funds' portfolios. With the portfolio companies of most private equity firms located in many different industries, private equity's expertise is typically financial, not operational. It takes advantage of economies of scale and market power and focuses on maximizing shareholder value at the level of the *PE firm* across all of its funds and portfolio companies.

At the level of the fund and its portfolio companies, private equity adopts the precepts of agency theory, which argues that concentrated ownership, the use of high levels of debt to discipline expenditure decisions, and managerial pay tied to shareholder value allows shareholders to monitor managers and better ensure that they act in the shareholders' best interests. But the PE model takes the idea of "concentrated shareholders" to the extreme by linking ownership more tightly to control: the general partner of the private equity fund decides which companies to acquire, sets the strategic direction for those companies, typically appoints members to the portfolio company's board of directors, and is also a member of the board himself. Executives of portfolio companies are handsomely rewarded if they meet performance targets set by the GP—and quickly dismissed if they fail. The investors, or limited partners in the PE fund, who are shareholders of each of the portfolio companies the fund owns, have little or no influence over which companies are acquired or how they are managed, but they may enjoy benefits not available to shareholders in publicly traded companies.

Our case studies show how this concentration of ownership and control allows the general partners to make money through financial engineering strategies that substantially increase the level of debt in portfolio companies as well as through business and operational strategies that reduce costs or add value to the enterprise. The relative mix of strategies depends importantly on the focus of the PE firm and the size of the portfolio company. Small and midsize companies, with enterprise values of under about $300 million, offer less collateral for leveraging debt and better opportunities for operational gains. Larger companies that already have professional managers and sophisticated systems in place, especially those with enterprise values over $500 million or $1 billion in value, offer fewer easy opportunities for operational improvements but have more assets that can be used as collateral to support high levels of debt. These larger companies offer more opportunities to use tax arbitrage, sell assets, cut costs, outsource operations, and access junk bonds for additional dividend distributions. In the years leading up to the 2007 financial crisis, private equity firms also made a lot of money by simply buying low and selling high, riding a rising stock market and the overall increase in the prices of operating companies in the bubble economy.

The financial crisis, however, undermined many of the assumptions of the classic private equity model, as we discuss in chapter 4. The high leverage that was critical to outsized earnings in good times left many PE-owned companies in financial distress when the economy contracted.

And while bankruptcies increased for publicly traded companies during the crisis, they skyrocketed for those owned by private equity because of the larger debt load they carried. And because exiting companies became harder, PE firms held on to companies longer than their three- to five-year targeted time frame. Fund-raising for new investments was also more difficult, and banks were less willing to make loans. As it became more difficult to find "good" companies to buy, PE firms ended up with unspent funds that the limited partners had already committed (known as "dry powder").

The poor performance of funds, slower exits, excess dry powder, and continued payment of management fees in the years following the financial crisis led to dissatisfaction among the limited partners. Private equity firms coped by devising a range of strategies. They refinanced many of their loans through "amend and extend" agreements; relied more on management fees than profits from the sale of their companies; and made greater use of dividend recapitalizations, loading portfolio companies with more debt in order to pay dividends to themselves and their limited partners. They made greater use of secondary buyouts—one PE firm selling a portfolio company to another PE firm. And they diversified their asset base by seeking funds from new investors, such as Sovereign Wealth Funds, while at the same time chasing new investment opportunities in emerging-market economies. Investments in distressed companies, which generally represented only 1 or 2 percent of PE investments prior to the crisis, increased somewhat during this period.

In the postcrisis period, many private equity firms tried to shift their emphasis to operational strategies. Given the difficulty in closing mega-deals, which had been much easier to pull off in the bubble years, they turned to the middle market. The middle market for private equity buyouts, however, is as amorphous as the middle class in U.S. politics. Deals valued at anywhere between $25 million and $1 billion are classified as the "middle market."

In chapter 5, we disaggregate the middle market into different segments and examine how differences in the size of private equity firms and the deals they make are associated with differences in the relative use of operational and financial engineering strategies. The classic large PE firm uses its financial skills for competitive advantage and focuses on maximizing short-term efficiencies to produce outsized returns. Smaller PE firms with fewer assets may be viewed as niche players with somewhat longer time horizons. They tend to buy smaller companies and to specialize in particular industries or areas of expertise. Opportunities for operational improvements are greater and collateral for leverage is lower in companies valued at less than about $300 million. In addition, banking deregulation has led to a consolidation of banks into large banks and "mega-banks" that are less likely to provide credit to small and midsize companies. Private equity has filled this vacuum,

often combining financing with access to management and industry expertise. Here the PE general partner can establish a strategic direction, provide
resources for operational improvements and expansion of the market to
a regional or national level, and help the company grow. Our cases also
show that making private equity pay off in this segment is difficult because
PE firms cannot rely on high levels of debt to boost returns; they also need
deep industry knowledge to set the strategic direction of the company and
guide operational and marketing improvements. While these strategies
are more common among PE firms operating in the middle market, we
also found many examples of private equity failures due to mismanagement or a cookie cutter–like reliance on financial engineering.

In chapter 6, we assess the evidence on private equity fund performance
and the returns to limited partners, net of management fees, expenses,
and carried interest. Because there is no publicly available or comprehensive data on private equity, all studies of performance suffer from
incompleteness and biases, and different methods of calculating returns
yield different results. That being said, some data sets and methodologies are more credible than others. Reports that PE funds substantially
outperform the stock market come almost entirely from industry sources,
and these reports use the internal rate of return as the measure of performance. This measure is deeply flawed for several reasons, including
the fact that it is an absolute rather than a relative measure—it does not
take into account the alternative uses of funds that might generate higher
returns. More rigorous academic studies compare the returns achieved
by private equity relative to one or another stock market index. Here
the results are far more modest: Although top-quartile funds do provide
outsized returns, most pension funds and other investors do not have
access to these PE funds. The top-quartile performing funds are largely
accessible only to the large institutional investors with deep relationships
with the leading PE firms. The returns earned by the majority of PE funds
do not compensate limited partners for the added risk and illiquidity of
PE investments.

Our review of the academic research covers the most credible studies
by top finance scholars, who in the main do not rely on the internal rate
of return to measure PE fund performance. Some studies report that the
median private equity fund does not beat the stock market, and others
show that returns for the median fund are only slightly above the market. The most positive academic findings for private equity compare
its performance to the S&P 500: They report that the median fund outperforms the Standard & Poor's 500 by about 1 percent per year, and
the average fund by 2 to 2.5 percent. The higher average performance is
driven almost entirely by the top quartile of funds—and particularly the
top decile. With the exception of the top-performing funds, returns do
not cover the roughly 3 percent additional return above the stock market

that is required to compensate investors for the illiquidity of PE investments. When PE funds are compared to indices of smaller publicly traded companies whose size is comparable to most PE-owned portfolio companies (the S&P 500 comprises much larger corporations), then the average PE fund barely performs better, and the median fund just matches stock market returns.

Our case studies also show the range of effects that private equity can have on the level of employment in the companies they own, a theme we turn to in chapter 7. Private equity typically acquires companies in which employment is growing. It has both created jobs through operational improvements and growth strategies and destroyed jobs via the closing of establishments, across-the-board cuts, downsizing, and outsourcing. Private equity's overall impact on U.S. employment is the net effect of job creation and job destruction, but it is difficult to construct national data to assess this question. We examine the small number of rigorous econometric studies using credible data that have been undertaken. Overall, these studies show that PE-owned companies destroy more jobs than they create relative to comparable publicly traded companies. In addition, these studies find that private equity firms tend to acquire healthy, better-performing companies rather than those suffering financial distress. That is, job loss in PE-owned companies is not due to the fact that these companies were distressed to begin with.

The union strategies of private equity firms are varied and complex, as demonstrated in our case studies across a wide range of industries and unions, from steel and autos to aerospace, food distribution, utilities, and hospitals. While some PE firms market themselves as union-friendly, others are hostile, and still others are agnostic. Their range of attitudes does not seem to differ substantially from those of U.S. employers more generally. Their control of employment relations is evident in the prominent role they have played in collective bargaining negotiations with unions. In some cases, negotiations between private equity owners and unions are constructive and produce positive outcomes for all parties, while in others, despite constructive relations, the leveraged debt model of private equity has left the company in financial distress, facing bankruptcy or a questionable future. In other cases, new PE owners have deunionized plants, while in still others unions have successfully mobilized against new owners and achieved successful contracts and more positive labor-management relations. What ties private equity employers together is their determination to extract higher-than-average returns compared to public corporations. For union workers, this often means giving up wages and benefits that they have fought hard to win and maintain. And in some cases, PE owners may be behind a portfolio company's decision to resort to bankruptcy courts and shift pension liabilities to the Pension Benefit Guarantee Corporation (PBGC).

U.S. unions have positioned themselves in a contradictory and complex relationship with private equity. On the one hand, PE owners often increase their returns by reducing head-count or wages or by jettisoning pension benefits for workers in the companies they control—a pattern we observe in chapter 7. On the other hand, public-sector and union pension funds have increasingly invested in private equity funds and now represent more than one-third of all investor commitments—the subject of chapter 8. In both cases, whether representing active workers or pension fund beneficiaries, unions are in an asymmetric relationship with private equity firms, which are in a more powerful position to dictate the terms of the agreements with unions. As limited partners in PE funds, pension fund trustees commit to invest in a fund for a period of ten years, during which time they typically pay an annual 2 percent management fee, but as previously mentioned, they have no say in investment decisions and may receive insufficient information regarding how decisions are made. This insufficient transparency in PE decision-making puts particular pressure on pension fund trustees to carry out due diligence and ensure that the PE fund is acting in the best interests of its current and future beneficiaries. We conclude by evaluating whether a series of reforms proposed by the Institutional Limited Partners Association (ILPA) are sufficient to improve the bargaining power of limited partners and their ability to act in the best interests of their fund participants.

In the final chapter of the book, chapter 9, we consider the role of public policy in reining in the excesses of private equity firms. In general, the financial engineering practices of PE firms are legal. Yet they may compromise the competitiveness of companies or even lead to financial distress or bankruptcy, eliminating jobs and pension benefits for workers and retirees. The policies we consider would retain the ability of private pools of capital to invest in and support the development of productive enterprises, while limiting the practices that undermine company sustainability and jobs. Our policy proposals would reduce the incentive to overburden portfolio companies with debt; improve transparency for limited partner investors; protect vendors, suppliers, and other unsecured creditors against the reckless transfer of portfolio company resources to PE owners; help ensure that PE firm partners pay their fair share of taxes; and update laws passed by Congress to protect workers so they take account of this new form of corporate ownership and governance, in which investors not only own but actively manage their portfolio companies.

In sum, private equity has emerged as a new financial player in the last forty years. Its business model represents an extreme form of the shareholder value model of the firm, substantially different from the business model of public corporations because of the moral hazard that is embedded in its approach to generating high returns. PE firms have benefited from lax regulation and a tax code that privileges debt over equity while the risks they take in pursuit of outsized profits affect the economic outcomes of thousands of companies employing millions of workers across the U.S. economy. The effects of their actions extend beyond the portfolio companies they own to suppliers, creditors, consumers, and communities.

In this book we document the investment and management activities of private equity, both where it has provided resources for operational improvements and growth and where it has extracted value at the expense of other stakeholders. We summarize the evidence regarding the economic returns to investors, the employment outcomes for workers, and the dilemmas for pension fund managers. Our policy discussion is meant to inform current debates and provide a roadmap for strategies to encourage the positive role of private pools of capital in the economy while constraining the moral hazard that leads to more negative results. Given the substantial and ongoing influence of private equity in the U.S. economy, it is in the interest of the general public, policy makers, and social science researchers to understand how the private equity business model works and how these investors have become managers.

═ Chapter 2 ═

Institutional Change and the Emergence of Private Equity

The private equity business model of the 2000s emerged out of the shareholder-value revolution and the leveraged buyout (LBO) movement of the 1970s and 1980s. Shareholder-value maximization represents a fundamental shift in the concept of the American corporation—from a view of it as a productive enterprise and stable institution serving the needs of a broad spectrum of stakeholders to a view of it as a bundle of assets to be bought and sold with an exclusive goal of maximizing shareholder value. Investor takeovers of corporations through leveraged buyouts—in which a small number of investors buy out other investors using high levels of debt—represent a direct form of maximizing shareholder value. These investors assume responsibility for managing the company, take it private, obtain maximum returns through high dividends, asset sales, and other innovative financial strategies, and exit the investment via a sale of the company to the public (an initial public offering, or IPO), to another company (a strategic acquirer), or to another private equity fund.

In this chapter, we examine how and why private equity emerged as an important force in the 2000s and why it is important today. To understand the origins of private equity, we begin with a brief discussion of how the prior managerial business model worked and why it unraveled. A series of institutional changes in the United States from the 1950s on—both outside and inside the industrial corporation—undermined the system of managerial capitalism established over the prior fifty years, facilitating the emergence of a financial model of business organization and management—or financial capitalism.

Externally, legal changes altered the financial environment in which firms operated. Financial deregulation ended the historic segmentation of the financial services industry, thereby fostering the disintermediation of basic banking services and the ensuing disruption of traditional relations between banks and corporations. Corporate, tax, and pension laws were modified in ways that enabled financial institutions to pool large amounts of capital and make it available for financial innovation rather than keep it tied to corporation-initiated equity and bond offerings. In accordance with their new deregulatory stance, government regulators chose not to regulate the new financial intermediaries created to assemble and manage large capital pools. Legal changes were accompanied by a new theory of firm management and control developed by finance economists to challenge prior legal theories. "Agency theory" provided the theoretical underpinnings for successive movements to replace corporate managers with investor-managers: the leveraged buyout movement in the 1980s and its sequel in the 2000s, private equity.

These developments in the external environment were complemented by fundamental shifts in the structure of power and decision-making within large corporations.[1] Labor's bargaining power weakened as trade liberalization put blue-collar workers in many industries in competition with low-wage labor in less-developed countries. And more aggressive anti-union strategies undermined unions' ability to organize or deliver contract gains. In the pivotal decade of the 1980s, a new generation of financiers invaded the management-controlled corporation through leveraged buyouts, installing the new models of financial engineering that are at the heart of finance-based models of management. In the 1990s, Wall Street thoroughly institutionalized the shareholder-value model of corporate management by diffusing this model across the nonfinancial sectors of the economy.

By the 2000s, multiple factors had combined to allow private equity firms to reemerge as a powerful force. The scandals of the LBO movement were forgotten, but the scandals associated with public corporations like Enron were fresh. The Public Company Accounting Reform and Investor Protection Act of 2002, also known as the Sarbanes-Oxley Act, had put new reporting requirements on public companies, spurring incentives to take them private. The junk bond market was firmly established, shareholder-value management was widely accepted, further banking deregulation had created even larger private pools of capital, and new unregulated financial instruments, such as derivatives and credit default swaps, had enhanced speculative activity. Private equity firms took advantage of this confluence of factors to reconstruct and expand the old LBO model of investor takeovers, increase its scale and scope, and become a powerful force in the economy in the 2000s.

The Managerial Business Model and Its Decline

The managerial model of capitalist enterprise depended on the market stability created by securities laws, which were put in place during the New Deal to limit speculative behavior. The structure of decision-making and the successful growth of large corporations depended on the separation of ownership and managerial control, which had emerged as an effective model in the railroad industry in the 1920s.[2] Because ownership shares were widely dispersed, shareholders had little influence over decision-making. In an ongoing debate from the 1930s on, Adolf Berle and Gardiner Means argued that the managerial model ignored shareholder interests, while Harvard law professor Merrick Dodd argued that the purpose of the corporation was to provide jobs and consumer goods and to benefit society more broadly.[3] By 1954, Berle admitted that the managerial model had won.[4]

Since then, business historians have shown that this separation of ownership and control enabled managers to control the accumulation of capital and use retained earnings for investments in technology, machinery, skills, and R&D or for the strategic acquisition of other companies.[5] They developed human resource practices, or internal labor-market rules, that allowed workers to accumulate firm-specific skills through job ladders that also provided secure jobs and built loyal workforces.[6] Corporations hired and internally trained professional managers and experts to develop new products and processes, enhance growth, and expand market share. Managers were motivated to advance innovations for long-term improvements because internal labor markets provided opportunities for promotion, income growth, status, and long organizational careers.[7] Their individual careers and identities were tied to organizational success. As Gordon Donaldson found in his study of Fortune 500 companies, managers did not seek to maximize shareholder wealth per se, but rather corporate wealth, or "the aggregate purchasing power available to management for strategic purposes during any planning period."[8] In the process, they created large-scale production facilities and mass distribution of goods and services to a growing middle class. They financed innovation and expansion primarily through retained earnings. Wall Street was at the service of Main Street as shareholders benefited from a steady stream of dividends,[9] and workers gained from rising wages that supported the growth of mass consumption.[10]

This argument is not meant to paint the managerial business model as ideal: large corporations have faced their share of opportunistic managers and labor-management conflict. In the postwar period, however, employers largely abided by labor laws, if grudgingly, and union contracts linked wage growth to productivity growth, fueling demand for mass-produced goods. Large non-union corporations imitated the employment practices of union firms to avoid unionization.[11] Relative prices tracked productivity gains, falling in industries where productivity rose.[12] As a result, employees and consumers shared in the gains from productivity growth.[13] At the same time, primary service industries such as banking, telecommunications, airlines, transportation, health care, and education were highly regulated, producing wide distribution of basic services, and service labor markets were primarily local and shielded from broader competition.

This managerial model prevailed from the 1950s to the 1970s. Its dismantling has been linked to the rise of the diversified conglomerate[14] and the fall in the rate of return on capital, which plummeted from about 12 percent in 1965 to just over 6 percent in 1979.[15] Diversified conglomerates emerged in part in response to the 1950 Celler-Kefauver Act, an antitrust law designed to limit the elimination of competition by firms through vertical integration (when companies acquire their supply and/or marketing chains) as well as through horizontal integration (when companies buy out their competitors). Corporations responded to Celler-Kefauver by diversifying into unrelated businesses, and some very large conglomerates soon emerged. This business model was viewed as economically profitable, as corporations used their retained earnings to buy and sell a portfolio of companies and spread risk across diverse industries.[16]

The new conglomerate model undermined the managerial model in several ways. First, companies that bought unrelated businesses often lacked the industry expertise or competence to run those businesses. Second, as stock options became a growing part of compensation for executives in top corporations by the 1960s and 1970s, their allegiance shifted from "managers of organizations" to "individualistic owners of shares" with less identification with long-term goals.[17] Third, in the internal struggle for control of the corporation, finance managers assumed a more powerful role in part because financial metrics could be compared across radically different lines of business and because profits dramatically fell in the 1970s. Whereas business unit managers had been measured and motivated by excelling in product-specific divisional performance, they now were "managed by the numbers."[18] With less control over their own budgets, line managers lost the power to affect the direction of their business units. Managerial incompetence and opportunism were also less visible in these sprawling organizations, and financial performance did decline. Moreover, under the conglomerate or portfolio model of the corporation, mergers and acquisitions (M&As)—the frequent buying and selling of companies—became a central focus, creating a new norm of viewing companies as assets to be bought and sold.[19] As these developments undermined the power of line managers to make strategic decisions, the concept of the enterprise shifted from that of a production and marketing function to that of a finance model in which chief financial officers (CFOs) gained control.[20]

Shareholder Value and Agency Theory as Solutions

The low profitability of U.S. conglomerates, coupled with the economic recession and stagflation of the 1970s, led to shareholder disgruntlement, a critique of corporate managers and the managerial model, and a movement to improve shareholder returns. That movement received academic approval in a widely influential 1970 article by Milton Friedman, published in the *New York Times*. His argument—that maximizing profits is the only responsibility of corporations—rapidly gained adherents and spawned a generation of writing on corporate law and economics. Michael Jensen and William Meckling and other economists applied economic theory to corporate law to develop an "agency theory" of the firm.[21] In this theory, shareholders are the "principals" and residual claimants of the corporation, while the directors and corporate managers are the "agents" who must act on behalf of the shareholders and maximize their profits.

Agency theory turned corporate law on its head, according to critical legal scholars, who argue that, by law and precedent, corporations are "juridical persons," and when they are established, the founders must appoint a board of directors that acts on their behalf and may issue stock. Corporations exist before shareholders. The corporate directors are the "principals" and the shareholders are the "agents" who enter into a contract to purchase stock, similar to others who have a contractual relationship with the corporation—bondholders, suppliers, or employees. Under law, corporations are required to conduct business in a legal manner and shareholder value is but one of many purposes. No court has sanctioned a board of directors for failing to issue dividends or maximize shareholder value.[22]

Agency theory nonetheless became the dominant perspective that guided corporate and investor actions in the 1980s and helped launch "shareholder-value management," which has become a taken-for-granted axiom. It legitimated the view that maximizing shareholder value—particularly share price—is the exclusive goal of the corporation. In this view, the principal cause of the low profitability of corporations is the principal-agent problem. Opportunistic managers (the agents), with control over decision-making, are able to make decisions that favor their own interests at the expense of shareholders (the principals) because the latter are dispersed and unable to sufficiently monitor or control managerial decisions.[23] When investment and other spending decisions are financed out of retained earnings, managers do not have to demonstrate that the payoff to such spending justifies the expenditure, as they would if they needed to borrow the funds. That is, managerial decisions about the use of retained earnings are not subject to a market test of whether they are in fact the best use of these funds. Managers, not markets, allocate capital.[24]

The agency theory argument is that managers, especially those in low-growth industries, should return free cash flow to shareholders and use debt to finance new investment. This approach subjects investment projects to scrutiny by financial firms and to a market test for efficiency.[25] Mature firms, in particular, are likely to have accumulated assets that can be used as collateral when they borrow, and their high free cash flow can repay the debt without creating financial distress.[26] Moreover, the necessity to repay debt keeps managers focused on cost reduction and maximizing shareholder value—what Jensen refers to as "the control function of debt."[27]

To curb managerial opportunism, shareholders need to take a more active role in controlling managers, according to agency theory. Corporate raiders do this directly by forming a small group of activist investors, purchasing the undervalued stock of a company, unseating the CEO and corporate board, and changing the company's management strategy. Raiders implement an investment strategy for the company that adheres to their approach in acquiring the company: financing the purchase of new companies through leveraged buyouts. By loading the acquired company and its new divisions with debt, raiders demonstrate that the company's new management is subject to the "discipline of the market." Thus, agency theory provided the rationale for the 1980s wave of hostile takeovers financed by LBOs. In turn, hostile takeovers provided all firms with the new model of management behavior required to satisfy financial markets—a model to be implemented by manager-agents whether or not activist investor-principals were directly involved in the implementation process.

New theories of compensation were handmaidens to agency theory. To make managers think and act like owners, one had to turn them into owners. By linking their pay to generous stock options, their self-interest and identities as individual shareholders trumped their identities as organizational professionals.[28] Incentives to increase share price in the short term outweighed incentives to invest retained earnings over the longer term in new technologies, work processes, or innovations. Following the 1990 *Harvard Business Review* article by Michael Jensen and Kevin Murphy promoting pay for performance, executive stock option pay exploded in the 1990s.[29] The logical flaw in the academic theory, however, is that unlike shareholders, top managers do not invest their own money—and thus there is no downside risk. In addition, virtually the only metric used to measure corporate performance is share price.

Finally, while agency theory and compensation theory addressed the restructuring of corporate management through the realignment of managerial interests with investor interests, they did not deal with business strategy. That came from strategic management scholars, who advanced a theory of competitive advantage based on the "core competency" model of the firm.[30] C. K. Prahalad and Gary Hamel argued that in contrast to the conglomerate approach, firms could become "best in class" by focusing their resources and talent on their core competencies and eliminating other lines of business.[31] This argument provided the business and organizational strategy for shareholder-value management. Selling off "noncore"—typically the less profitable divisions—provided immediate cash flow to shareholders. It also subjected the remaining core to more transparent shareholder scrutiny—something that institutional investors and securities analysts demanded.[32] The more focused model of organization also reduced the freedom of top managers. In the past, if one division faced a demand shock, the company could cross-subsidize it to create time for reorganization or the release of new products. The core-competency model eliminated this kind of buffering so that employees often absorbed the costs of restructuring through layoffs or work intensification.

Deregulation and Leveraged Buyouts as Precursors to Private Equity

These novel financial and management theories played themselves out in the actions of investors in leveraged buyouts and hostile takeovers in the 1980s. They were only made possible by a series of regulatory changes, from the 1970s, on that freed up large pools of capital for investment in the stock market as well as for leveraged buyouts, hostile takeovers, and mergers and acquisitions—and later, for new financial intermediaries such as private equity and hedge funds (HF). In the 1970s, for example, the Employment Retirement Income Security Acts (ERISA) of 1974 and 1978 allowed pension funds and insurance companies, for the first time, to hold shares of stock and high-risk bonds in their portfolios. The law and regulations nonetheless required the fiduciary to make pension allocations based on the judgment of a reasonable person (the "prudent man rule"). By 1992, however, the U.S. Department of Labor had adopted the "prudent investor rule," based on the assumption of modern portfolio theory that risk can be managed through diversification at the portfolio level. This encouraged pension trustees to invest in riskier assets in the belief that they could achieve higher returns without the associated risks.[33]

These institutional investors became critical actors from the 1980s on.[34] Their overall share in the stock market almost doubled, from under 30 percent in 1980 to over 50 percent in the late 1990s.[35] The Oregon, Washington, and Michigan state pension funds were among the first investors in LBOs in the 1980s,[36] and in 2013 some 35 percent of funds committed to private equity came from public and private pension funds. Gordon Donaldson argues that the rise of institutional shareholders was critical in shifting the balance of power in the 1980s from corporate stakeholders to shareholders.[37] Securities analysts also played a critical monitoring role,[38] with the number of analysts per company rising from eight in 1976 to eighteen in 1990, according to one estimate.[39]

Similarly, Reagan-era policies facilitated the mobility of capital and the breakup of conglomerates. The U.S. Supreme Court's overturning of state anti-takeover laws allowed corporate raiders more opportunities.[40] The Federal Trade Commission (FTC) made it easier to undertake horizontal mergers so that laws no longer favored the acquisition of companies across diverse industries. These changes gave rise to "the market for corporate control"—that is, the market for external actors to buy enough shares of publicly traded stock to take control of a corporation—which could occur through hostile takeovers or through "tender offers" in which investors bypassed the CEO and boards of directors and went directly to shareholders to buy their stock at a higher-than-market price.[41]

In addition, in 1982 Congress passed legislation (the Garn–St. Germain Depository Institutions Act) allowing savings-and-loan banks (S&Ls) to make commercial loans. This opened the door for investment in risky commercial activities, including junk bonds, a financial tool frequently used by private equity funds today. High-risk bonds are rated by credit rating agencies as below investment grade because they have a higher likelihood of default (while yielding higher returns). They are more speculative in nature, and hence "junk bonds." These legislative and judicial changes led to the emergence of large pools of liquid capital for junk bonds, which financed a great many leveraged buyouts and the purchase of large blocks of shares of publicly traded companies by corporate raiders. LBOs were used by investors to acquire companies using a small amount of their own capital and borrowing the rest based on the assets of the acquired company, which were pledged as collateral. With a debt/equity ratio of 80/20 or higher in the 1980s, target companies saddled with this level of debt often experienced distress or went bankrupt.

Reduced regulation opened the door for S&Ls to purchase junk bonds for use in financing the takeover of a firm in a leveraged buyout or the purchase of a large block of shares of a publicly traded company, since these qualified as commercial lending. In fact, only a few S&Ls engaged in these transactions; 69 percent of all junk bonds held by S&Ls were held by just eleven institutions tied to Michael Milken and the investment bank that employed him, Drexel Burnham Lambert (Drexel) (see box 2.1).[42] Although S&Ls are no longer able to hold junk bonds, the junk bond market continues to thrive. Having adopted the leveraged buyout model in the 2000s, private equity firms often use junk bonds to finance their own dividends, or "dividend recapitalizations," as we discuss in chapter 3.

The Leveraged Buyout Model

The private equity model of today traces its roots to a series of developments in this period that allowed the leveraged buyout model to thrive. The investment firm most credited with developing this model, KKR, is one of the largest private equity firms of today. With its purchase of Houdaille Industries in 1979, it launched a model of financial engineering that became the dominant LBO model for the decade and, later, for

---

Box 2.1   Michael Milken and the Junk Bond Market

Michael Milken is credited with almost single-handedly creating the junk bond market, beginning in 1982. Junk bonds made large, unregulated pools of capital available to investors who previously would have had to rely on banks for loans. Prior to Milken's involvement, high-risk, high-yield bonds were not popular because lenders viewed them as easy to manipulate and likely to default. To sell junk bonds Milken had to convince lenders that the yield on the junk bonds Drexel offered was substantially higher than the risks and that the bonds Drexel underwrote had a very high success rate.[43] With the help of the S&Ls that were close to them, Milken and Drexel had almost no defaults on their junk bonds. This success was ascribed to Milken's unique genius in evaluating and monitoring borrowers.

The bankruptcy of several S&Ls with close ties to Milken led to his downfall, however, and the legal case against him revealed his true strategy. Milken formed more than five hundred different partnerships that purchased securities underwritten by Drexel. These partnerships used thousands of accounts to make many thousands of purchases of junk bonds, thus ensuring that public offerings of junk bonds by Drexel were fully subscribed. They could mark up prices on the bonds before they were sold to the public, thus ensuring profits for participants in the partnerships. The success of these offerings encouraged institutional investors to participate. Defaults could be minimized by making loans to borrowers for more than they needed for a project, thereby guaranteeing that some of the initial proceeds from the loan would be available to make interest payments. More importantly, Milken used his links to S&Ls close to him to provide new long-term financing to bankrupt companies, thus reducing the observed default rate on junk bonds brokered by Drexel. The outstanding bonds of the bankrupt firms could be exchanged for new bonds from the S&Ls.

The apparently low rates of default fueled the rapid growth of the junk bond market.[44] By the time the FDIC brought a complaint against Milken and Drexel, institutions with close links to Drexel held $14 billion in junk bonds, and the three "captive" S&Ls that allowed Milken to trade in their accounts—Thomas Spiegel's Columbia S&L, Charles Keating's Lincoln, and David Paul's CenTrust—held $9 billion.[45] These junk bond portfolios represented a significant share of the assets of these institutions. In these deals, Drexel purported to represent the S&L, the counterparty, and itself. Milken's use of these captive S&Ls came to light through the efforts of Bart Dzivi, who supervised investigative auditors during the savings-and-loan crisis. The S&Ls had failed to carry out contemporaneous underwriting of such loans or to maintain a written record, as required by law, because Drexel made all the decisions. Records were created long after the fact. Noticing that some pages were not sequentially numbered, Dzivi ultimately unraveled the fraud.[46]

private equity.[47] By the end of the buyout decade, KKR held thirty-five companies worth $59 billion in corporate assets—fifth in size behind GM, Ford, Exxon, and IBM.[48]

Buyout firms began to be active in the 1960s and 1970s by harnessing a large amount of debt to acquire small, privately held companies in what were known as "bootstrap deals." It was an attractive exit option for aging founders in successful companies too small to be taken public. Robert Kohlberg clinched a small deal like this in 1964 when he bought a $9.5 million company with $1.5 million in equity—or 16 percent. By the 1970s, other elements of the model were in place. Banks were willing to lend, and investors were putting up equity, because the debt was secured by the assets of companies that threw off a lot of cash that could be used to pay down the debt. Contrary to the financial wisdom at the time, deals were evaluated on the basis of a company's cash flow—its ability to pay down debt—and not its profitability.[49]

Investors adapted the bootstrap model to large, poor-performing conglomerates in the 1980s. Although not all conglomerates were poor performers, most were viewed as having excess cash on hand and poor corporate governance practices that had allowed CEOs to become complacent and take advantage of perks and a privileged lifestyle.[50] For large corporations, cash reserves kept the cost of capital low for investing in new products and processes, but corporate raiders sought to "disgorge cash to investors" and return it to shareholders.[51] As William Lazonick states, the conflict was over the control of retained earnings: strategic managers wanted a low dividend/earnings ratio in order to finance investments internally, while shareholders wanted a high dividend/earnings ratio for higher returns.[52]

Central to the model—then and now—are three interdependent characteristics: acquisition of a company that has strong cash flow and solid fundamentals but is undervalued; high use of debt; and investor control of management post-buyout. The LBO-PE model rarely targets poor-performing or distressed companies to turn them around because speedy debt retirement requires high cash flow. Debt is central to the model because it magnifies returns: investors are able to acquire companies using other people's money, especially when interest rates are low and credit is easily available. Moreover, debt has large tax advantages. Debt also forces managers to gear all their efforts to paying down the debt to avoid defaulting. Houdaille was a Fortune 500 company with lots of cash on hand, little debt, and an undervalued stock price; KKR purchased it with 8 percent equity and 92 percent debt (see box 2.2).[53]

The importance of investor control over management post-buyout is driven home by the detailed analysis of the KKR model by George Baker and George Smith, who had unparalleled access to KKR's internal records and were able to interview the partners. They argue that KKR reintegrated ownership and control by creating owner-managed corporations.[54] From

---

Box 2.2   KKR's Leveraged Buyout of Houdaille

KKR's buyout of Houdaille Industries—a Fortune 500 conglomerate employing 7,700 people—is widely viewed as having altered Wall Street's view of financial engineering and launched the era of large leveraged buyouts.[55] The Houdaille deal yielded spectacular returns for shareholders and proved that corporations could be restructured and managed to maximize shareholder value. Large investment companies quickly entered the LBO game.

Houdaille Industries was a perfect takeover target. It grew from an auto parts supplier to a large conglomerate by producing a variety of unrelated products. Like many conglomerates in the 1970s, its revenues and profits were growing slowly and its share price was depressed. Houdaille's $22 million in debt was a small percentage of the firm's value, and it had cash reserves of $40 million. Pretax profits were $50.8 million, and the company paid $22.3 million in taxes. The company's stock, which traded at around $14.50 a share in early 1978, rose to about $25 a share on rumors of a takeover. KKR offered to buy the outstanding shares at a premium price of $40 a share, which set the expected value of the deal at about $335 million. KKR and its partners, including holdover Houdaille management, put up $25 million in equity; KKR's own contribution was just $1 million. About $300 million came from debt assumed by Houdaille and $10 million from preferred stock sold to banks.[56]

The deal exploited the tax-advantaged position of debt relative to equity. Interest on debt is tax-deductible. By loading the company with debt, KKR greatly increased its after-tax profits. This both increased Houdaille's value (and so appeared to "unlock its hidden value") and freed up income to pay much of the interest on its massive debt. Accounting rules allowed KKR to value the company's capital assets at current market value and to re-depreciate these assets for tax purposes. Not satisfied with this tax advantage, KKR adopted an approach to computing depreciation for tax purposes at Houdaille that made use of shell companies whose sole purpose was to further reduce the company's tax bill. For the life of the buyout, the company was expected to pay little in corporate income taxes, freeing up the forgone tax payments to service the company's debt.[57]

Between 1979 and 1981, KKR restructured Houdaille by shedding unprofitable product lines, retaining its profitable niche in machine tools, and acquiring John Crane Inc., a global leader in mechanical seals. The $204 million acquisition was financed with debt. KKR appeared ready to take Houdaille public again in 1984, but its debt burden placed it in a poor position to do so. A large chunk of its original cash reserves—$35 million—had been used to pay down debt, and its equity cushion was thin. Houdaille was ill prepared to face the deep recession of 1981 to 1982 or Japanese inroads into the machine tool industry, which accounted for one-quarter of its revenues. When the company's debt burden became unmanageable in 1985, Houdaille was again restructured to reduce its junk bond debt and interest expense. KKR divested seven divisions, including the machine tool group, with a loss of 2,200 high-skill, high-paid jobs.[58]

(*Box continues on p. 26.*)

Box 2.2   *Continued*

In 1986 Houdaille sold junk bonds rated CCC and paid almost 13.9 percent in interest in order to fund a dividend for shareholders that allowed unhappy equity investors to recover their initial investments. A year later, the company was taken over by the British firm Tube Investments Group PLC (TI Group), which paid $112 million and assumed $388 million of debt to acquire Houdaille. Baker and Smith report a deal value for Houdaille of $380 million, a holding period of 8.45 years, and a return on equity invested before KKR carry and management fees of 33.9 percent a year.[59] TI Group kept only the John Crane Houdaille division and disposed of the remaining six divisions. For all intents and purposes, Houdaille ceased to exist as a manufacturer of machine tools and industrial products.

Although the LBO paid off well for KKR and the other investors, the company failed. Burdened with debt and lacking an equity cushion, Houdaille—a major U.S. machine tool manufacturer—was unable to meet the Japanese challenge. As *Washington Post* business writer Max Holland chronicled in his book, *When the Machine Stopped,* Houdaille's machine tool division quickly shifted to a singular focus on generating cash to service the debt—failing to reinvest in new equipment and pushing orders out the door regardless of quality. The company's stellar reputation for quality evaporated in a short two-year window, and the company was sold off, piece by piece, giving the Japanese a larger share of the world market.[60]

---

his early deals onward, Kohlberg first made sure that his firm had control over investment and post-buyout decisions and that the investors in his fund were passive. Then, for each deal, KKR developed a projection for financial returns based on a financial structure for the deal (the relative proportion of senior and subordinated debt and equity) and a management plan matched to the specific conditions of the target company. To ensure implementation of the plan, KKR insisted that top managers risk a large portion of their own money. And as board directors, KKR partners "monitored their companies far more rigorously than did conventional corporate boards. They managed corporate financings and subjected managers to ongoing review."[61] More important, the post-buyout management plan—including which divisions would be cut, which assets would be sold, and so on—was "embedded" in the debt and equity structure of the buyout[62]: "The strict 'discipline of debt' allowed for no slack, no surprises, no deviance."[63] For the mega-buyout of Beatrice Industries for $8.2 billion, with 95 percent debt (including a substantial portion of junk bonds), "the entire post-buyout strategy for shrinking the headquarters, decentralizing markets, and selling off unmanageable operations was forced by the deal's capital structure. . . . Beatrice staged the largest corporate sell-off in history."[64]

Within a few years, the KKR model of leveraged buyouts had gained legitimacy. A total of 2,597 LBOs took place in the 1980s, representing 7.7 percent of all mergers and acquisitions.[65] Almost half of all U.S. public corporations experienced a takeover attempt in that decade.[66] Twenty-nine percent (144) of Fortune 500 firms in 1980 were subject to hostile takeovers in the following decade, and 125 of the attempted takeovers were successful. Firms that were less likely to be takeover targets had high market/book ratios, high debt, and more institutional ownership, while companies with finance CEOs were more likely to be targets, and older companies were more likely to be hostile targets.[67] At the same time, acquisitions during the decade were primarily horizontal mergers. Among Fortune 500 firms, the total level of diversification dropped by one-third between 1980 and 1990, and the level of unrelated diversification dropped by 44 percent.[68]

Labor Market Deregulation

Accompanying the deregulation of financial markets was the decline of organized labor as a countervailing force to financial power. The historically weak U.S. labor and employment laws, based on a system of decentralized collective bargaining and "employment at will," made the adoption of new, non-union business models relatively easy.[69] By the 1970s, corporations were aggressively attacking labor unions, demanding concessions, and disregarding prior norms of labor-management trust, reciprocity, and productivity pacts. Because U.S. labor institutions lack the rules or props to constrain quick exits from joint partnerships or productivity pacts, those voluntary deals have followed a "yo-yo" model of duration.[70] While some manufacturing unions had established pattern bargaining in their industry, and the more powerful unions were able to maintain industry standards, union power and membership eroded substantially. Increasingly firm-based or establishment-based, unions had to fight major corporations—or later, new private equity owners—on their own.[71] This decentralization of collective bargaining continued through the 2000s and weakened the ability of unions to shape the new business models and employment policies that have emerged in recent years.

The tough anti-union stance of the new era, legitimized by Reagan's firing of the PATCO air traffic controllers in 1981, became institutionalized as a model for corporate labor strategies in subsequent decades. Union density in the private sector stood at 6.6 percent in 2012.[72] The use of mass layoffs, a first response to the 1981 recession, subsequently became normalized as an ongoing business strategy, not just an adjustment to cyclical downturns.

Moreover, to the extent that firms began to increase their profits from financial activities relative to those from productive activities, the incentive to invest in workers' skills or human capital began to decline. The welfare of shareholders and managers became less intertwined with the welfare of employees. High union wages, which historically pushed firms to invest in new technologies and skills to improve productivity, began to play a smaller role in the economy. In leveraged buyouts both then and now, employees are viewed as more dispensable—a variable cost to be minimized or, more recently, outsourced or sent overseas. Of course, at the same time, the digital revolution and global competition have created countervailing pressures to compete on high-value-added products and skilled labor, but the idea of labor as a "quasi-fixed" asset,[73] or human capital as valuable and firm-specific,[74] have come under attack. Instead of investing in firm-specific skills, employers have turned to market-based solutions and urge employees to stay "employable" by investing in their own training.[75] In sum, the incentives that management traditionally had for investing in labor skills and engaging in productive labor-management relations began to unravel in the 1980s and have continued to do so.

The shareholder-value model of business organization and management emerged and prospered during the 1970s and 1980s owing to transformative changes in the governance of the American corporation. Declines in financial and labor market regulations created a new regulatory regime. The rise of institutional investors, the formation of new financial engineering strategies and intermediaries, and the activist elaboration of academic theories combined to provide the institutional opportunity structure for Wall Street to replace the management-controlled firm with the finance-controlled firm.

Setting the Stage for Private Equity and a Rebound in Leveraged Buyouts

By the early 1990s, companies acquired in leveraged buyouts and saddled with high debt burdens had filed for bankruptcy in record numbers. KKR met with disastrous results in its two mega-buyouts of Beatrice Industries and RJR Nabisco, eliminating over 45,000 jobs in the latter. And the LBO model of the 1980s itself was discredited and viewed as dead. Anti-takeover legislation in the early 1990s also reduced buyout opportunities. Despite these developments and their implications, other developments ultimately defined the 1990s as a decade in which market liberalization and the shareholder-value model became firmly established.

Public corporations, private investment firms, and the financial services industry more generally benefited from the ongoing deregulation and re-regulation of banking in a series of laws that ultimately repealed the Glass-Steagall Act of 1933—the law that separated commercial and investment banks in order to reduce speculative behavior following the 1929 Depression. These actions culminated in the 1999 Gramm-Leach-Bliley Act (GLBA), which allowed commercial banks, investment banks, securities firms, and insurance companies to consolidate. Nonbank financial institutions gained access to insured deposits at commercial banks and dramatically increased the pools of liquid capital available for trading and speculation. The financial industry also created new complex financial instruments—commercial mortgage-backed securities, collateralized debt obligations, collateralized loan obligations, credit default swaps, and other derivatives—that were unregulated. Collateralized loan obligations in particular became useful tools in the financial engineering strategies of private equity firms in the 2000s. The junk bond market also soon returned: it had declined in the late 1980s with the credit crunch, but returned to 1980s levels by the late 1990s.[76]

At the same time, institutional investors continued to grow in power as the capital they controlled expanded and they became more active in their monitoring role as corporate board members. Board-member vigilance increased in part because Securities and Exchange Commission (SEC) rule changes substantially reduced the cost to shareholders of mounting proxy contests to challenge management teams. The number of shareholder proposals initiated by institutional investors grew substantially. Based on one sample of 429 of the largest corporations, there were 100 such proposals in 1979, 350 in 1991, and 450 in 1995.[77] A 1992 SEC ruling also required more detailed information disclosure on executive compensation in relation to firm performance; this requirement shifted the attention of boards of directors and shareholders to stock performance.[78]

In response, corporations began to integrate shareholder-friendly policies into their repertoires, thereby making buyouts and hostile takeovers less relevant as a solution to poor financial performance.[79] They restructured voluntarily, without the threat of corporate raiders.[80] They integrated market discipline into their organizational practices through performance management and compensation programs that linked managerial pay to the extent to which returns on capital exceeded the cost of capital, thus focusing managerial attention on this cost. Stock options that tied CEOs to Wall Street, which had stood at 20 percent of CEO compensation in 1980, skyrocketed after Jensen and Murphy's influential 1990 article on executive pay.[81] It reached 50 percent by 1994, a dramatic increase in the sensitivity of CEO pay to performance.[82] Stock option pay realigned the interests and identities of managers—away from a focus on organizational stability and toward a commitment to managing share price to maximize shareholder value and their personal wealth as shareholders. Stock buybacks as a mechanism to increase share price also accelerated.[83]

Large corporations also became adept at using a range of financial and tax avoidance strategies to make money, thereby reducing their dependence on productive activities. They increased their use of debt financing, though it did not reach the levels used in LBOs. And like LBO-acquired companies, corporations with too much debt were significantly more likely to focus on cost-cutting initiatives such as downsizing or defunding pension funds.[84]

In addition, the heightened sensitivity to share price and the creation of shareholder value led to the increased use of derivatives and a variety of accounting and off-balance-sheet practices designed to obscure the real financial volatility and weakness of companies—practices that in the extreme were fraudulent. The result was another round of scandals in the early 2000s with the downfall of global corporations such as Tyco, Global Crossing, Enron, WorldCom, and the consulting firm Arthur Anderson.[85]

The new round of financial scandals in the early 2000s led Congress to pass the Sarbanes-Oxley Act in 2002 to rein in the worst excesses of earnings manipulation and fraudulent accounting behavior by corporations. The law strengthened corporate governance rules and prohibited auditors from involvement in consulting activities for their clients. Many have argued that these new rules provided incentives for companies to be taken private, an opportunity that private equity firms were quick to cash in on.

Private equity firms also benefited from the ongoing trend in financial deregulation, which continued despite the financial scandals and dot-com bust of the late 1990s. Congress, for example, refused to regulate new financial instruments that facilitated speculative activity. Under the 2000 Commodity Futures Modernization Act, Congress (at the request of the Clinton administration) explicitly excluded from regulation the complex financial instruments, such as derivatives and credit default swaps, that lacked transparency and had been tools for accounting fraud. While little attention was paid to it at the time, this exclusion allowed the entire derivatives market to be unregulated. The massive shift of funds from the regulated financial sector to the "shadow banking" sector set the stage for the financial crisis of the late 2000s. And in 2004 the SEC allowed investment banks to hold even less capital in reserve, thereby facilitating greater use of leverage in trading activities.

In the meantime, while media coverage of buyouts had all but disappeared, investment firms like KKR that had led the buyout movement had not. Deals were more difficult to close, however, and the debt available for buyouts had declined; the mix of successes and failures became more negative. KKR had a series of disasters with buyouts of Primedia, Regal Cinemas, and Spalding, which led it to reorganize into major industry groups and hire a broader array of industry and legal experts.[86]

Other firms began to specialize in particular industries or niches or to diversify into other types of investments. More broadly, buyout departments in large commercial and investment banks grew substantially, and leveraged buyout partnerships numbered some eight hundred in 1997.[87] Similarly, institutional investors had become accustomed to including higher-risk investments as part of their portfolios. By the 1990s, they regularly allocated funds to a broad array of alternative investments, including distressed investing and venture capital, which fell under the general category of "private equity." Baker and Smith date the use of the term "private equity" to this period.[88]

By the turn of the century, then, shareholder value management had become commonplace in public corporations, but these companies still differed in fundamental ways from the private equity model that reemerged in the 2000s. Corporations increased their use of debt, but not to the levels typically found in private equity buyouts. They engaged in financial engineering, but their actions were subject to legal, public, and shareholder scrutiny, which in fact led to the downfall of some major corporations and accounting firms in the early 2000s. Private equity firms, by contrast, lack transparency and legal and public accountability for many of their actions. Although their financial incentives for risky behavior are higher, they can walk away from the bankruptcies of their portfolio companies or the pension liabilities in multi-employer plans.

Until recently—with the passage of the 2010 Dodd-Frank Wall Street Reform and Consumer Protection Act—PE firms were not regulated at all by the SEC. U.S. public corporations and much of the financial services industry are governed by the Securities Act of 1933, the Securities Exchange Act of 1934, the Investment Company Act of 1940 (the Company Act), and the Investment Advisers Act of 1940 (the Advisers Act). The Securities Act prohibits fraud, requires registration and public reporting by publicly traded firms, and gives authority to the SEC to regulate the industry. The Company Act requires investment funds to disclose their financial policies, restricts activities such as the use of leverage and short selling, and requires a board structure with a substantial percentage of disinterested members. The Advisers Act requires the registration of fund managers, enforces compliance with fiduciary responsibilities, and limits the performance fees they may charge.[89]

Prior to August 2012, most private equity funds were able to avoid these regulations by limiting their funds' size to that which was defined as exempt under these laws (see box 2.3, taken from Bain Capital Partners' filing with the SEC). This exemption allowed them—in contrast to mutual funds, for example—to engage in financial practices such as selling securities short, making use of substantial leverage, and adopting performance-based fees that increase with fund gains but do not necessarily decrease with losses.

Box 2.3   Bain Capital Partners' SEC Filing

Bain Capital Partners, a private equity firm that sponsors PE funds, is registered with the Securities and Exchange Commission. The funds it sponsors,
however, are not required to register, and unlike the financial statements
of publicly traded companies, private equity fund financial statements
are not filed with the SEC. The following item is taken from Bain's Form
ADV: Part 2, on file with the SEC:

Item 4. Advisory Business

Bain Capital Partners, a Delaware limited liability company wholly owned
by Bain Capital, LLC ("Bain Capital"), provides investment advisory
services to pooled investment vehicles that are exempt from registration
under the Investment Company Act of 1940, as amended (the "1940 Act")
and whose securities are not registered under the Securities Act of 1933, as
amended (the "Securities Act") (the "Bain Capital Partners Funds"). As the
investment adviser of each Bain Capital Partners Fund, Bain Capital Partners,
along with each Bain Capital Partners Fund's General Partner ("General
Partners"), identifies investment opportunities for, and participates in the
acquisition, management, monitoring and disposition of investments of, each
Bain Capital Partners Fund.

This changed somewhat in 2010 with passage of the Dodd-Frank
Act, which now requires private equity and hedge funds with more
than $150 million in assets to register with the SEC and provide gen-
eral reports on basic organizational and operational information, such
as size, types of services, clients, employees, and potential conflicts
of interest.[90] Most general partners of private equity funds are now
required to provide regular reports on their operations; smaller funds
remain exempt from these reporting requirements. But these reporting
requirements are modest compared to those required of public corporations. And unlike the SEC reports of publicly traded companies,
the reports of PE fund advisers are confidential, thus ensuring that PE
transactions remain private and transparency remains an issue. The
reporting requirements have implications for staffing, record-keeping,
and controls on financial reporting at PE firms, but are not expected to
alter the business model of these firms.

Private equity also takes advantage of U.S. tax laws. The use of high
levels of leverage in buying companies reduces the tax liabilities of
PE-owned companies, since the interest on debt may be subtracted from
taxable income, whereas retained earnings or dividends are taxable as
profit. PE firm profits from their portfolio investments are defined as
"carried interest," which is treated in the tax code as capital gains and
taxed at a 20 percent rate (up from the 15 percent rate that prevailed until

2013) rather than at the top rate of 35 percent for corporate or individual taxes.[91] In addition, most PE firms and HFs avoid other taxes by registering offshore.[92] Legislative attempts to tax carried interest as ordinary income have failed in the past, but are likely to be raised again.[93] These minimal reporting requirements for private equity in the United States stand in contrast to the European Union's (EU) Alternative Investment Funds Managers Directive. The Directive instructs member states to adopt much more extensive reporting requirements as well as substantive rules to limit the use of leverage and implement risk management systems.[94]

At the level of portfolio companies owned by private equity, U.S. labor laws and institutions also make it difficult to hold private equity accountable for its actions. First, when PE firms acquire a company, unions representing those companies have no information or consultation rights—unlike their counterparts in Europe, where companies with more than fifty employees are required to have works councils that represent employees at the workplace and firm levels. Unions and works councils have information and consultation rights that allow them to influence the direction of negotiations over new ownership. European transfer-of-rights laws also require new owners to accept the union status of existing employees. These laws provide some points of leverage for unions to protect the rights of workers in the event of ownership transfers.[95]

Second, the U.S. pension system is a decentralized, employer-based system in both the public and private sectors, though some unions control members' pension funds under provisions of the Taft-Hartley Act of 1947. Unions and public-sector officials have a fiduciary responsibility to ensure that these multibillion-dollar funds have adequate returns, and many have invested in private equity in an attempt to achieve high returns. Pension funds invest an average of 7–8 percent of their portfolios in private equity.[96] This system has created dilemmas for U.S. unions. While they invest in private equity to gain high returns for retired members, they also encounter PE investors as owners of companies where they represent workers and thus may find themselves in conflicts around downsizing initiatives or derogation of contract rules. As a result, the U.S. labor movement as a whole has not developed a unified position or public approach to PE owners, in contrast to the unified opposition to private equity among European unions.[97]

In sum, some of the innovations introduced by LBO investors in the 1980s became diffused throughout U.S. corporations in the 1990s when they embraced shareholder value as the single most important performance metric. But several institutional, market, and organizational factors came together to allow private equity to reemerge in the first decade of the twenty-first century. Public corporations were discredited in the early 2000s in the way that LBO firms and junk bonds were in the early 1990s. The Sarbanes-Oxley Act created incentives to take some companies private. Hiding companies from public scrutiny had some appeal. And further banking deregulation gave private equity access to larger private pools of capital as well as collateralized loan obligations, junk bonds, and other speculative financial instruments. Private equity buyouts of public corporations were back in the news headlines as mid-decade buyouts surpassed what until then had been the largest buyout in history—KKR's takeover of RJR Nabisco for $25 billion.

Why Private Equity Matters: Scale and Scope in the 2000s

Private equity funds—many with roots in the leveraged buyout firms of the 1980s—emerged as a major source of unregulated private investment after the 2001 recession. The explosive growth of private equity in the 2000s took many by surprise. As of 2013, the Private Equity Growth Capital Council reports that the total number of PE firms headquartered in the United States is 2,797, while 17,744 PE-backed companies are headquartered in the United States.[98] How did a discredited business model become so successful in the 2000s?

Rechristened as private equity firms, KKR, Blackstone, Carlyle, and others were again able to raise large, unregulated pools of financial capital—from pension funds, endowments, sovereign wealth funds, and wealthy individuals—which they combined with extensive debt financing to acquire operating companies in leveraged buyouts. Leveraged buyouts include large deals that take publicly traded companies private; deals in which large divisions of publicly traded companies are taken private; deals in which independent private companies—often still owned by the family that founded them—are taken private; and secondary buyouts in which a portfolio company of one PE fund is acquired by another PE fund. Add-on deals are leveraged buyouts in which a portfolio company, together with the PE firm that controls it, acquires another firm as an add-on to the portfolio company. PE firms have often acquired companies to use as a "platform" to acquire a number of other companies as add-on deals via LBOs. Companies acquired as add-ons may fall into any of the four types of LBO deals.

Public pension funds became the largest group of investors in private equity funds in the 2000s. In the low-interest-rate environment of the 2000s, pension funds were lured by PE firms' promises of considerably higher returns than were available via investments in bonds or stock. In 2007, at the peak of the boom in PE buyouts, the top four investors in PE funds were CalPERS (California Public Employees' Retirement System), CalSTRS (California State Teachers' Retirement System), Pennsylvania's PSERS (Public School Employees' Retirement System),

Figure 2.1   Total Capital Invested in Leveraged Buyouts and Deal Count, by Year, 2000 to 2012

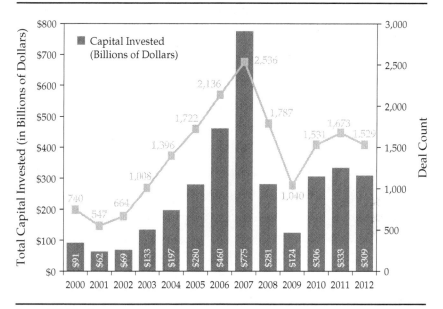

Source: PitchBook.

and the Washington State Investment Board.[99] Access to workers' capital in pension funds enabled PE firms to expand the scale and scope of their operations and to become global in their investment activities. Both the number and transaction value of leveraged buyouts by PE firms increased rapidly between 2002 and 2007 before the bubble economy burst.

The marked expansion of private equity investments is illustrated in figure 2.1, which plots the number of PE-leveraged buyouts and their total capital value, by year, from 2000 to 2012.[100] In 2002, for example, PE firms invested $69 billion in U.S. LBOs of 664 portfolio companies. The annual value of PE investments in LBOs doubled by 2003, and more than doubled again by 2005. PE LBOs continued to accelerate during the 2006 to 2007 boom years. Between 2005 and 2007, the number of deals rose by almost 50 percent, but the capital value of those deals rose by 175 percent, reflecting the fact that the average size of transactions increased and megadeals became more popular. These trends are broadly consistent with other data and estimates.[101] And nine of the top ten largest LBOs in history (see table 2.1) took place in the 2007 to 2008 boom period.

When the bubble burst, the financial crisis took a toll on private equity investments: the annual number of deals and capital invested in those deals fell after 2007 and reached their low points in 2009 before beginning to recover. Total capital invested in LBOs in 2009 fell below its 2003 level. A strong fourth quarter in 2010 for LBOs raised hopes of a robust

Table 2.1   Top Ten Largest Buyouts in History, as of 2012

Company	Deal Value (Billions of U.S. Dollars)	PE Investors	Date	Industry
TXU (Energy Futures Holding)	$43.80	KKR, Goldman Sachs Capital Partners, TPG	2007	Utilities/ energy
Equity Office Properties Trust	38.90	Blackstone Real Estate Partners LP	2007	Real estate
HCA, Inc.	32.70	Bain Capital, Inc., KKR, Merrill Lynch Global Private Equity	2007	Health care
RJR Nabisco, Inc.	31.10	KKR	1988	Food/tobacco
Alltel Corporation	27.87	TPG, Goldman Sachs Capital Partners LP	2007	Telecom
First Data Corporation	27.73	KKR	2007	Finance/ technology
Harrah's Entertainment, Inc.	27.40	Apollo Management LP, TPG	2008	Entertainment
Hilton Hotels, Inc.	25.80	Blackstone Group LP	2007	Lodging
Clear Channel Communications, Inc.	24.86	Bain Capital, Inc., Thomas H. Lee Partners	2008	Media
Kinder Morgan, Inc.	21.56	Goldman Sachs Capital Partners LP, AIG Global Asset Management, Riverstone Holdings, and Carlyle Group, Inc.	2007	Energy

Source: Pensions&Investments, "Largest Leveraged Buyouts," January 16, 2013. Available at: http://www.pionline.com/gallery/20130116/SLIDESHOW2/116009999/1 (accessed February 13, 2014).

recovery, but these hopes were disappointed as PE activity failed to maintain this pace, slowing further in the first half of 2012.

Private equity investors also branched out beyond leveraged buyouts in the 2000s, making investments in publicly traded companies (private investments in public equities, or PIPEs) and taking minority positions in various types of enterprises. This activity became more prominent in the postcrisis period as attractive opportunities for LBOs became more difficult to identify. Given our focus on LBOs and the portfolio companies that private equity controls, however, our data analysis does not include PE investments as minority owners.

Figure 2.2   Cumulative Inventory of Private Equity Investments by Year, 2000 to 2012

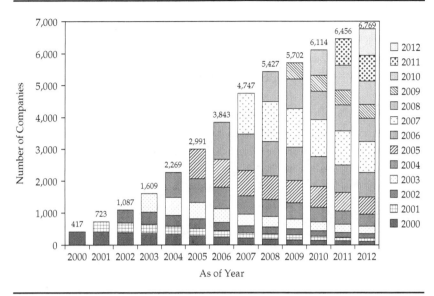

Source: PitchBook.

Cumulatively, private equity firms invested a total of about $3.4 trillion in leveraged buyouts of approximately 18,300 companies between 2000 and 2012. (These figures represent the sum of annual PE investments as shown in figure 1.1.) About two-thirds of these companies (11,500) were unique sales, while the remaining one-third were companies bought by one PE firm from another (secondary buyouts). Estimates of the number of employees who have worked or currently work for companies owned by private equity are more difficult to come by. For the period 2000 to 2010, private equity's industry association, PEGCC, estimated that PE-owned companies employed a total of about 7.5 million people.[102]

Our data also show that in 2012 the cumulative PE-owned inventory of companies was roughly 6,700 (figure 2.2). These are companies that PE firms have purchased since 2000, but had not yet sold by the end of 2012. Figure 2.2 also shows the percentage of PE-owned companies in 2012 by the year in which they were acquired. For example, roughly one-third of the companies purchased between 2000 and 2006 were still owned by PE firms in 2012. This is a pattern we discuss more fully in chapter 4 regarding the postcrisis period. The actual capital value of these companies is more difficult to assess. One estimate of the total value of the companies held in 2011 is about $1.3 trillion.[103]

Buyout activity also spread beyond manufacturing and retail to other industries in the 2000s. The two largest targets for private equity buyouts

Figure 2.3   Total Capital Invested, by Sector, 2000 to 2012

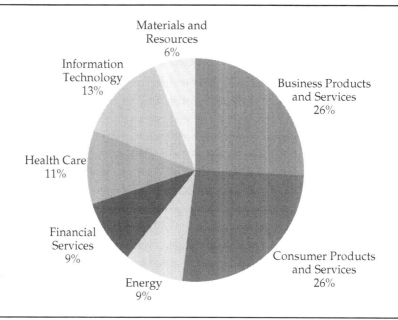

Materials and Resources 6%
Information Technology 13%
Business Products and Services 26%
Health Care 11%
Financial Services 9%
Energy 9%
Consumer Products and Services 26%

Source: PitchBook.

were business products and services and consumer products and services, representing 36 and 25 percent of total capital invested, respectively. Figure 2.3 shows the percentage of total investments, by sector, for 2000 to 2012. Investments in energy, financial services, and information technology companies represented between 9 and 13 percent of investments each, while health care represented 6 percent. These percentages do not differ substantially if we examine the total number of companies purchased rather than their capital value.

The patterns of investment did change somewhat over the course of the 2000s. Traditional investments in business products and services and in consumer products and services represented about 62 percent of investments from 2000 to 2005, but fell to 48 percent in the postcrisis years of 2008 to 2012. Investments in four other sectors—energy, financial services, health care, and information technology—became increasingly important. Together, they accounted for 30 percent of capital invested in leveraged buyouts prior to 2006, but rose to 46 percent during the boom years and maintained that level in the postcrisis period. Notably, average annual investments in financial services rose from 4 percent prior to the boom to 11 percent in the postcrisis period. Comparable figures for the energy sector are 6 percent and 10 percent, and for health care 8 percent and 13 percent.[104]

Figure 2.4   Total Capital Invested, by Region, 2000 to 2012

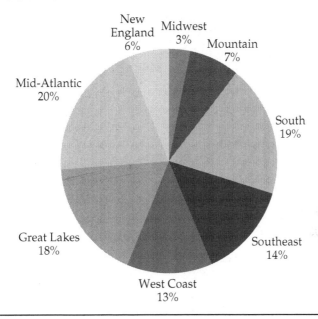

Source: PitchBook.

Private equity investment has also been dispersed by region, but some regions have received very little PE investment, as shown in figure 2.4.[105] The largest share of capital investment occurred in three regions: the Mid-Atlantic (20 percent), the South (19 percent), and the Great Lakes (18 percent). The West Coast and the Southeast each attracted 13 and 14 percent of all PE capital, respectively. Together, New England, the Midwest, and the Mountain states garnered only 16 percent of all PE investments during the period. This regional distribution of investments ebbed and flowed somewhat over the period but overall was relatively stable.

Taken together, the data suggest that private equity is now well represented in all sectors of the U.S. economy and in most regions. Its influence, as well as the example of its business model, is felt in nearly every industry and most regions of the country.

Conclusion

The last three decades have witnessed a fundamental shift in the nature of the U.S. economy as the power and influence of the financial industry has increasingly dominated the post-industrial restructuring of economic activity. Firms that used to make money by producing goods and services are increasingly used as investment vehicles—assets in the portfolio of a private equity firm, to be bought and sold to maximize shareholder value. This transformation has been facilitated by the deregulation of financial services; regulations, some in place since the 1930s, have been steadily repealed or relaxed. This transformation has made it possible for PE firms and other investors to accumulate large pools of private capital and to gain access to leverage, both on an unprecedented scale. Legal changes in the 1970s that allowed pension funds to invest in the stock market and undertake risky investments were critical to making available large pools of capital on which investors could draw. Spectacular returns from some leveraged buyouts in the 1980s inspired high-risk behavior, and although LBOs had been discredited by the end of that decade, many of the innovations piloted by the corporate raiders of that period have persisted. Aggressive tactics to maximize shareholder value and attacks on labor unions and their capacity to represent the interests of workers have led to a redistribution of the gains in productive enterprises from workers to investors. Agency theory, developed by finance economists, substantiated the view that managerial capitalism was inefficient and that maximizing shareholder value should be the exclusive goal of the corporation.

The 1990s witnessed the institutionalization of the shareholder value model among public corporations, which particularly embraced financial engineering, tax-avoidance strategies, core competency strategies and downsizing, and the pay-for-performance theories that became handmaidens to agency theory. By tying executive compensation, in the form of stock options, to corporate performance, investors largely succeeded in aligning CEO interests with their own. Unlike investors, however, CEOs had nothing to lose because they were not investing their own money. Stock option pay encouraged CEOs to fundamentally shift their allegiance from the corporation as a productive organization to their own interest in managing share price to advance their personal wealth.

While the shareholder-value model has diffused across the corporate landscape, private equity firms differentiate themselves by using higher leverage, adopting a broader array of financial engineering strategies, taking greater risks, and disposing of assets in short time horizons. They present a more extreme form of the shareholder-value model in which investors play an active role in managing the companies they own, without the transparency or accountability found in public corporations. PE firms have particularly relied on pension funds—the retirement savings of workers—as sources of capital for investment. The bubble economy years of the mid-2000s saw an explosive growth in PE funds and leveraged buyouts. Private equity has invested widely across the regions of the United States as well as across industry sectors, with investments in health care, financial services, energy, and information technology increasing in importance. Although PE firms reduced their activity in the economic slowdown and financial crisis of December 2007 through June 2009, they began to recover in 2010. The recovery slowed in 2012, then picked up in the last half of 2013. Private equity remains an important and ongoing force in the U.S. economy.

= Chapter 3 =

The Business Model: How Private Equity Makes Money

This chapter unpacks the business model that private equity firms use to make money. The model operates at two levels—the level of the PE firm and the level of the portfolio companies it acquires. The extensive use of debt to take over operating companies lies at the core of the private equity business model at both levels: the higher the use of debt at the portfolio level the higher the potential profits at the firm level.

Most private equity firms are partnerships. The firms sponsor investment funds that buy out operating companies using high levels of debt—so-called leverage. Partners in the PE firm assume the role of general partner (GP) of the PE funds. The structure of the relationship of the PE firm's partners with the firm's equity and debt suppliers concentrates the PE fund's gains in the hands of the fund's general partner, who, as noted, is a partner in the PE firm. The general partner of the PE fund makes decisions about which operating companies the fund should acquire and how much debt to use in acquiring them. The personal funds invested by general partners are a small fraction of the purchase price of the companies the fund acquires. Most of the PE fund's equity is supplied by pension funds, wealthy individuals, and other institutional investors who are the fund's limited partners (LPs). The majority of the purchase price of portfolio companies is financed with debt. Despite their small contribution of equity, a major share of fund gains accrues to the general partners. This asymmetric relationship creates a moral hazard problem: the general partner loses only a small amount if the investment sours, but realizes huge gains, magnified by the use of debt, if the investment is successful. With little to lose and much to gain by leveraging portfolio companies, the general partners in PE funds have incentives to engage in risky behavior and load excessive amounts of debt on the companies they acquire and control.

Julie Froud and her colleagues argue that private equity firms have successfully adopted the leveraged buyout (LBO) model of the 1980s and created "a hierarchy of ownership claims for debt and equity suppliers" that enables the general partner in the PE fund to capture most of the value extracted from the purchase, management, and sale of portfolio companies.[1] They characterize the operation of the PE business model at the level of the firm as the "control of ownership claims." That is, the PE firm distributes the gains accrued by a PE fund among the fund's general partners; its limited partners, who supply most of the fund's equity; and its debt providers, who contribute most of the financing for the deals to the advantage of the general partners.[2]

Before value can be captured by the private equity firm's partners, it must first be extracted from the operating companies acquired by PE funds. PE funds use a range of governance, operational, and financial strategies to manage, control, and direct their portfolio companies.[3] PE owners are both investors *and* managers of the portfolio companies they acquire, exercising "ownership with control" to maximize shareholder value for the portfolio company's owners over the PE firm's three- to five-year ownership horizon.[4]

PE ownership is painted by its enthusiasts as a superior form of business organization. In line with the prescriptions of agency theory, private equity concentrates a company's ownership in the hands of a few shareholders—the fund's general partner and the limited partner investors in the fund. The portfolio company is actively managed by the fund's general partner, who closely monitors the company's managers. In this telling, PE firms use their superior access to finance and management know-how to unlock the untapped potential in good companies or to turn around poorly performing or failing ones. The result is a net gain for the economy as well as outsized returns to the PE fund and its investors.

Ignored in these accounts are the cases in which general partners maximize returns for themselves and other investors in the PE fund through the use of financial engineering strategies. These may include excessive use of leverage, dividend recapitalizations, stripping of assets, tax arbitrage, and the strategic use of bankruptcy without regard for the effects of these actions on the long-term viability of the company and the impact on its workers, vendors, lenders, and community. The need to service high levels of debt may lead to unwarranted cost-cutting to achieve short-term results that jeopardize the company's long-term viability. These actions may increase the company's enterprise value, enrich the PE fund's general partner, and earn returns for the PE fund's investors, but they do not increase economic wealth or contribute to job creation in the larger economy. Instead, these gains come at the expense of other economic actors—notably workers, creditors, and taxpayers.

We draw on cases of private equity ownership of companies to illustrate the role that these investors play in managing the companies they take over. Our cases illustrate both private equity's use of business and operating strategies to increase value and its use of financial engineering strategies to transfer wealth from other stakeholders to the portfolio companies' PE owners.

The Business Model of Private Equity Firms

Private equity funds are financial intermediaries.[5] A PE firm raises capital from pension funds, mutual funds, insurance companies, university endowments, sovereign wealth funds, and wealthy individuals for a PE fund that it sponsors, and it invests this capital in the acquisition of a portfolio of operating companies. The general partner of the fund is a partner or group of partners in the PE firm. The investors in the PE fund are the fund's limited partners. Pension funds are the largest source of equity capital for PE funds, supplying more than one-third of all capital committed to U.S. PE funds.

A private equity firm may sponsor multiple PE funds and typically raises a new fund every three to five years. The PE fund acquires operating companies through leveraged buyouts, using the cash flow and assets of the company it purchases as collateral. Repayment of this debt is the responsibility of the acquired company; neither the PE firm nor the PE fund behind the purchase is liable to repay the debt. There are four routes to PE acquisitions: buying out publicly traded companies and taking them private; buying family-owned businesses from their founders; purchasing divisions of larger companies that want to divest these operations; and acquiring companies from other PE firms (secondary buyouts).

The New Diversified Conglomerate

There are several ways in which the legal and incentive structure of private equity firms resembles the much-maligned diversified conglomerates of the 1950s, 1960s, and 1970s.[6] First, the choice of which portfolio companies to acquire is based entirely on the potential for that company to generate profits for the PE fund and its investors. A good target for acquisition typically has demonstrated strong growth but has undervalued assets, generates a steady stream of cash, and has good prospects for a successful exit from the investment in a three- to five-year period. These acquisition criteria lead PE firms, via the funds they sponsor, to own a wide diversity of companies across many industries rather than, for example, companies in the same industry, in complementary product lines, or competing in the same product market. There are exceptions, of course, as a minority of PE firms do specialize (such as Silver Lake

Capital's focus on technology companies), and specialization strategies are more prevalent in PE firms that focus on small- and mid-market buy-outs (discussed in chapter 5). But larger PE firms own companies across a wide range of industries and resemble conglomerates: their portfolio companies are the equivalent of a conglomerate's operating divisions. Indeed, the KKR buyout model that emerged in the 1980s was referred to initially as an "LBO Association."[7]

Second, private equity firms pursue a strategy to limit their legal liabil-ity should things go wrong with one of the companies their funds have acquired; this strategy has the effect of contributing to the creation of a diversified conglomerate organizational structure. Regardless of the industry composition of a firm's portfolio companies, each fund and each company in a fund is set up as a separate legal entity. That is, each fund sponsored by a PE firm is a separate special-purpose entity that acquires a number of companies, and each deal in which an operating company is acquired for the fund's portfolio is structured as a separate corpora-tion. The purpose of this structure is to limit the legal liability of the PE firm and the fund investors. If a portfolio company of one fund experi-ences distress or enters bankruptcy, the partners in the fund will lose their stakes in this company and creditors can seize the property or business, but neither the PE fund nor the PE firm that sponsored it is liable to make good on the portfolio company's debts or losses.

An example of how this works is the 2006 private equity fund raised by Tishman Speyer and BlackRock to purchase the landmark Manhattan rent-regulated apartment complexes Stuyvesant Town and Peter Cooper Village. The $5.4 billion complex was purchased by the investors with 20 percent equity and 80 percent debt. Their intention was to turn the rent-controlled apartments into condos and market them in the booming Manhattan real estate market, but they were unsuccessful in driving renters out and converting the properties. When the PE owners defaulted on their loans in 2010, CWCapital Asset Management took control of the properties on behalf of the multitude of investors in commercial mortgage–backed securities that collectively held a $3 billion mortgage. Tishman Speyer and BlackRock lost their initial investment of $112.5 million, though the loss was offset somewhat by the $18 million a year in management fees they collected. The limited partners fared far worse. These included the Church of England, the government of Singapore, and three public employee pen-sion funds in California and Florida, which lost a total of $850 million. The PE firm had increased the rents, which turned out to be illegal, and at the time of bankruptcy, residents were owed $200 million in overpay-ments they had made to the PE owners. Tishman Speyer, however, with a $33.5 billion portfolio of projects on four continents and $2 billion in cash at the time of the default on the Manhattan properties, had no responsi-bility to make up the losses or reimburse the tenants. The failure of the

Manhattan project hardly made a dent in the firm's ten-year average annual returns.[8] A court settlement in November 2012 ordered CWCapital and Met-Life, the former owner, to pay $147 million to the 21,500 tenants whose rents were increased.[9]

This strategy to reduce legal liability creates an organizational structure in which the PE firm is in effect a holding company for its portfolio companies that exercises centralized control (as opposed to legal ownership) over their activities. Like the corporate headquarters of a multidivisional conglomerate, it makes decisions regarding which portfolio companies to provide with managerial and financial resources based on its view of what will maximize returns to the PE firm across all of its funds and all of the portfolio companies owned by those funds.

As with conglomerates, this common control enables PE firms to take advantage of economies of scale and make extensive use of the market power that derives from their ability to buy everything from copy machine paper to employee health insurance in bulk for all of their portfolio companies. For example, the Blackstone Group, a private equity giant, bought more than 50,000 Hewlett-Packard computers in 2011, using bulk buying to get discounted prices and save millions. Blackstone owns all or part of 74 companies that employ 700,000 people, while KKR owns 74 portfolio companies, and the Carlyle Group has investments in 200 portfolio companies that collectively employ around 675,000 people. Imitating the business practices of the large conglomerates, the large PE firms use their size and scope to put pressure on suppliers.[10] As was true of the conglomerates, having the PE firm make purchasing decisions for portfolio companies in very different industries and strong-arming suppliers to get lower prices may have immediate short-term cost-reducing benefits, but this "one size fits all" approach does not allow for the customization of supplier services to operating companies, which may be central to a company's value-added strategies. As discussed in the Mervyn's Department Store case later in the chapter, companies often develop important relationships of trust and collaboration with the contractors in their supply chains, and those relationships contribute to revenue generation and benefits far beyond the realized cost savings from centralization strategies.

There is a certain irony here: the difficulty of effectively managing a far-flung corporate empire played a critical role in the development of the private equity model. It motivated Jensen's development of agency theory and provided the rationale for the first wave of leveraged buyouts. There are, of course, differences in how private equity manages its portfolio companies and how conglomerates manage their subsidiaries. Conglomerates may use cross-subsidies, whereas private equity cannot. And private equity time horizons are much shorter: PE funds have a typical life span of ten years, with portfolio companies exited in just a few years after they are acquired. Publicly traded conglomerates have no such expectations.

Maximizing Shareholder Value

As we discussed in chapter 2, the exclusive reliance on shareholder value as the measure of corporate success is a central feature of the shift from managerial to financial capitalism. The conglomerate organization of PE firms reinforces private equity's single-minded focus on shareholder value, since the only common performance metrics across portfolio companies are financial ones, such as profit margins and quarterly internal rates of return. Moreover, given PE firms' promise to realize returns on limited partners' investments in a relatively short time frame, their focus is on short-term measures of shareholder value, not longer-term financial measures, such as market share or industry leadership, or intermediate measures, such as operational excellence or innovation.

The exclusive focus on short-term shareholder value is driven by several features of the PE firm's business model. During a PE fund's typical life span of ten years, the limited partners cannot withdraw their capital and new investors cannot join the fund. At the same time, the PE firm is under the gun to invest this capital in the first three to five years of the fund's life or return the uncommitted capital and relevant management fees to the LPs. Limited partners also expect to realize at least some returns within five years of investing in the PE fund; if they do not, they have fewer resources available to commit to subsequent PE funds raised by the firm. This puts additional pressure on the general partner to either exit a portfolio company within five years of acquisition or, if not, to make distributions to the LPs in the form of dividends collected from operating companies' cash flow or additional loans the operating company is required to take out using its assets as collateral. Exits can occur through the sale of the company to another company as a strategic acquisition or to another PE company (a secondary buyout), or via an initial public offering (IPO) on a stock exchange. Only at the end of a fund's lifetime, after all investments in portfolio companies have been realized, is it possible to calculate the actual asset values of the companies and the investment returns of the fund.

Beyond any one fund, however, the successful private equity firm depends on raising a series of funds—a new fund every three to five years—and sponsors three or even more funds at the same time. While the mechanism for PE firms to make money is the successful acquisition and exit of individual portfolio companies within a relatively short time frame, the PE firm's long-term success as a diversified conglomerate depends on maximizing returns across *all of its funds*. And it has considerable discretion in how it allocates investment opportunities among them in order to maximize returns at the PE firm level. The success of *any individual portfolio company* is a second-order concern to the firm's PE managers. Thus, the perspective of PE owners is radically different from that of owners of privately held companies or the managers of publicly traded corporations, whose primary investment or livelihood depends on the success of the company they own or manage.

Leverage Multiplies Private Equity Returns

The extensive use of debt—or leverage—is at the core of the private equity business model. High leverage in the acquisition of portfolio companies magnifies the returns earned on successful PE investments (see box 3.1). However, high debt levels simultaneously increase the risk of financial distress to the companies they acquire.[11]

Private equity firms buy businesses the way individuals purchase houses—with a down payment or deposit supported by mortgage finance. As we illustrate later in this chapter, this high debt is a key component of the PE business model. In the go-go 1980s, the PE fund's down payment or equity investment was typically 10 percent of the purchase price while 90 percent was borrowed. In subsequent decades, the equity portion increased to 25 to 33 percent on average. In the tight credit conditions in the years immediately following the onset of the financial crisis in 2008, equity investments rose as high as 40 percent for the typical PE fund.

The initial loans come from investment banks, hedge funds, or other large lenders. These are short-term loans—for example, a revolving credit facility or term loan—on which these lenders earn interest. These loans are quickly repackaged into bonds and resold—as collateralized loan obligations (CLOs) or, sometimes, as commercial mortgage–backed securities (CMBS), with the initial lenders collecting substantial fees for this service. Some of the bonds are sold to investors as senior secured notes that provide a claim on the acquired company's assets in case of financial distress; some are unsecured and sold to so-called mezzanine investors. Lenders receive a fixed return determined by the interest rate on this debt.

A critical difference between how an individual purchases a home and how a private equity fund purchases a portfolio company, however, is that homeowners pay their own mortgages, whereas PE funds require the companies they buy to assume the debt and pay it off. PE firms argue that this high debt burden can be serviced and paid down out of the acquired company's own excess cash (cash flow net of what the company needs to pay its bills) and from the higher earnings that result when the principal-agent problem is solved and greater efficiency is achieved.

A low-interest-rate environment reduces the returns to lenders and makes the use of very high leverage even more attractive to private equity funds. Looking at investment C in box 3.1, consider what happens to this investment when the interest rate is 5 percent rather than 10 percent. With a 5 percent interest rate, the interest payment would be $3.75 and the amount the investors would clear at the end of a year after selling the

---

Box 3.1   Leverage: A Double-Edged Sword

Leverage is a double-edged sword that magnifies the returns to investors from successful investments, but increases the risk that a company will face bankruptcy. The effects of leverage on the expected returns earned by investors can best be illustrated by comparing the following examples.

Investment A
   Buy a $100 company with $100 in cash
   Sell the company for $120 in cash after one year
   $120 – $100 = $20
   ($20/$100)*100 = 20 percent return on investment (ROI)

Investment B
   Buy a $100 company with $50 cash and $50 debt at 10 percent interest
   Make one interest payment of $5
   Sell the company for $120 in cash after one year
   Repay $50 loan
   $120 – $5 – $50 – $50 = $15
   ($15/$50)*100 = 30 percent ROI

Investment C
   Buy a $100 company with $25 cash and $75 debt at 10 percent interest
   Make one interest payment of $7.50
   Sell the company for $120 in cash after one year
   Repay $75 loan
   $120 – $7.50 – $25 – $75 = $12.50
   ($12.50/$25)*100 = 50 percent ROI

---

company for $120 would be $120 – $3.75 – $25 – $75 = $16.25. The return on investment would rise to ($16.25/$25)*100 = 65 percent.

PE-owned companies have substantially higher levels of debt than comparable publicly traded companies. One study of 153 buyouts between 1985 and 2006 by large PE firms found, for example, that these companies had an average net debt-to-enterprise value level of 67 percent, compared to 14 percent for comparable publicly traded firms. Average net debt to EBITDA (earnings before interest, tax, depreciation, and amortization) was 5.4 in the buyouts and 1.1 in the public firms.[12]

These high levels of leverage increase the risk of financial distress, especially in economic downturns and periods of slow growth. They increase the risk that a portfolio company will not be able to meet the payments on its debt and that the investment will fail. The result is that, "almost by design, more PE-backed firms will experience financial distress or go bankrupt in economic downturns."[13] It is well known in finance that the probability of financial distress rises as the debt-to-equity ratio increases and that the direct and indirect costs of such distress can be considerable.[14] Nevertheless, PE firms tend to ignore these risks and costs, presumably because they will not be held liable to repay these debts if the company fails. This willingness to ignore the risks may be due, at least in part, to the relatively low rates of bankruptcy of portfolio companies over long periods, although the fact that the 1980s wave of LBOs ended with many portfolio companies in default or bankruptcy was widely recognized.[15] A study of bankruptcy rates worldwide among PE-owned companies between January 1970 and June 2007, for example, found that these highly leveraged enterprises did experience higher bankruptcy rates than comparable publicly traded firms.[16] Per Strömberg found that for the LBOs that occurred between 1970 and 2002, the rate of bankruptcy or reorganization was twice as high as it was for publicly traded companies. For LBO deals completed by 2002, a total of 7 percent ended in bankruptcy or reorganization while the acquired company was in PE hands. Assuming that firms are held on average for six years, Strömberg calculated that this works out to an annual default rate of 1.2 percent a year; the annual default rate for publicly traded companies over this period was 0.6 percent.[17] In Strömberg's view, this higher risk of default is compensated for by the expectation of much higher returns.

This evidence that PE-owned businesses are twice as likely to experience bankruptcy as comparable public companies needs to be put in the context of another study that found that PE-owned companies that default on their debt are *less likely to declare bankruptcy* than their publicly traded counterparts.[18] In a review of about one thousand defaults since 1988, Moody's found that 47 percent of the LBO company defaults ended in bankruptcy compared to 63 percent on non-LBO company defaults.[19] The Moody's study attributes this finding to private equity's greater ability—or power—to get lenders to exchange distressed debt for new debt (so-called distressed exchanges) that will be due a few years in the future.[20] These "amend and extend" deals—less flatteringly referred to as "amend and pretend"—allow equity sponsors to restructure the balance sheets of the distressed companies they own to protect their equity stake. Distressed debt exchanges from 2008 to 2010 began to come due in 2012, when the inadequacies of this form of restructuring debt became clear in the form of follow-on failures. According to a separate Moody's study, a sizable percentage of these have failed. Between 25 and 45 percent of distressed exchanges are expected to fail.[21] If this occurs, it will bring the final bankruptcy rate for LBO company defaults to between 60 and 70 percent, comparable to the non-LBO company default rate.

The rate of financial distress for portfolio firms appears to be even higher for those bought out by more aggressive private equity firms.

Thus, the *Wall Street Journal*'s analysis of Bain Capital's performance found that of the seventy-seven businesses that Bain invested in from 1984 to early 1999, 22 percent either filed for bankruptcy reorganization or were liquidated by the end of the eighth year (12 percent by the end of the fifth year) following the investment[22]—a far higher percentage than the overall percentage of PE deals that ended in financial distress in the Strömberg study.

Strömberg's analysis does not cover the period of the financial crisis and its aftermath. In that period, operating companies held by PE funds came under intense pressure as they struggled to survive the economic downturn and weak recovery while servicing their high levels of debt. Many of the companies bought at or near the 2007 peak of the boom have struggled with high initial leverage and debt-financed dividend payouts to PE investors that have limited their ability to adapt during the recession.[23] Indeed, the largest bankruptcy of 2011 was NewPage Corporation.[24] NewPage, owned by the PE firm Cerberus Capital Management, is the largest North American maker of glossy magazine paper.[25]

A more recent study of highly leveraged firms, half of which were portfolio companies owned by private equity funds, found very high default rates among both PE-owned and non-PE-owned companies in the period 1997 to 2010. This is not surprising, as it is the high level of debt, not the PE ownership per se, that puts companies at risk. Default rates in this study varied from 12.3 percent for 2001 vintage LBOs to 31.6 percent for 1997 LBOs. One-quarter of the sample had a default between 2007 and 2010.[26]

The aggressive use of leverage to finance PE buyouts and the rise of LBOs in the years leading up to the 2008 financial crisis had repercussions beyond the portfolio companies that were bought and sold. As discussed more fully in chapter 9, private equity also contributed indirectly to the growth of the shadow banking system (lightly regulated financial institutions that perform some of the functions of banks) and, in this way, to the increase in systemic risk in the financial system. Between 2005 and 2007, banks made leveraged loans (that is, lower-quality loans rated below investment grade) valued at about $1.1 trillion to finance the transactions of PE funds. Nearly $634 billion of this was used by PE funds to finance a total of 956 leveraged buyouts and the rest was used for other transactions, such as refinancing companies already in the portfolios of PE funds.[27] The banks quickly "syndicated" the loans, selling them to other bank and nonbank financial institutions as collateralized loan obligations—that is, securities backed by the assets of portfolio companies. This growth of securitized loans, which were not subject to oversight by federal bank regulators, helped fuel the expansion of the shadow banking system.[28] The growth of shadow banking contributed to the increase in systemic risk that led to the 2008 financial crisis.

The Incentive Structure of Private Equity Firms: Low Risk, High Rewards

The private equity firm's relationships with the different classes of capital—limited partners and debt providers—are structured to ensure that the lion's share of the gains from successful investments are captured by the PE general partners. The bulk of the gains from successful investments accrue to the equity-holders—the general partner and the limited partners in the PE fund, and disproportionately to the GP. Rewards to the lenders, who have put up the majority of the capital used to purchase portfolio companies, are capped: lenders earn a fixed rate of return on the debt they hold.

The general partner receives three streams of income: management fees from the limited partners, profits from investments, and fees from the portfolio companies. The first two are specified in the contractual agreement between the LPs and the GP, the limited partner agreement (LPA). The typical agreement requires LPs to pay annual management fees of 2 percent of the total investment fund to the GP. Over a ten-year period, the GP collects 20 percent of the value of the fund as management fees, regardless of how well or poorly the fund performs. The LPA also stipulates that the GP will receive a share of the fund's profits, referred to as "carried interest," which is typically 20 percent of the gains from investments in the portfolio companies once the fund achieves the "hurdle" rate of return, typically 8 percent. Some PE firms, such as Bain Capital, claim as much as 30 percent of the profits made by the fund. GPs invest just $1 or $2 in the fund for every $100 invested by the fund's LPs, yet they claim 20 percent of the profit. This is often referred to as the "2 and 20" model.

In sum, general partners stand at the apex of a hierarchy of claims on the returns from investments in the portfolio companies. Below them are the limited partners, who not only pay management fees but hand over a disproportionate share of the fund's profits to the GPs, and the debt-holders, who put up most of the capital used in making acquisitions.[29]

General partners also hold decision-making power over a PE fund's investments. Limited partners are positioned as passive investors with no involvement in investment decisions, although they may voice concern when investments do not yield expected returns. The GP manages the fund's investments and makes all of the decisions about which companies to buy, how they should be managed, and when they should be sold. Good decisions result in good fund performance and in large payouts of carried interest. Thus, carried interest is performance-based pay similar to the bonuses earned by managers in publicly traded companies or to the sales commission earned by real estate brokers or wholesale sales representatives. Yet unlike these other forms of performance-based pay, which are taxed as ordinary income, carried interest is taxed at the lower capital gains rate of 20 percent rather than at the 35 percent marginal tax rate that high-income earners pay on ordinary income. These income streams, as we show next, are structured in a way that provides PE managers with high rewards relative to the risks they assume.

Management Fees

Because general partners receive an annual fee from limited partners regardless of how the fund performs, the risks associated with poor performance are shifted in large part to the LPs. They must hold capital that has been committed to the PE fund but has not yet been invested in liquid assets so that it is available when the PE firm is ready to use it. Thus, they bear most of the costs of investing in a poorly performing fund. In the case of a ten-year fund, a 2 percent annual management fee translates into fees over the life of the fund of 20 percent of committed capital, leaving only 80 percent available for investment. Thus, management fees are a significant cost to the LPs and a major source of income for the GP.

In recent years, limited partners have challenged this arrangement, and there is evidence that fees have declined somewhat, primarily for the larger and more influential investors (see chapter 7). In addition, PE funds that invest in small- and mid-market companies have tended to charge lower fees. A study of 144 PE buyout funds raised between 1993 and 2006, for example, found that the median level of lifetime fees was 12 percent.[30] This does not include, however, a onetime fee charged to LPs to cover the general establishment cost for the fund, which varies with the fund's size but is typically about $1 million.[31]

Despite changes in fee structure, management fees are still a major source of income for PE general partners. The pay packets of GPs, not including their share of carried interest, are quite high. Average senior GP pay in 2011 was nearly $1.4 million and ranged as high as $5 million. For a less experienced junior GP, average salary in 2011 was $270,268 and ranged up to $750,000.[32]

Andrew Metrick and Ayako Yasuda found that "close to two-thirds of the total revenues [of the PE firm] derive from fixed-revenue components, and about one-third from the variable-revenue components."[33] That is, in their study, management and other fees provided two-thirds of the income earned by a fund's general partner. Carried interest accounted for about one-third. An additional important finding of this study is that PE firms increase the size of their funds in successive rounds of fund-raising. Thus, the later funds of a PE firm are larger, leading to significantly higher revenue for the GPs because management fees increase with the amount of capital committed to the fund.[34] The study found that general partners in these later, larger PE funds have higher earnings "despite the fact that these later funds have lower revenue per dollar" of committed funds.[35]

This suggests a potential divergence of interests between the limited partners, who benefit from the higher revenue per dollar of committed funds earned by smaller PE funds, and the general partners, who pocket higher risk-free earnings from large funds with greater amounts of committed capital. We explore this issue further in chapter 7, where we examine the costs and benefits of private equity for the limited partners.

Carried Interest, Debt, and Moral Hazard

The carried interest portion of the general partners' pay is the most important dimension of the low-risk, high-reward incentive system in private equity firms. Recall that PE general partners typically put very little of their own capital at risk—$1 or $2 for every $100 contributed by the limited partners. Yet they receive 20 percent of all investment profits once a hurdle rate of return has been reached. This compensation formula creates perverse incentives for the GPs and encourages them to take on excessive risk—that is, more risk than is socially optimal—because their compensation is very closely tied to highly leveraged bets on the price at which the portfolio company can be sold a few years hence.

Debt, as we saw in the previous section, magnifies the returns to investing in portfolio companies. It increases the gains to the PE fund from successful investments in portfolio companies and raises the carried interest payout to the fund's general partner. As previously noted, if a portfolio company defaults, neither the PE fund nor its PE firm sponsor is responsible for repaying this debt; it is leveraged on the company. And having contributed only a fraction of the equity for the company's purchase, the GPs are largely insulated from losses if the portfolio company fails. While the gains accrue to investors in the PE fund, the losses fall mainly on the company's employees, customers, suppliers, creditors, and community. The fund's general partner—the decision-maker—has the least to lose in the event that a portfolio company becomes bankrupt. As a result, the GP can afford to focus on the gains from a risky strategy and ignore the possibility of losses—creating a classic moral-hazard situation. The upside gains, which in good times are substantial, accrue to the PE firm's partners and its limited partner investors; the losses on the downside fall overwhelmingly on the portfolio company's other stakeholders. In general, moral hazard leads to risky behavior on the part of the decision-maker. In the case of PE funds, it leads the GP to make excessive use of debt, increasing the risk of financial distress and bankruptcy for portfolio companies, with the costs absorbed not only by the immediate stakeholders but also by taxpayers and the economy more generally.

Fees Paid by Portfolio Companies

In addition to the fixed management fees paid by the limited partners and the share of the fund's profits claimed as carried interest, the general partner collects a range of fees from the fund's portfolio companies. These fees can have a detrimental effect on the portfolio companies' financial stability. An example comes from Bain Capital's investment in Cambridge Industries, a Michigan-based automotive plastics supplier, in 1995. Two years later, Bain owned the majority stake in the company. By 2000, Cambridge was in serious financial trouble, having lost money for three years and accumulated a mountain of debt. Bain Capital continued to collect nearly $1 million a year in "advisory fees" from Cambridge even as the company headed toward bankruptcy. Over the five-year period from 1995 to 2000, Bain collected more than $10 million in fees from Cambridge. In 2000, Bain took Cambridge into bankruptcy. The company was bought out of bankruptcy by Meridian Automotive Systems, which slashed more than one thousand jobs.[36]

Another example of abusive use of the ability to collect fees from portfolio companies comes from the case of Buffets Restaurant chain, described in more detail later in this chapter. A partner of the PE firm Caxton-Iseman, the general partner in the fund that acquired Buffets, collected an annual service fee of 2 percent of Buffets's earnings before interest, taxes, depreciation, and amortization (EBITDA), and the GP continued to collect this fee even as Buffets sank into bankruptcy. This fee was in addition to the dividends the PE fund's investors collected from Buffets. This behavior led to a lawsuit against Caxton-Iseman that accused the firm of, among other complaints, unjust enrichment.[37]

General partners collect two main types of fees from their portfolio companies.[38] Portfolio companies pay "transaction fees" that arise from events such as the acquisition of another company, the divestiture of a division of the portfolio company, the refinancing of the portfolio company's debt, and so on. They also pay "monitoring fees," usually on a quarterly basis, to compensate the PE firm's managers for monitoring the portfolio company's performance. This is in addition to the management fees paid by the limited partners to the PE firm for carrying out this management function. With the lack of transparency about PE firm operations, there is limited information available on the size of this revenue stream. Simulations done by Metrick and Yasuda suggest that they range from 14 to 21 percent of total management revenue.[39] Based on SEC filing data for three publicly traded PE firms (Apollo, Blackstone, and KKR) over the period 2005 to 2010, Peter Morris estimated that the median contribution to management fee income from fees charged to portfolio companies is 42 percent.[40] In principle, at least some part of the fees paid by portfolio companies is required to be shared with the limited partners. However, it is unknown what adjustments the PE firms make to the portfolio fees before sharing them.[41] In some cases, the limited partners may not receive any of the portfolio fees once these adjustments are made.[42]

Transparency

Another hallmark of private equity is that it operates with little transparency. As we discussed in chapter 2, prior to implementation of the relevant portions of the 2010 Dodd-Frank Wall Street Reform and Consumer Protection Act in August 2012, PE owners were not legally required to disclose any information about their own operations or those of their portfolio companies. The Dodd-Frank Act now requires most PE firms to file reports on their operations and finances with the Securities and Exchange Commission (SEC), but reporting requirements are thin. Dodd-Frank does not require PE firms to disclose the incomes of partners and senior managers, which companies they own, or financial information about their portfolio companies. Unlike publicly traded companies, which must conform to more rigorous, long-established reporting requirements, with information in the reports publicly available, PE firms must provide only a narrative rather than a quantitative report, and these reports are not made public. Thus, PE-owned companies remain shielded from public attention and accountability. There is no legal requirement to notify employees, unions, vendors, or other stakeholders when private equity takes over the ownership of a company or to publicly disclose the amount of leverage used in the acquisition.

This lack of publicly available data has repercussions for all stakeholders, including PE fund investors, as we discuss more fully in chapter 7 on limited partners and in chapter 9 on the policy implications of the lack of transparency in PE activities. A fundamental problem is that private equity claims about the rate of return on a fund's investments cannot be independently verified. PE firms typically use the internal rate of return as a measure of performance, but the validity of this measure has been seriously questioned in recent research in finance economics.[43]

General partners also estimate the value of a fund's portfolio of companies by including investments that have not yet been exited. That is, given that a fund normally has a life span of ten years, the true value of the fund's returns cannot be calculated until all investments from that fund have been exited. Since 2007, GPs have been required to report portfolio companies at "fair value"—essentially, a hypothetical exit price.[44] This is far better than the earlier guesstimates by GPs of the value of portfolio companies. However, GPs still have extensive discretion in determining the value of these companies. They are free to choose which valuation methodology to use and to make assumptions about financial measures that affect the estimated value of companies in the fund's portfolios. The focus of regulators is on the reasonableness of these assumptions and the GPs' consistency in applying the methodology, which still leaves room for subjectivity in these valuations. Indeed, a recent study found evidence that, despite these more stringent accounting standards, GPs can still manipulate valuations by underestimating the value of a fund's portfolio, so that LP investors are not disappointed when the portfolio companies are ultimately sold, and overestimating the fund's value when marketing a new fund to potential investors.[45]

The lack of publicly available, comprehensive data on private equity funds' track records limits researchers' ability to evaluate the attractiveness of PE investments. Academic studies necessarily rely on data sets that are very partial in nature. They may rely on access to fund performance obtained from a large limited partner with investments across a large number of funds[46] or on data from a software provider on the performance of investments by LPs who use this software for record-keeping and for monitoring their PE investments.[47] The lack of publicly available, comprehensive data on the financial activities of PE funds makes it impossible to know the biases that are built into the data sets used in analyses or the true returns to PE investments.

The PE Business Model for Portfolio Companies

Private equity firms take an active role in the governance, operations, and financial management of the companies they acquire. The general partner of the fund plays a large role in selecting the company's board of directors, which typically includes partners in the PE firm and outside industry experts appointed by the GP in addition to the company's CEO. Compared to publicly traded companies, PE portfolio companies have smaller company boards, hold more formal and informal meetings, and replace poorly performing management teams more rapidly than their non-PE-backed counterparts.[48] The GP actively advises and monitors the portfolio companies in the PE fund's portfolio.

The management plan for the portfolio company is driven by its capital structure—a feature of the PE model that builds on that of the leveraged buyouts in the 1980s (see chapter 2). At the direction of the general partner, managers of portfolio companies usually draft a "100-day plan" as an initial blueprint for restructuring the company's operations in order to service its increased debt burden and meet the PE fund's targets. In some instances, the GP puts its own management team in place to develop and implement a new business strategy.

The PE firm uses financial incentives to align the interests of an acquired company's top managers with those of its PE owners. Portfolio company managers are presented with a highly leveraged capital structure (the stick) and the promise of very generous performance-based pay (the carrot) if they meet targets established by the PE firm and substantially improve the portfolio company's profit margins. PE firms quickly replace managers who do not meet these expectations. In one study, new PE owners replaced more than one-third (39 percent) of CEOs in the first one hundred days after the LBO, and more than two-thirds (69 percent) at some point during the deal.[49] PE firms put great pressure on CEOs to perform or perish, as Emily Thornton put it in a *BusinessWeek* cover story.[50] As Metrick and Yasuda note, the primary goal of the PE business model is to maximize returns for investors—the PE firm that sponsors the buyout fund and the limited partners it recruits as fund investors.[51]

Research on private equity identifies various sources of gains for PE funds. These may be combined in different ways in various industry sectors, and their relative importance may vary as business cycle and competitive conditions change.[52] These strategies may be grouped into two general categories: business and operational strategies that add value to the portfolio firm, and financial engineering strategies that allow PE owners to extract wealth without necessarily adding value. Business and operational strategies are similar to those that are often used by public corporations, including investments in new processes, technologies, or human capital; growth via acquisitions or new marketing strategies; and restructuring and downsizing. Financial engineering includes the sale of assets, with proceeds going to PE investors; the aggressive use of debt to multiply gains, obtain tax advantages, or pay dividends to investors; and the use of bankruptcy to reduce debt, abrogate contracts with unions and suppliers, and rid the company's owners of workers' pension liabilities.

Some have argued that private equity firms shifted their role in portfolio companies—from "financial engineers" in the LBOs of the 1980s to "operational engineers" in the private equity boom of the pre-crisis 2000s.[53] But little evidence supports this claim. As noted in chapter 2, the capital structure in the KKR buyouts set the management plan after the buyout to achieve cost and revenue targets. In the 2000s, the large PE firms did use somewhat lower levels of debt than in the 1980s, and they did employ more industry experts and look for operational gains, but their business model did not shift to focus on operations. As we show more clearly in chapter 5, the balance between financial and operational strategies depends on the capital structure of the deal, and this varies by the value of the portfolio company.

The greatest opportunities for strategic and operational improvements occur in small and midmarket companies (under $500 million in enterprise value and frequently much smaller), which often lack professional management and modern financial accounting and information technology systems. They may be too small to attract the top management talent that could help them grow. Private equity owners can bring big company experience to these small and midsize enterprises. Acquisitions of large midmarket portfolio companies with an enterprise value of $500 million to $1 billion or megadeals for companies with an enterprise value of more than $1 billion provide few opportunities for value creation through operational engineering.[54] These very large, mature corporations already have professional management, accounting, and IT systems in place and typically have the resources and expertise to invest in growth and operational improvements. Private equity has fewer opportunities to make improvements along these lines, but the larger assets and cash flow of these corporations can be used to support very high levels of debt, to return dividends to PE investors, and to engage in other financial strategies.

Two further general points about the PE business model at the level of the portfolio company deserve mention: the role of a bull market or stock market bubble in boosting PE returns and the distinction between the profit-seeking and rent-seeking activities that private equity can use to generate returns.

A bull market for stocks, in which share prices rise across the board and price-to-earnings ratios increase, is a boon to private equity. The rising stock market allows PE firms to exit investments in operating companies at a price that is a higher multiple of earnings than the earnings multiple at which the company was purchased. This can lift returns for PE firms, but has little to do with the actions of PE firms and is more akin to successful stock picking or to timing the market.

The conceptual distinction between profit-seeking and rent-seeking activities is straightforward. Profit-seeking activities generate profit by creating value and increasing wealth—a process of value creation and economic growth that increases the size of the economic pie as well as the size of the slice that goes to profit. Rent-seeking activities, in contrast, generate company profits via changes in the structure and/or financing of the firm not related to wealth creation. Such efforts maximize the flow of revenue to a company's bottom line without simultaneously increasing value and "generate social waste rather than social surplus."[55] These actions fail to increase the size of the economic pie, but instead increase the size of the profit slice at the expense of other stakeholders.

We turn next to a detailed discussion and illustrative examples of how private equity uses business and operating strategies and financial strategies to make money.

Business and Operating Strategies

Private equity firms can add value to the companies they acquire through the development and effective implementation of a business strategy that takes the company to the next level or through improvements in operations that increase earnings and profit margins—for example, better supply chain management, new retail channels, technology modernization, process improvements, and worker engagement. Successful companies use this repertoire of strategies for organic growth and competitive advantage, but few PE firms offer any particular expertise in these areas. Rather, they rely on expert consultants as needed to provide guidance in these areas.

Anticipating Industry Growth Potential

The sweet spot for private equity is acquiring a company with a respectable earnings record in an industry whose fortunes are about to improve dramatically. Implementing a business strategy that positions the acquired company to benefit from pending developments in the industry can yield huge gains for PE investors without the necessity of large investments in operational improvements. Some of the most successful PE firms are much admired for the ability of the firm's partners to pick winners.

Hospital systems, especially those with a leading market position in the geographic area they serve, appear to meet these criteria. Health care is a stable, noncyclical industry. Medicare and Medicaid payments typically make up half or more of hospital revenues, and these are likely to increase as the population ages, ensuring both a rising demand for hospital services (though not hospital admissions) and increased revenue from these government programs. In the last decade, private equity has invested heavily in hospital systems that include outpatient and other facilities: six of the twelve largest hospital chains were acquired by private equity by the late 2000s, though several have since become publicly traded companies.[56] In 2010, forty PE firms established the Healthcare Private Equity Association (HCPEA), representing 500 member companies with $200 billion in revenue and over 750,000 employees in the health care industry.[57]

For example, Cerberus Capital Management created a hospital acquisition arm called Steward Health Care System. In 2010 Steward acquired highly regarded Caritas Christi Health Care, a six-hospital Roman Catholic health care chain in Boston known for its strong CEO, Ralph de la Torre, an MIT-trained engineer and cardiac surgeon.[58] Warburg Pincus acquired the well-positioned RegionalCare Hospital Partners in 2009; the network has since bought several other not-for-profit hospitals. Blackstone Group and Metalmark established Vanguard Health Systems as a vehicle for acquiring a large number of not-for-profit hospitals, including, in December 2010, the Detroit Medical Center.[59] Vanguard Health Systems has since had a successful IPO and is now a publicly traded company, although its PE owners continue to be major shareholders. Indeed, according to *PitchBook News*, PE firms have invested in eighty-four companies in the hospital and inpatient services industry since the beginning of 2007.[60] The passage of the Patient Protection and Affordable Care Act (ACA) in 2010 established requirements for hospitals that favor larger hospital systems and require more sophisticated management and capital strategies to compete effectively. Many not-for-profit hospitals lack the ability to obtain financing for investments in electronic health records and in the infrastructure it would take to provide the comprehensive patient care required by the Affordable Care Act. Many not-for-profit hospitals understand the consolidation taking place in the industry and recognize the need to be part of a larger hospital system in order to survive. The result is a large group of motivated sellers and attractively priced hospitals from which PE firms can choose those with a leading market position or strong brand name. The ACA's requirements have created the opportunity for private equity to make operational improvements with broad benefits for society.

Health care reform promises to provide many uninsured Americans with access to health insurance and to reduce the unpaid charity care that currently drains hospital resources. While not without risks, it creates a huge potential upside for the hospital industry. The seven largest publicly traded hospital companies by market capitalization wrote off about $7.4 billion in unpaid hospital bills in fiscal year 2011, a year in which they had about $5.5 billion in pretax income. Reducing the number of uninsured patients is expected to significantly benefit these hospitals.[61] Shares of publicly traded hospital companies, including Vanguard Health Systems, surged between 5 and 9 percent on the day the U.S. Supreme Court upheld the Affordable Care Act.[62] The price at which these companies now trade relative to their earnings has increased.

If it all works out as anticipated, the PE owners will make investments in technology and patient management infrastructure and improve hospital operations and the quality of care. Both they and the public will benefit. As the price of the hospitals they acquire increases in relation to the hospitals' earnings, they will be able to exit their investments in these hospitals at a profit. Skeptical observers, however, have raised two caveats. First, some part of the cash flow of the acquired hospitals is committed to servicing the high debt that was used to acquire them, raising questions about the steps that hospitals may need to take to increase revenues, reduce costs, and increase cash flow. Second, industry experts note that hospitals receive on average 97 cents for every dollar of services provided to a Medicare patient and 93 cents for Medicaid patients.[63] As part of the negotiations over health care reform, hospitals agreed to $155 billion in cuts in government payments.[64] Operating improvements will have to result in cost savings sufficient to cover these revenue shortfalls or PE owners will have to find other means of increasing revenues and reducing costs for this business strategy to succeed. The continuing efforts of opponents of the Affordable Care Act to defund the law in 2012 and 2013 introduced additional uncertainties in the hospital sector, considerably slowing PE investments in this sector during those years.

Turnaround Investment in Distressed Companies

Distressed investment can be tricky. It is no small feat to identify companies experiencing financial distress that have the potential to be turned around, to make them more competitive, and to yield healthy profits for investors. Most PE funds prefer to acquire healthy companies, and indeed, the evidence suggests that distressed investing is a tiny sliver—about 2 percent prior to the financial crisis—of PE industry investments.[65] We examine distressed investing in more detail in chapter 6; here we briefly highlight a case in which a PE firm correctly anticipated a change in an industry's fortunes and successfully invested in failing companies and turned them around.

The U.S. steel industry was buoyed in the 1990s by strong worldwide economic growth that fueled a high demand for steel. After nearly two decades of decline, steel prices rose, companies were profitable, and employment in the industry increased. This brief interlude came to an end in 1997, when world demand for steel collapsed. The openness of the U.S. economy to trade made this country a prime target for foreign steel producers to dump steel at prices below production cost. China's accession to the World Trade Organization (WTO) in December 2001, which opened U.S. markets to Chinese steel, exacerbated the situation. Forty-five U.S. steel companies declared bankruptcy between 1998 and 2001.

Wilbur Ross, whose investment firm owned the political daily *The Hill*, was aware that President George W. Bush was contemplating the imposition of tariffs on imported steel in response to the illegal dumping. In 2002 his PE firm, WL Ross, formed the International Steel Group (ISG) as a vehicle to purchase major bankrupt steel companies. It bought LTV Steel in February 2002, and a month later President Bush imposed a 30 percent temporary tariff on fourteen categories of steel. The tariff led to a dramatic reversal in the fortunes of the industry and allowed WL Ross and the steelworkers' union time to restructure and consolidate a major part of U.S. steelmaking capacity and turn the companies around. WL Ross sold its steel companies a short time later, earning some $4.5 billion on the investment (see chapter 6 for a full discussion of this example).

Operational Improvements

Increasing a company's earnings makes it possible to sell the company at a higher price than the price paid to buy it, even if the multiple of earnings—the price-to-earnings ratio—at which it is sold is unchanged. For example, a company bought at a price that is six times earnings will be sold at a higher price if earnings increase even if the multiple remains at six. The potential for making operating improvements and increasing earnings is what makes investments in small and midsize companies attractive.

In considering the purchase of privately owned companies, especially those owned by the founding family, private equity looks for companies that are well established, have a strong track record, and are large enough to have proven themselves. Often the company's founder is the CEO and the company lacks a professional management team. There are usually operational problems that need to be fixed, and private equity's greater access to financing for expansion may facilitate the implementation of a larger vision or a more aggressive business strategy for the company. A common strategy is the acquisition or add-on of another small company that offers the potential for synergy and scale. In other cases, private equity may provide capital for expansion and management expertise to a regional company whose deep knowledge of its products and processes provides the potential for growth to a national or global enterprise.

Axle Tech, headquartered in Troy, Michigan, with manufacturing operations in Oshkosh, Wisconsin, was highlighted by the Private Equity Growth Capital Council as a great example of how private equity helps companies increase sales revenues and earnings. The Carlyle Group did help Axle Tech develop a winning business strategy and increase earnings, but the story of PE involvement in the company does not begin with Carlyle and, as described in box 3.2 is more complicated than it first appears.

Investing in midsize companies presents risks as well as opportunities for private equity. It may be difficult to take a smaller company to scale. Integrating merged companies creates its own challenges. And even if the investment is successful, it may be difficult to exit. The strategy may be successful in terms of establishing a large and profitable enterprise, but it may not lead to a high-priced sale of the portfolio company, as illustrated in box 3.3 by PE efforts to consolidate the water sports industry.

Positioning a Company for Rapid Growth

Private equity firms operating in the low end of the market that acquire firms with an enterprise value between $25 million and $100 million or even lower typically make money through growth strategies rather than through financial engineering or dividend recapitalizations. Although successfully implementing a growth strategy can be challenging, helping a small portfolio company implement a strategy for rapid growth in revenue and EBITDA pays off for PE investors in two ways: the higher earnings lead to a higher price at exit even if the multiple of earnings is unchanged, and the demonstrated potential for growth also enables the PE firm to sell the company at a higher multiple of earnings than the multiple at which it bought the company. This is an important source of potential gains for PE firms that invest in technology or other companies

---

Box 3.2   Axle Tech

Axle Tech was a regional manufacturer of axles, brakes, and other drivetrain systems and components for off-highway and specialty vehicles for the military and commercial markets. It was a midsize company with 450 employees when it was acquired in a leveraged buyout by the Carlyle Group on October 3, 2005, for $345 million, including $80 million in equity (23 percent) and $260 million in debt (77 percent) leveraged on the company. Three years later, in December 2008, when it was purchased as a strategic acquisition by General Dynamics, it was a leading global supplier of heavy-duty axle and suspension systems.[66] Carlyle and Axle Tech CEO Mary Petrovich focused the company's development efforts on the fast-growing military sector and the commercial aftermarket, doubling employment and tripling revenue.[67] Carlyle reports that, working with Petrovich, it increased Axle Tech's capital investment, executed three add-on acquisitions, doubled worldwide production capacity from 2,399 to 4,600 axles per month, and doubled employment to approximately 900 employees in Michigan, Wisconsin, Illinois, France, and Brazil, including 300 unionized employees represented by the United Auto Workers. Carlyle attributes Axle Tech's success to targeting the fast-growing military sector, expanding its range of offerings in the commercial aftermarket, strengthening its management team, and improving its financial reporting capabilities.[68] The pressure that Carlyle put on Petrovich to achieve these performance gains—and the pressure she put on her senior managers—is documented in Emily Thornton's *BusinessWeek* article.[69] Turnover of top management was very high. Six of the seven top executives who reported to Petrovich had been replaced by 2006, and four of the new recruits were gone by November 2007.[70]

Carlyle succeeded in helping a regional manufacturing company develop and execute a business strategy that enabled it to grow into a global supplier of axles for heavy-duty, specialty vehicles. But the story of Axle-Tech's success is not quite so benign.

When Carlyle acquired Axle Tech in 2005, it did so by buying the company from another private equity firm, Wynnchurch Capital. Axle Tech had been a neglected division within a larger vehicular supplier when Wynnchurch acquired it in December 2002. Its revenues had declined over the previous four years, and Wynnchurch and a minority investor were able to buy it for $5.5 million. It was Wynnchurch that hired Petrovich as CEO, and it was Petrovich who, almost immediately after taking the job, extracted major concessions from union workers that reduced workers' pay and benefits.[71] As noted in the *Milwaukee Journal Sentinel,* "Autoworkers at AxleTech International in Oshkosh [members of UAW local 291] . . . agreed to cut their wages, to pay more toward health insurance and to drop medical coverage for retirees."[72] As Wynnchurch reported, Petrovich "transformed the company's cost structure."[73] Lower pay for workers and initiatives in procurement and product development led revenues and profits to rise dramatically during Wynnchurch's ownership of the company and positioned Axle Tech for a highly profitable sale to Carlyle.[74]

Box 3.3   Consolidation in the Water Sports Industry

The water sports industry, which was growing rapidly in the 1990s, was largely fragmented, with small companies manufacturing one or a few items—whitewater rafts, kayaks, stand-up paddle boats, canoes, life jackets, and other accessories—and marketing the products through mom-and-pop specialty stores. The private equity firms Arcapita Bank and American Capital Strategies (now American Capital) established platforms in 1998 to acquire a number of these small companies. Arcapita bought Perception Kayak and Dagger Canoe and merged the two companies to form the Water Sport Division of Watermark Paddlesports as Arcapita's vehicle; American Capital established Confluence Watersports. Their strategy was to consolidate operations such as purchasing and to develop a new retail channel for marketing these products—the big-box stores, which had found it difficult to deal with a large number of small suppliers. Their major thrust, however, was to sweep up the smaller specialty dealers and force them into the buying programs that the PE firms were already using for the larger box stores. Privately held Johnson Outdoors, which had earlier acquired Ocean Kayak and Carlisle Paddles, also went into buying mode and purchased Necky Kayaks and Extrasport Lifejackets.[75]

All three groups tried to become dominant, putting pressure on the retailers who carried these brands and competing aggressively with each other. The result was chaos in the water sports market. Some specialty retailers dropped various competing lines from other producers and focused on a limited product mix supplied by one or another of the PE-owned companies. Other retailers became frustrated with the tactics used to push them into the buying programs and refused to "play ball," which ultimately led to some stores losing distribution lines and sales. The competition among the three large producers led to prices being slashed. Nobody made any money. Caught in the fallout were some of the remaining specialty manufacturers whose brand labels could not compete and who could not survive the price wars; they ultimately went out of business.

Private equity's entry into the water sports market created serious problems for smaller specialty brands and for the small retailers that carried them. Nevertheless, some of these specialty companies, still owned by the founding family, managed to survive and, ultimately, to thrive. Among these was NRS, which is still family-owned. Despite the difficult environment, NRS was able to take advantage of specialty retailers' reluctance to adopt the new business model pushed on them by Watermark Paddlesports and Confluence. NRS adjusted its product lines, sales methods, and business relationships, which it could more easily do than its competitors. NRS now markets to more than one thousand small shops as well as specialty retailers such as REI, EMS, and LL Bean.[76]

Confluence acquired Wave Sport, Mad River Canoe, and Wilderness Systems in 1998 and 1999. Six years later, in 2005, it acquired its less successful rival, Watermark Paddlesports, reportedly for less than Arcapita

---

Box 3.3   *Continued*

Bank had paid for it. In this deal, Arcapita exited its water sports investment by selling the portfolio company to another PE firm in a secondary buyout, the most common type of exit in the recreational goods industry, according to PitchBook.[77] Today, according to PitchBook, Confluence is a profitable company. It employs 650 people and designs and distributes canoes and kayaks in the United States and Canada. It manufactures a range of products for the canoe and paddling industry as well as canoeing and kayaking accessories, paddles, flotation devices, and apparel.

Whether by choice or circumstance, American Capital still had not exited its investments in Confluence in 2013, fifteen years after it made its first acquisition in the water sports industry.

---

with high growth potential. New Capital Partners' acquisition of a very small company—the health IT company Awarix, Inc.—in a leveraged buyout in January 2006, described in box 3.4 provides an example.

Financial Engineering Strategies

Financial strategies are a significant source of private equity earnings, notably in megadeals in which private equity acquires large operating companies. Indeed, in the financial market conditions that prevailed from 2002 to 2007—low interest rates and easy access to borrowed funds, a bull market in stocks, and a real estate bubble—strategic and operational improvements were relatively unimportant. In this financial environment, enhancements in operations accounted for only a fraction of PE firms' earnings. Financial engineering—the use of high levels of debt, tax arbitrage, and dividend recapitalizations—rather than operational improvements explains much of private equity's financial success during the bubble years. High levels of debt put pressure on managers to cut costs and increase cash flow by firing employees or slashing wages and benefits. This led to higher profit margins, but had little to do with increasing efficiency. What is striking is how little the earnings of the PE funds (as opposed to the competitiveness or sustainability of their portfolio companies) depended on business strategy or improvements in operations during this period.[78] The exceptions can be found in midmarket deals by smaller PE funds—which, as illustrated earlier, put greater emphasis on business and human resource strategies to drive revenue and earnings growth—and in some turnaround deals. Even in these cases, however, the use of relatively high levels of debt to acquire companies boosted returns to their PE owners.

Box 3.4   Awarix, Inc.

Awarix's software provides hospitals with a patient care visibility system that enables clinicians to coordinate clinical and location information to better and more efficiently care for patients simply by looking at large-screen displays. The technology lets nurses know about patients' needs—whether they need medication, are waiting to be taken for a test, or are ready to be discharged. Housekeeping staff can see when a patient is about to be discharged and more quickly prepare to clean the room. In addition, management can monitor employees' work performance electronically.

The technology also allows patients to be moved smoothly through the treatment process by preventing the unnecessary delays caused by backups when rooms are not ready for them to be admitted or when patients are being transferred from one unit of a hospital to another. These problems often lead to overcrowding in the emergency room or to ambulances being diverted to other hospitals. A study by the Government Accountability Office found that a major cause of overcrowding is the inability to transfer patients from the emergency department to an in-patient bed.[79] Awarix's software seeks to address this problem by streamlining various processes—such as reducing the time a patient is kept in the hospital waiting to have tests done, reducing the time between discharge authorization and actual discharge, reducing the time for housekeeping staff to learn that a room is vacant and in need of cleaning. Such streamlining increases a hospital's capacity utilization.

Awarix was a very small company when it was established in September 2003, with fewer than a dozen employees. Awarix technology had been implemented in two Alabama hospitals when New Capital Partners led an investment of $3 million at the end of 2005. Over the next eighteen months, under the direction of a PE firm, the number of hospitals that implemented Awarix grew to nineteen—a notable rate of adoption in an industry with long investment cycles. The PE firm exited its investment in Awarix via the sale of the company to a strategic buyer, McKesson Corporation, eighteen months later, in July 2007, for four times what it had paid.[80] McKesson, a publicly traded company, is one of the largest suppliers of solutions to improve health care delivery and the patient experience.[81] After its acquisition by McKesson, it had more than four hundred McKesson sales reps available to market its software.[82] In a short period of time, New Capital Partners had demonstrated Awarix's growth potential and prepared it to be acquired by a large enterprise.

New Capital Partners is a PE firm that focuses on acquiring successful companies with growth potential at the micro end of the acquisitions market. It also specializes in particular sectors, mainly health care and financial services. Its current fund focuses on deal sizes in the $10 million to $20 million range; its earlier fund bought even smaller companies. The firm seeks out

Box 3.4   *Continued*

investments with high growth potential that it can acquire at a good price, typically five times EBITDA, financed with 40 to 50 percent debt and 50 to 60 percent equity. The small size of the acquired companies and their modest revenues make growth the only viable strategy for achieving high returns for investors: with relatively few employees, there is not much room to cut costs, and their small size presents few opportunities for financial engineering.

New Capital Partners is able to guide portfolio companies like Awarix in implementing a growth strategy because it has deep industry expertise and over the years has developed a network of professionals and talented managers it can recruit to fill key positions in the portfolio firm. It takes an active role in building the management team and hiring experienced industry professionals to fill top positions. Because of its proven track record in growing small companies into much larger ones, New Capital Partners is able to recruit extremely talented managers—CEOs, CFOs, COOs, and top sales and marketing professionals—who otherwise might not be interested in joining a small enterprise. As in the case of Awarix, this human resource strategy is key to the PE firm's success in achieving the rapid growth of its portfolio companies and selling them as strategic acquisitions to large, publicly traded enterprises.[83]

New Capital Partners also develops a deep knowledge of the companies it acquires, sometimes facilitated by personal relationships of trust. New Capital Partners acquired Awarix from its CEO, who had started two other businesses and was known to the PE firm's partners. He was creative and very good at coming up with elegant solutions to problems that also had commercial applications and could be implemented. He was not as equipped, however, to take the company from a small success to a large enterprise and was willing to bring in both equity partners and additional management talent while retaining an equity interest in the business.

> We liked what he had developed, but we knew it needed to be professionalized. It needed professional management and a high-level team of sales professionals. We hired a CEO that we knew who had previously run a company with this type of sales force. We increased the number of sales reps—guys making $200,000-plus a year—from one to six. . . . We weren't ready to sell the business after just eighteen months—we were in negotiations with both McKesson and GE to partner on distribution of Awarix's IT solution. But McKesson wanted to buy it now so they wouldn't have to pay more later— and was willing to pay future value for our business today.[84]

Selling the company to McKesson for four times what it had paid in just eighteen months yielded a very high rate of return for New Capital Partners and its LP investors. And the founder and former CEO of Awarix cashed out of the business to start another entrepreneurial venture.

Writing candidly in the *Financial Times* during the 2012 U.S. presidential campaign, Luke Johnson, chairman of the private equity firm Risk Capital Partners, described the PE model in the following terms:

> Stating the obvious, private equity is so-called because it does not operate in the public arena. It is a pure capitalist pursuit in which investors buy companies and try to sell them for a capital gain. There is an intense focus on returns for shareholders and rather less concern for citizens as a whole. Generally speaking, corporate social responsibility, sustainability, disclosure and environmental issues are not as much a priority as they are to public companies, charities and government.
>
> Buyout houses such as Mr. Romney's Bain Capital use debt to acquire companies, and in doing so pay less corporation tax than might otherwise have been the case. These companies are run to maximise profits for the owners, rather than for the creation of jobs. Of course private equity can be healthy for an economy, but as a career it is probably at the opposite extreme from the public services in terms of motivations. Attention is not directed towards the common wealth, but enriching the management, buyout partners and their institutional backers. That is the nature of the game. To argue otherwise is bogus.[85]

Earlier in this chapter, we saw how private equity can maximize investor returns by enhancing the performance of portfolio companies and creating economic wealth. We turn now to a discussion of the means by which shareholder returns can be increased not via an increase in economic wealth but as a result of redistribution from other stakeholders to shareholders.

Transfers from Portfolio Companies

Transfers from portfolio companies to PE owners can be an important source of private equity gains. These take two main forms: making dividend payments to the PE owners, and stripping the operating company of its real estate or other assets.

Dividend Recapitalizations Dividends are recapitalized when a company takes on new debt in order to pay a special dividend to shareholders. Dividend recapitalizations have exploded in use in the last decade as private equity owners have used loans to pay themselves dividends, typically in the form of junk bonds. In this way, PE owners transfer resources to themselves that could have been used to improve portfolio company operations. Dividend recaps return much—or even all—of the initial equity investment to investors. They increase pressure on the portfolio company to reduce costs and make it more likely that the company will lay off workers. According to Standard & Poor's, dividend recapitalizations damage credit quality, may increase defaults, and may drive portfolio companies into bankruptcy.[86]

Dividend recapitalizations are controversial, even among PE investors. Traditionally, private equity owners wait for an exit event—such as a sale of the business or a return to public trading on a stock exchange—before generating a return. Not only do dividend recaps undermine the argument that PE returns are due to improvements in company performance, but in several instances PE firms have been accused by creditors of "bleeding out" the company and causing it to become insolvent. Creditors of the bankrupt restaurant chain Buffets, which at its peak operated more than six hundred restaurants under a variety of brand names and employed thirty-six thousand workers, sued PE firm Caxton-Iseman (since renamed CI Capital Partners) and Sentinel Capital Partners, charging that the dividend recapitalizations and annual service fees they charged Buffets resulted in losses and the 2008 bankruptcy of the once-profitable company. The PE investors had put up $130 million in equity toward the $643 million purchase price for Buffets in 2000; in June 2002, they took $150 million out of the company and distributed the money to themselves. Over the years, the PE owners collected $250 million in dividend recapitalizations. The lawsuit alleged that Caxton-Iseman and the minority shareholders had drained millions of dollars in transfers that were detrimental to Buffets and its unsecured creditors. In September 2010, the PE investors settled the case for more than $23 million.[87] CI Capital Partners is not the only company to face such accusations. Sun Capital faced similar accusations in relation to the bankruptcy of the Mervyn's Department Store chain, while TPG Capital faced a similar complaint in the case of TIM Hellas.[88]

PE owners uncertain of a profitable exit from a portfolio investment may resort to dividend recapitalizations in order to recoup their original investment despite the increased risk of distress for the portfolio company. The retailer Urban Brands (Ashley Stewart & Marianne Stores) was bought out by TSG Capital Group in April 1996 for $30 million. Six years later, in January 2002, unable to resell the company for what it had paid, TSG took a dividend recapitalization. It ultimately sold the company to another PE firm, Trimaran Capital, in April 2004 for $20 million. Urban Brands eventually went bankrupt and was bought out of bankruptcy in November 2010 by the PE firm GB Merchant for $15.7 million.[89]

Harry & David, the food and gift mail-order business, provides another example. It was acquired in 2004 by Wasserstein & Co. and Highfields Capital Management for $253 million, with $82.6 million in equity and $170 million in debt. A year later, in 2005, the PE owners took a dividend of $82.6 million, and then two more dividends totaling $19 million. This guaranteed the investors in Harry & David a 23 percent return no matter what happened to the company. In March 2011, the company—sinking under a debt load of $200 million—declared bankruptcy.[90] The federal Pension Benefit Guaranty Corporation assumed responsibility for the retirement benefits of 2,513 Harry & David's employees and retirees.[91] Note that both Urban Brands and Harry & David were small companies that should have provided opportunities for operational improvements and growth; instead, PE firms extracted dividend recapitalizations, resulting in bankruptcy in both cases.

Although dividend recapitalizations increase the debt load of portfolio companies, they do not usually end in bankruptcy. Hospital Corporation of America (HCA), a publicly traded, for-profit hospital chain at the time it was acquired by private equity, was taken private in a leveraged buyout in 2006 by a consortium that included Bain Capital Partners, KKR, Merrill Lynch Global Private Equity, Citigroup, Bank of America, and HCA's CEO. These PE firms and the limited partners in their funds put up $5.5 billion in equity and leveraged the remaining 75 percent of the $21 billion deal. The investors had planned to return HCA to the public market in 2010 via an initial public offering in the stock market. Their goal was to sell one-fifth of the company via shares valued at $4.6 billion. This would have enabled the PE owners to recoup 75 percent of their original $5.5 billion investment while retaining an 80 percent share in the company.[92]

The slowdown in the IPO market that year led the PE owners to delay. Instead, HCA's PE investors recouped nearly all of their equity investment in the hospital chain by paying themselves a total of $4.25 billion in three dividend recapitalizations in 2010. The last dividend was financed in part by junk bonds issued by the new holding company, HCA Holdings, because debt issued by HCA had reached limits set by existing debt covenants.[93] The debt received a Caa1 rating from Moody's—seven levels into speculative, or "junk," status. This type of debt was highly risky for the lenders because it was issued by the holding company, HCA Holdings (which had no assets), was unsecured by collateral from HCA Holdings' operating subsidiaries (mainly the HCA hospital chain), was subordinate to the existing debt of those subsidiaries, and contained no negative pledge covenants against the issuance of future debt or dividends.[94] As of December 31, 2010, HCA's debt level was $25.4 billion—or almost ten times its cash flow from operations for that year.[95] On March 9, 2011, HCA went public, selling 126 million shares at $30 and raising $3.79 billion.[96]

Seaworld Entertainment is another recent example in which the private equity owner was able to more than recover its investment through dividend recapitalizations and an IPO while still retaining a 63 percent ownership share in the company. Blackstone purchased Seaworld in 2009, with $1 billion of its own equity and $1.3 billion in leveraged loans. From 2009 to 2012, it extracted some $627 million through fees and two dividend recapitalizations—$100 million in September 2011 and $500 million in October 2012. In April 2013, it launched an IPO and sold 16 million of its shares in Seaworld, which yielded at least an additional $432 million for the PE firm.[97] Taken together, these returns more than offset Blackstone's initial investment. Industry analysts also point to other ways in which Blackstone made money from Seaworld. It received $17 million for "strategic advice" during the first three years it owned the company; Seaworld then used some of its own proceeds from the IPO to pay Blackstone $47 million to end that agreement for strategic advice. Blackstone also made $2.1 million for its role in underwriting the IPO.[98]

The OpCo/PropCo Model In the OpCo/PropCo model, private equity firms divide a portfolio company into two companies: the operating company (OpCo) and the property company (PropCo). They typically sell the property company, return the proceeds to the PE investors, and then require the portfolio company to lease back and pay rent on the property it used to own—often at rents above the market price. Sale-leaseback arrangements can make sense when the proceeds of the sale go to the operating company, but in these instances the proceeds go to the PE investors. The OpCo/PropCo strategy has been widely used in such industries as retail, restaurant chains, nursing homes, and other businesses rich in real estate assets.

In the nursing home industry, although the practice of selling off real estate assets became fairly common among publicly owned chains in the 1990s, the returns were used to buy additional nursing home operations—that is, they were typically used to finance growth. Private equity adapted this strategy in the 2000s to return dividends to itself, thereby undermining the growth potential of its portfolio companies. Moreover, PE firms have combined this strategy with another: separately incorporating each facility in a nursing home chain, thereby shielding the PE fund from legal liability in the event of negligence or medical or other errors. Not only is it impossible for a patient to sue the PE firm sponsor or the investors in the fund that acquired the chain, but the resources of other members of the nursing home chain are also shielded. Combining these two strategies—selling off nursing home assets and separately incorporating each home in a chain—ensures that the operating company has legal liability in the case of negligence or medical errors, but very little in the way of resources to satisfy patients' claims against it. Separating real estate assets from the operating companies is a strategy for minimizing exposure to patient litigation. The 2007 acquisitions of the HCR Manor Care chain by the Carlyle Group and of the Genesis Health Care chain by Formation Capital and FER Partners provide examples of this widespread practice. Joseph E. Casson and Julia McMillen approvingly explain why these practices are important:

> In the context of nursing home ownership and operation, legal entities such as corporations, limited liability companies and limited liability partnerships can be formed to benefit nursing home companies by limiting the financial liability and Medicare and Medicaid exclusion exposure of the

real estate investors and business owners. . . . The business entities can also prevent litigants from obtaining judgments against related companies, and the owners personally, in proceedings alleging Medicare or Medicaid over-payments, false claims, or negligence.[99]

The OpCo/PropCo strategy has played out somewhat differently in the retail and restaurant industries. There, businesses traditionally pre-ferred to hold little debt and to own the properties where their businesses were located because doing so allowed them to handle the inevitable downturns in the business cycle, sudden changes in consumer tastes, or periods of weak consumer spending. This business model gave retail-ers and restaurant owners the flexibility to survive the inevitable bad times. Private equity often turns this business model on its head when it acquires businesses with valuable real estate holdings. The real estate assets are mortgaged to finance the leveraged buyout of the company being acquired. The new owners require the operating company to sign long-term leases and lease back the property and facilities that it pre-viously owned from the property company—at market and sometimes above-market rents. After holding the real estate long enough to qualify for favorable capital gains treatment, the PE owners sell these assets to a real estate investment trust (REIT) or other buyer—paying off the debt and in many cases recouping their initial equity investment and more. The operating company receives little or none of the proceeds from the sale of what had been its property. Without the buffer provided by the real estate or other assets, and with the added expense of rent or lease payments, the risk of financial distress or even bankruptcy increases for the portfolio company (see the case of Mervyn's Department Store in box 3.7). The business may have to shutter some stores or restaurants, or even close down entirely. This is the likely explanation for the finding that the pace of job destruction in PE-owned retail establishments is far greater than in comparable non-PE-owned establishments.[100]

In 2007, just before the collapse of the commercial real estate bubble and the onset of the recession, lawyers from Kirkland and Ellis LLP published an article in *Venture Capital Review* extolling the advantages to private equity firms of using real estate sale-leaseback agreements to finance lev-eraged buyouts.[101] The growth of REITs facilitated the dramatic increase in these transactions. The law firm's website lists sale-leaseback transac-tions to finance the LBO of a ski resort business, a portfolio of theaters, a department store chain, a chain of 186 bowling centers, and a chain of 65 restaurants.[102] For the PE owners, sale-leaseback agreements are a way to quickly monetize assets and recoup all or part of their initial equity investment. For an operating company in a cyclical industry, however, such an agreement dramatically increases the difficulty of surviving a fall in consumer demand.

Transfers from Workers

Companies acquired in a leveraged buyout have high debt burdens that they must service by making interest payments and, in some cases, amortizing the debt. Managers of portfolio companies must quickly achieve an increase in predictable cash flow. Failure to do so, and to meet debt payments, endangers both the financial viability of the company and, as we saw earlier in this chapter, the jobs of the CEO and the company's other top executives. The temptation to cut costs by squeezing labor, discussed in greater detail in chapter 6, looms large in many cases. Thus, a third source of private equity gains is a transfer from workers to PE investors when employees at healthy companies are laid off and those who remain are subjected to an intensification of work. In addition to downsizing, employee wages and benefits are often reduced; collective bargaining agreements may be abrogated; plants and other facilities may be closed; work may be shifted from union to non-union facilities; and work may be outsourced or offshored. Although some of these actions may be justified at distressed firms in need of a turnaround, so-called distressed investing, as we noted earlier, is a thin sliver of PE investments.[103] Outsourcing, downsizing, and other practices implemented so that cash flow and profit margins can be quickly increased and high debt levels can be serviced are applied far more widely. Even previously healthy firms acquired in a leveraged buyout can struggle to increase net revenue while making payments on their debts, provoking CEOs to slash employment even as they implement business and operations strategies intended to improve performance.

Hertz is a global car and equipment rental company that was acquired in December 2005 by a consortium of PE firms led by Clayton, Dubilier, & Rice (CD&R) and including the Carlyle Group and Merrill Lynch Global Private Equity. The case (box 3.5) illustrates how the effects of debt on a company's net revenue lead to job losses even as PE firms earn rich rewards and changes in business strategy and operations improve performance. Eventually the high levels of debt resulting from the leveraged buyout at Hertz would leave the company in a weak position to deal with the global recession of 2008 to 2009 and lead to significant reductions in its workforce.

Transfers from Taxpayers

Yet another source of private equity gains is a transfer from taxpayers to private equity—what one state economic development officer termed "taxpayer financed capitalism." The leverage used to acquire the portfolio company alters its debt structure, increases its debt, and, because of the favorable tax treatment of debt compared to equity, reduces the company's tax liabilities. Lower taxes raise the bottom line and increase the enterprise value of the company by 4 to 40 percent, thus increasing the returns to private equity

---

Box 3.5   Hertz Car and Equipment Rental Company

In December 2005, a consortium led by Clayton, Dubilier, & Rice (CD&R) completed a successful bid to acquire Hertz from Ford. Hertz, which employed 32,100 people, was attractive because of its strong brand, market leadership, consistent revenue growth, low debt, and strong profit performance. CD&R believed that there were opportunities for high returns for investors, both from restructuring Hertz into separate fleet and operating companies and from improving operations.[104] The CD&R group immediately split Hertz into two companies: a fleet company (FleetCo) that owned the domestic and international automobile rental fleets, and an operating company (OpCo) that owned the equipment rental assets and conducted all rental transactions. OpCo leased the cars it rented from FleetCo. Hertz was acquired from Ford for $14.8 billion, with the CD&R group contributing $2.3 billion in equity. Debt was used to finance the remaining 84 percent of the sale price—$5.6 billion in corporate debt and $6.9 billion in asset-backed securities levered on the vehicle fleet. The deal price was seven and a half times Hertz's EBITDA of $2.7 billion.[105]

On the financial engineering side, payments from OpCo to FleetCo for the use of the cars would finance FleetCo's debt. On the operations side, CD&R prided itself on acquiring neglected divisions of large parent companies and improving their operations by providing management leadership and active oversight.[106] The increased cash flow from operational improvements would be available to service the corporate debt.

The PE investors did quite well. Less than seven months after acquiring Hertz, without much time to improve operations, and before recruiting a new CEO to run the company, the CD&R group filed to sell shares in an initial public offering. Just weeks before that filing, uncertain of the response they would get in the market, the PE owners had Hertz take out a $1 billion loan and pay the proceeds to them as a dividend, ensuring that they would recoup nearly half their equity investment.[107] In November 2006, the owners took Hertz public, selling shares representing 27.5 percent of the company at $15 a share and raising $1.3 billion. With a market capitalization of $4.8 billion and debt of $12 billion, Hertz's enterprise value had increased to nearly $17 billion in less than a year. Proceeds of the IPO were used to repay the $1 billion loan and to make a second dividend payment of $260 million to the PE owners.[108] In an interview with Andrew Ross Sorkin of the *New York Times*, Mark Frissora, the Hertz CEO hired by CD&R in July 2006, explained this increase in the company's value from $14 billion to nearly $17 billion this way: he attributed one-third of the increase in value to market timing. Hertz had benefited from increased air travel, as had other travel-related companies. "It had nothing to do with private equity," Frissora noted.[109] Another third of the increase in value was due to the performance of the equipment rental business, which rented to the construction industry and benefited from the housing bubble. And finally, the CD&R group had bought Hertz at a discount because Ford needed cash quickly when it sold the company.

Box 3.5   *Continued*

Operational improvements—better internal processes in the equipment rental business—accounted for a small share of the $3 billion increase in Hertz's enterprise value, according to the company's CEO.[110]

In June 2007, a little more than six months later, the CD&R group completed a secondary offering of an additional 14 percent of its shares. The shares priced at $25.03 and yielded $1.2 billion for the PE owners, who retained a 55 percent ownership stake. None of the proceeds went to Hertz.[111] In eighteen months, the PE owners had received more than their initial equity investment in the company.

While the PE investors did very well financially, public market investors who bought shares in Hertz in the initial and secondary public offerings did not fare so well. Hertz shares peaked at $26.72 on July 6, 2007, before declining sharply; they traded in a range between $10 and $15 from July 2010 through 2012. Further offerings of debt and stock in 2009, 2010, and 2011 reduced the ownership stake of the CD&R group to 39 percent. On July 17, 2012, Hertz's share price was just under $12.50, market capitalization was about $5 billion, total debt was about $11 billion, and the enterprise value of the company was $16 billion.[112] The company's share price finally exceeded its July 2007 level in September 2013, before sinking below $22 a share in early November of that year.

Following the buyout, the PE owners worked with Hertz management on the company's business strategy and operations. Process improvements—for example, in the cleaning and processing of rental cars on their return—increased the number of cars available for customers. Hertz reduced the cost of its fleet by increasing the share of cars it bought rather than leased. In terms of business strategy, Hertz took steps to increase its market share in the leisure segment of the car rental market. It targeted these price-sensitive customers by offering discounts for reserving cars online and using self-service kiosks. Revenue continued to increase in the first two years after the leveraged buyout, as it had under Ford. Net income declined, however, as a result of the higher interest payments on the debt used to acquire Hertz. Interest payments rose from 6.7 percent of revenue in 2005 to 11.2 percent in 2006 before declining somewhat to 10.1 percent in 2007.[113]

Net income declined by two-thirds between 2005 and 2006, from $350 million to $116 million, putting pressure on Hertz to cut costs. To help reduce costs, the company cut its workforce by about 9 percent, from 32,100 employees (22,700 in the United States) at the end of 2005 to 29,350 (20,550 in the United States) at the end of 2007. Most of the job cuts came in 2007.[114] The first round of layoffs in January, which eliminated 200 jobs at the company's New Jersey headquarters and its Oklahoma City service center, was projected to save the company about $15.8 million a year in compensation costs. A second wave of layoffs in March, which cut 1,350 jobs primarily in car rental operations in the United States, was expected to bring annual savings of about $125 million in compensation costs.[115] In all, these layoffs were projected to

(*Box continues on p. 76.*)

Box 3.5   *Continued*

reduce Hertz's wage and related costs by more than $140 million. The savings in labor costs contributed to an increase of $149 million in Hertz's net revenue in 2007, to $265 million.[116] The workforce was further reduced in 2008 as the company outsourced functions, including procurement and information technology.[117]

Highly leveraged companies like Hertz lack a buffer of equity that they can draw on to get through difficult times. The slowdown in business and consumer travel during the global recession of 2008 to 2009 reduced both the number of rental deals and prices. Faced with the necessity of making payments on its outstanding debt, Hertz needed to look for cost savings elsewhere. In January 2008, the company announced that it would cut more than four thousand jobs, about 12 percent of the company's workforce. By January 2009, including those four thousand jobs, Mark Frissora had eliminated 32 percent of Hertz's workforce since becoming CEO in August 2006.[118]

In May 2013, seven and a half years after acquiring Hertz from Ford, Hertz's private equity owners sold the last of their shares in the company and cashed out.[119]

without any increase in economic wealth.[120] In addition, the PE firm is more likely to be able to make aggressive use of tax arbitrage to legally avoid taxes.[121] Some acquisitions are made for this purpose rather than as strategic acquisitions intended to provide synergies and create value.

Leverage Leverage is an important source of private equity earnings, owing in part to the favorable treatment of debt (leverage) in the tax code. Because a company's interest payments on its debt are tax-deductible, its tax liabilities are reduced. There are no compelling legal, administrative, or economic rationales for this treatment of debt. Indeed, this tax treatment raises concerns about the economic efficiency of the corporate tax code and the possibility that tax-induced distortions in business decisions lead to inefficient allocations of capital. The tax benefits of debt encourage companies to employ inefficiently high debt levels and to engage in tax arbitrage to reduce tax payments.[122]

The tax advantages of debt hold, of course, for any company, not just companies owned by private equity. But as we have noted, PE-owned companies carry much higher debt loads than public companies—often two to three times the level. Private equity's high use of leverage is typically unrelated to the factors (size, R&D intensity) that explain the capital structure of publicly traded companies. Rather, low interest rates and the availability of financing appear to drive the capital structure in a leveraged buyout.[123] The average leverage ratio during the 2005 to 2007 boom was 75 percent debt. In contrast, the capital structure of a publicly traded company was 75 percent equity.[124] Thus, PE-owned companies receive a relatively greater tax benefit than other companies from the use of leverage.

The reduction in taxes from the higher interest deductions increases the PE portfolio company's enterprise value. Interest deductions can explain between 4 and 40 percent of the company's value, with the higher figure applying in the case where the debt is permanent and personal taxes provide no offset.[125] Steven Kaplan and his colleagues estimated that lower taxes due to increased leverage would likely account for 10 to 20 percent of the company's value. Thus, the enterprise value of the company, and the gain to its PE owners, is increased without a corresponding increase in economic wealth. These increased earnings for PE investors represent a net loss for the taxpaying public, which must either pay higher taxes or face cutbacks in services as a result.

In addition, tax savings from the increase in debt can offset the interest payments on the debt. This is especially true of the huge increases in leverage in the case of public-to-private transactions. The debt-to-equity ratio generally rises substantially when publicly traded companies, subject to greater financial reporting pressures and oversight by the Securities and Exchange Commission, are taken private and are no longer subject to more stringent SEC regulations and to scrutiny by outside investors.

Tax Arbitrage Tax arbitrage is the use of tax strategies to reduce the federal and state taxes a company is required to pay. In restructuring a company or its financial structure for the primary purpose of reducing tax payments, tax arbitrage can generate substantial tax savings that pass through to the bottom line and benefit a company's shareholders. Although legal, its only purpose is to alter tax structures to provide investors with greater gains. These strategies are not unique to private equity, as attested by GE's ability to minimize its federal tax payments and Microsoft's actions to reduce its tax payments to Washington State.[126] But they are employed more widely in PE-owned companies than in similar publicly traded companies.[127]

Many companies lack the scale, resources, and political clout of GE or Microsoft and are not able to successfully pursue tax avoidance strategies: the costs of hiring the necessary tax experts are too high and the risks of running afoul of the Internal Revenue Service (IRS) are too great. By contrast, large PE sponsors—such as KKR, Blackstone, Bain, Carlyle, and Apollo—can well afford the elite law firms and tax specialists required to aggressively engage in tax arbitrage. Smaller PE firms can engage specialist tax advisers to help them and their portfolio companies engage in tax avoidance (see box 3.6). More importantly, the benefits of a more complex organization designed to reduce tax payments must be weighed against any increase in transaction costs that results from this gamesmanship.

Box 3.6   McGladrey Case Study of Tax Avoidance

The McGladrey firm specializes in providing tax, audit, mergers and acquisitions, and IPO work for private equity firms. The following case is taken from the company's website.[128]

Reducing Costs Through Tax Incentives
McGladrey's state and local tax advisors identified and helped a private equity firm obtain fully refundable credits worth more than $9 million over 10 years for a target acquisition.

The client: A private equity firm focused on the industrial services and manufacturing sectors.

The issue: The firm was acquiring a recreational vehicle manufacturer and wanted to maximize potential tax savings.

The solution: McGladrey's mergers and acquisitions knowledge and deep industry experience made us an ideal fit to design and implement all tax aspects of the acquisition.

Because our state and local tax professionals had significant knowledge of various tax credit and incentive programs in the target company's home state, McGladrey was able to identify and obtain an agreement with the state for fully refundable tax credits worth more than $9 million over 10 years, allowing the private equity firm to reduce its investment cost and increase the return to its investors.

Benefit of working with us: Recently, the firm decided to pursue a roll-up and IPO exit with four of its companies. In designing the roll-up, McGladrey put in place a structure allowing each separate management team and co-investor group to rollover their interests tax-free, while also providing a partial liquidity event to the private equity firm on the combination.

For a large PE firm that owns many portfolio companies, the payoff can be considerable.[129] Talent and resources that could otherwise be used to produce economic wealth are instead diverted to the highly remunerated but socially unproductive activity of reducing the tax payments of portfolio companies. This produces gains for the PE owners of the portfolio companies, but at the expense of the taxpaying public.[130]

Brad Badertscher, Sharon Katz, and Sonja Rego provide some insights into the tax avoidance strategies utilized by PE-backed portfolio companies.[131] They found that PE-backed companies more often engage in sale and leaseback transactions that result in higher deferred taxes. They also found that portfolio firms are more likely to use tax avoidance strategies related to intangible assets. Finally, they found that PE-backed portfolio companies have significantly more subsidiaries in low-tax countries, including tax havens, than non-PE-backed firms. Moreover, once a formerly PE-backed firm is taken public, it increases the number of its subsidiaries located in tax havens. Tax avoidance through foreign operations appears to be an important tax arbitrage strategy for PE-backed firms. These researchers concluded that PE firms view tax planning as an additional source of returns to investors from investments in portfolio firms.

Former Massachusetts governor Mitt Romney's release of two years of his tax returns during his unsuccessful campaign for the presidency of the United States in 2012 provides further insight into how the use by businesses of offshore entities located in tax havens like Bermuda and the Cayman Islands to avoid paying taxes can enhance the incomes of investors.[132] Romney's company, Bain Capital, is located in the United States, but some of its private equity funds, as well as other Bain entities, are located in the Cayman Islands and other offshore locations. Some of the funds have bought out overseas companies that they now control—investments that might well trigger certain federal taxes that would have to be paid by the funds' investors as a result of their controlling interest of these foreign companies. Other offshore Bain entities are "blocker corporations"—so called because they block taxes that would otherwise have to be paid.

Although the income of pension funds and other nonprofit investors is generally tax-exempt, this exemption does not apply to "unrelated business income" from investments that use debt financing. Pension funds, foundations, and other nonprofit organizations would ordinarily have to pay taxes on this income. However, if this debt-financed investment income is paid to a blocker corporation, it can pay dividends to the pension fund. This dividend income paid to the pension fund is not subject to taxation in the United States; the pension fund pays only the much smaller Cayman Islands taxes. Still other entities are used to buy up the steeply discounted debt of the bankrupt portfolio companies owned by the PE firm. When a company buys up the defaulted loans of a company it owns, taxes to be paid by the insolvent company on the "canceled debt" can be triggered. It is possible to avoid triggering these taxes, however, by setting up a company unrelated to the troubled portfolio company in an offshore location that does not allow withholding taxes on interest. This special-purpose entity then buys up the portfolio company's debt. This can save the struggling portfolio company millions of dollars and enhance investors' returns, but the savings come at the expense of taxpayers, who are essentially subsidizing these PE investments.[133]

Thus, the corporate tax code provides private equity firms with opportunities to increase the returns to investors in PE funds beyond what public corporations typically do and apart from any improvements in efficiency. The tax deductibility of interest means that PE firms, with their superior access to financial markets, are able to increase the value of the companies they acquire via the extensive use of leverage. Large PE firms also have the resources to promote the increased use of tax arbitrage at their portfolio companies. This reduces tax payments and increases profit at these companies, thus increasing their value and the price at which they can be sold when the PE firm exits the investment. Both the use of leverage and the successful implementation of tax avoidance strategies increase returns to investors whether or not PE ownership has led to the creation of greater economic wealth.

Transfers from Creditors

The easy access to credit that fueled the boom in private equity buyouts in the 2002 to 2007 period burdened some of the acquired companies with debt loads that quickly became unsustainable when the economy slowed. As the specter of bankruptcy loomed for some of the most highly leveraged large companies that were taken private in megadeals at the height of the boom, PE firms were able to reduce the debt burdens of these companies and restore their prospects at the expense of the creditors whose loans had financed the buyout. The bondholders "took a haircut," and the PE firm's portfolio company got a new lease on life. There were two main ways in which this was accomplished—through the PE firm buying back its own debt at a discount, or through a debt exchange.

Buying Back Debt at a Discount Although portfolio companies are privately held and ownership shares cannot be traded, the debt issued by these companies is freely traded among banks, mutual funds, hedge funds, and other investors. When a company gets into financial difficulty and bondholders begin to fear that the company may seek bankruptcy protection, the company's debt trades at a steep discount to its face value. The company can then quietly buy back its own debt in the open market for corporate bonds for pennies on the dollar. If the bonds are trading at 50 cents on the dollar, for example, then the purchase of bonds with a total face value of $600 million reduces the company's outstanding debt by this amount at a cost of only $300 million. In 2009 a number of corporations took advantage of depressed prices for their bonds to buy back their own debt and save millions of dollars in interest and debt repayment costs. These included the portfolio companies of the PE firm Apollo Global Management Group: Hexion Specialty Chemicals Inc. and Harrah's Entertainment Inc.[134]

Debt Exchange A debt exchange is a type of deal in which bondholders forgive part of their debt in exchange for a higher interest rate on new notes or a more senior position in the capital structure. In 2008, as the recession threatened the solvency of highly indebted companies, creditors exchanged $36 billion of debt for a lesser amount, according to the credit rating agency Moody's.[135] Bondholders were willing to take the haircut rather than risk having the debt-strapped companies file for bankruptcy protection, in which case they would recoup even less. The following example shows how it worked.

The successful chip-maker Freescale Semiconductor was taken private in 2006 by a consortium of PE firms consisting of Blackstone Group, Texas Pacific Group, Permira Funds, and the Carlyle Group in the largest buyout of a technology company up to that time. The company was acquired for $17 billion, with $7 billion in equity and $10 billion in debt. At the time of the deal, Freescale was profitable, had a rich technology base, owed little debt, and generated cash flow of about $1 billion a year. Overnight the chip-maker's debt rose from less than $1 billion to more than $10 billion owed to creditors who had bought the company's bonds or otherwise loaned it money. The onset of recession in 2007 led to a decline in demand for Freescale's chips; sales dropped 10 percent in 2007 compared with 2006. Its high debt burden put the company in serious trouble despite cash flow that year of $1.5 billion. In 2008 the company closed a plant and laid off 10 percent of its workforce—2,400 workers. Its bonds were trading at a discount, and Freescale bought back $85 million of its own bonds on the cheap. This reduced the company's debt, but was not enough to put it on solid footing. Its bonds continued to trade among investors at a deep discount as fears of bankruptcy rose, and in 2009, after closing two more plants and laying off 5,000 workers, Freescale made a debt exchange offer to its bondholders. The company was able to persuade a group of creditors who were owed $2.85 billion to exchange that debt for a loan of $924 million that had priority over other debt and would give these creditors a greater chance of collecting if Freescale went bankrupt. The debt exchange lowered Freescale's debt by $2 billion and substantially reduced its interest payments, allowing the company to survive and protecting the ownership interests of the company's private equity owners.[136]

Apollo Global Management's Fund VI provides another example. The $10.2 billion fund, established in 2005, joined the PE firm TPG Capital in the buyout of the casino operator Harrah's Entertainment Inc. in January 2008, for $30.7 billion—one of the largest PE deals ever made. The company's debt load doubled to $23.9 billion as a result, leaving Harrah's with an interest bill of $2.1 billion. To service the debt, Harrah's cut costs. Among other steps it took to save money, the company reduced the number of cashier windows and cut dealers' hours and benefits.[137] The decline in consumer spending on gaming in 2008 made it impossible for Harrah's to service its high debt load, and the company proposed a debt exchange with its creditors. In December 2008, the company exchanged bonds with a face value of $2.2 billion for new ones worth $1.06 billion, giving bondholders a little less than 50 cents on the dollar. Bondholders took the deal because Harrah's bonds were trading in the bond market for 20 cents on the dollar. Then, in April 2009, Harrah's exchanged $5.5 billion of additional bonds for new bonds worth $3.6 billion. At the end of these exchanges, Harrah's had reduced its debt by a total of $3 billion.[138]

Apollo Global Management is a publicly traded PE firm that, like other public companies, is required to file certain forms with the Securities and Exchange Commission. The noted independent analyst Peter Morris has analyzed Apollo's S-1 filing dated March 21, 2011.[139] In that filing, Apollo reports that, "as of December 31, 2010, Fund VI and its underlying port-folio companies purchased or retired approximately $18.7 billion in face value of debt and captured approximately $9.3 billion of discount to par value of debt in portfolio companies such as CEVA Logistics, Caesars Entertainment, Realogy, and Momentive Performance Materials."[140] Using this information, and making the reasonable assumption that Apollo used leverage of three-to-one on the $11 billion of capital that the fund invested, Morris estimates that the fund may have borrowed $33 billion in order to buy companies with a cumulative enterprise value of $44 billion. Information provided in the filing shows that as of December 31, 2010, the value of these companies had declined to $40 billion. A range of organiza-tions (banks, bond funds, and so on) had loaned the $33 billion to help Apollo's Fund VI buy a group of companies. But for $18.7 billion of these loans, lenders ended up receiving only $9.3 billion, or 50 cents on the dollar. The creditors lost $9.3 billion on their loans to Apollo Fund VI companies. From Apollo's point of view, however, it managed to negotiate $9.3 billion of savings for the investors in its Fund VI.

What are the implications of this financial engineering for Apollo's investors? As Morris explains it:

> Suppose Apollo had done no financial engineering. In that case, the com-panies would still have debt of $33 billion. The value of Fund VI's equity investments would therefore be $7 billion. Fund VI would therefore have lost about $4 billion, or one-third, of its initial value ($11 billion). But instead of being worth $7 billion (down one-third), Fund VI's $11 billion invest-ment is worth $15 billion: an *increase* of one-third. This is entirely due to financial engineering: "capturing" the debt discount. More than one-half ($9 billion) of Fund VI's $15 billion value at December 2010, and all of its positive investment return, had been extracted from lenders.[141]

Bankruptcy for Profit

The possibility of using bankruptcy for profit was first observed in the 1980s in the waves of financial activity related to junk bonds and lever-aged buyouts.[142] Bankruptcy for profit occurs when a PE firm takes a port-folio company into bankruptcy and then buys it out of bankruptcy. The PE firm is still the owner, but the debts of the company have been slashed and its pension liabilities have been transferred to a government agency, the Pension Benefit Guaranty Corporation. The PE firm comes out ahead, but lenders take a haircut and workers face job loss and reduced pensions.

In a paper that examined the savings and loan crisis of the late 1980s, George Akerlof and Paul Romer considered the possibility that some firms may engage in bankruptcy for profit.[143] It is not possible to know whether some bankruptcies of companies while in private equity hands fit this description. But there are some unusual cases. In their study of private equity and the financial distress of portfolio companies, Per Strömberg, Edie Hotchkiss, and David Smith note that "only a small minority of pre-default [PE] owners retains control of companies" following bankruptcy.[144]

Sun Capital, however, was able to do this in several cases. Following the bankruptcy of Friendly's, the iconic ice cream parlor and family restaurant, Sun Capital managed to hold on to the restaurant chain. Immediately after Friendly's closed 65 stores, laid off 1,260 workers, and sought Chapter 11 bankruptcy protection in November 2011, a second Sun Capital affiliate announced its intention to acquire the restaurant chain. A third Sun Capital unit came forward to provide a loan to finance the chain's operations while it was in bankruptcy. This made Sun Capital both the owner of Friendly's *and* its largest creditor, and it put Sun in position to retain ownership of Friendly's when it emerged from bankruptcy with fewer liabilities. Under bankruptcy law, the owners of a bankrupt company are last in line to be repaid and generally lose their equity investment. This is intended to motivate them to avoid taking the company into bankruptcy and risk losing their money along with the jobs and pensions of their workers. Lending Friendly's money to keep operating while in bankruptcy put Sun Capital in a position to retain ownership of the company—a tactic that thwarts the goals of bankruptcy law.[145]

With less than two months between the bankruptcy announcement and the date set for the auction of Friendly's, no other bidders came forward. In December 2011, Sun Capital was allowed to "buy" Friendly's in a "credit-bid" sale—that is, Sun Capital was able to hold on to ownership of Friendly's by wiping out the $75 million loan that one of its units had previously made to see the restaurant chain through the bankruptcy period and by assuming some of Friendly's liabilities.[146] A key part of Sun Capital's restructuring plan involved shifting liability for the Friendly's pension plan to the federal government's Pension Benefit Guaranty Corporation. Sun Capital ended the year as the owner of Friendly's but with much of the company's debt forgiven and without responsibility for the chain's pension obligations to its nearly six thousand employees and retirees.[147]

A review of PitchBook company reports uncovered three more cases of bankruptcy of Sun Capital portfolio companies that followed the same pattern—Fluid Routing Systems, Big 10 Tire, and Anchor Blue. A fund sponsored by Sun Capital acquired Fluid Routing Systems in a leveraged buyout in May 2007. The company filed for Chapter 11 bankruptcy protection in February 2009. A Sun affiliate provided Fluid Routing Systems with a $12 million loan to keep it operating. In March 2009, another Sun Capital affiliate bought the company out of bankruptcy by having Sun Capital forgive $11 million of the loan. Big 10 Tire was acquired in a leveraged buyout by a Sun Capital–sponsored PE fund in November 2006. The company sought bankruptcy protection in April 2009. A Sun Capital affiliate provided a $27.9 million loan to finance operations during bankruptcy. In July 2009, another Sun Capital affiliate bought the company out of bankruptcy and reopened "targeted" stores. In May 2011, the restructured Big 10 Tire was sold to The Pep Boys for an undisclosed sum. Retail chain Anchor Blue was acquired by a Sun Capital–sponsored PE fund in a leveraged buyout in 2003 with $2 million in equity. In August 2005, Anchor Blue paid its PE owners a dividend recapitalization via the sale of a 25 percent interest in the company for $70 million. This gave the Sun Capital PE fund a return of 3,400 percent. Between 2005 and 2009, Anchor Blue closed many stores, reducing the number from 252 to 177. In June 2009, the retail chain sought Chapter 11 bankruptcy protection. It was bought out of bankruptcy by another Sun Capital unit in August 2009. But in January 2011, it again entered bankruptcy, closing the remaining 117 stores and laying off 1,446 workers.

Sun Capital is not the only PE firm to retain ownership of a company that has entered bankruptcy. The Stant Corporation is a leading manufacturer of closure caps, onboard vapor recovery components, and engine and transmission cooling components for the automotive original equipment market and for automotive aftermarket customers. Stant was acquired from Tompkins by H.I.G. Capital in June 2008 for an undisclosed sum. A year later, in July 2009, Stant filed for bankruptcy. H.I.G. Capital provided the financing to keep Stant operating while it was in bankruptcy. Two months later, in September 2009, the Stant Corporation was acquired by another affiliate of its owner, H.I.G. Capital, for $81 million.[148]

In yet another example, Black Diamond Capital Management retained ownership of its bankrupt portfolio company PTC Alliance with a credit-bid of $100 million plus some additional funds. And while not all purchases of bankrupt companies via credit-bids are by private equity firms seeking to retain ownership, it is worth noting the recent huge increase in these deals. In 2006 to 2008, there were just nine credit-bids, with a combined debt value of $768 million. This increased to 171 deals, with a combined debt value of about $6.8 billion, in 2009 to 2011.[149]

Breach of Trust

Breach of trust occurs when implicit understandings between managers and workers, vendors, lenders, and others are not honored. Stable enterprises depend on implicit contracts between managers and stakeholders for their continued success. Private equity can get a quick boost to a portfolio company's bottom line by reneging on implicit contracts, but doing so undermines the trust necessary to the long-term sustainability of the portfolio company.

In their analysis of the sources of increased returns following a hostile buyout of a company, Andrei Shleifer and Lawrence Summers distinguished between the value-creating and value-redistributing effects of such takeovers.[150] Although they do not deny that such takeovers can improve efficiency and create value, they argued that the redistribution of rents from other stakeholders is also an important source of increased financial returns in a leveraged buyout. The redistribution of value in such takeovers arises from the willingness of the new owners to behave opportunistically and breach the implicit contracts with stakeholders entered into by managers on behalf of the former owners.

Similar arguments can be made about takeovers by private equity buyout funds. As Andrew Metrick and Ayako Yasuda observe, the overriding goal of a PE fund is to maximize financial returns to the fund's partners.[151] To achieve this goal, the fund's general partners closely monitor and manage the portfolio company and align the interests of its top executives by offering them generous financial incentives if the targets set by its PE owners are met. Implicit contracts—that is, the discretionary commitments made previously by the firm's managers to employees, vendors, suppliers, or the community—may, from this point of view, be seen as instances of opportunistic behavior that divert earnings away from maximizing investor returns. Defaulting on these implicit obligations can benefit shareholders.

Although many public corporations have clearly defaulted on implicit contracts—through downsizing and mass layoffs, among other practices[152]—private equity owners have more incentives to default on such contracts and fewer constraints against doing so. Recall that the PE general partners disproportionately gain from the returns to PE investments and that the negative reputational effects of a portfolio company's downfall accrue to that company and not to the PE partner pulling the strings. In addition, PE general partners often do not have a clear enough understanding of how implicit contracts undergird business success to worry about them—as is well illustrated in the PE buyout in 2007 of EMI Music by Terra Firma, a PE fund headed by Guy Hands. After the buyout, Hands went on a cost-cutting drive that alienated established artists such as Paul McCartney and the Rolling Stones, who left the label. But the EMI business model critically depended on retaining established artists and using their reputation to bring in a pipeline of new artists. Unaware of the importance of trust and implicit contracts, Hands destroyed the foundations on which the business model rested.[153]

Because new private equity owners are focused on short-term returns and lack firm-specific skills and knowledge, they are more likely to introduce a lower trust model that breaks with previously accepted norms[154] and undermines established stakeholder relationships and interests.[155] The experience of Mervyn's Department Store chain, in which implicit contracts with workers, vendors, and the community were broken, is

Box 3.7   Mervyn's Department Store Chain

Mervyn's Department Store chain—a major U.S. midtier retailer that in 2004 had 30,000 employees and 257 stores, including 155 that were owned by the company—was a good candidate for a PE buyout. The chain, while profitable, had suffered from neglect by corporate management since its acquisition years earlier by the Target Corporation. Target's share price rose on news of the divestiture,[156] and Mervyn's employees were promised that the new PE owners would spruce up the stores, bring in new management to strengthen operations and business strategy, and improve the chain's performance in an increasingly competitive market.[157]

The leveraged buyout of Mervyn's by a consortium of PE firms in September 2004 for $1.2 billion followed a common pattern in retail.[158] The PE consortium (made up of Cerberus Capital Management, Sun Capital Partners, and Lubert-Adler and Klaff Partners) immediately split Mervyn's into an operating company (Mervyn's Holdings LLC) and a property company controlled by the investors (MDS Realty) that owned the firm's valuable real estate assets. Mervyn's received little or no financial benefit from this transaction. The PE partners put in $400 million in equity and funded the balance of the buyout by using the chain's real estate as collateral to borrow $800 million through Bank of America. The loan proceeds were paid to Target, with Mervyn's receiving no compensation and no residual interest in the property. The bank quickly securitized the loan—bundled it with other loans—and resold it. MDS Realty then leased the real estate back to Mervyn's stores at high rents in order to service the debt and extract value over time.[159] A year later, having held the properties long enough to obtain capital gains tax treatment, MDS Realty sold the stores, most of them to two large real estate investment trusts—Developers Diversified Realty Corporation and Inland Western Retail Real Estate Trust.[160] None of the proceeds went to Mervyn's, which had been required by its PE owners to sign individual twenty-year leases for each store at high rents that were scheduled to rise further each year.

While failing to keep pace with its main competitors, Mervyn's nevertheless had net operating income of $160 million in 2003, its last full year of operation under Target. The chain's employees expected the new PE owners to invest in turning the stores around, thereby raising operating income and profits. The PE investors made modest improvements by broadening product selection, closing stores in unprofitable regions, and focusing on the West and Southwest, where the chain was strongest. The president, CEO, CFO, finance vice president, CIO, and supply chain manager were replaced—all of the "C group," according to a former Mervyn's executive.[161] Nevertheless, the chain's new executives had difficulty making it competitive—partly owing to the high rents the PE owners committed the stores to paying. In addition, the company's PE owners took resources out of the stores by paying themselves dividends out of the stores' cash flow in 2005 and 2006.[162] Skeptical of the PE owners' commitment to the company,

Box 3.7   *Continued*

---

four CEOs entered and exited the retail chain in four years. Key to the ultimate downfall of the company, however, was the PE owners' breaching of implicit contracts with key stakeholders—vendors, employees, and the communities from which Mervyn's drew its customers.

To meet the high rent payments that were necessary to service the debt used to purchase Mervyn's, the PE owners needed to quickly increase cash flow. Laying off workers, intensifying work for those who remain, and cutting pay are common ways to quickly and predictably increase cash flow. The chain's new owners took over in August 2004 and in mid-September called an off-site meeting of all finance directors—for marketing, purchasing, logistics, financial services, stores, and each subdivision. According to a former high-level manager at Mervyn's headquarters:

> The finance directors were told they needed to cut 10 to 15 percent out of all budgets, including employee payroll. We were told that we need head-count cut—out of fifty people, we need ten people to go. They didn't want to understand what people did—just decided they were overstaffed and needed to cut. Yes, we needed change, but not this drastic. That was our first experience; they didn't care; they just wanted head-count cuts. . . . They looked at my area. We were a profit center—we were making money for the company—but they were more interested in head-count.[163]

Customers noticed the cutbacks in janitorial and maintenance staff and complained about the lack of cleanliness in the stores on customer satisfaction surveys. Warehouse operations were switched over to a third-party management company. The corporate executive explained:

> They did head-count reduction in the warehouse, and a lot of employees with many years in those jobs lost their jobs. There were a lot of complaints about this from the stores. Service went down with the new third-party arrangement. Cost went down as well—the company saved money. But the third-party employees didn't have the same commitment that internal staff would have. . . . In terms of corporate strategy, all decisions were made for short-term gain. The PE investors had no interest in the long-run future of the company.[164]

Mervyn's had a pay-for-performance system for supervisors and managers, and bonuses depended on the evaluation an employee received. As the high-level manager described it, her rankings were gone over with a fine-tooth comb:

> With employees, we were more or less told how to rate employees. We always had standards at Mervyn's and were expected to have so many employees in each category. But we never had this type of oversight before. I would submit my spreadsheet that included evaluation, proposed raise, and proposed bonus. Then I would be told I had to cut planned payroll by 1 percent—without knowing anything about my employees. Once I did this, they would come back and say, "Well, we agreed to 1 percent, but now we need another 1 percent." It was as bad as buying a car. Some of my supervisors

(*Box continues on p. 88.*)

Box 3.7   *Continued*

---

and managers were working fourteen- or fifteen-hour days, and it was hard to lower their scores. I felt it was very unfair to lower their pay and bonuses. For me, I put a lot into each employee review; they had no idea how capable my employees were or how much effort and overtime they put in.

This manager remained with the department store chain, but she reported that "many finance directors left early on because they could see the writing on the wall."[165]

The chain's commitments to the communities in which its stores were located were also broken to quickly increase cash flow. Mervyn's did a lot of community work. There was an active volunteer committee at the chain's headquarters, and volunteer committees at the stores as well. According to this manager:

We did lots of community work . . . including a kids' breakfast club that fed kids breakfast in summer and holidays. Mervyn's was a huge sponsor of this. . . . We were a sponsor of the San Francisco AIDS walk. We would bus people up—hundreds of thousands of dollars were raised for AIDS this way in the name of Mervyn's. We were really proud of this, and the company used it when they went out to recruit new employees. . . . [The volunteer committee] had a budget and would make decisions about supporting projects. At headquarters, [Mervyn's] adopted three or four schools in Hayward—supported tutoring, mentoring, building a new baseball field. In some years we supported St. Jude [Children's Research Hospital]. . . . Each store had a volunteer coordinator with a budget and would support the local community. At headquarters the budget was $100,000; this was cut to $10,000 afterwards, and [the volunteer committee] had to go to the CFO to get approval—even if we wanted to give fifty books, we couldn't make the decision.[166]

Mervyn's managers viewed these activities as important for building customer support and loyalty in the communities in which the chain's stores were located.

It was the breach of trust with the department store's vendors, however, that led most directly to the chain's bankruptcy. Trust plays a critical role in the operations of a department store. Buyers place orders with manufacturers for merchandise to be produced and delivered, but pay for the merchandise only after they receive the goods. This may not be a problem for large suppliers. But for many vendors, this process is facilitated by a financial intermediary, known as a "factor," that advances funds to the manufacturer to produce the goods and is repaid when the retailer pays for the merchandise. In order to advance funds to the manufacturer, the factor must have confidence that the retailer will pay for the goods that were ordered.

Mervyn's relied extensively on CIT Group to guarantee its transactions with vendors.[167] In five decades, the company had built strong relationships with its vendors and CIT. As the recession took hold, the retail environment became more difficult, and like many retailers, Mervyn's struggled to survive the downturn. In 2007, according to court documents,

Box 3.7   *Continued*

---

the company suffered a $64 million loss—less, it should be noted, than the $80 million annual increase in its rent payments following the LBO.[168] The chain's attempts to renegotiate store leases failed. In early 2008, CIT grew concerned about the chain's ability to pay for the merchandise it ordered and turned to Sun Capital, the company's main shareholder, for reassurance. As Shleifer and Summers note, to "convince stakeholders that implicit contracts are good, shareholders must be trusted not to breach contracts even when it is value maximizing to do so."[169] Failing to get the reassurances it sought, CIT started cutting back on its dealings with the department store chain, raising fears among other vendors about its trustworthiness and impairing the chain's ability to contract with suppliers.[170] This left Mervyn's without the merchandise it needed for the important back-to-school selling season.[171]

Unable to maintain a flow of merchandise into the stores, the company's days as a going concern were numbered. On July 29, 2008, the chain's owners took the company into bankruptcy. The high rents, which the chain's landlords refused to lower, proved a stumbling block to the sale of the company. Unable to emerge from bankruptcy, Mervyn's closed its remaining 177 stores, dismissed its remaining 18,000 workers, and was liquidated.[172] Mervyn's told its managerial workforce that their pensions were now in the hands of the bankruptcy court—a statement that was untrue, as their pensions were in a 401(k) plan. It took the efforts of a law firm to get the pension accounts returned to the employees.[173] Mervyn's owed the Levi Strauss Company more than $12 million, and owed all of its vendors, taken together, in excess of $102 million—debt that was unsecured.[174] The private equity owners, however, were little affected. Profits realized through the real estate deals far exceeded losses on the retail side.[175]

In September 2008, at the request of its vendors, Mervyn's sued Target, the PE firms, and others involved in the transaction. The complaint alleged that Target and the other defendants engaged in a fraudulent transaction by knowingly causing the company's real estate to be transferred either with intent or without adequate consideration of the effect on creditors. The complaint also alleged that Mervyn's owners breached their fiduciary duties to Mervyn's and its creditors by various actions, including paying themselves a dividend at a time when Mervyn's, despite positive cash flow, was essentially insolvent.[176] Target and the PE owners filed a motion to dismiss the complaint, but in March 2010, the Delaware court surprised observers by allowing the case to proceed. In October 2012, without admitting guilt, the PE firms Cerberus Capital Management and Sun Capital Partners and the real estate investment firm Lubert-Adler and Klaff Partners agreed to pay $166 million to the department store's vendors and other unsecured creditors. The settlement is one of the largest against private equity companies accused of fraudulent conveyance (illegal asset stripping) and breach of fiduciary duty.

illustrative of this process. The PE owners lacked the requisite motivation and knowledge to maintain the prior relations of trust that were central to the chain's business success and long-term stability.

Conclusion

Private equity presents itself as a new, more efficient, and more productive form of business ownership and governance. Its claim is that it creates value that increases the returns to shareholders and benefits all of society. The reality is more complex, and the implications for companies and employees are often much darker. PE firms may provide strategic and managerial direction to the companies they acquire for their funds' portfolios. In that way, they sometimes improve efficiency, increase the enterprise value of portfolio companies, create economic wealth, and enlarge the economic pie. But this is rarely the only—or even the main—source of PE earnings. The use of high levels of debt to magnify returns and reduce tax liabilities, the payment of dividend recapitalizations by portfolio companies to PE owners, and the negotiation of debt exchanges with creditors—strategies often referred to as financial engineering—are widespread among PE firms. These financial strategies are in essence rent-seeking behaviors that increase the earnings of investors in PE funds, but at the expense of other stakeholders. During boom times—when interest rates are low, credit flows easily, and stock markets are rising—private equity's gains from leverage and dividend recapitalizations dwarf those from operational improvements. Indeed, the high debt levels typical of financial engineering put pressure on portfolio company CEOs to downsize their workforces and reduce wage and other labor costs. These actions, which flow directly to the bottom line, are often taken immediately after the new PE owners take over. New directions in business strategy and improvements in operations take longer to show results. The high debt levels also increase the risk of financial distress, default on loans, and bankruptcy when the business cycle turns and the economy contracts. Debt swaps with lenders who fear the even greater losses associated with bankruptcy help some portfolio companies avert disaster, but at a high cost to creditors.

The "hierarchy of claims" on the rewards from investing in portfolio companies guarantees that the general partners of PE funds will capture a disproportionate share of the value extracted from these companies. At the level of the PE firm, the PE business model channels the rewards so that they differentially benefit the general partners, the limited partners, and the debt providers—and enrich the general partners who are principals in PE firms.[177]

In the period since the onset of the recession and financial crisis, financial engineering strategies have become more difficult to carry out.

Lenders have required higher equity investments by private equity, and less use of leverage. Target companies are more difficult to identify in tough economic times. Competition for promising companies has made it difficult to purchase them at attractive prices. Difficulty finding buyers for older portfolio companies has slowed PE firms' exits from investments. PE firms are holding on to portfolio companies for longer periods of time and need these companies to demonstrate success. To succeed in this new environment, private equity firms may need to rely more on providing portfolio companies with improvements in business and operating strategies. We examine developments in the PE business model in the postcrisis era in the next chapter, and developments in midmarket investments with their greater opportunities for promoting growth and improving performance in the chapter that follows.

$=$ Chapter 4 $=$

The Effects of the Financial Crisis, 2008 to 2012

The bursting of the housing bubble in 2006, the onset of recession in December 2007, and the financial crisis that erupted in 2008 led to the most serious contraction of the U.S. economy since the Great Depression. In a technical sense, the contraction ended during June 2009 with the upturn in the country's gross domestic product. On other measures, however, such as slow economic growth and continued high unemployment, the U.S. economy was still mired in the doldrums during 2013, with limited prospects for rapid improvements in job creation. Median household income adjusted for inflation fell during the recession from $54,916 in December 2007 to $53,508 by June 2009; it fell further during the economic recovery to $50,964 in June 2012.[1] While poor macroeconomic conditions since 2007 created challenges for businesses and workers in general, this economic context also greatly increased the risk of financial distress for highly leveraged companies.

These conditions threatened to undermine the private equity business model because, as we saw in the previous chapter, extensive use of leverage is central to achieving the high returns that PE funds promise. But leverage not only provides tax advantages and magnifies gains—it also increases the risk that a company's debts will need to be restructured or that it will face bankruptcy or even liquidation. The expectation that portfolio companies will *occasionally* need to restructure debt or seek bankruptcy protection is built into the notion that PE funds hold a portfolio of companies, some of which will yield spectacular gains when sold and some of which will fail. And PE deals are structured to minimize investors' losses should a portfolio company need to seek bankruptcy protection. The sharp downturn and slow recovery from the recession, however, reduced revenues far below expectations; many highly leveraged companies had to "amend and extend" their loan agreements with creditors, and many did go bankrupt.

High rates of bankruptcy reflect poorly on private equity firms, however, and in this climate, limited partners began to reassess their relationships with their PE partners. Beginning in 2008, the financial distress and high-profile bankruptcies in PE-owned companies made LPs more cautious, made fund-raising by PE funds more difficult, and led stakeholders to be more resistant to being acquired by PE funds.

In the immediate postcrisis period, private equity also found it difficult to acquire or exit from portfolio companies. Credit availability shrank as the financial crisis left banks' balance sheets in need of repair and limited their willingness to make credit available to borrowers. Credit, however, is the lifeblood of the PE model and is vital to private equity's ability to use leverage to acquire operating companies. Selling portfolio companies was also more difficult: the stock market's sharp decline in 2008 and the volatility of share prices once the market recovered made it more difficult for PE firms to exit existing investments via initial public offerings in the years immediately following the onset of the crisis. The recession and continued slow recovery also affected the price at which portfolio companies could be sold. The falloff in demand and the reduced revenues and earnings of portfolio companies put downward pressure on the prices that strategic buyers were willing to pay, making this exit route less attractive to PE funds as well. These difficulties began to abate somewhat beginning in 2010, but serious problems for PE firms persisted through 2012. It was not until 2013 that things began to look up for the industry. As a result of these developments, many portfolio companies have been held for longer than the PE firms' preferred three- to five-year time horizon, and the number of so-called mature investments in the portfolios of PE funds has increased. Some of these have turned into "zombie" investments: few prospects are available to the PE funds to ever exit from these investments.

The recession and weak recovery also took a toll on companies that were potential acquisition targets and made attractive takeover targets scarce. Competition for the limited number of desirable target companies raised the price at which private equity could acquire these companies, making high returns at exit more problematic. Fewer viable targets also made it difficult for PE firms to put the capital committed to their funds to work within the time frame available for making acquisitions and left them with an overhang of capital still waiting to be invested.

In sum, the economic recession set off a chain of events for private equity that persisted until 2013. Financial distress and bankruptcies in portfolio companies led to poor returns and dissatisfied limited partners. Difficulties acquiring new companies and exiting from existing portfolio companies led to the accumulation of large amounts of uncommitted capital, making it more difficult to raise new funds from impatient LPs. PE funds held on to companies longer than they intended and sought to undertake operational improvements to keep these companies viable. Increasingly, PE funds exited investments in portfolio companies by selling them to other PE funds (secondary buyouts), and they increased their investments in emerging markets. Despite all of these challenges to the PE business model, it remained fundamentally unchanged.

Reliance on leverage as a driver of high returns has made the private equity business model especially sensitive to credit market conditions. With the onset of the recession and the financial crisis, PE deal-making collapsed as total capital invested declined by more than half between the fourth quarter of 2007 and the first quarter of 2008. Highly leveraged PE-owned companies faced difficulty generating sufficient cash flow to both meet debt obligations and undertake the expenditures necessary for the business to succeed. Cash flow that was assumed to be forthcoming when the portfolio companies were acquired failed to materialize for many of them, especially in highly cyclical sectors such as hotels, retail, and construction.

Boom-Bust Cycles in Private Equity Investing

Practitioner accounts, corroborated by the available empirical evidence, suggest that the private equity industry is highly cyclical. Kaplan and Strömberg identified two major cycles of PE leveraged buyouts. The first, which began in 1982 or 1983, ended in 1989; the second began in 2003 or 2004 and ended in 2007. PE activity was muted in the early 1990s; it recovered somewhat toward the end of that decade, then dipped substantially from 2000 to 2002 before beginning to rise again.[2]

The economic conditions in the boom years of the 2000s and their impact on leveraged buyout activity also differed from conditions in the 1980s. Both the number of deals and the aggregate value of deals were higher in the boom period of the 2000s than in the 1980s. Private equity firms paid more for acquisitions in the latter period—that is, the prices paid were a higher multiple of EBITDA (earnings before interest, taxes, depreciation, and amortization). Debt levels, while still much higher in general for PE-owned companies than for other companies, were somewhat lower in the 2000s than in the 1980s. For large LBOs, the share of equity used to finance the acquisition of portfolio companies in the 1980s was typically 10 to 15 percent, with debt accounting for 85 to 90 percent of the purchase price. In the 2000s, the equity share was typically 25 to 30 percent of the price of the acquisition, with debt used to finance 70 to 75 percent of the leveraged buyout.[3] At the peak of the boom, fund managers were able to negotiate so-called covenant-lite loans, which typically lack the covenants that require regular reviews of the borrower's operating performance and that can trigger a default if performance deteriorates. Lenders anxious to get in on the action during the boom were more willing to let underwriting standards become lax and to provide loans that gave them less control over borrowers.

Figure 4.1   Total Capital Invested in Leveraged Buyouts and Deal Count, Quarterly, 2007 Q1 to 2012 Q4

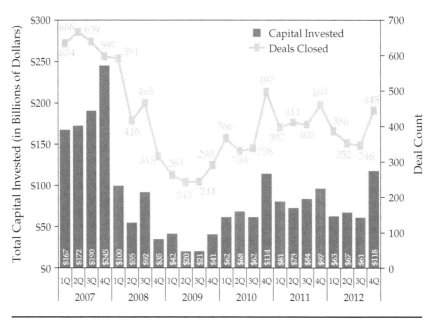

Source: PitchBook.

The boom-bust cycle in private equity was particularly evident during the financial crisis. As we saw in chapter 2, total capital invested by private equity in leveraged buyouts of U.S. companies peaked in 2007, as did the number of deals closed, and capital invested climbed more rapidly than deal activity as the number of megadeals increased. With the onset of the recession and the financial crisis, however, PE deal-making collapsed. Total capital invested in leveraged buyouts of U.S. companies declined by two-thirds between the fourth quarter of 2007 and the first quarter of 2008, and it reached its low point in the second quarter of 2009. New PE investments fell from $245 billion to just $20 billion between the fourth quarter of 2007 and the second quarter of 2009 (see figure 4.1). The number of LBO deals also fell over this period. Deals closed and capital invested in buyouts of companies recovered somewhat in 2010, reaching postcrisis peaks in the fourth quarter of that year before slowing somewhat in 2011. Both capital invested and the number of deals declined further in the first three quarters of 2012, with the amount invested falling more rapidly than the number of deals closed as the focus of many PE firms turned to smaller "midmarket" deals.

The increased emphasis in the postcrisis period on midmarket deals has meant that the share of megadeals in which large, publicly traded companies are taken private has declined. Nevertheless, private equity investors have not given up entirely on deals to take large companies private. The largest of these buyouts was the takeover of Samson Investment Company by a KKR-led consortium for $7.2 billion. This topped Apax Partners' $6.1 billion purchase of Kinetic Concepts.[4] Nevertheless, these deals do not compare to the $21 billion buyout of hospital chain HCA in 2006 or the $48 billion buyout of the energy company TXU (now EFH) in 2007.

The availability of cheap financing affects booms and busts in private equity activity because the extent of leverage in buyouts is driven by the low cost of debt rather than by firm- and industry-specific factors. In periods of easy financing, deal volume and capital invested increase. Megadeals are easier to finance, and the valuations of firms targeted for acquisition by PE funds increase; at 70 percent debt financing, inflated purchase prices mean more debt levered on the acquired companies. Ultimately, this results in an increase in troubled investments, as over-priced and highly leveraged companies, whether PE-owned or not, are more likely to experience financial distress during economic downturns. Many companies acquired by private equity in leveraged buyouts at market peaks experience distress during the subsequent contraction.

Distress and Bankruptcy in Portfolio Companies

The year 2007 was clearly a bellwether year for private equity. By the end of that year, however, the ominous signs of an impending sharp increase in defaults on loans and in bankruptcies among highly leveraged companies had appeared. By 2008, highly leveraged companies—whether public or PE-owned—were in serious trouble. Debt defaults quadrupled in 2008 compared to 2007. In the first nine months of 2008, eighty-six companies around the world had defaulted on their debt, but notably, a disproportionate number of them—fifty-three (62 percent)—were owned or backed by private equity.[5] By the end of 2008, forty-nine PE-owned U.S. companies had filed for bankruptcy.[6]

The private equity owners—the PE firms that sponsored the funds, the PE funds, and the limited partners in the funds—were not responsible for repaying the outstanding debt owed to the creditors of distressed portfolio companies. As discussed in chapter 3, PE owners' losses are limited to their original equity investments, which typically, in the boom years, account for one-quarter to one-third of the total transaction value of the leveraged buyout, though sometimes much less. The lucrative management fees paid to the PE fund's general partner by the limited partners and the monitoring fees paid to the general partner by the portfolio companies largely shielded the general partners' PE firms from major losses during the economic crisis.[7] In addition, the general and limited partners in PE funds substantially reduced their losses in some cases by paying themselves dividend recapitalizations prior to any bankruptcies. They frequently financed these dividends by issuing further debt, which was loaded onto their portfolio companies, often in the form of high-yield junk bonds. The same low interest rates and easy credit that fueled the housing bubble made debt-financed dividend recaps look like easy money to many PE firms, and they were widely used as late as the second quarter of 2007.[8]

Debt-financed dividend recaps in the precrisis period, in turn, contributed to financial distress in portfolio companies during and after the crisis. Moody's Investor Service singled out private equity firms TH Lee and Apollo for drawing dividends from one-third of their portfolio companies in the first year following the leveraged buyout. By 2008, a high proportion of companies acquired by these two firms experienced financial distress in meeting their debt obligations.[9] Similarly, the PE firms CI Capital Partners and Sentinel Capital Partners used dividend recaps to more than repay their initial equity investment in the Buffets Restaurant chain, which we described in more detail in chapter 3. Burdened by its high debt load, the restaurant chain could not meet its financial obligations and declared bankruptcy in January 2008. Many Buffets restaurants were closed and workers lost their jobs, but the PE owners nevertheless saw a positive return on their investment.

Even portfolio companies that did not go bankrupt found it difficult to meet the payments on their ballooning debts. Of the nine all-time largest PE-leveraged buyouts, eight occurred in the peak boom years of 2006 and 2007. Many of these companies struggled in the aftermath of the recession and financial crisis.[10] Harrah's Entertainment, the world's largest casino company with 30,440 unionized employees, was acquired by the Apollo Group and the Texas Pacific Group (TPG) in 2006 for $30.7 billion, paying $90 per share and assuming the company's $10.7 billion debt. By June 2007, the casino company's long-term debt had more than doubled to $23.9 billion. The gambling industry slumped in the recession, and Harrah's (now known as Caesar's Entertainment Corporation) struggled under its debt burden. The company cut staff, reduced hours, outsourced jobs, and scaled back operations.[11] It scrapped a plan for an IPO announced in November 2010 that would have offered shares at $15 to $17 per share, owing to low investor interest in the money-losing, debt-burdened company. In February 2012, the company returned to the public markets, selling shares at $9 a share in its IPO to raise much-needed cash.[12]

Clear Channel Communications, owner of the largest network of radio stations and a major player in outdoor advertising, was acquired in 2008 by Thomas H. Lee Partners and Bain Capital in the largest buyout to occur in the media and entertainment business.[13] The company, which was profitable prior to its acquisition by private equity, faced falling revenue and cash flow in 2012, which made it difficult to meet the payments on its $19.9 billion in long-term debt. The need to service this debt led to extensive cost-cutting. The company reduced the number of radio stations it owned and laid off more than 8,000 of its 30,900 employees.[14] In addition, the company was sued in March 2012 by an investor, who accused it of improperly moving $656 million from Clear Channel Outdoor to the parent company in order to meet payments on its debt.[15] While the situation remained difficult, Clear Channel bought itself some breathing room by selling a total of $1.75 billion in secured notes, due in 2021, which it used to pay off debt that matured in 2011.[16]

The credit card processor First Data Corporation agreed to be taken private by Kohlberg Kravis Roberts (KKR) in 2007. The deal, valued at $29 billion, closed in 2008.[17] In 2006, before the takeover was announced, First Data employed about 27,000 people and had profit of $1.51 billion on revenue of $7.08 billion. The company, with about $23 billion in debt in 2011, posted substantial losses in 2009, 2010, and 2011. Payroll declined by nearly 10 percent at the struggling company, to 24,500 in 2011. The *Wall Street Journal*'s "Deal Journal" labeled KKR's acquisition of First Data as one of the biggest private equity flops.[18]

Debt burdens that resulted when companies were acquired by private equity weighed especially heavily on retailers, as we saw in the Mervyn's case in chapter 3. Retail is a cyclical business that experiences sharp declines when the economy contracts. Traditionally, retail store chains had little debt and owned the real estate that housed their operations. This made it easier for them to survive the slack periods. Among the early companies to experience distress, Linens 'n Things, a specialty retailer taken private in a leveraged buyout by Apollo Management in 2006, filed for bankruptcy in May 2008 and went into liquidation in October when it was unable to find a buyer. Debt-holders questioned the company's quick demise following Apollo's acquisition.[19] In addition to Mervyn's and Linens 'n Things, other PE-owned retailers that filed for bankruptcy in 2008 included Steve & Barry's budget clothing chain (owned by TA Associates), Whitehall Jewelers (Prentice Capital Management), Goody's Family Clothing (GMM Capital and Prentice Capital), Fortunoff Fine Jewelry and Silverware (Trimaran Capital and Kier Group), Wickes Holdings furniture stores (Sun Capital, Rooms to Go, and StoneCreek Capital), Sharper Image (Crystal Capital and a PE consortium), Value City Department Stores (Bain Capital), Home Interiors and Gifts (Hicks, Muse, Tate & Furst), and the online retailer Lillian Vernon (Ripplewood Holdings and ZelnickMedia).[20] Retailers continued to struggle during the prolonged period of slow growth. In 2011, two years after the official end of the recession, PE-owned retailers Anchor Blue (Sun Capital), Appleseeds Clothing (Housatonic Partners), Harry & David (Wasserstein), Signature Styles (Patriarch Partners), DSI Stores (Lee Equity Partners and a consortium),

HomeForm Group (Phildrew Ventures), and Sportcraft (Heller Equity Capital) all filed for bankruptcy protection.[21] As is clear, a wide range of PE firms were involved in these buyouts that ended in bankruptcy.

According to *The Deal Magazine*'s reckoning, 100 portfolio companies owned or backed by private equity filed for bankruptcy protection in 2009, 69 filed in 2010, and 42 filed in 2011—similar to the 49 that filed in 2008. In all, 260 PE-owned companies entered bankruptcy during the 2008 to 2011 period. Five of the portfolio companies that entered bankruptcy in 2011 were owned by Sun Capital Partners and its affiliates, the largest number of any PE firm.[22] While the PE funds and their sponsors were not on the hook for the debts of these companies, limited partners' expectations that they would cash out in a big way on these deals were disappointed. Dividend recaps and IPO exits slowed during these years, and opportunities to cash out were delayed, if they didn't evaporate entirely.

The financial crisis and recession made highly indebted companies in industries other than retail vulnerable to failure as well. The shocking bankruptcy of the magazine and publishing icon *Reader's Digest* (owned by a PE consortium led by Ripplewood Holdings) in 2009 was brought about by the debt piled on it by investors who took it private in 2007 in the failed belief that projected revenues would be sufficient to meet the company's obligations. Company revenues fell rapidly, however, owing both to the recession and to rapid changes in the media industry that the PE investors failed to understand.[23] The biggest bankruptcy of a PE-owned company in 2011 was NewPage Corporation, the largest coated-paper manufacturer in North America based on production capacity. The company, which produces paper for magazines, was acquired in a leveraged buyout by Cerberus Capital Management in January 2005. NewPage and its affiliated companies employ about six thousand people, 70 percent of them members of labor unions. The companies, headquartered in Ohio, had $3.4 billion in assets and $4.2 billion in debt when NewPage sought bankruptcy protection six years after its acquisition by private equity.[24] Coach America, a bus tour operator that operates in twenty-six states and employs about six thousand people, provides another example. The company suffered from a liquidity shortfall that caused it to defer capital improvements and lose customers.[25]

The solvency of highly leveraged companies is very much affected by changes in macroeconomic conditions, which can affect demand for the companies' products or services and thus operating cash flow. As Hotchkiss, Smith, and Strömberg observe, PE proponents have identified the potential sources of gains from leveraged buyouts by private equity funds, but "relatively less attention has been given to the potential downside of these transactions, namely that their high debt levels greatly increase the risk of financial distress. The most recent LBO boom, ending abruptly with the beginning of the financial crisis in 2007, has left a record number of PE-owned firms in default."[26]

Amend and Extend

Debt defaults and bankruptcies are not limited to PE-owned companies. Highly leveraged companies, whatever their ownership structure, are at especially high risk of default when general business conditions sour. From January 1997 through April 2010, Hotchkiss, Smith, and Strömberg followed 2,156 highly leveraged companies whose high debt level made them high-credit-risk companies. About half of these firms (1,062) were PE-backed at some point during this period. They found that 5.1 percent of PE-backed companies and 3.4 percent of non-PE-backed companies defaulted over the entire period, with the higher default rate for PE-backed companies being due to their higher leverage and lower credit ratings. Compared to other companies with similar credit ratings, PE-backed companies experienced rates of default on their debts that were similar to those of other highly indebted companies, but on average PE-backed companies were more highly leveraged and more risky. This study of highly leveraged companies found that following the financial crisis these companies—both those backed by private equity and those without PE investment—experienced "an explosion in defaults. . . . Over the period 2007–2010 Q1, roughly 25% of all firms in the leveraged loan sample default on their debt."[27] The default rate fell markedly between January 2010 and January 2012.[28]

Post-default, PE-backed companies enjoy several advantages over other distressed companies as a result of their PE sponsors' greater access to financial markets and strong relationships with other financial investors. Hotchkiss, Smith, and Strömberg found that, among firms that defaulted on their debt, PE-backed firms were less likely to be sold to another company or liquidated, and that on average they were able to complete reorganizations four months earlier than other companies.[29] In a separate review of about one thousand defaults between 1988 and 2011, two hundred of which were in firms acquired by private equity in a leveraged buyout, Moody's found that the PE-backed companies had two advantages. First, prepackaged bankruptcies, in which the plan and financing to exit bankruptcy is established before bankruptcy protection is sought, are more frequent among PE-backed companies. Second, and importantly, PE owners of a company in distress have a greater ability to get lenders to engage in a "distressed exchange"—that is, to exchange distressed debt for new debt due a few years in the future.[30] These "amend and extend" deals—less flatteringly sometimes referred to as "amend and pretend"—allow PE sponsors to restructure the balance sheets of companies owned by their funds to protect investors' equity stakes.

In the case of a PE-backed company unable to make payments on its debt, both the banks and the PE owners of the firm have incentives to undertake a distressed exchange. Bank debt usually does not experience default, as it sits at the top of the capital structure of a company experiencing financial distress. Moody's found, however, that the PE-backed companies acquired in leveraged buyouts had smaller cushions of subordinated debt that would protect bank lenders from default.[31] In a distressed exchange, the bank does not have to write off the bad debt, the PE owners get to protect their equity in the distressed company, and the relationship between the bank and the PE sponsor of the leveraged buyout is preserved. Other creditors also have an incentive to amend and extend loan agreements. In the low-interest-rate environment that has prevailed in the years following the economic crisis, creditors may not be able to find superior alternative reinvestment opportunities and so may be willing to extend loan agreements even for marginal borrowers.

Extend-and-amend exchanges of distressed debt enable the portfolio company that defaults on its debt to avoid declaring bankruptcy and gives the company a chance to implement a turnaround. In its study of firms that defaulted between 1988 and 2011, Moody's found that fewer than half (47 percent) of the defaults of PE-owned companies were bankruptcies, compared with nearly two-thirds (64 percent) of other companies.[32] If business conditions continue to be difficult, however, a company that uses a distressed exchange to avoid bankruptcy may again face distress when the new debt becomes due a few years hence. A good example of this problem is the 2007 leveraged buyout of Texas Utilities Corporation, now Energy Future Holdings (EFH), by KKR & Co., the Texas Pacific Group (TPG), and the PE arm of Goldman Sachs. The largest buyout in history, valued at $48.1 billion in 2007, left the company with $52.2 billion in debt, compared to $44.1 billion in assets, in 2012. As we discuss in greater detail in chapter 6, the repeated use of amend-and-extend agreements has staved off bankruptcy, but in 2013 analysts were predicting a 91 percent chance of default.

In 2010, Moody's estimated that more than $700 billion of the total new debt would become due in 2012 to 2014.[33] Some of the distressed debt exchanges that averted bankruptcy in 2008 to 2010 have experienced a second round of failure. As a financial consultant specializing in corporate finance and restructuring observed,

> Moody's recorded approximately 100 distressed exchanges in the three-year period that began with the 2008 credit crisis—many of which were arranged by private equity sponsors attempting to quickly de-lever the balance sheets of troubled investments while minimizing the dilution to their equity positions. Creditors were often accommodating because their recovery prospects in a bankruptcy scenario amid a time of economic turmoil

were usually highly impaired. . . . Distressed exchanges are often band-aid remedies for companies that have become chronically uncompetitive.[34]

The ratio of distressed debt to total high-yield corporate debt—an indicator of future defaults—remained high in 2012, suggesting that a not insignificant share of distressed exchanges may have delayed, rather than avoided, bankruptcy.

Private Equity's Challenges

The increase in financially distressed portfolio companies and the large number of high-profile bankruptcies in the postcrisis period, together with continuing poor macroeconomic performance (slow GDP growth and job creation), pose major challenges to private equity deal-making. Finding "good deals" on new companies is difficult because the slow growth of the economy limits the number of potentially lucrative targets—increasing their price as competition heats up. Overpaying for a portfolio company at purchase can sharply reduce returns at exit. In the years following the crisis, many private equity funds were sitting on high levels of committed capital that they were not able to put to work earning returns for limited partners (so-called dry powder). For more than a few PE funds, this problem still persisted in 2012, saddling them with large amounts of dry powder that they were under intense pressure to invest.

Exits were also problematic because many PE funds were unable to exit their portfolio company investments without incurring losses or lower-than-anticipated returns and thus were limited in their ability to distribute profits to the fund's general and limited partners. Unable to sell mature investments to the market—either through an initial public offering on a stock exchange or to another company as a strategic purchase—PE firms increasingly turned to selling portfolio companies to other PE firms. As a result of these challenges, some PE firms had difficulty attracting limited partners and raising new funds. They looked for greater participation from hedge funds and sovereign wealth funds. Established, "brand-name" private equity firms fared better than newer funds, but even some well-known PE-fund sponsors had to set more modest fund-raising goals for their new funds. We now take a closer look at these challenges.

Dry Powder, Mature Investments, and Secondary Buyouts

The large inventory of funds that had been committed by limited partners but not invested—the dry powder—arose from the difficulties in acquiring new portfolio companies because of the lack of desirable targets, high prices, and tight credit. While cost-cutting measures raised profits at many businesses, weak sales performance during the recession and continued weak revenue growth in many industries limited the availability of good targets for acquisition. Tight credit during the crisis made borrowing to finance acquisitions difficult. And despite low interest rates in the postcrisis period, creditors remained wary and loans were more difficult for PE firms to obtain. Continuing high rates of unemployment and declining household incomes for many consumers in the years following the crisis created a difficult economic environment for private equity. And as we have noted, prices for attractive companies were bid up, with purchase price premiums similar to those at the peak of the boom period.

Private equity's classic strategy of buying low and selling high also did not work in the postcrisis period. In the past, PE firms could identify undervalued companies and make money on the "buy"—that is, they could buy companies cheaply, paying a low multiple of the company's earnings, and then resell the enterprise a few years later at a higher earnings multiple, pocketing a profit without the need to do much in the way of making operational improvements. As sellers became more familiar with PE deal-making, they were unwilling to part with operating companies that PE firms found attractive at bargain prices. Lenders also became less willing to provide the leverage that PE firms needed to make high returns. Chastened by high rates of default and bankruptcy on highly leveraged investments, lenders required PE investors to put up as much as 50 to 60 percent in equity during the crisis and its immediate aftermath. This requirement eased considerably by 2011—and especially for large, brand-name PE firms—but the situation remained problematic. As recently as the second quarter of 2013, the median amount of equity in new deals was 43 percent,[35] and leveraged financing for larger deals continued to be difficult to obtain.[36]

Unable to find attractive investment opportunities in the postcrisis period, PE funds were sitting on dry powder—the large amounts of committed funds that they had not been able to invest. As of November 2011, PE funds still held large amounts of dry powder, estimated variously to be $376 billion[37] or more than $400 billion.[38] Dry powder peaked at $473.7 billion in 2008, according to PitchBook, then dropped to a still massive capital overhang of $328.4 billion at the end of 2012. More than $70 billion of this dry powder came from funds launched in 2007 and 2008, with more than three-quarters of this capital overhang held in funds with $1 billion or more in capital commitments.[39] By 2012, funds launched in 2007 and 2008 were approaching the end of their investment window. The problem became so acute that some PE firms returned money to investors that they were unable to put to work.[40]

The relative mix of realized capital, unrealized capital, and dry powder shifted dramatically following the crisis, as illustrated in figure 4.2. In the early 2000s, realized capital constituted the majority of total funds

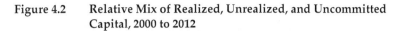

Figure 4.2   Relative Mix of Realized, Unrealized, and Uncommitted
Capital, 2000 to 2012

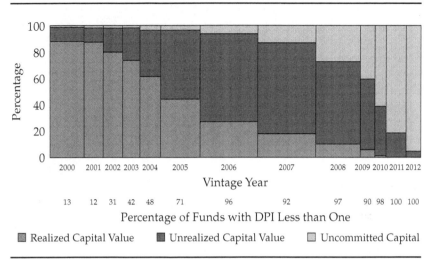

Source: Preqin, reprinted from Bain & Company, Inc., *Global Private Equity Report 2013.*
Note: DPI is the ratio of distributed to paid-in capital.

committed by limited partners. From 2005 to 2009, unrealized capital represented the highest proportion. That is, private equity firms invested heavily in this period, but had not yet exited those investments. As is typical of newer funds, from 2010 to 2012, dry powder was the highest category. PE firms anticipated exiting investments made in 2007 or earlier at least by 2012, but that did not happen. Instead, the proportions of unrealized gains and dry powder in relation to capital committed to private equity increased.

Exiting mature investments was also more challenging in the postcrisis years (2008 through 2012) because portfolio companies—notably those in cyclical industries—performed poorly during the recession. For many, their value fell below or remained near their original purchase price, and their PE owners were reluctant to sell under those conditions. PE general partners usually cannot collect their share of the funds' profits unless a "hurdle" rate of 8 percent return is achieved. With many investments still underwater in 2011 and 2012, PE firms had an incentive to hold on to the companies in their portfolios. The cofounder of the PE firm TPG, David Bonderman, suggested that if things did not improve, hurdle rates might need to be eliminated and investors might need to ratchet down their expectation that PE investments would yield 20 percent returns.[41]

In some cases during those years, PE owners were willing to sell the portfolio company but strategic buyers, usually publicly traded companies, had difficulty obtaining debt financing to carry out the acquisition.

In addition, volatility in the stock market created an uncertain environ-ment for taking PE-owned companies public again and exiting via an IPO. The result, as we saw in figure 2.2 (which shows the number of companies owned by private equity each year from 2000 to 2012, by year of investment), is that PE funds were holding large inventories of mature investments that were not able to exit in their preferred three- to five-year window. In line with this preferred holding period, the median holding period for portfolio companies in 2007 was 3.49 years. But the number of companies held more than five years has increased dramatically since then. For example, 531 portfolio companies acquired in 2005 had still not been exited seven years later in 2012. Of 6,769 companies acquired between 2000 and 2006, 2,269 (34 percent) had not been exited by mid-2012.[42] Of the 25 top mega-buyouts from private equity's "golden age" (1995 to 2008), 14 still remained in the hands of private equity in 2012.[43]

Changes in the tax code effective January 2013 spurred a flurry of exit activity in the second half of 2012 as PE funds moved up exits to avoid the increase in taxes on carried interest. The result was a record number of exits in 2012. Exits fell dramatically, however, in the first half of 2013, which was on track for the least number of exits since 2009.[44] Anecdotal evidence suggests that exits may have picked up at the end of 2013 spurred by the run-up in the stock market to new highs in the final months of that year.

The slowdown in both acquisitions and exits reduced the investment returns to the limited partners. Distributions to limited partners were delayed because of the large overhang of mature investments that PE funds were unable to exit at a profit, combined with dry powder that they were unable to invest. Globally, more than 90 percent of funds launched in 2006 and 2007 had distributed less to limited partners by 2012 than the LPs had paid into the funds.[45] General partners were under great pres-sure both to exit mature investments and to put accumulated dry powder to work.

Secondary buyouts (one PE firm selling its portfolio company to another PE firm) became more frequent after the crisis because they helped solve the slowdown in deal-making that affected all PE firms. They enable PE firms to help each other out. Secondary buyouts are more easily com-pleted than IPOs or sales to strategic buyers, and they are subject to less scrutiny of the price paid or the wisdom of the deal that comes with bid-ding on a company not owned by private equity. More importantly, these transactions solve two problems for PE firms: they allow PE funds on the buy side to invest some of their huge overhang of dry powder, and on the sell side PE funds can reduce their large inventory of mature portfolio companies and make distributions to limited partners. This is impor-tant, since limited partners cannot give much new money to PE funds until such distributions are made. One of the largest of these deals in the

United States was the 2010 leveraged buyout of MultiPlan Inc., a health care business that puts together medical networks for major health care insurers. The company was acquired by the PE firms BC Partners and Silver Lake Partners from Carlyle Group and Welsh, Carson, Anderson & Stowe in a transaction that valued the company at $3.1 billion.[46] Smaller companies, too, were the targets of secondary buyouts. Intelligrated, a company in Mason, Ohio, that designs, manufactures, and installs material handling automation solutions, was sold by the PE firm Gryphon Investors to the PE firm Permira Funds for $500 million in August 2012.[47]

Secondary buyouts rose in the postcrisis period,[48] increasing from 26 percent of PE exits in 2009 to 45 percent in 2012.[49] They spiked in the fourth quarter of 2012, accounting for more than 50 percent of the record 230 exits in that quarter in advance of the January 2013 increase in the tax rate on carried interest from 15 to 20 percent.[50] In 2013 (through September 30), secondary buyouts accounted for 40 percent of PE exits.[51]

The advantages of secondary buyouts for the PE firms are clear, but the benefits to limited partners are questionable. Large public pension funds and sovereign wealth funds that invest in multiple funds of multiple PE firms may find themselves involuntarily on both sides of the secondary buyout. Although they receive a distribution from the PE fund that sells the portfolio company, they may now own the company via another PE fund (in which they have invested) that has just purchased the company; the PE fund that bought the company probably paid a higher price than the original price, however, and this may limit gains when the second PE fund exits the investment. Moreover, LPs who are on both the selling side and the buying side in these sponsor-to-sponsor deals pay fees and carried interest to both PE firms involved, which again reduces returns to the limited partners. Thus, some LPs are concerned that while secondary buyouts may be less risky investments, the high valuations in a secondary buyout, along with the transaction fees, limit the returns that can be earned. In addition, the secondary buyout gives the operating company's management team an opportunity to cash out their ownership shares in the company, raising questions about their commitment to the company after the transaction occurs.[52]

Not all secondary buyouts are motivated by the desire to reduce the amount of dry powder or dispose of a mature investment. A secondary buyout can sometimes be a strategic acquisition intended to increase the scale of a portfolio company's operations or to complement its product or service offerings. An exit via a strategic acquisition by another PE fund can make sense for the fund selling the company as well. A sale to a strategic acquirer, whether to another PE fund or to another type of company, is often desirable. According to a managing director in a PE firm that focuses on midmarket companies, a strategic buyer is "likely to be more thoughtful and to be willing to pay more for a quality-compliant operating company." According to this informant, the natural life span of an operating company in a PE fund's portfolio is five years. The PE firm managing the investment looks five years out and makes a plan that identifies how the operating company will develop over this period. At the end of five years, market dynamics are likely to have changed, and it may be necessary to refresh the plan. At that point, it may well make sense to sell the operating company to the PE fund of another private equity firm. While this is sometimes the case, the PE firm managing director also noted that the increase in secondary buyouts in recent years owes a lot to the fact that PE funds have grown larger and have unspent committed funds while the universe of attractive companies available for PE investments is declining.[53]

The Challenge of Raising New Funds

Private equity experienced a steep decline in almost every aspect of its business in 2009 as the global financial crisis took a toll on an industry whose lifeblood is credit. The situation was especially bad in fund-raising, which fell sharply that summer. Just thirteen funds with a total of $12 billion in committed capital closed in the third quarter of 2009. This compares with forty-seven funds and total committed capital of $74 billion in the third quarter of 2008, and sixty-three funds and total committed capital of $84 billion in the same quarter of 2007.[54] The decline in fund-raising paralleled the deep drops in deal-making and exits.

Fund-raising remained sluggish in the period from 2009 to 2011 as industry activity, despite a rebound at the start of 2011, remained depressed. Following a relatively strong first quarter, fund-raising was subdued for the remainder of that year. Although pension funds and other limited partners generally did not reduce their commitments to private equity as a share of their investment portfolios, the slow pace of exits kept the industry from meeting expectations for the return of capital to these investors. Returns to the LPs in most PE funds proved disappointing from 2008 to 2011, which made raising new funds more difficult. Such payouts are a major source of capital that LPs can commit to subsequent PE funds. As a result, the capacity of LPs to take on commitments to new funds was weak in 2010 and 2011. The uptick at the start of 2011 soon fizzled out.[55] Newer or less successful PE firms had difficulty raising successor funds as older funds matured. Even established firms faced difficulty attracting limited partners, and in 2011 some even failed to attain the hurdle rate of return at which they could claim a share of the profits.

In January 2011, eighteen months into the economic recovery and with investment activity rising, PE firms were "on the road" trying to get capital commitments to new funds. Globally, more than 1,600 new funds, with an aggregate target value that exceeded $600 billion, were actively engaged in fund-raising. This was more than twice as much capital as they had brought in during 2010.[56] The target proved to be overly optimistic. The overhang of dry powder meant that many limited partners still had billions in previously committed capital that had not yet been invested, which made them cautious about committing more capital to private equity. LPs became much more selective and, in a flight to quality, placed commitments with a narrow set of PE managers. The result was a high level of fund-raising success in 2011 for an elite group of PE firms, while the large majority faced lackluster results.

Even some established PE firms with a record of success, however, had difficulty raising new funds in those years. Large investors such as the bigger pension funds have become less enthusiastic about investing in the large buyout funds because of their high fees and disappointing performance.[57] Mega-funds proved unpopular; LPs favored funds that specialize in midmarket acquisitions and focus on growth.[58] Fund-raising continued to be weak at the start of 2012 as capital previously committed to older funds remained tied up, picked up in the second quarter,[59] and then fizzled out, making 2012 a weak year for fund-raising. Just 112 funds closed in 2012, the lowest total since 2003.[60]

Not until 2013 did fund-raising by PE firms begin to pick up. The number of funds raised is now back to the level of the best preboom years; however, the popularity of smaller funds has combined with the low interest in mega-funds to bring a more modest recovery to total capital raised by PE funds.[61] Despite the smaller size of PE funds, raising funds now takes longer. Funds closed in 2013 have taken 18.5 months on average to reach a final close, compared to just 11.3 months on average for funds that reached a final close in 2006.[62]

Increased use of dividend recapitalizations in 2012 was another strategy used by private equity firms to deal with the sluggish exits and the slow rate of payouts on their investments. According to Moody's, PE firms completed forty-nine dividend recaps worth a total of more than $16.5 billion in the first three quarters of that year.[63] The largest of these was an eye-popping $1 billion dividend recap by Booz Allen Hamilton, a publicly traded company that is majority-owned by private equity. The dividend resulted in a huge windfall for the PE firm Carlyle Group, which owns 75 percent of the company's common stock. Booz Allen Hamilton already carried a much higher debt load in relation to its equity than most other publicly traded companies; Moody's cut the company's credit rating following the dividend recap.[64]

The use of debt-financed dividend recaps contributes to a weakening of company finances and, as we have seen, leaves companies less able to weather a deterioration in business conditions. Indeed, Moody's downgraded the credit rating of many of the companies that carried out a dividend recap in 2012, noting the increased risk that resulted.[65]

The falloff in fund-raising in the United States in the postcrisis period was most evident in the largest and smallest funds—the mega-funds with at least $5 billion of committed capital and the micro-funds with less than $100 million. In 2008 mega-funds accounted for 47 percent of the capital raised by PE; in June 2012, they were just 10 percent, although they still held $100 billion in committed capital in aggregate. At the other end, funds with less than $100 million accounted for 13 percent of committed funds in mid-year 2012. Midmarket funds—with committed capital in the $100 million to $250 million range, in the $250 million to $500 million range in the core middle market, and in the $500 million to $1 billion range at the high end of the middle market—saw increases.[66] There was a shakeout in the PE industry during the financial crisis. Between 2007 and 2012, 427 U.S. private equity firms failed to raise a new fund. At the end of August 2012, just 81 of those firms were actively raising capital for a new fund.[67]

The Lure of Distressed Investing

Distressed investing emerged as another strategy for using dry powder in the postcrisis period. It increased somewhat in these years as some PE firms failed to find a sufficient number of attractively priced, good-quality acquisitions and turned to investment opportunities in distressed companies. Even in these conditions, however, it is important to note that private equity did not mainly engage in buying up failing companies and turning them around. The emphasis in the media and by PE firms on efforts to turn around failing companies is substantially out of proportion to the frequency of these activities. The reality is that distressed investing remains a small fraction of PE investments.

Nonetheless, private equity may play an important role in turning around companies. It is high risk for PE funds and difficult to do, as it requires a different set of skills than investing in healthy companies—a greater emphasis on operations than on financial engineering and access to different sources of debt financing. A small set of PE firms specializes in distressed investing and has been successful in turning around companies. Others, however, have bought companies out of bankruptcy on the cheap and dismembered them for cash or bought up the debt of companies in order to acquire them cheaply, only to load them with more debt and exacerbate their problems.

In the traditional approach to distressed PE investing, a PE fund acquires a company in financial distress at a low price, brings it out of bankruptcy, and takes it private in order to restructure it, away from public view. A company that has defaulted on its debt, that is under bankruptcy protection, or that is heading in that direction is a potential target for such an acquisition. In a successful turnaround, the PE firm saves the company and exits the investment at a much higher price, earning a handsome return. Some PE firms sponsor funds that specialize in these "special situations" or "turnaround investments." Experienced partners in these firms seek out mismanaged companies that have hidden strengths—a good business strategy, strong products or services—and can be returned to profitability through improvements in financial accounting practices and business operations. These PE firms see their role as providing superior access to the managerial talent and financial markets that enable a struggling company to become a viable economic enterprise.

TMB Industries and Insight Equity are examples of private equity firms that specialize in buying distressed companies in order to turn them around. TMB acquires distressed Midwestern industrial businesses with revenues between $30 million and $500 million in the automotive, medium- and heavy-duty truck, and engineered products sectors. Almost all of the firm's managing directors have an operating background rather than a financial one, and the company invests substantial amounts of its own capital in the companies it acquires. Insight Equity, whose recent acquisitions include companies specializing in industrial site maintenance or civil construction, has a similar approach. It invests in underperforming or distressed companies with an enterprise value between $50 million and $500 million and revenues up to $1 billion, and it takes a hands-on approach. Both firms specialize in acquiring underperforming companies that are strategically viable. Rather than focusing on financial engineering, both TMB and Insight Equity have reputations for focusing on providing management and other services to enable their portfolio companies to reach their potential.[68]

Not all PE firms that invest in distressed companies operate this way. Some approach investing in distressed firms as an exercise in financial engineering or as an opportunity to pick up a company cheaply and dismember it—breaking it up, closing establishments and facilities, selling off real estate, disposing of machinery and equipment—a strategy that has earned these firms a reputation as "vulture" funds. In other cases, the goal is to take advantage of opportunities to rid the distressed company of its debts. Creditors are left in the lurch as the new PE owners profit from opportunities for financial engineering. The case of Extended Stay Hotels described in box 4.1 provides an example of this approach.

In contrast to the megadeal orchestrated by private equity firms in the Extended Stay Hotels case, distressed midmarket companies with enterprise values in the $100 million to $500 million range are generally the most attractive targets for these buyouts. An example is the purchase out of bankruptcy by the PE firm Gores Group LLC of NEC Holdings, the parent of San Francisco–based National Envelope Corporation—in 2010, the largest North American envelope-maker.[69] In April 2006, National Envelope had received $220 million in debt financing from several PE

Box 4.1   Extended Stay Hotels

Extended Stay Hotels has 685 locations in the United States and Canada. It is the largest chain of company-owned and -operated extended stay hotels in North America and employs approximately nine thousand people in its headquarters and hotel properties. It is operated and managed by HVM LLC.[70]

In 2004, BHAC Capital IV LLC, a private equity fund sponsored by the Blackstone Group, acquired Extended Stay America, a publicly traded hotel chain, in a leveraged buyout for just under $2 billion and the assumption of $1.1 billion in debt. The transaction took the hotel chain private. At the same time, the Blackstone Group PE fund acquired Homestead Village Management, whose name subsequently changed to HVM LLC. At the time, Extended Stay America had 483 hotels. By 2005, Blackstone had combined these properties, along with the 111-hotel group Homestead Village that it had purchased in 2001 and other properties it had acquired, into a hotel chain now known as Extended Stay Hotels. HVM managed Blackstone's Extended Stay Hotels chain, which at the time controlled more than one-third of the extended stay market.[71]

In June 2007, at the peak of the real estate bubble, Blackstone sold Extended Stay Hotels along with HVM to the Lightstone Group for $8 billion. At the time the chain was sold, it consisted of 644 hotels located in 44 states. Yet, according to a report prepared for the U.S. Bankruptcy Court, "the new owner . . . had no experience operating any hotel chain or an entity of this size and magnitude, nor were there any expected synergies or strategies that the new owner was bringing to the organization that could be called 'consideration.'"[72]

Lightstone acquired the Extended Stay Hotels chain using $7.4 billion of debt, $200 million of Blackstone rollover equity (which reduced the cash price of the acquisition to $7.8 billion and allowed Blackstone to retain a $200 million ownership interest), and just $400 million of equity assembled from Lightstone and two other investment firms, Arbor and a subsidiary of Prime Group Realty Trust. Lightstone's own contribution was $200 million, just 2.5 percent of the purchase price.[73] After adjustments, the final cash purchase price was $7.75 billion, and the $7.4 billion in debt financing was 95.4 percent of the purchase price paid to Blackstone. This level of debt was almost five times higher than the median debt ratio of 19.2 percent for lodging C-corporations, and over twice the median ratio of 43.5 percent for lodging REITs.[74] Extended Stay Hotels was already a low-cost provider of hotel accommodations with little room for cost-cutting to meet payments on its debt; only under very rosy assumptions about revenue growth would the chain be able to service this unusually high debt load.

Saddled with $7.4 billion in debt as part of the leveraged buyout that transferred ownership to Lightstone, the hotel chain was unable to weather the recession that began in December 2007. Facing falling occupancy rates and revenue, Extended Stay Hotels could not make the required payments

Box 4.1   *Continued*

on its debt and defaulted. In June 2009, the chain filed for bankruptcy protection—the largest bankruptcy ever in the hotel industry.[75] Extended Stay Hotels ran into trouble partly because of the downturn in the hotel industry, but its major problem was its debt. At the time of the bankruptcy, Extended Stay Hotels had $7.1 billion in assets and $7.6 billion in debts.[76]

The financial distress facing the hotel chain did not, however, prevent Lightstone from engineering cash distributions—dividend recapitalizations—and making dividend payments to itself and the other equity holders. Despite falling short of the stipulated performance criteria required to make such distributions, Extended Stay Hotels made distributions of $2.7 million in cash to an entity controlled by Lightstone's founder in August 2007 and $6.2 million in cash to an entity controlled by Prime Group Realty Trust in several payments from July to December 2007. Extended Stay Hotels filed for bankruptcy despite the fact that the chain's creditors had received a $100 million personal guarantee from Lightstone's founder requiring him to pay that amount if the hotel chain filed for bankruptcy.[77] The high price paid by Lightstone to Blackstone and the cash taken out of the struggling hotel chain to make cash distributions to Lightstone and Extended Stay Hotels' other owners led some lenders to question whether the original LBO was designed to fail.

The failed hotel chain quickly became an attractive target for private equity distressed investing. It was a major player in its segment of the hotel industry, and its problems were on its balance sheet and not in its operations. Centerbridge Partners, a private equity and distressed-debt investor, saw that the struggling hotel chain had a good business model but was burdened with too much debt and a complex financial structure. Centerbridge bought up a big chunk of Extended Stay Hotels' debt at a steep discount in a move designed to give the PE firm control over the hotel chain's bankruptcy reorganization and to position the firm to take control of the chain as it emerged from bankruptcy. For this latter purpose, Centerbridge assembled a consortium that included Paulson & Co. and, perhaps surprisingly, Blackstone Group. Despite competition from another consortium of PE investors, Centerbridge and its partners prevailed. Extended Stay Hotels backed the Centerbridge offer to buy the hotel chain out of bankruptcy in preference to a rival bid from a consortium consisting of Starwood Capital Group, TPG Capital, and Five Mile Capital Partners LLC.[78]

The chain was bought out of bankruptcy by the Centerbridge/Blackstone/Paulson group for $3.925 billion in a deal that reduced Extended Stay Hotels' debt load by almost $5 billion, down from almost $8 billion when it filed for bankruptcy in 2009.[79] The deal was approved by the bankruptcy court in July and concluded in October 2010 after Starwood Capital Group, one of Extended Stay Hotels' creditors and also a rival bidder in the May auction for the chain, dropped its objection to the transaction.[80] For Blackstone

(Box continues on p. 114.)

Box 4.1   *Continued*

Group the distressed investment allowed it to regain an equity interest in Extended Stay for 50 cents on the dollar compared to the $8 billion Blackstone received when it sold the hotel chain in 2007.

Among the creditors to lose a substantial amount of money was the U.S. taxpayer, since one of the lenders was Bear Stearns, whose loans to Extended Stay Hotels were assumed by the Federal Reserve after Bear Stearns collapsed in March 2008. The Fed held a total of $897 million of Extended Stay Hotels' debt. Other creditors to take large losses were Wachovia Bank (now Wells Fargo) and Bank of America.[81]

The bankruptcy examiner's report raised serious questions about whether the conditions of the very highly leveraged sale of Extended Stay Hotels and Homestead (HVM) by Blackstone's private equity fund to Lightstone in 2007 caused the previously profitable hotel chain to become insolvent. The examiner left open the question of whether the terms of the sale left the chain with assets hopelessly below liabilities, but concluded that they "left ESI [Extended Stay Hotels] and Homestead unable to meet their obligations as they fell due in the ordinary course of business."[82] Further, the examiner questioned the cash dividend distributions made to Lighthouse Group in 2007 following the acquisition of the hotel chain, noting that Extended Stay Hotels was almost certainly insolvent at the time the dividend recapitalizations were made.

Extensive litigation followed Extended Stay Hotels' emergence from bankruptcy in the hands of a group that included Blackstone. In June 2011, Blackstone Group and Lighthouse Group were sued over the $8 billion 2007 LBO, which, according to the plaintiffs, "was tainted start to finish."[83] Blackstone and the other defendants were accused of taking all the cash they could get and paying themselves millions of dollars following the acquisition in a deal that was structured to fail. The suit, filed by the creditors of the hotel chain, claimed that Blackstone Group skimmed $2.1 billion from the sale of the chain to Lightstone and sought restitution plus punitive damages because it alleged malicious breach of duty to Extended Stay Hotels' creditors. The lawsuit claimed that Lightstone put up little of its own cash and that the terms of the 2007 deal burdened Extended Stay Hotels with an excessive amount of debt. This debt load, plus restrictions on its finances, led to the hotel chain's bankruptcy just two years later. According to the creditors' complaint, participants in the leveraged buyout knew or should have known that the terms of the deal would make Extended Stay Hotels insolvent and unable to repay its creditors.[84]

Notwithstanding the ongoing litigation against Blackstone and Lightstone over their alleged financial profiteering, the new owners led by Centerbridge announced their own dividend recapitalization in November 2012. They planned to raise $3.5 billion in debt financing in part to pay for a $700 million dividend to themselves.[85]

Box 4.1   *Continued*

Finally, in June 2013, the creditors accepted a settlement of $10 million from Blackstone plus $200,000 from one of the PE firm's financial advisers. In accepting the settlement, the creditors noted that recent court rulings had made it very difficult for creditors to challenge bankruptcy protections.[86]

Earlier that year, lenders to Extended Stay Hotels made plans to securitize the loans and cash out. In preparation for this move, each of the properties in the chain was appraised. As of November 2012, the hotel chain had increased in value by $900 million—to $4.82 billion—since being bought out of bankruptcy.[87]

In July 2013, the hotel chain filed with regulators to raise up to $100 million in an initial public offering, a figure that was increased to $500 million in October. On November 15 the company went public at $20 a share, raising $565 million and valuing the chain at $4 billion.[88]

---

firms. The Gores Group bought the company out of bankruptcy in a leveraged buyout for $92.3 million plus assumption of some of the company's outstanding debt, putting the company's valuation at $149.9 million.[89] Another example of this trend is Shapes/Arch Holdings LLC, a leading supplier of industrial and building products and one of South Jersey's largest employers, which was bought out of bankruptcy for $95 million in August 2008 by an affiliate of the PE firm H.I.G. Capital. H.I.G.'s distressed-investing arm typically targets companies with a total enterprise value of up to $400 million.[90] PE firms have been active participants on both sides of this process as a result of their position as equity owners in some of these troubled companies and as potential acquirers of others.[91] For example, Stant Corporation, which filed for bankruptcy protection in 2009, was in the hands of the PE firm H.I.G. Capital at the time of the bankruptcy filings.[92] H.I.G.'s distressed-investment arm, meanwhile, was busy over the same period acquiring other distressed or bankrupt firms.

Turnaround investing is fraught with challenges that make buying distressed companies a risky undertaking. The stakes are high when a PE firm takes control of a distressed company and tries to turn it around because of the likelihood of hidden liabilities that can derail the turnaround. The PE firm needs to be able to correctly identify the problems facing the troubled company and to solve the numerous operational and strategic challenges—financial and managerial—that it faces. Not every distressed company that is bought out of bankruptcy succeeds. To take one high-profile example, Fortunoff Fine Jewelry and Silverware LLC filed for bankruptcy in February 2008 with an agreement to sell substantially all of its assets to an affiliate of the PE firm NRDC Equity Partners

LLC. But Fortunoff went bankrupt again a year and a half later, while in PE ownership, and its assets were liquidated.[93]

Buying up failing companies and successfully turning them around is an important function that private equity may play in the economy. The successes show PE investment at its best; the inevitable failures are a good-faith effort by these firms to save a company in trouble. As past president Bill Clinton put it when he explained what is good about private equity on the PBS *NewsHour* in 2012:

> I've got a friend who buys failing companies, and he tries to turn them around. And he's turned a bunch of them around, but not all of them. So sometimes he tried and failed. The effort was honorable. That's a good thing.[94]

A less productive approach to distressed investing has also emerged in recent years. Private equity funds have traditionally bought up the equity in a company (distressed or not) in order to manage its operations, but some are now buying up the debt (rather than the equity) of distressed companies in order to control the restructuring process. In an early example of this, in 2006, the PE firm Yucaipa Companies bought up about half the unsecured debt of Allied Holdings, Inc., the largest North American vehicle transporter. Allied had filed for bankruptcy protection in 2005. As a result, Yucaipa became the single largest holder of Allied's debt and was able to use its debt position to control Allied's restructuring. A case study of Allied's bankruptcy found that, "when the dust settled, Allied emerged from bankruptcy with approximately $200 million less debt, a new secured financing facility, a modified labor contract, and a new controlling shareholder—Yucaipa."[95]

In this circumstance, it is large creditors, rather than the debtor's managers, that make key decisions in the restructuring process—potentially to the disadvantage of the debtor company, its employees, and its other stakeholders. This is a recent development in the United States, where the management of financially troubled companies has historically remained in control of the company through the restructuring process.

Private equity investments in the debt of distressed companies is part of a new "loan to own" strategy that puts the PE firm or fund that purchases this debt in position to gain control of the company as it restructures and emerges from bankruptcy. PE firms with deep pockets, such as Blackstone Group and KKR & Co., have joined hedge funds and distressed-debt firms such as Oaktree Capital Management and Crescent Capital Group in investing in the deeply discounted debt—rather than the equity—of distressed companies. The goal is to obtain a favorable position for themselves as owners after the distressed company passes through bankruptcy—that is, PE firms are buying the distressed debt of struggling companies with the goal of positioning themselves to own the assets.

The high leverage used by private equity to acquire companies puts the companies, as we have seen, at increased risk of default and makes them likely targets for distressed investing. Typically, the ownership of defaulting companies changes hands, and both the creditors of such companies and the partners in the PE funds that formerly owned the bankrupt companies experience losses. In what may strike some as a remarkable development, however, some PE firms are now buying the debt of companies that their funds own—specifically, second-lien debt—in order to gain a claim on equity and a chance at continued control of the company should the debt burden prove too much and the company go into bankruptcy.[96] First-lien holders get paid in cash if the bankrupt company has any. Second-lien holders get a claim on equity in the company. Apollo Global Management's Fund VI joined with Texas Pacific Group's TPG Partners Fund V in the disastrous buyout of casino operator Harrah's Entertainment Inc. (now Caesar's Entertainment). In 2009, concerned that Harrah's would declare bankruptcy, TPG and Apollo began buying up second-lien notes for 37 cents on the dollar. The purpose of this type of investing in distressed debt is to position fund sponsors to claim a major equity stake on the cheap in the bankrupt companies owned by their own PE funds. As we saw in chapter 3, this maneuver can greatly enhance returns to PE investors at the expense of the creditors who loaned the money that financed the initial leveraged buyout of the company.

Adapting to a Changed Environment

While the economic recession has posed serious challenges to the private equity business model and its returns on investment, the evidence does not suggest that the $1.3 trillion industry is in decline. It was continuing to rebound in 2013, and the largest players held billions of dollars in assets under management (table 4.1). Some of these funds were now invested in more diverse areas beyond private equity. Others specialized in particular industries, such as the mining-focused firm Resource Capital Funds, and Riverstone Holdings with its expertise in the energy and power sectors. At the end of 2013, the largest U.S. private equity firm, the Blackstone Group, held $248 billion in assets under management, followed by the Carlyle Group ($180 billion), Apollo Global Management ($113 billion), and KKR (over $90 billion).

Private equity firms adapted to the changed environment following the economic crisis by shifting into less-exploited arenas. Three strategies are noteworthy. They shifted toward acquisition of midmarket companies, where financial engineering plays less of a role and strategic and operational improvements are more important. They diversified into other alternative investments, such as hedge funds and real estate investment trusts (REITs). And they expanded their geographic focus away

Table 4.1   U.S. Private Equity Firms with Assets Under Management
Valued at More Than $20 Billion, 2013

Investor Name	Active Investments	Investments in the Last Five Years	Assets Under Management (Millions of Dollars)
Blackstone Group (BX)	172	202	$248,000
Carlyle Group (CG)	255	220	180,400
Apollo Global Management (APO)	66	82	113,100
Kohlberg Kravis Roberts (KKR)	120	173	90,200
Goldman Sachs Capital Partners	119	122	76,217
Oaktree Capital Management	80	100	74,900
Bain Capital	69	110	70,000
GTCR Golder Rauner	39	75	69,732
CVC Capital Partners	41	51	68,034
TPG Capital	100	129	60,551
Apax Partners	62	96	46,619
Warburg Pincus	144	116	39,370
Resource Capital Funds	17	12	34,000
Lone Star Funds	15	17	30,830
Kelso & Co.	24	35	27,000
Providence Equity Partners	54	66	27,000
Silver Lake Partners	29	61	25,962
Riverstone Holdings	67	66	23,445
Cerberus Capital Management	57	42	23,000
Lexington Partners	5	9	22,500
New MainStream Capital	1	2	22,000
First Reserve	51	41	20,897
Hellman & Friedman	26	54	20,800
Black Canyon Capital	6	8	20,000
Centerbridge Partners	23	40	20,000
Welsh, Carson, Anderson & Stowe	55	47	20,000

Source: PitchBook.

from the United States and the United Kingdom and toward emerging markets—especially China, India, and Brazil. These arenas are expected to provide ongoing opportunities for private equity investments in the coming years.

Attempts at Strategic and Operational Improvements

In the boom years 2003 through 2007, private equity funds could rely on a combination of factors to generate high returns. GDP growth provided an expanding market for the products and services of the portfolio firms they acquired. A buoyant stock market with rising price-to-earnings multiples made it easy to sell a company at a higher multiple of earnings than the price at which it had been acquired. The easy availability of credit, as well as debt markets that welcomed leveraged buyouts, facilitated ever-greater leverage in PE acquisitions. Cost-cutting strategies to free up cash to service these debts were also common. Mainly, PE firms made money for their investors by choosing the right sectors to invest in and the right time to make the investments. For the most part, adding value to an operating company by providing superior access to management talent and financial markets played a small supporting role in generating returns for PE funds.

That changed in the postcrisis period. The recession battered the balance sheets of many operating companies, reducing the pool of attractive acquisition targets. Competition among PE firms for the companies drove up purchase prices and the multiple of earnings at which companies were acquired, making it unlikely that there would be large increases in the multiple at which the companies could later be sold. Slow economic growth and more cautious debt markets following the economic crisis also threatened PE investor returns. Many publicly traded companies and privately held businesses reduced staff and engaged in cost-cutting during the recession, leaving new PE owners with few options for further reducing operating expenses. And as discussed in greater detail in the next chapter, PE firms increasingly turned to investments in midmarket companies, where future returns from acquiring portfolio companies depend far more heavily on developing business strategies for growth and providing superior management and operational improvements.

This focus on business strategy and performance improvements has always been more common among smaller PE funds—those that have committed capital under $500 million and focus on investments in smaller companies. These funds invest in companies with a relatively small enterprise value—generally too small for the company to have been publicly traded. Their size tends to limit the assets these companies have available for collateral and hence the degree of leverage that can be used to acquire them. And they often lack modern management know-how. The use of debt remains very important for boosting returns to PE investors, but with fewer opportunities for high leverage and greater opportunities to bring managerial know-how to bear, the PE general partners in these funds are more likely than in large or mega-buyout funds to have relied on strategic and operational improvements to generate returns. These funds were also less likely to suffer losses during the financial crisis. This made smaller funds more attractive to investors.

Since the financial crisis, some large PE firms have added partners who are focused on operations and have experience running companies; these firms have also developed teams that specialize in particular industry sectors—specialist teams within large generalist PE firms that can identify opportunities for growth and performance improvement. At the "SuperReturn 2012" conference in Boston in June, Terry Mullen, cofounder and partner of Arsenal Capital Partners, made the point that PE firms know investors are looking to invest in funds that create value this way. Operational excellence is the new measure of top performance, he noted, and "80 percent of buyout funds claim this is what they do."

These claims are wildly exaggerated, as many at the SuperReturn 2012 conference acknowledged. But the private equity model did begin to change as a result of the economic crisis. Partners were recruited with operational expertise. PE firms tried to build well-articulated and replicable strategic approaches. Whether PE firms that succeeded in the boom years when a rising stock market lifted all ships can be successful in the new environment in focusing on midmarket investments and implementing strategic and operational improvements is not clear, as some of the cases in chapter 5 illustrate. Questions remain about the role played by PE partners with operational expertise, as compared to those with investment expertise, in identifying target companies for acquisition, in going through the acquisition process, and in developing relationships with portfolio company managers. Three decades of research on effectively implementing superior management practices shows that deep investments in skills and work organization and extended time horizons are needed to bring about substantial change in operational performance.[97]

There is also the question of how permanent the shift away from financial engineering and toward operational improvement will prove to be and whether PE firms are just biding their time, waiting for the traditional sources of PE returns to recover. The healthy credit markets and low interest rates of 2012 led to an uptick in the use of leverage in LBOs. By the end of 2012, the percentage of debt used in buyouts had almost returned to its 2007 level of 70 percent, according to Thomson Reuters,[98] and based on an analysis of Capital IQ data, the ratio of debt to EBITDA in buyouts had returned to 2007 levels as well.[99] In mid-2013, according to PitchBook, the median percentage of debt was almost 60 percent, which is consistent with an average debt ratio approaching 70 percent.[100] Examples of highly leveraged deals include a 2012 $5 billion leveraged buyout by Carlyle of DuPont Performance Coatings in which Carlyle put down about 25 percent in equity.[101] And in 2013, Bain and Golden Gate Capital put down only 18 percent cash in the buyout of BMC Software for $6.9 billion. The last two times equity contributions were this low were the buyout of Clear Channel Communications in 2007 and the buyout of Harrah's Entertainment in 2008, both of which suffered from oversized interest payments that led to operational cutbacks.[102]

Diversifying Types of Investment

PE firms that had diversified into a range of other businesses were better able to earn positive if lackluster returns in the 2008 to 2010 period than firms that concentrated exclusively on leveraged buyouts. In the late 1990s, Blackstone Group was almost the only PE firm to have diversified into other lines of business, including real estate, credit, and hedge funds as well as consulting. Its 2010 profit was driven in large measure by imputed gains in its property portfolio, which was up substantially for the year; investments in distressed real estate proved exceptionally successful as a source of returns that year. In early 2013, Blackstone committed $116 million to help build a hydroelectric dam on the White Nile in Uganda, an investment that the firm expects will generate years of reliable income.[103]

In the early 2000s, a number of large PE firms—Texas Pacific Group (now TPG), Carlyle Group, and KKR—expanded into hedge funds and other asset management businesses. Fortress Investment Group provides an example of the importance of diversification. The $2.5 billion PE fund raised by this investment firm in 2006 was seriously underwater in 2010, as some of its largest portfolio firms faced financial distress. While the limited partners in its PE fund faced significant losses at that time, Fortress itself remained profitable because the firm's investment vehicles include a number of hedge fund and credit businesses in addition to its PE funds.[104]

Today, many PE firms—especially the top-tier players—are reinventing themselves as multi-platform alternative investment companies to better weather challenges in financial markets and to protect themselves (if not their limited partner investors) from the risks associated with the highly leveraged buyouts undertaken by the PE funds they sponsor.[105] PE firms have diversified into a range of other businesses—hedge funds, credit operations, and REITs—while PE funds have added new forms of investment, including private investments in publicly traded enterprises (PIPEs), minority investments in privately held companies, and add-on investments by companies already in their portfolios. The reinvention of PE firms has been facilitated by the new requirements in the federal financial reform act, the Dodd-Frank Wall Street Reform and Consumer Protection Act of 2010. Under this new legislation, banks are required to shut down most of their proprietary trading operations. Brand-name PE firms have been successful in recruiting top trading teams from banks such as Goldman Sachs and Credit Suisse Group and are adding proprietary trading in publicly traded companies to their lines of business.

In 2004 leveraged buyouts accounted for 51 percent of private equity transactions. Add-ons brought this total up to 80 percent. Minority investments in private companies accounted for only 17 percent of transactions. The share of LBOs has declined since then and through the third quarter of 2013 accounted for only 33 percent of all transactions, while the share of minority investments increased to 25 percent.[106] With the continuing need to invest dry powder and the keen competition for target companies to add to PE fund portfolios, private equity is likely to continue to seek minority investments in publicly- and privately-held companies.

Investing in Emerging Markets

Investments by private equity firms in the BRIC nations (Brazil, Russia, India, and China) grew during the boom years from 2003 to 2007. China, India, and Brazil, in particular, offered attractive opportunities for deals, with the greatest amount of investment in China. As in the developed economies, activity peaked in 2007, then dropped somewhat in 2008, and slowed more dramatically in 2009. PE activity recovered strongly in these markets in 2010 as these economies emerged from the global recession more quickly and experienced more robust growth than the United States or the United Kingdom. Nevertheless, total investment in PE activities in these emerging economies remained very small in relation to the volume in the advanced industrial nations. By mid-2013, slower economic growth in these countries as a result of the lackluster recovery from the recession in the United States, the United Kingdom, and Europe, plus tax reform and other political and economic changes and challenges, led to a falloff in PE investment.

During the period of economic retrenchment in the advanced economies, the governments in China, India, and Brazil signaled that they were receptive to private equity investments. China's government, for example, while hostile to offshore, dollar-denominated funds that buy out Chinese companies and evade restrictions on foreign ownership, has welcomed PE investments in Chinese companies via Chinese-currency-denominated funds as part of its plan to strengthen the nation's financial services industry and deepen its capital markets.[107] U.S. hedge funds and PE funds have responded with major new investments. Despite the numerous challenges associated with investing in China that can complicate deal-making and undermine returns—the rule of law is weak, ownership of companies is often unclear, and public and private data may be unreliable—PE firms have sought deals there.

In the years following the financial crisis, general and limited partners of PE funds were reported to be most bullish on China, with India right behind. The PE firm TPG, which has a long history of investing in Chinese companies via offshore, dollar-denominated funds, teamed up in 2010 with two big Chinese cities, Shanghai and Chongqing, and created the investment firm's first Yuan-based funds. Similar joint ventures to set up local currency funds were made between the Blackstone Group and the Shanghai government and between the Carlyle Group and the Beijing government. Carlyle agreed in January 2010 to establish a ¥1 billion PE fund, which was launched later that year. KKR wrapped up a $1 billion fund targeted to investments in small, fast-growing companies in China. Smaller PE firms have also expressed interest in China.[108] According to the investment bank China First Capital in Shenzhen, global

PE funds as well as Chinese funds completed nearly ten thousand deals worth a total of $230 billion from 2001 to 2012.[109]

But investing in China has been problematic for PE firms, as they have found it difficult to exit their investments. At the start of 2013, about 7,500 of the 10,000 PE deals made from 2001 on had not been exited. The traditional exit route for these investments has been an IPO in the United States, but the interest of U.S. investors in Chinese companies has waned as a result of accounting scandals and other difficulties. And regulators in China have essentially shut down the Chinese IPO market for the time being, making exiting PE investments in 2013 very difficult and leading to a slowdown in PE investments in that country.[110]

India was presumed to have certain advantages over countries such as China, including better-trained managers and more corporate transparency, as well as the oldest stock market in Asia and the largest number of listed stocks. Investment firms successfully exited from PE investments in Indian companies via IPOs, and Indian courts were considered capable of fairly deciding disputes that involved investor rights. As a result, the country was viewed favorably by investors. Nevertheless, India has had its own challenges for foreign investors that have limited the extent of PE activity. Government restrictions on foreign investment make it very hard for foreign PE investors to acquire 100 percent ownership of Indian companies. The families that control Indian businesses often resist their sale to foreigners. In addition, the leverage that makes PE deals attractive in the United States and Europe and makes it possible to take public companies private is difficult to obtain in India. The result is that global firms doing business in India are more likely to take a minority stake in a company rather than try to acquire the entire company. Warburg Pincus entered the Indian market as early as 1999, acquiring an 18 percent stake in Bharti Tele-Ventures, a top cell-phone company. By 2005, major U.S. and U.K. firms, such as Blackstone Group, Carlyle Group, General Atlantic Partners, and Actis, were active in the Indian market. Blackstone began investing in India in 2005 and in 2010 had about $1.2 billion invested there in twelve companies, including Gokaldas Exports and Intelenet Global Services.[111]

By 2013, the expectation that India would provide robust returns for private equity investors was extinguished. The India private market consultant for JPMorgan asset management, Avneet Kochar, characterized the situation as follows: "Current global sentiment about the Indian private equity market is about as negative as it has been since the inception of the industry." Much recent PE investment went into infrastructure, energy, and real estate, sectors plagued by poor decision-making, cost overruns, and excessive leverage. In addition, private equity tends to be the minority investor when it acquires Indian companies, and the majority investors do not share private equity's hurry to exit investments. The result, according to Kochar, is that "most limited partners who believed in the India growth story in the last cycle are looking at a rather poor outcome from their prior commitments. The entire PE market is in a state of logjam with investors either sitting on unrealized losses or a lack of liquidity or exits from the reasonably performing portfolio companies."[112] Currently, causes for optimism about PE investing in India are largely aspirational.

Brazil, which emerged from the global economic crisis early and with a strong recovery, became an attractive focus for PE investing. The country has a large and stable economy, robust capital markets, the Bovespa stock exchange—which makes it possible to exit from PE investments via an IPO—and a financial system that escaped the crisis. In addition, Brazilian regulations allow pension funds to invest up to 20 percent of their funds in alternative investments. As a result, pension funds have fueled the growth of private equity in that country. Brazil is the most-favored Latin American location for PE activity and has been central to PE activity in that region.[113] Two out of every three PE acquisitions on the continent are located there, and the country has attracted investments by major players, including the Carlyle Group and Warburg Pincus. Warburg Pincus opened its office in São Paulo in February 2010 and in September made its first investment in Omega Energia, whose business is buying small hydropower plants. Blackstone Group entered Brazil via its acquisition in September 2010 of a 40 percent stake in São Paulo–based Patria Investimentos, a diversified investment firm whose activities include PE investments. Smaller U.S. firms, such as the Boston PE firm Advent International and the Silicon Valley company Draper Fisher Jurvestson, were also actively investing in Brazil in that period.[114]

But the economic situation has changed dramatically in Brazil. The country recovered strongly from the global financial crisis and registered a 7.5 percent growth rate in 2010. Two years later, in 2012, a sluggish economy and high inflation reduced the growth rate to just 0.9 percent. Growth in 2013 was on track to increase to 2 percent. Even apart from these economic issues, the country faces problems of corruption, insufficient infrastructure, and poor services. The economic optimism of the years immediately following the crisis has turned to pessimism among many investors. Some private equity firms are encouraged by the promise of reform, however, and attracted by Brazil's size and potential. This includes 3i Group, which is increasing its commitment to the region, and H.I.G. Capital, which made two investments in the country in July 2013.[115]

Economic prospects for China, Brazil, and other emerging markets weakened in 2012 as global demand for products slowed, and investing in companies in these markets faces many other risks as well. The legal, tax, regulatory, and environmental frameworks are in flux as these countries' economies evolve. Debt markets are still developing. Workers with the requisite skills may be in short supply. And management and accounting standards at companies targeted for acquisition by PE funds may be want-ing, making it more difficult for the PE firm to evaluate the target compa-ny's potential. The risks loom larger if the macroeconomic context becomes less forgiving. Although there may be the potential for high returns, recent experience with the risks raises questions about whether returns on invest-ments in emerging markets will live up to expectations.

Conclusion

The threat of bankruptcy did not appear particularly worrisome to pri-vate equity investors in the bubble economy of the mid-2000s, when credit was readily available, stock prices were generally rising, and the higher default risks faced by highly leveraged firms were more than off-set by the very high payoffs from successful exits from portfolio compa-nies. Occasional bankruptcies had little effect on the overall returns to PE investors, and even less on returns to PE firms. With each PE fund structured as a separate partnership, and each portfolio company as a separate corporation, the most that the PE firms and the funds' investors could lose was their equity stake in a portfolio firm that went bankrupt. Such losses may have been offset by dividend recapitalizations that let the PE owners take money out of the company prior to bankruptcy and by the fees that the portfolio company was required to pay to the PE firm. Creditors could seize the property or business, but the PE partners were not liable for the portfolio company's losses or for repaying its debts, and creditors were often big losers in a bankruptcy.

The higher incidence of financial distress and bankruptcy among highly leveraged companies during and following the onset of the eco-nomic crisis in December 2007 cannot be dismissed so lightly by private equity firms. Fear of losses has increased the difficulty that PE firms faced in obtaining credit in financial markets and in recruiting limited partner investors. The large overhang of committed funds that PE firms have not yet invested (dry powder) and the increased reliance of PE firms on sec-ondary sales (sales of a portfolio company to another PE firm) are indica-tions of the challenges that PE funds faced in finding and deploying new capital commitments and in exiting mature investments.

Private equity activity experienced a slowdown—in fund-raising, deal-making, and exits—following the onset of the economic crisis. It has gradually recovered; in 2013—five years after the crisis began—fundraising had clearly improved, but PE activity was still far below its previous peak. PE firms in the industry responded to the changed environment in the postcrisis period in a variety of ways. There were increases in distressed investing, including purchases of the debt of trou-bled companies at prices well below the face value of the loans, as well as acquisitions of such companies at deeply discounted prices. Distressed investing is premised on the assumption that the economy will begin to grow more rapidly and demand for the goods and services provided by struggling companies will increase. PE funds that specialize in turning failing companies around require a greater focus on, and experience with, operational improvement. This is a skill set more commonly found among PE firms that specialize in acquiring midmarket or smaller companies, where opportunities for leverage and financial engineering are limited because such companies have fewer assets that can be used as collateral. Increased attention to strategy and operations and less reliance on financial engineering—at least for the time being—have become more prominent goals of PE funds.

PE firms have adapted to the changed economic environment in two other ways as well: they have diversified the types of alternative investments that they make, with the larger PE firms adding hedge funds and REITs to their investment platforms, and PE funds are investing in less conventional assets. Recent fundraising success means the industry has more dry powder to put to work. Minority investments in publicly traded and privately held companies are likely to continue until the economic recovery becomes more robust and a greater number of attractive takeover targets become available. Finally, PE firms have diversified geographically, beyond the PE hub of the United States, the United Kingdom, and Europe. Investments in emerging markets, especially China, India, and Brazil, increased in the immediate aftermath of the economic crisis, but results have not lived up to expectations.

= Chapter 5 =

The Middle Market—Increasing
Focus After the Crisis

The private equity business model has several unique characteristics that distinguish it from the way that public corporations do business. As discussed in chapter 3, these attributes include the promise of outsized returns to the limited partners, the short time horizon for achieving higher-than-average returns, the greater use of leverage and financial engineering to increase returns, the active involvement of the PE firm in the business decisions of portfolio companies, the lower tax liabilities, and the lack of transparency when companies are taken private.

The ability of private equity firms to execute this business model, however, varies with different market conditions, as we saw in chapter 4. Notable megadeals that captured the public imagination in the precrisis boom years became financial disasters during and after the economic crisis of 2007 to 2008. PE investments in portfolio companies in the middle market, which relied less on debt, fared better in those more challenging economic conditions. Limited partners expressed a clear preference for these investments, and PE funds responded. Smaller PE funds capitalized on their successes by buying out midsize companies; large PE funds added operations professionals and tried their hand at taking over small and midsize companies, with mixed results. PE investments are particularly sensitive to the business cycle, as the ability to make deals and exit them successfully depends on the availability of credit, trends in the stock market, the confidence of investors, and creditors' willingness to take risks.

This chapter examines another source of heterogeneity in private equity firms' success: how the size of the portfolio companies that private equity acquires influences the application of the basic PE business model. Size matters because it shapes the capital structure of the buyout deal and influences the range of opportunities available to create and extract value from the portfolio company. Small and midsize companies with fewer assets than large corporations are not able to provide the collateral to back high levels of debt, so leverage and other forms of financial engineering contribute less to returns when private equity takes over these companies. At the same time, small and midsize companies offer a range of growth opportunities that larger corporations are likely to have already exploited. Thus, the relative payoff from operational versus financial strategies depends on variation in the enterprise value of the acquired company—from small or midsize deals to large- or mega-market deals.

Our line of argument is consistent with the strategic perspective of Robert Hoskisson, Mike Wright, and others, who argue that private equity firms vary along two dimensions: in their relative reliance on debt versus equity, and in whether they pursue a "focused" or a diversified strategy. PE firms that buy out small and midsize companies use less debt and typically pursue a focused strategy centered on a particular industry: they are "niche players" with relatively longer-term equity positions. Large buyout firms, by contrast, rely more on debt and their own financial expertise and pursue a diversified strategy across different sectors. They are "short-term" and "efficiency-oriented players."[1] A central question in the postcrisis period is whether "the giants can learn to dance."[2]

What is referred to as the "middle market" includes a wide swath of companies with an enterprise value ranging from $25 million to $1 billion—a definition widely used in the industry, as well as by PitchBook.[3] The entire private equity market is typically segmented into small (less than $25 million), lower middle ($25 million to $100 million), core middle ($100 million to $500 million), upper middle ($500 million to $1 billion), and mega-market (more than $1 billion). The mega-market has received most of the media attention over the last decade and accounts for roughly 40 percent of all capital invested in deals. Thus, the small- and middle-market portfolio companies are an important and relatively neglected part of the PE story.

In the immediate aftermath of the financial crisis, limited partners in private equity funds became more interested in middle-market deals, as risky mega-deals often performed poorly. As we saw in chapter 4, LPs and lenders alike became cautious about backing megadeals after the spate of defaults on debt obligations, amend-and-extend agreements, bankruptcies, and even liquidations that occurred during the crisis and immediately afterward. Surveys of LPs in the postcrisis period found a strong preference for investing in new funds that promised to focus on the middle market. These deals proved more resilient during the financial crisis and were less likely to be underwater in the years after the crisis ended. Preqin's December 2011 survey of limited partners found that small- to middle-market buyout funds were the most attractive to investors: 45 percent of respondents felt that these funds presented the best opportunities at that time, and 49 percent reported plans to invest in such funds during 2012. Only 15 percent of LPs viewed large funds and mega-funds as presenting the best opportunities, and just 16 percent planned to make such investments.[4]

As a result, PE investment did shift to the middle market, but it was particularly concentrated at the high end—in deals between $500 million and $1 billion rather than in smaller deals. As we discuss later in the chapter, large deals and megadeals still represented 55 percent of the value of PE investments between 2008 and 2012. Thus, the majority of capital investment in the postcrisis years has continued to be in large enterprises.

Despite the resilience of large buyouts, however, it is in the small and midsize companies—those with an enterprise value *under* $500 million, and most often under $300 million—where private equity can most often contribute to business growth and innovation. That is because the leverage used in deals between $500 million and $1 billion more closely resembles that used in megadeals than the debt used in deals under $300 million. In this chapter, we compare the trends in PE investment across all market segments and then focus on cases of small and midsize companies bought out by PE firms.

The demand for private equity financing in these small and midsize companies has grown in part because of the institutional vacuum created by banking deregulation. Historically, small or independent commercial banks made loans to small-business owners who were trusted customers—customers whom they knew well enough to be able to evaluate their ability to repay—to finance new investments in facilities and equipment. Revolving loans typically provided small businesses with cash flow to cover prepaid inventory or supplies until customers paid for final products.

The deregulation of the banking industry, however, spurred the consolidation of banks into large and "mega" financial institutions, which are significantly less likely to lend to small businesses than are small or independent banks.[5] The differences in the loan preferences of large and small banks are due, at least in part, to differences in the availability of information. Small businesses are "informationally opaque" in that they do not have the kind of "hard," publicly available information—such as financial audits, credit scores, collateral ratios, and the like—that large banks typically use to assess risk in large corporations.[6] As a result, lenders need to rely on the accumulation over time of "soft" information about the reliability and trustworthiness of the small-business owner to assess the risk and the company's creditworthiness. Small banks have the organizational capacity to engage in this type of "relationship lending" because they tend to be located near the small businesses they serve, have fewer levels of management, and are able to directly monitor the loan officers in charge of small-business loans. These features tend to eliminate the agency problems that might arise between loan officers and higher-level management. Longer relationships also lead to lower interest rates and lower collateral requirements for small businesses.[7]

For large banks, by contrast, relationship management is costly; they also lack the organizational capacity or interest to engage in the kind of relationship lending needed to loan funds to small firms. Large banks rely much more on "hard" data in transactions-based lending—that is, on quantitative public information as the basis for approving loans. Allen Berger, Lawrence Goldberg, and Lawrence White, for example, found that markets with higher shares of large banks and more complex banks are significantly less likely to lend to small businesses than are smaller and simpler banks.[8] In addition, mergers and acquisitions among large banks have led to a decrease in small-business lending, although mergers among small banks have had a positive effect. These findings are consistent with a series of prior studies.[9]

This institutional vacuum created space for private equity and other private pools of capital to fund small-business innovation and growth. Not only do the small and midsize PE firms that buy out small and midsize companies have the financial resources to invest, but at least some of them have also developed a relationship management approach that is similar to that practiced by independent banks. They often have accumulated relationships and reputations in particular sectors that allow them to combine financial resources with consulting expertise in their industries or areas of specialization. Large PE funds have also entered this segment, buying small and midsize companies, with mixed results. The skill set required for successful investing in this market segment is very different from the type of financial engineering typically undertaken by the larger PE funds.

PE firms deal with the problem of information opacity in small and midsize companies by conducting very careful due diligence. This partly explains why private equity has filled only a small share of the demand by small and midsize companies for financing. According to recent survey research, only 15 percent of businesses that had attempted to tap private equity were successful.[10] That is due in part to the high selectivity of PE firms: in general, they select the most promising small businesses, not those that are financially distressed. Two Pepperdine University faculty members, John Paglia and Maretno Harjoto, analyzed the correlates of PE investment in midmarket establishments and compared the means of establishments with and without PE financing.[11] They found that PE investors are significantly more likely to invest in establishments that are subsidiaries of larger companies (especially if the parent company has multiple establishments); to invest in establishments with government contracts; and to invest in establishments that pay their bills promptly. PE investors are significantly less likely to invest in companies that are corporations compared with other types of establishments (for example, subsidiaries of companies or family-owned businesses) or in businesses that have female, non-Caucasian, or foreign-born owners.

For these reasons, the demand for private equity investment in small and midsize companies over the last decade or so has been robust. Because they are often privately owned (sometimes by the founder), they have difficulty finding other sources of funding, and they are attracted to private equity for the combination of financial resources and management expertise that PE firms may be able to offer. This combination can provide these companies with the cash and the know-how to invest in new technologies, IT and accounting systems, work processes, human capital, marketing, or acquisitions to help the company grow. When PE owners play this kind of role, they can be an important catalyst for taking these companies to a qualitatively new level of development and competitiveness.

Media analysts and academics alike often compare private equity to venture capital based on the role that private equity can play in fostering business growth. But conflating the two asset classes is misleading, as they are quite different in their business models. Although both assume substantial control over the companies they invest in, venture capital provides seed money for early-stage, high-risk start-ups; takes an equity position in the company; and, importantly, does not load the company with high levels of debt or use the other financial engineering strategies that are central to the PE model.

It is worth pointing out that while PE firms in the middle market tend to focus more on operational improvements as a source of returns on investment, leverage and financial engineering strategies still play an important role in meeting promised levels of returns to their limited partners. Successful execution of the operational role is difficult and not always reliable as a source of returns. Beyond raising substantial pools of capital, PE firms in this market space need general skills in areas such as human resource management, finance and accounting, and marketing, as well as specialized industry knowledge to help guide strategic and operational decisions in the portfolio companies. Not all PE firms have these kinds of skills, capacity, or patience to implement operational improvements or innovations. As some of our case studies demonstrate, heavy reliance on leverage and financial engineering—a kind of one-size-fits-all approach—is not uncommon in the middle market, with unsurprising results.

The upshot is that large private equity firms have had incentives and opportunities to move into the middle market. The empirical question is whether they have developed the operational and industry-specific skills needed to shift from short-term efficiency players to long-term equity players—which they must be in order to improve the performance and competitiveness of small companies. Some large PE firms have brought in former CEOs and industry experts as partners to execute this approach. The business model of large PE firms—building a portfolio of firms in disparate markets to exploit financial opportunities as a type of diversified conglomerate—is not well suited to advising small and midsize companies in particular industry and product market niches.

Size, Scope, and Trends
in the Middle Market

From 2000 to 2012, middle-market leveraged buyouts totaled some 12,317 deals, valued at $2.42 trillion, according to PitchBook data.[12] These sums include deals valued at between $25 million and $1 billion, but not small deals under $25 million or megadeals over $1 billion. The trends in private equity deal-making in the middle market look quite similar to those for the PE industry as a whole as the market changed from the early 2000s to the mid-decade bubble years, and then into the crisis period and beyond. As shown in figure 5.1, from 2000 to 2007 the number of deals and the value of the capital invested by private equity in the middle market grew steadily—particularly accelerating in the boom years of 2006 and 2007—before plummeting in 2008. The number and value of deals hit their low point in 2009 (when they fell back to their 2003 level), but rebounded thereafter, although not to their bubble-year highs. Between 2010 and 2012, the annual number of deals averaged 62 percent of their high point in 2007, while their value averaged 69 percent.

During this period, PE-leveraged buyouts of middle-market companies occurred across all industry sectors. The share of deals in each industry sector varied by one or two percentage points from year to year, but remained fairly consistent. In 2011, 32 percent of companies acquired by private equity provided goods and services to other businesses; 21 percent provided goods and services to consumers; and 7 percent were in the energy business, 10 percent in financial services, 12 percent in health care, 13 percent in IT, and 5 percent in materials and resources.[13]

The investment pattern of private equity in different market segments is of interest to management and employment scholars as well as policymakers because it indicates which types of companies have been most affected by PE-leveraged buyouts and how that has changed over time. The distribution of PE investment across market segments can, in part, provide insights into the relative importance of operational and financial engineering strategies because the opportunities for these strategies vary by company size.

Table 5.1 shows the total number of U.S. leveraged buyouts and their value by market segment for the period 2000 to 2012. During this period, PitchBook documents over 18,300 buyouts at just over $3.4 trillion. The largest number of buyouts occurred in small and midsize companies, but the capital invested in these deals was relatively small. Thus, buyouts of companies valued at under $25 million accounted for nearly one-third of the deals but only 2 percent of the capital invested. Similarly, just under one-third of other deals were completed in the $25 million to $100 million segment, but these accounted for only 11 percent of all

**Figure 5.1   Middle-Market Leveraged Buyout Deal Flow,
by Year, 2000 to 2012**

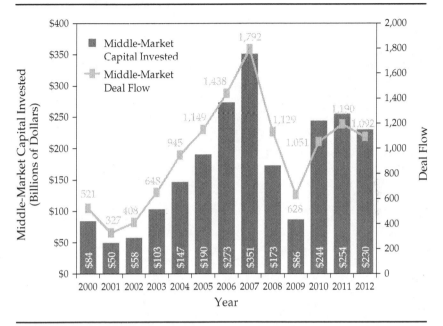

Source: PitchBook.

**Table 5.1   Total Number and Value of U.S. Leveraged Buyouts,
by Market Segment, 2000 to 2012**

Market Segment	Total Number of LBOs	Percentage Deal Count	Total Capital Invested	Average Percentage Capital Invested
$0 to $25 million	5,639	32%	$56.67	2%
$25 million to $100 million	5,701	32	287.70	11
$100 million to $500 million	5,307	28	1,105.72	36
$500 million to $1 billion	1,309	6	852.59	25
$1 billion or more	352	2	1,122.75	25
Total	18,308	100	3,425.42	100

Source: PitchBook.

capital invested. At the other end of the spectrum, buyouts of companies valued at $500 million or more represented only 8 percent of deal-making activity but 50 percent of all capital invested by PE firms.

Figures 5.2 and 5.3 show the patterns of deal-making and capital investment in different market segments on an annual basis. Activity in the bubble years of 2006 and 2007 was heightened in every market segment, in terms of both the number and value of leveraged buyouts. The relative proportion of investments, however, shifted from deals of less than $500 million to deals of higher value. Subsequently, in the immediate postcrisis years, the lower market segments recovered, while deal-making above $500 million or so fell off markedly and did not recover until later.

Some analysts have pointed out that deal-making in the postcrisis years shifted considerably to the middle market because megadeals were more difficult to complete. But it is important to look more closely at different segments of the middle market. In terms of total capital invested, deals of less than $500 million represented 59 percent of private equity investments before the bubble years, fell to 32 percent during the bubble (2006 to 2007), and rose to an average of only 45 percent of activity between 2008 and 2012. Large deals and megadeals averaged 68 percent of the value of LBOs during the bubble years and 55 percent of the activity from 2008 to 2012. Thus, the majority of capital investment in the postcrisis

Figure 5.2   Leveraged Buyouts by Market Segment, 2000 to 2012

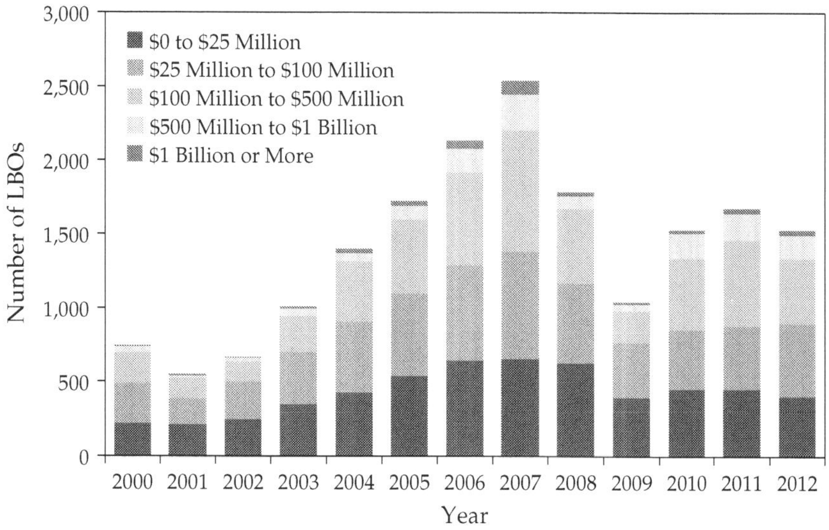

Figure 5.3   Capital Invested in Leveraged Buyouts by Market Segment, 2000 to 2012

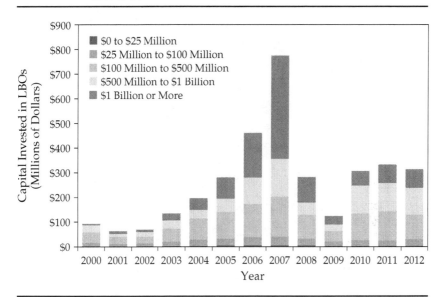

Source: PitchBook.

years has continued to be in large enterprises. What has changed since the crisis is the relative distribution of capital invested in large deals as opposed to megadeals. In the bubble years, megadeals equaled about 47 percent of the value of *all* deals, but that fell to 26 percent in the period 2008 to 2012. Because megadeals were more difficult to negotiate after the crisis, large PE firms shifted some of their activity to the $500 million to $1 billion market: the percentage of capital invested in this segment rose from 21 percent of all activity in the bubble years to 29 percent since 2008.

In 2013 large deals continued to recover, while megadeals remained far below their bubble-year peaks, although they have not disappeared. A total of 489 PE deals closed in the third quarter of 2013, of which 70 percent—or about 325—were leveraged buyouts; 10 were deals of $1 billion or more.[14]

Changes in market conditions over the decade also affected the pattern of exit activity to some extent. For all deals for which exit data are available between 2003 and 2012, over 50 percent of exits occurred through corporate acquisitions, while some 37 percent occurred via secondary buyouts and only 9 percent via IPOs. The patterns changed somewhat between the pre- and post-crisis periods, with a rise in the relative use of corporate acquisitions and secondary buyouts and a decline in IPOs (from 13 percent before the crisis to 7 percent afterward).

Figure 5.4   Exits by Market Segment, Pre- and Post-Crisis, 2003 to 2012

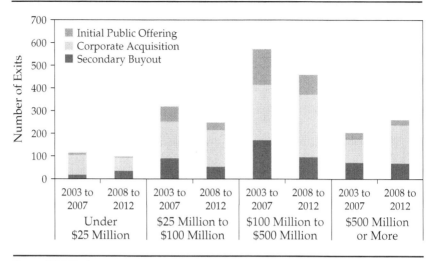

Source: PitchBook.

Exit activity by market segment is shown in figure 5.4.[15] In each segment, corporate acquisitions represent the largest share of exits, followed by secondary buyouts and then IPOs. IPOs were the most successful for investments in the core middle market ($100 million to $500 million), followed by the lower middle market ($25 million to $100 million). Comparing exit activity in the pre- and post-crisis periods, it was lower in all market segments after the crisis—except, surprisingly, in the large- and mega-market segments. There, corporate acquisitions increased considerably, perhaps because large corporations had cash on hand to invest in proven enterprises but were unwilling to expand their own businesses given market uncertainties.

Pricing and Financing Deals in the Middle Market

The variation by market segment in the pricing and financing of deals is important because it influences the business models pursued by private equity firms in their portfolio companies. The pricing and financing of deals differs by segment in two primary respects. The first is the price paid to acquire the portfolio company, as measured by the multiple of the company's earnings (EBITDA). Companies in the small and lower middle market generally are purchased at a lower multiple of the company's earnings compared to larger corporations. Second, the proportion of debt that PE firms lever on the companies they buy is lower for smaller

Figure 5.5   Debt and Equity Multiples by Market Segment, Pre- and Post-Crisis

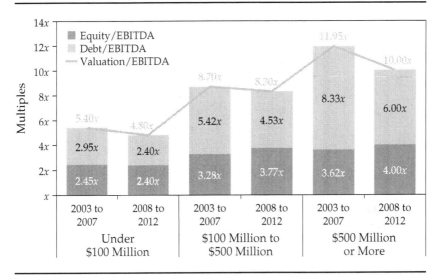

Source: PitchBook.

companies than for larger ones. Both of these factors imply that large- and mega-market acquisitions are under more financial pressure to recoup their investment, since the debt load is greater and the higher price paid to purchase a company increases the difficulty of exiting the investment at a profit. These differences in financial factors shape, to some extent, the relative importance of operational versus financial strategies for making money in mega- versus middle-market deals.

The cost of acquiring the portfolio company—the multiple of a company's earnings (EBITDA)—depends on market conditions as well as the valuation of the company. Despite the fact that earnings multiples and the prices paid to buy portfolio companies reflect the volatility of the market, the multiples for large acquisitions are consistently higher than those for smaller companies. This pattern is illustrated in figure 5.5. First, for each market segment, the overall multiples paid to purchase companies were higher in the precrisis years of market growth compared to the postcrisis years. And second, the multiples paid on average increased by market segment. In the precrisis period, they averaged 5.40 times EBITDA for deals valued at under $100 million, 8.70 times in the core middle market ($100 million to $500 million), and 11.95 times for mega-market deals. In the postcrisis period, the multiples dropped in each segment, but the differences across segments remained similar: 4.80 times EBITDA for deals under

$100 million, 8.30 times for the core middle market, and 10.0 times for mega-deals. By 2013, however, deal multiples had rebounded to levels last seen in 2008. Higher multiples mean that PE funds are paying higher prices across market segments to acquire portfolio firms in 2013—the result, according to PitchBook, of "willing lenders providing debt at low interest rates, aging dry powder and the continued dearth of attractive opportunities."[16]

The proportion of debt to equity in a private equity deal can also be understood in relation to the earnings multiples. Consider a company that sells for a price of nine times earnings. This is often broken down into a debt multiple and an equity multiple. The company may have a debt multiple of six times earnings and an equity multiple of three times earnings. That is, the company was purchased with two-thirds debt and one-third equity. If the debt multiple increases to seven, then the company would be purchased with 78 percent debt and only 22 percent equity.

Figure 5.5 illustrates the variation in the use of the debt multiple by market conditions and market segment. First, across all of the segments, the average reliance on debt financing was greater before the crisis compared to afterward. That is, debt was cheaper and more available in the growth and bubble years leading up to 2007. Second, PE firms made greater use of leverage the higher the valuation of the deal. For investments under $100 million, leverage represented 55 percent of valuation precrisis and 50 percent postcrisis. For the core middle market, the comparable figures were 62 percent versus 55 percent. The leverage used in large- and mega-market deals jumped to an average of 70 percent before the crisis and 60 percent thereafter.

In sum, the lower relative price that private equity firms pay for small and midsize companies compared to larger ones, coupled with the lower proportion of debt that the portfolio companies assume, leads the PE firm to focus on operational improvements and growth as the source of investor returns for these smaller companies. As one investment professional we interviewed noted, things are much saner in the middle market: "Leverage is important, but prudent leverage is even more important."[17] The smaller size of these portfolio companies also limits the opportunities to enhance the bottom line via cuts in employment or in wages and benefits, which are typically less generous to begin with than in larger companies.

Nevertheless, the more restricted opportunities for debt financing and dividend recapitalizations in the small and middle markets do not eliminate the use of financial engineering in these contexts. New business strategies and improvements in operations may be used in conjunction with dividend recapitalizations and aggressive tax planning to boost returns for investors. Failing to focus on approaches that add value, however, and relying instead on leverage and financial engineering for investor returns can prove disastrous in the case of small- and lower-middle-market portfolio companies. Such an approach puts the portfolio company and its workers, creditors, and customers at great risk.

How Private Equity Adds Value: Management, Operations, and Access

Private equity firms acquire healthy small and midsize companies that typically want to grow but do not have the capacity, resources, or know-how to shift to a qualitatively different level of size and competitiveness. PE firms that specialize in acquiring such companies meet this demand by combining the expertise of both financial and management consulting firms. The most successful examples respect the expertise of existing managers or founders, bring in professional managers with complementary skills, and combine these skill sets with the financial and industry expertise of the PE firm.

First, private equity firms provide general management expertise in areas such as strategic planning, leadership, and professionalization of management functions. Small companies often lack the systems of finance, accounting, and auditing needed to manage larger corporations. Information technology systems may need to be upgraded. The PE firm can economize by introducing similar systems across all of the small businesses it acquires as well as by applying its sophisticated knowledge of tax law to minimize its portfolio companies' taxes. PE firms also introduce more sophisticated human resource systems, including systematic and "best practice" approaches to recruitment, hiring, retention, incentive compensation, and performance management. In addition, they may help redesign the organization so that it can handle rapid growth.

Second, successful private equity firms in the middle market often have industry-specific knowledge to help companies in that industry develop bolder and more effective business and operational strategies. They may place industry leaders on the corporate board of a portfolio company, as well as hire managers with proven industry experience in executive positions. They may undertake research on competitors and help develop new product and marketing strategies. They may finance product innovation or provide the expertise and investment capital for operational improvements, such as modernizing existing facilities, upgrading technologies and work processes, and investing in employee skills—with gains for workers and communities as well as investors. They may also introduce supply chain management techniques and offshore manufacturing or service operations to low-wage countries, with more mixed outcomes for other stakeholders.

Third, private equity firms use their well-developed networks, reputation, and relationships with lenders and industry specialists to help portfolio companies navigate the broader market. This guidance may include giving a small or midsize business access to financial markets so that it can acquire another company or adding on companies with complementary products or established relationships in new markets. Or it might involve establishing the portfolio company as a "platform" and acquiring ("rolling up") competitors to achieve economies of scale through consolidation. PE firms also help guide the portfolio company through the IPO process or, alternatively, help negotiate the sale of the portfolio company to a larger corporation.

The strategy of add-ons to help companies grow is most prevalent in small- and mid-market deals under $100 million, but the value of those deals represents a relatively small portion of the capital invested in add-ons. For the period 2000 to 2012, 64 percent of all add-ons occurred in transactions of less than $100 million, but these accounted for only 19 percent of the capital invested in add-ons. The core middle market is where the greatest amount of capital was invested in add-ons. This market segment accounted for only 22 percent of all add-on deals but 44 percent of capital invested in add-ons. By contrast, large- and mega-market deals accounted for only 4 percent of add-on activity, but 36 percent of capital investments in add-ons.[18]

An example of the add-on strategy comes from InterMedia Partners, LP, a private equity firm that is active in the media industry and has investments in television, radio, publishing, the Internet, and marketing. The firm focuses on providing content to niche or underserved markets. In March 2007, the PE firm acquired a division of PriMedia in a leveraged buyout and renamed the portfolio company InterMedia Outdoors. InterMedia Outdoors provides information and entertainment to sportsmen and outdoors enthusiasts. It has a network of websites devoted to hunting, shooting, and fishing; owns numerous magazines that serve these audiences; and produces television programs geared to these viewers. In August 2008, InterMedia Outdoors acquired Barrett Productions, an award-winning producer of outdoor and adventure television programs, from its founder, John Barrett, via a leveraged buyout of the company by InterMedia Partners. Barrett Productions, which had been an independent private company, was acquired as an add-on to InterMedia Outdoors to enhance its TV production capability.[19]

These types of activities are evident in Berkshire Partners' takeover and development of the children's apparel company Carter's Inc. As a middle-market PE firm, Berkshire makes investments in the range of $50 million to $500 million (acquisitions valued at $200 million to $2 billion). It invests in companies that are market leaders and have a strong financial history and noncyclical earnings growth. Berkshire purchased Carter's Inc. from InvestCorp in 2001 for $450 million, with an equity investment of $130 million, or 28.9 percent. Carter's, which had suffered profit losses in the early 1990s, had undertaken cost reductions, initiated offshore outsourcing, and returned to profitability in the mid-1990s, when it was bought out by InvestCorp for $208 million.[20] Its total net sales grew from $300 million to $500 million between 1996 and 2000. When Berkshire Partners acquired Carter's, it focused on strategic planning and further development of offshore outsourcing, which allowed for the expansion of sales into mass-market retail channels. Berkshire also provided advice to Carter's in its first IPO process in 2003, followed by secondary offerings in 2004, 2005, and the acquisition in 2005 of Osh-Kosh B'Gosh (Carter's major competitor) for $312 million.[21] Berkshire Partners owned 85 percent of the company before its IPO in 2003. Its stake fell to 25 percent after the secondary offering in 2004, then to 13 percent after the secondary offering in 2005; it exited the company with the 2006 secondary offering.[22] Berkshire made a 600 percent return on its four-and-a-half-year investment.[23]

Given the demands of business in the small and middle markets, it is evident that the skill sets required for successful investing in these segments are quite different from those typically found in PE firms that focus on large leveraged buyouts of established corporations. PE firms that focus on small- and lower-middle-market deals usually have partners with industry expertise (often former CEOs) who are on par with the firm's partners engaged in finance and deal-making. Unlike venture capital, which invests in a portfolio of start-ups aiming to hit a home run with one of its investments and unperturbed if the others go bust, PE firms investing in the small and lower middle markets seek out businesses with established track records and good prospects and aim for more modest, but consistent, success in every deal.[24] These firms can attract and retain a cadre of experienced executives who are usually unwilling to work for small and midsize companies but are attracted to the potential for substantial upside gain when private equity buys out such businesses.

An alternative approach to securing the needed expertise in industry-specific skills is that taken by the Riverside Company, one of the largest private equity firms focusing on the small and lower middle market. Founded in 1988 and now a global firm with $3.5 billion in assets under management and over three hundred completed deals, Riverside buys and sells companies with an enterprise value under $200 million. Riverside is a generalist PE firm with expertise in small-business development through organic growth or add-ons.[25] Riverside combines its own small-business generalist expertise with that of specialized consulting firms—the Riverside "Toolkit"—which it hires to provide advice for its portfolio companies on key issues such as lean manufacturing, sourcing, pricing optimization, and sales and marketing.[26]

Given private equity's heightened emphasis on growth strategies and lower use of debt in this market segment, we would expect that employment in small- and middle-market companies bought out by private equity also would be likely to increase. The empirical evidence on this point is thin, but one recent study is informative. Paglia and Harjoto examined the effects of PE financing from 1995 to 2009 on sales and employment growth in small and midsize business establishments. The businesses in the study tended to be small, with average annual sales revenues of $15 million to $16 million in the year or two prior to investment by private equity and average employment of 147 to 155 employees.[27]

In view of the selectivity of private equity in choosing its investment targets and how difficult it is for small businesses without PE backing to get access to capital, it would be surprising if the PE-backed companies did not have faster sales and employment growth than those without such backing. In fact, Paglia and Harjoto did find differences between companies with and without PE financing, but not for the reasons one might expect. In the five years after PE investment, both sales revenue and employment grew more rapidly in the PE-backed establishments than in those without it. This was true even though sales, employment, and growth rates were about the same for the two groups of establishments in the two years prior to PE investment. The authors reported that "the average increase in [inflation adjusted] net sales for establishments with PE financing during the entire five years after financing is approximately $11.8 million compared to a $4.9 million increase in sales for control establishments without PE financing."[28] They also found that at the end of five years PE-backed establishments employed thirty-six more people than did those without PE backing.[29]

However, the authors did not discuss the reason for these differences, which are evident in table 5 of their report.[30] Among the PE-backed companies, sales and employment growth were strongest in PE-financed establishments in the year of acquisition. Then the rate not only slowed down, but the rate of employment growth was actually slower in the years following the year of PE financing than in the years preceding it. In fact, the differential employment growth in favor of PE-backed establishments was due to a far more dramatic drop in the rate of employment growth in non-PE-financed establishments, where employment growth fell from annual growth rates of 6 or 7 percent to growth rates of 2 percent or less. Thus, employment was higher in PE-backed establishments, despite a slowdown in employment growth in the five years following PE financing, because of the precipitous decline in employment growth in non-PE-backed businesses.

To better illustrate the different ways in which private equity adds value in the small and midsize companies it acquires, we examine two very different cases—Aidells Sausage Company and Milestone AV Technologies.

Aidells Sausage Company: Private Equity Buyout of a Small Family Business

Aidells Sausage Company represents a private equity buyout of a small family-owned business with a very successful product serving a local market. The goal of the PE acquisition was to expand the company's size and market, and the PE firm offered several resources to achieve this: professionalization of management functions in order to handle a larger company; financial resources to invest in new technologies that improved product quality and shelf life; expertise to expand marketing and distribution networks; and know-how to position the company as a strategic acquisition. The company's owner, whose expertise focused on daily operations, did not have the resources to embark on the series of complementary management, operational, and distribution changes needed to take the company to a qualitatively different level of production and distribution.

Aidells Sausage Company, an iconic brand in the San Francisco Bay Area, was founded in 1983 by Bruce Aidells, a microbiologist and foodie. Chicken apple sausage, the company's first product, is still among its most popular offerings. Aidells developed an artisanal line of chicken sausage products. In 1993 Ernie Gabiati, whose family had been in the sausage business for three generations, joined the company as chairman and chief executive officer. Eventually, Gabiati bought the company, becoming its owner as well as its CEO. In April 2007, when it was acquired by the PE firm Encore Consumer Capital, Aidells was a premier sausage and meatball products company, mainly serving the Bay Area and with limited distribution beyond. Encore prefers to acquire established, privately held businesses that have a good track record and strong growth potential, and Aidells fit this profile.

According to a PitchBook report on Aidells, in 2006, in its last full year of operation prior to its acquisition by private equity, the company employed 140 people and had total revenue of $26.6 million.[31] Information about the deal size was not disclosed, but portfolio companies of this size typically are priced by PE buyers at 1.3 times revenue,[32] which suggests an approximate enterprise value of $34 million for Aidells at the time it was acquired. Like many small PE firms, Encore Consumer Capital typically acquires portfolio companies using debt to finance 50 percent or less of the enterprise value. Most of the proceeds from the transaction went to Aidells' former owner, Ernie Gabiati.

Although Aidells was a successful company and the brand had a large and loyal following, its distribution under Gabiati's ownership was largely confined to San Francisco and a few communities beyond the Bay Area. Bob McHenry, who ran the day-to-day operations at Aidells under Gabiati, and his management team saw the potential for expanding Aidells into a company with a national presence in club stores as well as in high-end grocery stores and restaurants. But for Gabiati, Aidells represented nearly all of his net worth. Ownership of the company enabled him to create sufficient cash flow for himself, and he ran the business conservatively. It would not have made sense for him to risk his major asset to pursue an aggressive growth strategy.

As a private equity company, Encore Consumer Capital has a very different risk profile. Because the PE firm has a portfolio of companies, it is willing to take a more aggressive posture and manage the companies it buys—companies that typically have revenues of $10 million to

$100 million—for growth.[33] While family-owned companies may be satisfied with business growth of 5 to 7 percent a year, Encore's goal is to increase the size of the companies it buys to two to three times their original size. Encore recognized that Bob McHenry and his team at Aidells had a compelling plan for expanding the company, and it set about providing the strategic direction that would enable the Aidells management team to succeed.

One of the first things Encore did was to introduce a more sophisticated financial management system at Aidells. At the time of the acquisition, finance and accounting consisted of a single employee working on QuickBooks. Under Encore's ownership and direction, Aidells invested in a new financial system and increased the finance and accounting function to several people. As a company that was poised for growth, Aidells would need more checks and balances as well as a professional staff to manage its finances. Encore also built a top-tier board for Aidells that included a board member with a long career at Safeway and another who came from Clorox and Del Monte. The board was able to provide advice and guidance to McHenry and the company's management team as they pursued their plans for growing the company and developing a national distribution network. Compensation practices also changed: approximately one dozen of the managers responsible for the company's operations received stock options.

Encore also encouraged the Aidells staff to explore the development of new technology. Aidells wanted to improve its products in two ways: reduce the sodium content of its meats and eliminate the use of preservatives. The goal was to make Aidells products all-natural without reducing their shelf life or increasing food safety risks. Food production in specialty meats (and other food products) is outsourced to specialized manufacturing contractors. Aidells found that meeting its goals using the available technology would require an investment of several million dollars in the production capabilities of its main contractors. This was too expensive an investment, so Aidells staff set about working closely with the company's suppliers to find a different solution. The result was the development of a new technology for cooking sausage using a specialized pasteurization technique. The use of this technology made the meat products safer, increased their shelf life, and reduced their sodium content. The decision to invest in the development of a new technology for making sausage entailed considerable risk; it was a decision that the prior owner might not have been willing to make, but that the company's PE owners were able to undertake.

As part of the strategy for developing an expanded marketing and distribution network designed to get Aidells products into broad distribution channels throughout the West—and later throughout the country—Aidells ramped up staff between 2009 and 2010, more than doubling the number of employees. The largest group of employees consisted of workers who did in-store demonstrations of the company's products. This, not advertising or promotions, was viewed as the most effective means of marketing Aidells sausages and other meat products. Aidells believed that anyone who tried its product on the end of a toothpick would be likely to buy it. In 2010 the number of people employed at Aidells had increased to 350 and its total revenue, according to PitchBook, was $66.5 million.[34] Employment and revenue had increased to two and a half times their values at the time Encore acquired the company. It was time for Encore Consumer Capital to begin looking for an exit.

Acquisitions in the lower middle market are typically financed with about 50 percent debt and 50 percent equity, far less than the 75 percent debt typical of larger private equity deals at that time. Encore's purchase of Aidells was no exception. Unlike some of the PE firms that undertake large deals or megadeals, Encore focuses on paying down the portfolio company's debt and managing its working capital. Leverage plays a role, but the bulk of Encore's returns come from the growth of its portfolio companies' sales and revenue.

Encore prefers to exit its investments via a sale to a corporate acquirer, and Sara Lee looked like a good fit for Aidells. In 2009 Sara Lee began an internal review of its product lines and discussion of its future direction. The corporation decided to focus on its international coffee and tea business and on its top-branded specialty meat business. Over the next few years, it divested its household and body care product lines and sold off its bakery and refrigerated dough products. By 2011, Sara Lee—famous for its cakes and baked goods—was no longer in the "flour" business. In January 2011, Sara Lee announced that it would spin off its international coffee and tea business and its North American meat business into two independent, "pure play," or single-focus, businesses. The North American Meat Company owns such well-known brands as Hillshire Farm, Jimmy Dean, and Ball Park. These brands hold strong positions in their categories in the retail and food service distribution channels. Acquisition of Aidells Sausage Company would provide Sara Lee with a growth brand in the high-end specialty meat business. In May 2011, Sara Lee announced its acquisition of Aidells Sausage Company.[35]

Sara Lee's acquisition of Aidells Sausage Company was completed on May 27, 2011, for $87 million. The sale price valued the enterprise at 1.3 times revenue.[36] In addition to synergies with its existing brands, Aidells was attractive to Sara Lee because of its innovative technology. Aidells also found the acquisition by Sara Lee attractive, and it saw further opportunities for rapid growth via access to Sara Lee's extensive retail and restaurant distribution networks. In addition, Sara Lee agreed to treat Aidells as a separate center of excellence within its North American Meat Company business and did not see a need to restructure it. The entire Aidells team remained in place.

The sale of Aidells to Sara Lee was highly profitable for the private equity company. Encore did not disclose the terms of the transaction, so the exact gain is not publicly available. We can use what is generally known about such transactions, however, to provide hypothetical estimates. On the assumption that Encore Consumer Capital acquired Aidells in 2007 for about $34 million—1.3 times its 2006 revenue—and that it used 50 percent equity and 50 percent debt, we can examine the relative contributions of leverage and growth to the returns reaped by the PE investors when they exited the investment in 2011. The calculation is a simplification—we do not know how much of the debt used to acquire Aidells was repaid, and we do not know whether Aidells paid management fees to its PE owners. And there may be other relevant information that is not publicly available. The main facts about Encore's acquisition of Aidells and its sale of the company to Sara Lee, however, are either known or can be reasonably estimated.

The higher price Encore received from the sale of Aidells to Sara Lee compared to the price the PE firm paid for the specialty meats company was due to the growth of Aidells' revenue. Aidells' revenue more than doubled between 2007 and 2011 and drove the high returns that Encore and its investors earned. Leverage magnified these returns. We can see this by comparing Encore's returns with the use of leverage to what returns would have been if Encore had paid entirely in cash when it acquired Aidells.

Encore Consumer Capital, based on our assumptions, probably acquired Aidells with $17 million of equity and $17 million of debt. The $87 million Encore received when it sold Aidells to Sara Lee would have been used to pay Aidells' debt-holders the $17 million owed to them and to repay the $17 million initially invested by the PE owners. Thus, the net proceeds from the sale would have been $53 million. After four years, Encore's net earnings would likely have been 312 percent of its initial investment $(53/17 * 100 = 3.12 * 100)$.

Now suppose that Encore and its investors did not use any debt to acquire Aidells but put up the entire $34 million in cash. Net proceeds from the sale to Sara Lee would have been $53 million ($87 – $34). After four years, net earnings would have been 156 percent of the initial investment $(53/34 * 100 = 1.56 * 100)$. Without leverage, Encore's return would have been 156 percent rather than 312 percent. This is the part of the return earned by Encore that is due to "operational value added"— the part due to Encore's strong contributions with respect to business strategy and operational improvements that resulted in value creation at Aidells. However, the use of leverage was also important: it doubled Encore Consumer Capital's returns. Thus, both the robust growth of Aidells' revenue and Encore's use of debt were important contributors to Encore's returns.

In this case, a small operating company was acquired by a small PE fund sponsored by a firm whose partners included both professionals with expertise in the operating company's industry and professionals with expertise in finance. The PE firm added value to the operating company, grew its revenue and employment, and exited successfully with a win for all of the company's stakeholders.

Milestone AV Technologies: Strategic Add-ons in the Middle Market

Milestone AV Technologies illustrates the role of private equity in identifying and facilitating complementary acquisitions for portfolio company growth and development.[37] Although the company's founding owner was successful in manufacturing for a specific product market, he did not have the expertise to expand and develop the company's potential. The PE firm professionalized the management functions, shifted a major portion of production to offshore Asian locations, conducted market research, and expanded the company's mass-market distribution through the strategic acquisition of a retail partner.

Chief Manufacturing, founded in 1978, began as a niche manufacturer making stands for slide projectors. The company expanded its product line as technology changed and by 2002 was manufacturing technology-mounting solutions for plasma television units and LCD projector mounts. Chief was serving the professional market, producing highly engineered products with a high degree of customization, when it was acquired by a consortium of private equity companies led by Friedman Fleischer & Lowe Capital (FFL) for an undisclosed sum in a leveraged buyout in January 2003. Chief Manufacturing's products had a great reputation and were the most preferred by professional installers because of the company's intense focus on customer service and ease of installation. The company was led by a strong entrepreneur, did all of its manufacturing domestically, and achieved a 38 percent margin on earnings (EBITDA).

The successful company caught the eye of the PE firm FFL because of its established customer base and its potential for rapid growth. FFL focuses on the acquisition of growth companies in the U.S. middle market with enterprise values in the range of $30 million to $500 million.[38] The PE firm anticipated that consumer demand for the flat-screen TV, still in its infancy in 2003, would grow exponentially. FFL's market research found that the professional market for technology mounts would grow at a 24 percent compound annual growth rate over the period 2002 to 2006; however, the consumer market was projected to grow at a compound annual growth rate of 65 percent over the same period. The difficulty was that Chief Manufacturing lacked the knowledge and the networks to enter the retail distribution channel and reach this market. FFL, many of whose partners came from companies with strong retail connections and whose major investments included manufacturing companies that served the consumer market, recognized the opportunity this presented. FFL becomes actively involved in the companies it acquires for its portfolio, providing leadership in strategic planning, strategic acquisition of add-on companies, development of the capabilities of the management team to achieve strategic objectives, process improvement, and the assumption of day-to-day operating roles to fill in urgent gaps in management.

In terms of strategic planning, FFL saw that Chief, which had only one retail outlet, would require a culture shift and new infrastructure in order to enter the retail market at a scale commensurate with the nascent but rapidly growing demand for mounts for thin-screen TVs. Human capital development of the management team—who, as in many small-scale operations, did many things but did not do all of them well—was important. The increase in scale that FFL anticipated would require greater specialization and professionalization of management functions. FFL filled important gaps in management capabilities by bringing in a new head of sales and a new head of operations. Scott Gill, who would later become president and CEO of Chief, was brought in to head operations. FFL also brought in what it considered to be "big business process expertise" in manufacturing and sourcing to its midmarket manufacturing company acquisitions—focused especially on bringing outsourcing into this family-owned business.

In addition, the strategic acquisition of a retail-oriented company was urgent to facilitate development of this distribution channel and provide expertise in marketing to consumers. To this end, Chief Manufacturing and its PE investors acquired SANUS Systems in October 2004 for an undisclosed sum in a leveraged buyout. Dale Glomsrud, founder and CEO of Chief Manufacturing, became the CEO of the merged company, and Jim Wohlford, founder and president of SANUS, became general manager of SANUS, reporting to Glomsrud.[39] The add-on acquisition of SANUS, a leader in retail audio-video furniture, mounts, and accessories systems, brought complementary product offerings and a deep knowledge of retail distribution channels.

FFL understood that the integration of two companies with such different cultures would be challenging and was sensitive to the cultural tension. The merged company was named Milestone AV Technologies, but there were no brand changes—Chief products continued to be marketed under the Chief brand, and SANUS products under the SANUS brand. Chief and SANUS also retained their respective headquarters. The expertise of each company's leadership was respected, and integration bonuses were paid to key contributors to keep them from leaving for other jobs. Not everything worked out as planned: Milestone wanted to make a European acquisition, but the attempt was unsuccessful.

Relationships with retailers were critical to Milestone's success. Under the guidance of FFL and the PE firm's chosen chief operating officer, Scott Gill, the company relaxed its gross margin for its retail business, accepting a lower gross margin to win a larger share of the retail market. FFL's analysis showed that increasing production volumes and moving quickly down the cost curve would give it a strong competitive advantage. To meet the pricing requirements of mass marketers, FFL also believed that outsourcing manufacturing to Asia would be necessary. In 2003, when FFL acquired Chief, less than 1 percent of sales were sourced from Asia. This increased to 60 percent in 2008, the company's last year in FFL's hands. Milestone succeeded in having major retailers—Best Buy, Target, Walmart, and Costco—carry its product lines. Another challenge in using these retail channels was to manage conflicts among them. Milestone successfully did this by producing private-label products for different companies and, in the case of Best Buy, developing a direct import program for the retailer.

To address the human capital needs of the merged company, FFL revamped the organization chart, a process it began in 2003 when it first acquired Chief. In 2005 Scott Gill, who had been installed at Chief Manufacturing as chief operating officer by FFL, became the CEO of Milestone Technology AV; Dale Glomsrud was eased out of that position and became chairman of the board. A new CFO was added in 2006.

Leverage also played an important role in FFL's approach to the growth of its portfolio company. In 2006 Milestone had long-term debt of $214.6 million; its total liabilities exceeded its total assets by $80.2 million, which gave its shareholders negative equity. Nevertheless, the company was profitable, earning (EBITDA) $37.9 million on total revenue of $204 million (19 percent) in fiscal year 2006. Despite its already high level of indebtedness, Milestone took on a further $37.5 million in debt that year in a leveraged recapitalization to support its operations.[40]

In September 2007, Milestone announced its intention to return to the public market via an IPO. The company hoped to sell shares at $14 to $16 a share, but even after dropping the price to $12 to $14 a share it failed to garner sufficient shareholder interest. Instead, Milestone was sold for an undisclosed amount to a privately held company, the Duchossois Group.[41] The Duchossois Group is a family-owned company with holdings in the consumer products, technology, and service sectors. Founded by Richard L. Duchossois, currently chairman of the board, and led by its CEO, Craig J. Duchossois, the firm is both an investment company and an operating company. Milestone AV Technologies, which is wholly owned by the Duchossois Group, is one of its main operating companies. In April 2011, Milestone and the Duchossois Group made an additional significant add-on acquisition by purchasing Da-Lite Screen Company, which produces commercial and residential projection screens.[42]

In this case, the private equity firms that acquired Chief Manufacturing provided it with the necessary expertise to enable it to acquire SANUS, a company with an extensive retail distribution network that Chief needed in order to expand into this rapidly growing market. The merger of Chief and SANUS, with their very different cultures, was successful owing in part to the expertise provided by FFL. To exploit the retail market, however, FFL advised Milestone (the merged company) to outsource to Asia the production of standardized products for the retail market. Clearly, Chief Manufacturing's PE owners were instrumental in helping the company grow rapidly and expand into a new market. In terms of sales revenue and market share, Chief (as part of Milestone) gained from PE ownership. Nevertheless, when Milestone filed to go public in 2007, the financial reports the company filed with the SEC showed that its long-term liabilities exceeded its long-term assets. The company's PE owners failed to get sufficient interest to take the company public, even after lowering the share price at which the company was offered. Milestone was subsequently bought by a private company, so there is no information on how the company is actually performing today. More generally, the lack of transparency in the transactions undertaken by FFL—what it paid for Chief and SANUS and what it received when it sold Milestone to the Duchossois Group— make it impossible to know whether this was a successful investment for FFL and the limited partners in the PE fund it sponsored.

The Perils of Mismanagement and Financial Engineering

Lack of industry expertise and experience is a potential source of failure for private equity firms when acquiring small and midsize portfolio companies. According to a recent survey by KPMG and Directorbank of over three hundred directors of PE-backed companies, 41 percent rated the quality of PE managers' input as poor or average. Moreover, 78 percent said that the interests of the PE firm and their managers were aligned at the completion of the deal, but one-third said that those interests diverged thereafter.[43] Classic problems of mismanagement and financial engineering, which lead to financial distress or bankruptcy, are also common in the middle market. Midmarket companies offer opportunities for operational improvements, but not every PE firm has the focus and capabilities to successfully guide such businesses through a process of growth and expansion.

Many of the PE-owned portfolio companies that we discussed in chapter 4 were small- and middle-market companies that went bankrupt in the postcrisis period. Retail chains were particularly hard hit when the PE owners purchasing them during the bubble era loaded them with debt and, in some cases, sold off real estate assets or added more debt in order to pay dividends to themselves and their investors. There were many lower- and core-middle-market retail companies (with enterprise values between $25 million and $500 million) that suffered bankruptcy under these circumstances, including: Steve and Barry's budget clothing chain (owned by TA Associates), Fortunoff Jewelers (Trimaran CP and Kier Group), Home Interiors and Gifts (Hicks, Muse, Tate & Furst), HomeForm Group (Sun Capital), Deb Shops (Lee Equity Partners, Palladin Capital, and Gordon Brothers), Coach America (Fenway Partners), Whitehall Jewelers (Prentice Capital Management, Holtzman), Wickes Holdings furniture stores (Sun Capital, Rooms to Go, StoneCreek Capital), Anchor Blue (Sun Capital), and Harry & David's (Wasserstein & Co.).

Retail chains continue to be an attractive acquisition target for PE funds. Juicy Couture, known for its fashionable track suits, was acquired by PE-backed Authentic Brands Group in October 2013.[44] The acquisition was seen as part of a broader trend in PE involvement in the retail industry, in which the focus is on high-potential, high-end assets.[45]

Small restaurant chains also have been very popular targets for private equity firms because they are viewed as simple businesses that are in high demand, they throw off a steady flow of cash that can be used to pay dividends to the new owners, and many have real estate assets that can be sold off (and then leased back to the company). Mitt Romney and Bain Capital were the first to set the model with Domino's Pizza in 1997. Restaurant chains also are viewed as a safe place to park dry powder. In the special case of restaurant chains that are franchise operations, there is also the advantage that they require little capital investment and guarantee the franchisor a profit of 5 to 6 percent off the top.[46] From the perspective of restaurant chains, a majority of which are small or midsize businesses, private equity offers capital for expansion or renovation and cover from Wall Street for chains that need a facelift.

There have been two large buyout waves in the restaurant industry: in 2005 and 2006, before the financial crisis, and again since 2010, after the crisis. According to one analysis of thirty buyouts between 2005 and 2007, 30 percent went bankrupt and over half went bankrupt, had "technical defaults," or were sold at a large loss.[47] The restaurants under Chapter 11 were all small- and middle-market companies and included Barnhill's Buffet, Bugaboo Creek, Charlie Brown's, Claim Jumper, Friendly's, Perkins/Marie Callender's, Real Mex, Sbarro, and Uno's. The PE owners overleveraged the companies at acquisition, with an average enterprise value to earnings (EBITDA) multiple of 7.4 times. In addition, two companies (El Pollo Loco and Quiznos), which announced covenant breaches, were acquired with an average enterprise value to earnings (EBITDA) of 10.8 times. Another three companies (Sizzler, Pat & Oscar's, and Cheeseburger in Paradise) were sold via management buyout with an estimated large loss to the PE investors. This industry analysis concluded that the failures were not due to excessive multiples alone, but "that lack of menu renewal, lack of effective marketing budget size, lack of capital spending and older site locations were factors."[48] Not enough time has passed to assess the outcomes of the restaurant buyouts since 2010, but at least one chain, bought in 2010, seems to be following a classic PE pattern. Apollo-owned CKE (parent of Carl's Jr. and Hardee's) was unable to launch its IPO in August 2012, reportedly because investors were worried about its debt load of $1.5 billion as well as its poor growth prospects. Apollo had used junk bonds to purchase the chain and then added $190 million to its debt in 2011 in order to pay itself dividend recapitalizations.[49]

Another private equity analyst reached similar conclusions in assessing the buyouts of Sbarro, Friendly's, Real Mex, and Perkins Restaurant/ Marie Callender's. MidOcean Partners invested $120 million of its own cash to buy Sbarro in an LBO valued at $450 million, thereby loading the company with $330 million in debt. Sun Capital invested $199 million in an LBO of Real Mex valued at $359 million. Sun also acquired Friendly's for $337 million in 2007. And Castle Harlan acquired Marie Callender's Restaurant & Bakery in 1999 for $152 million and merged it with Perkins Restaurant, which it purchased for $245 million in 2005.

> While each of these restaurants struggled with distinct difficulties, a common failing emerged: poor stewardship by management and their private equity owners. As the combined effects of weighty debt obligations and soaring food prices began to take their toll, the restaurants began cutting corners, opting to funnel cash into debt payments while neglecting menu upgrades and other store improvements.[50]

Not all PE-backed restaurants did poorly, however, during and after the financial crisis. One example is the Ignite Restaurant Group, which operates 120 Joe's Crab Shacks, which compete in the casual dining seafood market. In 2006, J. H. Whitney Capital Partners bought the company in a leveraged buyout valued at $192 million and six years later sold 30 percent of the company in an IPO valued at $80.8 million. Stock sold at $14 a share at the IPO and had climbed to $16 as of March 2013.[51]

In sum, these examples of bankruptcy among small- and middle-market companies in the restaurant industry demonstrate that the middle market is not immune from the downside of financial engineering in private equity buyouts. While small- and middle-market portfolio companies provide private equity with ample opportunities to engage in growth strategies and make operational improvements, there is no guarantee that private equity will take advantage of these possibilities. PE firms that overleverage their acquisitions, pay prices that are too high on the bet that the stock market will continue to rise, take dividend recaps, or simply fail to pay attention to the needs of the business will not succeed in this market space. We now examine two cases that illustrate how lack of focus on adding value can lead to failure in the middle market.

Golden Guernsey Dairy: Mismanagement in an Industry Leader

Golden Guernsey Dairy represents a classic case of a private equity firm investing in an industry it knew nothing about. Golden Guernsey, a leading company in the Midwest dairy industry, was acquired by OpenGate Capital, whose portfolio of investments across myriad industries and continents strongly resembles the operations of a diversified conglomerate. OpenGate expected to use Golden Guernsey as a platform for acquiring other companies in the same industry, but in less than two years it closed the company without warning or explanation.

Golden Guernsey Dairy was started in 1930 as a farmer-owned cooperative in the Milwaukee area. It grew to be a major supplier of milk and milk products to schools, grocery stores, convenience stores, and major retailers in Illinois, Michigan, and Wisconsin. In 2009 Dean Foods, one of the nation's largest producers of milk and milk products, purchased two Wisconsin milk-processing plants in Waukesha and DePere from Foremost Farms USA for $35 million. Products from the Waukesha dairy, which opened in 1955, continued to be marketed under the popular Golden Guernsey brand.[52] The two plants provided more than 50 percent of the school milk purchased in Wisconsin and Michigan's Upper Peninsula, and, in addition, Dean owned 60 percent of the milk-processing plants in Wisconsin. Concerned that Dean Foods controlled too much of the milk supply, attorneys at both the Wisconsin and U.S. Departments of Justice brought suit to require Dean to divest the Waukesha facility.[53] Despite describing the consumer products division of Foremost Farms (including Golden Guernsey) as a "failing division" in the antitrust lawsuit,[54] Dean Foods strenuously fought the lawsuit in an effort to keep the dairy.[55] In the end, Dean capitulated and settled the antitrust lawsuit by selling the Golden Guernsey Dairy to the Los Angeles–based private equity firm OpenGate Capital on September 12, 2011. The result, as a local news commentator observed, was that "instead of the local facility being run by the industry leader, it would now be run by money managers in California."[56]

OpenGate Capital heralded its 2011 acquisition of the Golden Guernsey brand and dairy in a news release announcing the purchase. Andrew Nikou, OpenGate Capital's founder and managing partner, commented, "OpenGate has acquired a solid platform for growth with our new dairy processing plant and its associated brands. We look forward to working with Golden Guernsey plant management to accelerate its expansion opportunities and uphold its high standards for quality and excellence in milk products."[57] Less than a year and a half later, on January 5, 2013,

OpenGate abruptly and unexpectedly closed the dairy without warning and filed a request in bankruptcy court to halt all operations, close permanently, and liquidate the company's assets. OpenGate provided no explanation for choosing this route rather than taking the more usual path with a failing company of seeking bankruptcy protection to restructure the dairy's operations and finding a buyer for it.

When Nikou founded OpenGate Capital in 2005, he was a twenty-seven-year-old who had worked at the private equity firm Platinum Equity and was a fan of Formula One auto racing. The firm is headquartered in Los Angeles and has offices in Paris, France, and São Paulo, Brazil. According to the OpenGate website, its investment strategy is to "acquire stranded, underperforming or non-core businesses that are divisions of Fortune 1000 companies." Acquisitions have been made across a diverse group of industries, including divisions of companies as different as Dean Foods, Philips, Le Monde, Cascade, French Connections, Schlumberger, and Getronics International. Not only are OpenGate's investments in diverse industries, but they are scattered across several continents and include a telecom company in Brazil, a Finnish paper mill, and a European modeling agency. The firm's website notes that Nikou "currently serves as chairman of the board for each portfolio company where he provides the strategic and financial guidance necessary for the businesses to thrive."[58]

OpenGate appears to be reinventing the much-maligned diversified conglomerate strategy of the 1950s and 1960s, in which corporations diversified into unrelated businesses and ended up controlling a portfolio of companies. Nikou faced challenges managing OpenGate's portfolio of companies that were not unlike those confronting the CEO of a corporate conglomerate whose distance from the companies the conglomerate controlled and inability to be expert in the market and competitive conditions facing its various divisions created numerous management dilemmas. Nikou's position as chairman of the board of each of OpenGate's portfolio companies raises the same concerns that the early advocates of private equity raised in the 1970s about the diversified conglomerates of that time. Moreover, Nikou's interests extend beyond providing strategic leadership to OpenGate's portfolio of companies: at the same time that OpenGate was working on the deal for Golden Guernsey, Nikou was pitching a reality show in which he would mentor entrepreneurs and small businesses with revenues of between $20 million and $25 million—a show described as a cross between *Undercover Boss* and *The Apprentice*.[59]

OpenGate purchased the Golden Guernsey Dairy for an undisclosed price, rumored to have been very low.[60] Whatever OpenGate's hopes for accelerating the growth of the Waukesha plant may have been, the PE firm had purchased a facility in a segment of the dairy industry described by the director of the Center for Dairy Profitability at the University of Wisconsin at Madison as a tough business—fiercely competitive and with thin margins. The publisher of a dairy industry magazine noted that profits are slim in the school-milk business. Industry experts noted that bottled milk is a commodity where price matters more to consumers than the brand name. Moreover, consumer tastes have shifted in recent years; nationally, milk sales in 2011 fell to their lowest level since 1984.[61] Ice cream had been one of Golden Guernsey's more lucrative product lines, but Dean Foods managed to remove these operations and retain them when the dairy was sold to OpenGate.[62] In the view of a dairy industry magazine publisher, OpenGate's lack of experience in dairy doomed it to failure: "They were a novice in a brutal industry."[63]

Employees showing up for work on January 5, 2013, found themselves locked out of the plant, unable even to collect their tools and personal belongings. Milk haulers were unable to pick up product for delivery to schoolchildren and to customers throughout the region. Tens of thousands of gallons of milk and other dairy products sat inside Golden Guernsey. In the days immediately following the shutdown, no explanation for the sudden closing was given to the media or the workers. In an interview at the end of that week with Fox 6 News in Waukesha, Nikou blamed the dairy's closing on milk suppliers who refused to renegotiate contracts and lower their prices and on expensive union contracts.[64] Nikou claimed that OpenGate made "vigorous efforts" to discuss measures to reduce the dairy's expenses with its suppliers, vendors, and labor union, but that these efforts were rejected.[65] The PE firm further claimed that the prospect of bankruptcy was raised several times with all of these groups.[66]

Golden Guernsey's labor union objected to these assertions. Officials of Madison-based Local 695 of the International Brotherhood of Teamsters rejected Nikou's suggestion that the union was unwilling to cooperate with Golden Guernsey leadership to reduce costs and keep the dairy operating. According to the union, OpenGate Capital never expressed an interest in renegotiating the labor contract. As for reducing costs, when the union found an alternative health insurance plan in 2012 that would have reduced Golden Guernsey's annual premium costs by $180,000 while maintaining comparable coverage for employees, OpenGate did not approve the change in the health insurance plan. The union offered to amend the terms of the labor contract without reopening the agreement, but was rebuffed. According to union officials, the PE firm met only once with the Teamsters and paid little attention to the union's efforts to ensure the survival and viability of the plant. Local managers and union leaders at the dairy did work together, but their efforts were largely ignored by the company's PE owners. At the time of OpenGate's takeover of the dairy, the union had worked with local managers at the plant to maintain the plant's stability. The union agreed to set aside work rules in an effort to ensure a smooth transition and keep everyone employed. Later, in August 2012, the union sent a letter to OpenGate to let the dairy's owners know that the union was ready to sit down and discuss the plant's viability. According to the union, there was no response. At the time OpenGate terminated the plant and locked out the workers, the union and local management were actively working together to make Golden Guernsey a viable operation and to maintain employment in Waukesha.[67] The sudden closing of the plant came as a complete surprise to the company's union, workers, suppliers, and milk haulers and to community as well as state and local officials. It took a week and a half before about thirty truckloads of milk and milk products stranded in the plant were finally shipped to food banks in Milwaukee and elsewhere in Wisconsin.[68]

In violation of Wisconsin state law, OpenGate failed to give notice of the shutdown to city and state officials sixty days prior to closing the plant and may be liable for fines of $500 a day.[69] The firm also failed to provide such notice to Golden Guernsey's 112 workers, as required by federal and state law, and is liable for sixty days' severance pay for each of these employees. The Wisconsin Department of Justice filed a $2 million lien against Golden Guernsey for unpaid wages for the dairy's 112 employees.[70]

Charles Stanziale, appointed as bankruptcy trustee by the Delaware Bankruptcy Court, began immediately to aggressively seek a buyer to get the plant running again.[71] According to documents filed with the bankruptcy court, in consultation with Golden Guernsey and with the company's two primary secured lenders, the trustee concluded that it would be in the best interest of lenders and the community if Golden Guernsey was sold as a turnkey operation to another milk and dairy products company. The largest secured creditor was Accord, which provided Golden Guernsey with a term loan and also acted as a financial intermediary for the dairy, and was owed $7.9 million, secured by a second mortgage on the plant's property and by a lien on accounts receivable, inventory, and equipment. Accord had a validity guaranty from Andrew Nikou. The second-largest creditor was Foremost Farms, which was owed $1.1 million for unpaid invoices and damages for breach of a milk supply agreement, secured by a mortgage on the plant's property. The dairy was kept running while a buyer was sought, with operating funds provided by Accord and Foremost Farms.[72]

The bankruptcy trustee received an offer from the parent company of the Ohio milk producer Superior Dairy to purchase the Golden Guernsey Dairy plant for $5.5 million. The offer rejected both the union contract and the contract with milk suppliers.[73] The bankruptcy sales process would give a potential new owner the ability to operate the dairy free of the unsecured debts, liens, and other claims on the company—an advantage for any new owner, but a cost to the dairy's suppliers, vendors, and workers, who, according to bankruptcy court filings, were owed up to $4.8 million. This included vacation, severance, and sick pay owed to workers and commissions owed to independent sales representatives.[74] In addition, the Milwaukee-area schools began contracting with an Illinois milk producer,

Prairie Farms Dairy, suggesting that the loss of some jobs and contracts for dairy farms, milk haulers, and dairy workers would be permanent.[75]

In May 2013, Golden Guernsey was acquired at auction by Lifeway Foods for $7.4 million, substantially above the offer from Superior Dairy. Lifeway, best known for its kefir and related probiotic products, was expanding and preferred to buy an existing plant rather than construct a new one. Lifeway will not make traditional milk products at the plant, but the dairy's facilities can be used to produce kefir. Lifeway has not agreed to resume the union contract but has pledged to hire as many of the former workers at the dairy as possible.[76]

KB Toys: Financial Engineering in the Middle Market

The leveraged buyout of the midmarket toy retailer KB Toys is a case in which financial engineering was the major strategy adopted by private equity. The company was taken over by Bain Capital on December 8, 2000. Bain put down $18 million in equity for the $304 million buyout and leveraged the remainder; KB Toys was financed with just 6 percent equity and 94 percent debt. Even by the standards of PE buyouts, this was a very aggressive use of debt and far exceeded the 50 percent debt typical of buyouts of middle-market companies. A year and a half later, Bain gained approval by KB Toys' board of directors for a $121 million stock redemption (partially funded by a $66 million bank loan); $83 million of this was used to pay a dividend recapitalization to Bain and its PE investors. Investor returns from the dividend recap—$83 million on an investment of just $18 million, or a net gain of $65 million—were about 360 percent in less than two years. In January 2004, KB Toys filed for reorganization under Chapter 11 bankruptcy protection and eliminated almost half of its 1,200 stores located across the country. PE firm Prentice Capital Management bought KB Toys out of bankruptcy, its brand tarnished and its value diminished, for just $20.3 million on August 30, 2005. Three years later, in 2008, KB Toys returned to Chapter 11 status and closed its remaining 431 stores.[77] In all, 10,000 workers lost their jobs.

KB Toys became part of a public debate after Newt Gingrich ran a video arguing that Bain had destroyed the company by burdening it with debt through its leveraged buyout and dividend recapitalization. Some industry analysts defended Bain, arguing that KB Toys was a troubled company with an outmoded business model and could not keep up with the changing pace of the industry or the prices of competitors like Target, Toys 'R' Us, or Walmart. It was a "small mall" toy store that carried brand-name toys plus closeout items at a discount; its problem, these analysts argued, was that it could not carry enough inventory and it did not sell sporting goods or videos. In this view, KB Toys, like many other retailers, went under in the recession of 2001 and its aftermath; Bain's highly lever-aged buyout had nothing to do with the outcome.[78]

Other industry analysts, however, tell a very different story. In 2000, KB Toys was the second-largest mall retailer of toys after Toys 'R' Us. In 1999 profits had surged 50 percent over 1998 returns. The company was known for its innovations in products and marketing. Founded in 1922 by the Kaufman brothers in Pittsfield, Massachusetts, as a candy and fountain supply store, the company acquired a toy store in the forties and quickly diversified into that niche during the war, when the cost of producing candy skyrocketed. The Kaufman brothers continued to expand the busi-ness, switched to retailing in 1973, and by 1976 had opened sixty-five stores. In 1982, KB Toys was purchased by Melville Corporation, which acquired three additional toy store chains and more than tripled KB Toys' retail outlets. KB Toys withstood the structural changes that occurred in the industry in the 1970s and 1980s by attracting customers with brightly colored, well-designed stores and bargain prices on discontinued items. It carried higher-end products that could be sold once customers were in the door. Its corporate philosophy emphasized family values, and it sponsored pre-K reading programs and literacy programs for the disadvantaged; in 1994, after a child was shot by a policeman who thought his toy gun was real, the company withdrew all guns from its stores.[79]

In the 1990s, KB Toys remained competitive by undergoing major restructuring, closing 250 less-profitable stores, and opening larger ones. It expanded its product lines to include videos and adult sporting goods, and it opened a new line of stores, Toy Works, which offered a colorful race-course design to differentiate itself from Toys 'R' Us and other competitors. Net revenues of $1 billion in the early 1990s climbed 6.4 percent by 1996. In that year, KB Toys was bought out for $300 million by Consolidated Stores Corporation, a leading retailer that specializes in closeout merchandise. Consolidated also owned Big Lots Furniture, MacFrugal's, and Pic 'N' Save, among others. KB Toys provided a 50 percent return on Consolidated's investment in the first nine months and increased Consolidated's revenues by 70 percent in 1997. In 1998 its sales revenues grew to $1.6 billion, and it launched KBKids.com, which became an award-winning online merchan-dising operation offering toys, videos, video games, and software. Its 1999 profits were 50 percent higher than those of 1998.[80]

When Bain Capital acquired KB Toys in 2000, KB Toys' fundamen-tals seemed to be in order. The company had made tough decisions to close stores and restructure throughout the 1990s. It changed its product offerings, came up with creative marketing strategies, and launched the highly successful KBKids website. Yet Bain Capital failed to build on this legacy. While 2001 and 2002 were difficult years for the economy, KB Toys had successfully weathered recessions in the 1970s, 1980s, and 1990s. Yet it could not survive the downturn of the early 2000s.

The profile of KB Toys raises important questions about private equity's self-proclaimed role in performance improvement and company turnarounds. Bain was supposedly an expert in company turnarounds. It had the opportunity to redirect the company's business strategy, cut costs and consolidate stores, and, most importantly, work with an experienced, skilled workforce with years of expertise in product and marketing innovation in the toy industry. Instead, Bain engaged in financial engineering, loading the company with an amount of debt in the leveraged buyout that was high even by PE standards and then taking resources from the company to pay itself and its investors a dividend at a time when KB Toys faced a difficult economic environment. The PE firm had little knowledge of the toy industry, and according to employee accounts of the PE firm's management approach, it didn't put its efforts into innovation and creative marketing, but instead saddled them with paperwork and reporting requirements.[81]

After loading the company with debt and extracting some 400 percent on its investment, Bain let the company go bankrupt. Bain's financial engineering exacerbated the company's economic condition and shifted the costs of bankruptcy to others. Its actions redistributed wealth from the company, workers, and creditors to itself. The toy company's executives also benefited. CEO Michael Glazer received $18.4 million, senior vice president Thomas Alfonsi $3.3 million, and CFO Robert Feldman $4.8 million.[82] Over the course of Bain's ownership, more than ten thousand workers lost their jobs. In addition, creditors absorbed the costs. In 2006 the creditors sued Bain Capital, alleging that the PE firm's dividend recap plan had caused the bankruptcy. The lawsuit was settled, and Bain paid KB Toys' creditors $27 million to settle the litigation.[83] The penalty amounted to just one-third of the dividend recap paid to Bain and its investors, who still had a net gain of $38 million on their initial $18 million investment.

Conclusion

Small and midsize companies in the United States have a substantial need for sources of funding and management expertise to help them realize their growth potential and compete in national and international markets. Banking deregulation over the last three decades has encouraged large bank consolidations and decreased the number of small and independent banks that provide commercial loans to small businesses. This institutional vacuum has been filled, in part, by small and midsize private equity firms, which have succeeded in raising PE funds for this market and combine financing with management and technical expertise.

These companies offer a set of distinct challenges for private equity firms, which cannot make money as easily by relying on increases in the stock market or on financial strategies such as the use of high leverage or dividend recapitalizations. Instead, they need to rely more heavily on developing smart business strategies and providing companies with expertise in specialized areas—from marketing to work process improvements to supply-chain management—in the context of specific industry conditions. Supply-chain management in steel is not the same as supply-chain management in apparel or financial services. Although small and midsize companies provide ample opportunities to enhance performance via strategic and operational improvements, creating and extracting value in this way is much more difficult and takes much more time than generic financial engineering. Making money through add-on strategies appears straightforward, but more add-ons and acquisitions fail than succeed.[84] The cases in this chapter demonstrate how and why some PE firms have been successful in taking over small businesses and developing them to the next level of competitiveness and performance. They have done so by using lower levels of debt, relying less on financial engineering, and developing expertise in specialized industry niches. These PE firms build relationships with industry players, continuously expand their knowledge of products and services that are key to growth, and develop a reputation for trustworthiness.

There is nothing magical about the middle market, though in the post-crisis period it has gained almost cultlike popularity. Every private equity firm advertises that it is investing in the middle market, just as all but the top 1 percent of Americans report that they are in the "middle class." The evidence in this chapter suggests, however, that private equity LBOs in the middle market can often turn out badly—not only for the portfolio companies and their employees but for PE firms and their investors. One-size-fits-all financial recipes do not work very well. Moreover, the large variation in the financial conditions of middle-market companies, as well as the variation in product markets, labor markets, and industry conditions, prevents the PE firms that succeed in this market from relying on a diversified conglomerate approach dominated primarily by financial calculations.

=== Chapter 6 ===

How Well Do Private Equity
Funds Perform?

Whether private equity investments deliver on their promise of returns that are substantially above the stock market has been a controversial issue, with industry participants publishing very positive reports and finance economists providing more modest empirical results. Central to this controversy is the fact that private equity's lack of transparency makes independent analyses of its data all but impossible. And as we saw in chapter 4, limited partners became disgruntled in the postcrisis period over excessive management fees and the poor performance of funds; as a result, they slowed their commitments to new funds. They also signaled their preference for smaller funds that invest in the middle market, which appeared to be more recession-proof than the mega-market deals of the boom years, as described in chapter 5.

Notwithstanding these critiques, the commitments of institutional investors to private equity have slowly rebounded since the financial crisis, and the number of public pension funds with investments in private equity has continued to grow. The expectation that investments in PE funds will outperform investments in public equities—in publicly traded companies—by a wide margin makes these investments attractive to pension funds, endowments, and other limited partners despite their greater riskiness and lack of transparency. This is especially true of pension funds, which hold the retirement savings of millions of workers—so-called workers' capital—that these funds invest in order to fulfill their obligations to pension plan participants.[1]

In the boom years of 2005 to 2007, and sometimes earlier, many employers failed to make the required contributions to pension funds, counting instead on the run-up in the stock market to ensure that they could meet pension obligations. The financial crisis left these pension plans underfunded, and today they are seeking yield as they face a series of continuing challenges: the unwillingness or inability of employers to make up the shortfall in assets via higher contributions, the maturing of their participant base as the share of retirees increases, and the low interest rates on riskless Treasury securities. Thus, Réal Desrochers, the head of PE investing at CalPERS, the California Public Employees Retirement System, is reported to have answered the question of private equity's role in the pension fund as such: "Private Equity should be producing 300 basis points (3 percent) above equities. That's its role. It's the alpha provider for the whole [pension] system."[2] That is, CalPERS is relying on its PE investments to provide the yield it needs to meet its overall target returns.

In this chapter, we assess the evidence on private equity fund performance and the returns to limited partners, net of management fees, expenses, and carried interest. Our findings may be summarized as follows. Because there is no publicly available or comprehensive data on private equity, all studies of performance suffer from incompleteness and biases, and different methods of calculating returns yield different results. But some data sets and methodologies are more credible than others. Reports that PE funds substantially outperform the stock market come almost entirely from industry sources that use the internal rate of return as a measure of performance. This measure is deeply flawed, for reasons examined in this chapter, and many finance scholars reject its use. Industry reports are also biased, as they rely on the data and methods of self-interested parties.

Our review covers the most credible research by top finance scholars, who use different data and methods. They report much more modest returns to private equity funds, with some showing that the median fund does not beat the stock market and others showing that returns for the median fund are only slightly above the market. The most positive findings for private equity generally compare it to the S&P 500 and report that the median fund outperforms the S&P 500 by about 1 percent a year, and the average by 2 to 2.5 percent. According to these studies, the higher average performance is entirely driven by the top quartile of funds—and particularly the top decile. With the exception of the top-performing funds, returns do not cover the roughly 3 percent additional return above the stock market that investors typically calculate is required to compensate them for the added risk and illiquidity of PE investments.

The use of the S&P 500 as the stock market index to beat may also be misleading and lead to exaggerated views of PE performance. When PE funds are compared to indices of smaller publicly traded companies of comparable size to PE-owned companies (the S&P 500 is made up of much larger corporations), then the average PE fund barely performs better and the median fund just matches the stock market.

The result is that the majority of investors will not receive "outsized returns." Large institutional investors with deep relationships with the leading PE firms have been in the best position to invest in those PE funds with a history of outperforming the stock market, and historically the funds of PE firms with a good track record have tended to perform better. A number of studies, notably one undertaken by Steven Kaplan and Antoinette Schoar, have found a pattern of persistence in the outperformance of funds by some PE firms over other firms.[3] That is, they found that PE firms with top-quartile-performing funds in one period tend to have similar success with subsequent funds. These firms, in turn, have an easier time raising subsequent funds—even in a weak market—while other PE firms struggle. Limited partners want to invest in the PE firms or general partners with the best track record. A recent study, however, raises doubts about the persistence of outperformance.[4] Reiner Braun, Tim Jenkinson, and Ingo Stoff focused on the performance of sequences of funds raised by particular GPs. Their results confirm the persistent success of the best performers for funds launched through the end of 1998, a period that corresponds to the period analyzed by Kaplan and Schoar.[5] In that period, a GP's past performance did predict subsequent performance. From 1999 on, however, the authors found no statistically significant relationship between prior and subsequent performance. In more recent years, they found that past performance does not predict subsequent returns—a statement that is generally true of financial investing.

Measurement Issues in Evaluating Limited Partner Returns from Private Equity Investments

Before turning to recent academic studies of PE fund performance, two important measurement issues need to be addressed. The first concerns the valuation of companies in fund portfolios that have not yet been sold. In their seminal article on PE performance, Kaplan and Schoar measured PE fund performance in terms of *realized returns*—actual cash paid out to LP investors by funds that had exited all investments and closed.[6] But as it typically takes a decade to exit all investments, investors do not want to wait that long for information on their returns. They want to know about the returns to active funds in a more timely fashion. These calculations necessarily rely on estimates of *unrealized returns*, that is, estimates of the value of companies still in PE portfolios. Thus, studies of PE performance within the last decade rely on estimates provided by the funds' general partners of the value of companies still in PE portfolios—so-called net asset value, or NAV. New accounting standards implemented in 2008 require PE funds to report portfolio companies at "fair value." While this is an improvement over earlier valuations of portfolio companies, problems with this measure remain.

The second difficulty is that commercially available data providers, such as Cambridge Associates, and industry associations, such as the Public Equity Growth Capital Council, measure performance using the internal rate of return (IRR). Private equity firms tout the internal rate of return of existing funds when marketing new funds to pension plans and other LP investors. Similarly, limited partners rely on high IRRs to demonstrate that their PE investments have paid off. As we show later, however, there are serious problems with using the IRR as a measure of fund performance. For this reason, academic researchers generally prefer to use the public market equivalent (PME), which estimates the returns earned by investing in private equity relative to what LPs would have earned if they had invested the same capital over the same period in a stock market index, such as the S&P 500 or the Russell 3000.

Fair Value Accounting and Reported Values of Unsold Companies in Private Equity Portfolios

Since 2008, private equity firms have been required to report the value of portfolio companies at fair value, which is defined in the relevant accounting standard as "the price that would be received to sell an asset or paid to transfer a liability in an orderly transaction between market participants at the measurement date."[7] Prior to issuance of this standard, PE funds valued their illiquid investments in portfolio companies at the cost of acquiring them. General partners would adjust the value up or down only if there was a subsequent round of financing that placed a different value on the company. Valuing companies at cost, however, is incompatible with the concept of fair value.[8] The new accounting regulations therefore establish a reporting standard for situations in which unobservable inputs are used in determining the fair value of the investment, such as an illiquid investment in a portfolio company. The standard requires unobservable inputs to incorporate the assumptions that a market participant would use in developing an exit price. The PE fund can use its own data to develop the unobservable inputs used to arrive at the estimated fair value, and the assumptions, but not the data, must be disclosed.

As a result, a PE fund must outline a clear valuation process and must inform regulators and limited partners of any changes in the assumptions underlying the determination of fair market value. The PE firm, however, has full discretion in choosing the approach, choosing the unobservable inputs, and setting the range of values for the inputs.[9] CFOs doubt the value of this math given that these marks will always be pretty subjective. Discounted cash flow and market-comparable companies are the two approaches used in valuing portfolio companies.[10]

The upshot is that there is still a lot of guesswork embedded in assumptions about the range of values that each unobservable variable can take on, and especially in determining where in this rather wide range the portfolio company falls. Clarification of the rules for fair value measurement issued in May 2011 makes it clear that PE funds do not have to provide quantitative sensitivity disclosures to investors. That is, PE funds do not have to report to investors the potential impact of various assumptions on the valuation (NAV) arrived at for the investment.[11] Thomas Duffell reports that many limited partners are not satisfied with the level of transparency or consistency in the valuation methods used by general partners. He cites a 2011 Northern Trust survey that found that 70 percent of LPs believe that the fair valuation of PE assets is not yet up to par with industry accounting standards. They are particularly concerned about whether the GP uses the same evaluation method across portfolio companies and over time. However, LPs rarely challenge the documentation or the choice of comparable companies used in arriving at valuations.[12]

Despite these changes in accounting requirements, PE firms are still able to value portfolio companies opportunistically—underestimating the value of portfolio companies so that LPs are not disappointed with distributions when the fund is liquidated and overestimating the fund's value when marketing a new fund to potential investors.[13] Somewhat counterintuitively, low net asset values early on for companies that continue to be held in a fund's portfolio increase the fund's internal rate of return.

Passage of the Dodd-Frank Act in 2010 increased the scrutiny facing the private equity industry. General partners in most PE funds must now register with the Securities and Exchange Commission. In late 2011, the SEC began an informal inquiry into the PE industry. It was particularly concerned about whether PE firms use inflated valuations of current investments in portfolio companies when seeking to attract new investors to new funds.[14] Erroneous evaluations of portfolio companies can distort measures of a fund's performance in the years prior to its exit from all of its investments.

In March 2013, the SEC reached a settlement with the private equity unit of Oppenheimer & Co., which it had accused of inflating the valuation of one of its investments in order to help market a new fund. The settlement requires Oppenheimer to be censured, to pay a penalty of $617,579, and to return approximately $2.27 million in capital commitments to investors it had misled. In January 2014, the SEC barred and fined a former fund manager for inflating the fund's value.[15]

The lack of transparency and the continued high level of subjective judgment of fund valuations create problems for the measurement of fund performance.

The Internal Rate of Return as a Measure of Private Equity Fund Performance

The internal rate of return is the dominant measure of PE fund performance used by PE industry associations, PE firms, limited partners, and industry analysts. It is widely used by money managers who manage the assets of pension funds, foundations, and so on, to make decisions about how those funds should be allocated to various financial assets.

For example, David Swenson, who formerly managed Yale University's endowment, famously claimed that the annualized internal rate of return on the endowment's "PE" investments was 30.4 percent since the inception of Yale's alternative investment program in 1973.[16] Yale's report—clearly far above the gains from investments in the stock market—led many other institutions to follow the "Yale model."[17] IRR, however, is a deeply flawed measure for tracking and comparing PE fund performance, in view of the fact that the timing and payouts to limited partners may vary widely over the life span of a particular fund and between funds. In the following sections, we explain how the internal rate of return is calculated and used, and then demonstrate why it is an inaccurate measure that misleads investors about what their actual returns are. The use of this measure compromises reports that seek to compare private equity as an asset class with other asset classes.

What Is the Internal Rate of Return?

The internal rate of return is a type of interest rate that is widely used by chief financial officers (CFOs) of corporations to determine whether it is worth investing in a particular corporate project. Let's say that a steel mill is considering buying a piece of equipment that costs $100 million. The equipment is expected to have a useful life of twenty years and to generate a certain stream of income over the twenty years: $11 million a year in net revenue in each of the first ten years, and $8 million a year in each of the remaining ten years. At the end of twenty years, the equipment can be sold for $10 million. The return in the twentieth year is $8 million + $10 million, or $18 million.

To determine whether the investment is worthwhile, the CFO asks the following question: Suppose I took the $100 million and used it to buy a bond. What rate of interest would that bond have to pay in order to yield a stream of income equivalent to the stream of income that would result from buying the piece of equipment? That interest rate—which is referred to in economics and finance as the "discount rate"—is the project's internal rate of return. The CFO would then compare the IRR for the project with the best interest rate available on a twenty-year bond. If the IRR exceeds the interest rate on the bond, the project is worth investing in. Of course, the CFO might be considering multiple possible projects that the company could carry out. Computing the IRR for each project would enable the CFO to rank the projects from highest to lowest IRR. Projects with an IRR below the rate of interest available on bonds would not be carried out. If funds were limited, the CFO would allocate investment to those projects with the highest IRR.

A computer using an iterative process can easily calculate the IRR in this rather simple example. If the other projects under consideration also require an investment of about $100 million and generate a fairly steady pattern of net revenues, then using the IRR to rank investment projects is also straightforward. However, if the returns generated by an investment are highly volatile and vary widely from year to year, the iterative process can break down. The iterative search for the IRR may not converge to a solution. Or it may converge to multiple solutions. Moreover, the IRR cannot provide a meaningful rank ordering of projects if the investments are of different scales—say, for example, that one project requires an investment of $10 million, another requires $100 million, a third requires $500 million, and a fourth requires $1 billion. Using the IRR to order these projects may lead to a misallocation of company resources. These problems with the internal rate of return are well known in finance.[18]

The IRR has been borrowed from corporate finance and is now widely used by the private equity industry and the general public to evaluate the performance of a particular fund, the relative performance of different funds, and the performance of PE investments as an asset class compared to investments in stocks or other assets. In the case of private equity, the analogy to the revenue earned by the steel mill in each period as a result of buying the equipment is the cash flow generated in each period as a result of the initial commitments by LPs in a portfolio of companies. Capital commitments are invested at different times over the first few years of the fund's life span, and the fund receives distributions as the portfolio companies pay dividends or are sold. These are the fund's cash flows. For a fund that is still active and has unsold companies in its portfolio, the return in the last year of the period being analyzed is the fund's cash flow that year plus the value of any unsold companies still in the portfolio. Thus, the valuation of unsold companies (the NAV) plays an important role in determining a fund's IRR.

Some of the general problems with the internal rate of return as a measure of performance apply to its use in private equity calculations. Returns can be highly volatile, and even negative in some years. And different PE funds will choose to operate at different scales: some buy portfolio companies in the lower middle market, while others make acquisitions in the core middle market, the upper middle market, or the mega-market. These characteristics of PE returns make it problematic to calculate meaningful IRRs or to compare IRRs across funds.

The CFO who is evaluating an investment project has an alternative measurement approach available if these problems arise. He or she knows the interest rate at which the company can borrow funds—an interest rate that may vary depending on the amount being borrowed ($10 million or $1 billion, for example) and on the length of time for which it is being borrowed. The CFO can use this interest rate as the discount rate and ask a somewhat different question to evaluate whether the investment is worthwhile. Let's consider again whether an investment of $100 million that generates the income stream described earlier over twenty years should be undertaken. The CFO uses the discount rate that corresponds to the rate of interest the company would have to pay to borrow $100 million for twenty years and asks how large an investment would have to be made to generate this stream of income.[19] If the answer is more than $100 million, then buying the piece of equipment for $100 million is a bargain and the company should do it. If the answer is less than $100 million, then the piece of equipment is too expensive under current market conditions and the company should not invest in it. This approach to evaluating projects only works, however, because the CFO knows what the company's cost of capital is—what interest rate it has to pay when it borrows money. The PE fund's general partner may also know the rate of interest at which the fund can borrow for particular investments, so this calculation can be relevant for determining whether a particular investment is worth undertaking. It cannot be used, however, to show investors how well the investment is performing—and a fund's performance is, of course, the main concern of investors. Thus, PE funds rely on the IRR in evaluating the performance of a particular acquisition and the overall performance of the fund, which is misleading.

The Internal Rate of Return: The Case of Private Equity

Measuring private equity returns using the internal rate of return yields what appear to be impressive returns.[20] But there are problems with this measure. The general difficulties that can arise when calculating the IRR, if they are acknowledged at all, tend to be dismissed by PE firms and limited partners in PE funds as not very important. Most investors believe that the internal rate of return is a "good enough" measure of PE performance, and the ease of using this measure outweighs any consideration of these problems. There are additional characteristics of private equity, however, that make the use of the IRR as a measure of performance especially hazardous.

Unlike our example of investment in a piece of equipment for a steel mill, which generates a pattern of fairly steady returns, returns to investment in a PE fund tend to be highly volatile—very high in some years and very low in others. Let's take a simple example of a fund, Fund X, which begins at time zero with an initial investment of $100 million, which it uses to purchase several portfolio companies. One year later, having sold some of these companies, it receives $150 million. The next year it neither makes any further investments in portfolio companies nor sells any that it has, so its cash flow is zero. In year three, it exits its remaining investments in portfolio companies for $50 million.

The cash the fund returns to its investors is called its "distribution"; the capital invested by the fund is "paid in" by the fund's partners. The ratio

Table 6.1   Hypothetical Net Cash Flow Data from Funds X, Y1, Y2, and Z

Year	Fund X	Fund Y1	Fund Y2	Fund Z	Fund XYZ
0	−100	−100	−100	−100	−400
1	150	0	0	0	150
2	0	0	0	0	0
3	50	0	0	0	50
4	0	0	0	0	0
5	0	100	100	50	250
6	0	0	0	0	0
7	0	0	0	0	0
8	0	100	100	0	200
9	0	0	0	0	0
10	0	0	0	0	0
11	0	0	0	0	0
12	0	0	0	10	10
Internal rate of return	68%	11%	11%	−8%	12%
Multiple (distribution to paid-in capital)	2.00	2.00	2.00	0.60	1.28

Source: Phalippou 2008, 18.

of the distribution to paid-in capital is called the DPI. In this example, where the distribution equals $200 million ($150 million + $50 million) and the paid-in capital equals $100 million, DPI equals 200/100, or 2. The DPI is the investment multiple.

In this case, the procedure for computing the internal rate of return yields an annualized IRR of 68 percent. But that may not be the actual return that investors in the fund receive at the end of the third year when the fund is liquidated. In order for the partners in the fund to actually receive that high IRR, the $150 million distribution to the fund at the end of the first year would have to be reinvested in something that yields a 68 percent return in each of years two and three so that it grows to $420 million by the end of year three. If it is not feasible to get $150 million to grow to $420 million in just two years, then the actual rate of return received by investors in Fund X will be less than the annualized IRR of 68 percent. The spread between the IRR and the actual rate of return that investors in the fund receive will depend on the interest rate at which the money received by the PE fund and distributed to its limited partners can be reinvested.

Table 6.1 presents hypothetical cash flow data (in millions) for four funds—Fund X, Fund Y1, Fund Y2, and Fund Z. Private equity funds report investment multiples as well as IRR. It can be useful to know whether a fund doubled its investment (Funds X, Y1, and Y2) or returned less than was initially invested (Fund Z). But it is also important to know whether this occurred in three years (Fund X) or eight years (Funds Y1 and Y2). The IRR takes into account how long it takes to double an investment and the pattern of the cash flow over time. Hence, the IRRs for Funds X and Y1 or Y2 are very different.

The average IRR for multiple PE funds is calculated by adding the individual IRRs and dividing by the number of funds. In general, this average IRR is different from the IRR that an investor would get by actually investing in each of the funds. In the case where there is little volatility in the pattern of returns from each fund's investments, the difference is relatively small. However, returns from investments in PE funds—as dividends are paid or portfolio companies are sold—can be highly volatile, raising serious issues related to aggregating returns from multiple funds.

For Funds X, Y1, Y2, and Z in table 6.1, the average IRR is 21 percent ([68 + 11 + 11 − 8] ÷ 4). However, if a pension fund or other limited partner invested in all four funds, it would receive a much smaller return than this. The column headed "Fund XYZ" aggregates the investments and subsequent returns (cash flows) of the four funds. The IRR for this aggregate investment is just 12 percent—a little more than half (0.57) of the average IRR. Thus, an investor in all four of the funds would not earn the average IRR for these investments, but only about half that amount. Calculating an average IRR for a PE firm with multiple funds is likely to yield a rate of return that exaggerates the firm's performance. This is especially true if some of the funds take much longer than others to sell all their portfolio companies, which generally results in a lower IRR for that fund.

Two factors are critical to understanding why funds that take longer to exit investments in portfolio companies have a lower IRR: good investments are usually sold more quickly than those that are struggling, and the IRR calculation assumes that proceeds from successful early sales of companies will be reinvested at the same high rate of return. Thus, averaging performance across a PE firm's multiple funds when one fund exits investments early may produce an exaggerated view of the firm's performance.

Other problems can arise when the IRR is used to evaluate the performance of a PE firm. Consider a PE firm that has successfully exited its first fund and, on that basis, has raised two subsequent funds. Suppose that the PE firm's first fund is Fund X, which exits all its investments in year three with a 68 percent IRR. In year four, the firm launches its second fund, Fund Y1, which exits all its investments in year twelve. Finally, in year thirteen, it launches Fund Z, which exits its last investment in year twenty-five. As discussed earlier, the IRR for its first fund is 68 percent, the IRR for its second fund is 11 percent, and for its third fund the IRR is −8 percent. With a track record like this, the PE firm is likely to have difficulty raising another fund. But there is a way around this for the PE firm: it can group these three funds end to end, treating all of its investments and returns (its cash flows)—from time zero, when the first investment was made, to year twenty-five, when the last portfolio company was sold—as if they were one fund. Calculating the IRR for a fund with this pattern of cash flows is a very high 47 percent. Clearly, this result creates an entirely different impression of the PE firm among potential investors in funds that it sponsors. As Ludovic Phalippou observed, "This shows the hazard of treating the IRR as a rate of return. Doing so leads to very misleading impressions."[21]

Finally, IRR is influenced by the timing of cash payouts.[22] Assume that a fund buys a portfolio company for $100 million and a year later that company is worth $150 million. The PE fund can sell the company, or it can hold it for another four years, during which time the portfolio company increases in value another 20 percent a year. In year five, the company could be sold for $311 million. The best alternative investment that the fund's LPs could make if the company is sold and the $150 million is distributed to them yields just 12 percent. Clearly, it is in the best interests of the LPs for the fund to hold the portfolio company until year five. If the fund does this, however, the IRR from this investment will be 25 percent, whereas if the fund sells the portfolio company at the end of the first year, the IRR from this investment will be 50 percent. If GPs want to have a higher IRR to show for their fund's investments, they may decide to exit the investment after only one year.

Alternatively, the GPs might decide to have the portfolio company declare a dividend of $100 million at the end of the first year. The dividend could come from the portfolio company's cash flow. Or the portfolio company might be required to undertake a dividend recapitalization, selling $100 million in junk bonds to finance the dividend. This transfer of resources from the portfolio company might well reduce its future performance; perhaps, in this case, the company increases in value by just 10 percent a year for the next four years instead of 20 percent. Taking the dividend would not be a good economic decision, and it would not maximize returns to the fund's limited partners. It would, however, lead to an IRR for the fund's investment in this company of 28 percent, compared with 25 percent with no dividend, if the fund holds the portfolio company to year five, despite the fact that much less value is created at the portfolio company by this action.

General partners who are concerned about recording higher IRRs—perhaps because their bonus is tied to this metric or because their PE firm is marketing a subsequent fund—thus have an incentive to strategically time their cash flows. Some GPs may be discouraged from manipulating cash flow to prop up the IRR, since selling a company prematurely or extracting dividends from it may reduce profits and hence the GP's carried interest. We have no way of knowing whether or to what extent GPs strategically time dividends and other distributions to LPs as a way to boost returns as measured by the IRR. Certainly, funds sponsored by some PE firms make extensive use of dividend recapitalizations. In any case, the incentive to boost the IRR is clearly present. The fact that this could possibly happen once again highlights the hazards of using IRR as a measure of performance.

These concerns about the use of the internal rate of return as a measure of private equity fund performance have led PE funds, limited partners, and academic researchers to report investment multiples (such as the DPI) as well as IRR when discussing fund performance.[23] Investment multiples have the advantage in that they measure the amount of cash a limited partner actually gets back for a given investment in a PE fund. This is, after all, what LPs care most about. The multiple, however, does not incorporate a time dimension: it does not vary according to the timing of distributions, a key aspect of performance. It matters to investors whether they get back twice what they invested in six years or in twelve years.

Private Equity Industry Performance Reports

Private equity industry performance is reported quarterly by PitchBook, Cambridge Associates, Preqin, and Thompson-Reuters, and all four organizations take a similar approach.[24] First, the organization chooses a time horizon. Typically, performance is reported for one-, three-, five-, and ten-year time horizons. Second, the organization adds up the values of all the unexited investments in the portfolios of each of the funds in its database to get the net asset value at the starting date (one year ago, three years ago, and so on). It treats the NAV as the initial investment amount. Third, for each fund in its database, it calculates the net cash flows (distributions coming into a fund minus capital paid out by a fund as it acquires companies for its portfolio or makes other investments) on a quarterly basis, up to the last quarter. It then aggregates these cash flows. Fourth, for each fund in its database, the organization adds the NAV at the final date to the cash flow in the final quarter and then adds this up for all the funds to get the return in the final quarter. Fifth, using this stream of cash flows, the organization computes the IRR for the industry over the particular time horizon.

For example, Cambridge Associates reports the following horizon IRRs for the U.S. private equity industry as of June 30, 2013:

- One-year: 15.57 percent
- Three-year: 15.50 percent
- Five-year: 8.22 percent
- Ten-year: 14.12 percent
- Fifteen-year: 11.33 percent
- Twenty-year: 13.39 percent[25]

These returns look pretty impressive. Computing stock market returns using the same end-to-end methodology, however, and calculating the resulting IRR for publicly traded stocks, shows that private equity has lagged the broad stock market in recent years—falling behind it for the one-, three-, and five-year periods. Private equity beats the broad stock market for the ten-, fifteen-, and twenty-year periods.

The advantage of using the IRR to calculate industry performance is that it provides timely, up-to-date performance information for the industry. The drawbacks, however, should be evident. First, the accuracy of the measure depends on general partners' valuation of the unsold companies in their portfolios at their actual market value, or close to that. As a practical matter, this may be difficult for GPs to do. Moreover, as we have seen, GPs may have an incentive to underestimate the value of their remaining portfolio companies. Valuing portfolio companies conservatively both provides an upside surprise to LPs when the investments are sold and boosts the fund's IRR. The resulting conservative estimates of initial NAV also increase the IRR for the industry.[26] Second, the hazards involved in using IRR as a measure of performance discussed earlier apply here as well. The methodology for computing horizon IRRs is similar to the end-to-end method that gave misleading results when the three funds, X, Y1, and Z, were reported this way. Most important is the assumption built into the computation of IRR that distributions from investments sold early in the investment period are reinvested and earn the same rate of return as the initial investments earned. As Phalippou points out, it is possible to correct for this distortion, but the industry does not currently make such corrections.[27]

Summing Up: The Intrinsic Problems with the Internal Rate of Return as a Measure of Fund Performance

Although the internal rate of return is widely used by all participants in the private equity industry as a measure of individual fund performance and as a measure of performance of the asset class, it is a deeply flawed measure. We have discussed its limitations and now turn to a summary of the main weaknesses of IRR as a measure of PE performance.

- *Computational difficulties:* The calculation of the IRR is an iterative process carried out by a computer. Under certain conditions, the iterative process either does not converge, and thus no value for the IRR can be computed, or it yields multiple results for the IRR. This happens when the timing and/or amounts of returns are highly volatile. This is especially true if cash flows change direction (from positive to negative or negative to positive) more than once. Volatility is quite common in private equity cash flows.

- *The IRR calculation assumption that distributions are reinvested at the same IRR rate:* In the calculation of the IRR, the high IRR earned from an early distribution is assumed to apply to the distributed funds in subsequent periods. That is, the mechanics of the IRR computation assume that the distribution can be reinvested at the same high IRR.

- *Opportunities to game the calculation:* The IRR is sensitive to the timing of distributions from a PE fund. This provides GPs with an incentive to engage in early sales of portfolio companies or large dividend recapitalizations even when these do not make economic sense or are not in the best interests of the limited partners.

- *Which vintage?* General partners have some wiggle room in determining which vintage a fund belongs to. The launch of the fund can be dated from the first close (after a substantial amount of the target capital for the fund has been committed), from the final close (after which no other institution or person can join the fund as a limited partner), or from the first call on the limited partners for commitments.

All of these intrinsic problems with the IRR affect not only investors' views of returns from this asset class but also the relative ratings of individual funds as well. This may help explain how it is possible for so many PE funds to make the claim that they are a top-quartile fund—that is, in the top quarter of funds in their vintage year.

There is one further problem with the internal rate of return: it is an *absolute* measure of fund performance. It does not take into account that limited partners have alternatives to investing in private equity. They can, for example, buy shares of publicly traded companies in the stock market. What matters to investors is the *relative* performance of PE funds—that is, the performance of investments in private equity relative to investments in the stock market. And like stock market returns, the returns to investments in private equity are highly cyclical. PE funds performed quite well in the first half of the 2000s. Since 2009, however, the performance of U.S. PE funds has been outpaced by the run-up in the S&P 500 index, leaving the industry to argue that it is long-term returns that matter.[28] Thus, another important problem with the IRR as a measure of fund performance is that it is an absolute measure of fund performance while what investors need to know is how PE investments perform relative to the stock market.

The recent experiences of two major limited partners in private equity funds illustrate the importance of measuring returns from private equity relative to alternatives such as the stock market. Investigative reporter Gina Edwards obtained public records of Florida's state pension fund and analyzed the pension fund's PE returns.[29] Her analysis shows that the Florida state pension funds would have gained higher returns had they invested in publicly traded companies in the Russell 3000 stock market index over the relevant periods (see box 6.1).

Box 6.1   Returns to the Florida State Pension Funds, 1988 to 2011

The Florida State Board of Administration (SBA), which oversees the state's $132 billion pension fund for teachers, police, and other public workers, provided data to reporter Gina Edwards on returns from the six private equity funds that have closed.[30] Edwards obtained information about the period for which capital was committed to the fund, the amount committed, the amount actually contributed, the amount distributed back to the Florida pension fund from its PE investments, and the amount of gain or loss on the investment. In total, the Florida public pension fund contributed $836.4 million to the six PE funds and received distributions of nearly $1.2 billion, for a gain of $351.5 million on investments from 1988 to 2011.[31]

Florida's SBA selected the Russell 3000 stock index plus 3 percent as the benchmark against which to measure the performance of its private equity investments. This is more appropriate than the S&P 500 because most PE funds are too small to be able to purchase companies as large as those in the S&P 500. The small and midsize companies in the Russell 3000 more closely resemble the size of the companies these PE funds can acquire.[32] Thus, Florida's SBA requires investments in private equity to earn at least 3 percent above the Russell 3000 in order to compensate for the greater risk and the lack of liquidity of its PE investments. Its investments in private equity will have to beat the stock market—that is, the Russell 3000—by 3 percent or more for these riskier, illiquid investments to be worth undertaking. In *absolute* terms, the Florida pension fund appears to have gained from its investments in private equity. Edwards's analysis, however, shows that investments in the Russell 3000 yielded *even larger gains* over the investment period. Thus, Edwards's analysis suggests that Florida's pension fund would have gained far higher returns had it invested in the Russell 3000 index of publicly traded stocks rather than in these six PE funds.

A second example of the difficulty that PE investments have had beating the public stock market in recent years comes from the Harvard Management Company, the group responsible for managing Harvard University's very large endowment. In a public letter, Harvard Management Company's chief executive, Jane Mendillo, complained about the Harvard endowment's returns from its investments in private equity over the previous ten years. Commenting on returns for the fiscal year ending June 30, 2013, Mendillo wrote:

I would characterize our Private Equity performance this year as fair. Private Equity (which includes venture capital) returned 11.0% for the year, a strong nominal return, but well below the return on public market equity, and only slightly above our benchmark. When we invest in private equity, we lock up Harvard's money for multiple years. In exchange for that lock-up we expect to earn returns over time that are in excess of the public markets—an "illiquidity premium." Over the last ten years however, our private equity and public equity portfolios have delivered similar returns. While this asset class still presents unique opportunities for attractive returns, it has gotten much more crowded and there is less of an illiquidity premium. As a result, we are actively focused on honing our private equity strategy.[33]

As these examples make clear, limited partners need to know how the returns on investments in private equity funds compare with other alternative investment opportunities. They need this information—not the internal rate of return—in order to evaluate PE returns and decide whether the performance warrants locking up capital for ten years in a PE fund.

Academic Studies of Private Equity Fund Performance and Returns to Limited Partners

Rather than using the absolute performance measure that practitioners rely on, the internal rate of return, academic researchers have typically used relative measures of performance, and their results are generally more modest for private equity performance relative to the stock market. Relative measures, such as the public market equivalent described in this section, take into account the performance of other assets—such as shares of stock in publicly traded companies—that might have been purchased with the funds that were committed to private equity.

We review two types of academic studies: those that measure the returns to fully liquidated funds (those in which all investments have been exited and the fund closed), and those that measure interim returns using the estimated net asset value of funds. Studies of fully liquidated funds are the most accurate but can only be done for PE funds that are at least ten years old. Thus, studies of performance that include more recent vintages of PE funds must use NAV to estimate the value of unsold companies that are still in funds' portfolios.

The Performance of Fully Liquidated Funds and the Public Market Equivalent

Limited partners in a private equity fund commit a certain amount of capital to the fund and are typically locked into the investment for a ten-year period. The key metric for them is how much money they get back by the end of the ten-year period relative to their initial investment, and how that compares with the return they would have earned if they had invested the same amount of capital in some other way—perhaps in the shares of companies that trade in the stock market. In their seminal and widely cited 2005 study of private equity returns, Kaplan and Schoar carried out just such an analysis by examining funds in which all (or virtually all) portfolio firms had been sold and the fund had been liquidated.[34] Their analysis showed that the returns to limited partners from these investments are highly variable and on average are slightly lower than what they would have earned by investing in the S&P 500 index. Limited partners in top-performing PE funds earned returns that beat the stock market, but most funds did not.

Unlike publicly traded stock and mutual funds, whose values can easily be tracked, there is no comprehensive and widely available database that can be used to analyze PE fund performance. Researchers have had to utilize very partial data sets that rely on self-reported data from the general and/or limited partners in PE funds. In their study, Kaplan and Schoar relied on data provided by Thompson Venture Economics (TVE) that consists of voluntary reporting of fund returns by PE firms and their limited partners.[35] Kaplan and Schoar analyzed data for the period 1980 to 2001, which includes the dot-com boom and the bursting of the stock market bubble in 2000 but does not include the much more severe economic crisis after the housing bubble burst in 2006. Importantly, their analysis focused on funds that had reached the end of their life span and were liquidated by 2001. Thus, their calculations were based on *actual* returns to the limited partners and not on the subjective estimates of interim returns for portfolio investments not yet exited in funds not yet liquidated. These researchers measured performance using the public market equivalent, which compares returns from investing in private equity with returns from comparable investments in the S&P 500 index. If the PME is equal to one, the return from investing in the PE fund just matches the return from an equivalent investment in the stock market. A PME greater than one indicates that the return from investing in the PE fund was greater than what could have been earned in the stock market; a PME less than one indicates a return from PE investments that is less than the stock market return would have been.

Kaplan and Schoar found that PE fund returns vary widely, with some funds "beating the market"—that is, yielding a higher return than the stock market—but most funds failing to do so. The researchers found that, net of fees and carried interest, PE investors earned on average 93 to 97 percent of what they would have earned by investing in the S&P 500 index. Returns for funds at the twenty-fifth percentile were less than two-thirds of the return of the S&P 500; returns at the median were four-fifths of those of the S&P 500; and returns at the seventy-fifth percentile were 12 percent higher than those of the S&P 500. On a size-weighted basis, the returns at the twenty-fifth percentile were about three-quarters (72 percent) of what could have been earned by investing in the stock market, while at the median they were about four-fifths (83 percent).

PE funds at the seventy-fifth percentile outperformed the stock market by 3 percent. This study, which has been widely cited, showed that investments in top-performing funds outpaced the returns that could be earned in the stock market. For the rest, limited partners would have been better off investing in a stock market index fund. Moreover, Kaplan and Schoar found that fund performance is persistent—firms that sponsor a fund that outperforms the stock market in one period are likely to outperform with follow-on funds as well. One recent study that incorporates data beyond the years studied by Kaplan and Schoar found that top-quartile funds no longer persistently outperform the stock market, though they commonly did so in the period covered by the Kaplan and Schoar study.[36]

In any case, the problem for limited partners is that not everyone can invest in the top-quartile PE funds. Endowments and pension funds that were early participants in PE funds have the greatest access to funds with proven track records. Most investors are not able to gain access to these funds, especially investors who are new to private equity. For these investors, the Kaplan and Schoar study suggests that investments in PE funds are likely to underperform the broad market. And this is without taking into account the higher risk associated with the greater debt, less liquidity, and lack of transparency of PE investments.[37]

More recent academic studies of private equity returns, including research by Steven Kaplan, have raised questions about the quality of the TVE data and turned to other data sources. Here we examine these studies in detail, after a discussion of some of the common challenges in evaluating PE fund performance.

Caveats Common to Studies of Private Equity Performance

There is no comprehensive data set that accurately captures private equity activity, and there are biases in each data set that must be acknowledged when interpreting results. Earlier research, such as Steven Kaplan and Antoinette Schoar's 2005 study and Ludovic Phalippou and Oliver Gottschalg's 2009 study, used TVE (now Thompson VentureXpert) data, which are incomplete and do not accurately identify the funds that are liquidated.[38] These earlier studies also focused on funds with vintage years (initial start dates) from 1980 to 1995 and necessarily excluded those formed in the second half of the 1990s and early 2000s. Many of these more recent funds exited investments in the boom years of the last decade and can be expected to have performed well. These data issues potentially bias downward the results for fund performance in the Kaplan and Schoar and Phalippou and Gottschalg studies. Three recent studies—by David Robinson and Berk Sensoy, by Robert Harris,

Tim Jenkinson, and Steven Kaplan—as well as research by Jenkinson, Miguel Sousa, and Rüdiger Stucke—and by Chris Higson and Stucke—have attempted to address these issues by using other data sets and by including the performance of more recent vintage funds.[39] Nonetheless, these authors themselves acknowledge that problems remain with data sources, the choice of benchmarks, and the inclusion of funds that still hold many unsold portfolio companies.

- *Data sets available to researchers are improving, but there is still no comprehensive, unbiased, and widely available data set that can be used to evaluate PE performance.* All of the studies of PE performance suffer from sample bias. In the Jenkinson, Harris, and Kaplan study, the sample consists of funds with limited partners who use the Burgiss system to track and monitor their investments and who have agreed to have their track records included.[40] Investors who have backed underperforming PE funds may be less likely to agree to be part of this database. Robinson and Sensoy's data come from one investor whose long track record and willingness to share his data suggest that his PE fund investments were successful.[41] Interestingly, this investor greatly reduced his commitments to more recent vintage funds. Data for the Jenkinson, Sousa, and Stucke study cover the entire history of 761 fund investments—of which 291 were PE buyout funds—made by CalPERS, the pension fund for California public employees.[42] CalPERS is the largest U.S. investor in private equity and enjoys access to funds sponsored by top-performing PE firms that are not available to smaller LP investors or those that began investing in PE funds more recently—including other pension funds. Higson and Stucke utilize the Cambridge Associates database of funds' cash flow—which contains data on 60 percent of U.S. buyout funds by value—and extend the sample by collecting self-reported information on additional buyout funds from a number of limited partners.[43] The resulting sample is the most comprehensive to date and, according to the researchers, captures approximately 85 percent of the funds raised by the U.S. buyout industry back to 1980. Despite the broad coverage of this data set, it includes self-reported returns for one-quarter of the funds in its larger sample and omits returns from about 15 percent of U.S. buyout funds in the PE universe. These funds may very well be underperformers about which LPs prefer not to volunteer information. A further issue is that, unlike most other data sets used in academic research, Cambridge Associates reports gross returns rather than returns to LPs net of fees and the carried interest paid to the general partners. Higson and Stucke "infer the fees and carried interest . . . by making reasonable assumptions about the terms of the partnership agreements."[44]

- *It is not possible to determine how representative any of the data sets are.* As Robinson and Sensoy note, "Assessing representativeness [of a sample of PE funds] is inherently difficult because the universe of private equity funds (and portfolio investments) is not available, making representativeness a concern that applies to all research in private equity."[45]

- *Including PE funds that are still active in the analysis makes PE fund returns sensitive to estimates of net asset values.* PE funds from vintages formed in 2002 and later continue to hold investments in their portfolios. Vintages since 2003 still hold between 70 and 98 percent of investments in their portfolios.[46] This is not a problem if NAVs are good estimates of the market values of companies still in PE fund portfolios. The implementation in 2008 of fair value accounting has given some researchers greater confidence in these estimates; others are skeptical, however, pointing out that GPs have wide discretion in making these estimates. Relying on quarterly cash flow reports from LPs does not solve the problem of GPs exercising considerable discretion in calculating NAVs because it is the GPs, not the LPs, who make this calculation. And as we saw in the previous section, the evidence suggests that GPs can—and sometimes do—manipulate these values.

- *Examining a subsample of funds that have liquidated also poses problems.* A study of PE returns based on all funds (or a randomly drawn sample of funds) that made their first investments between 1985 and 2000, virtually all of which would be liquidated at the present time, would avoid the problems described so far. Beginning with an incomplete sample of funds, however, necessarily introduces problems of selection bias and lack of representativeness, particularly given the cyclical nature of PE performance. Selecting a subsample of funds that have liquidated may create a bias toward higher performance outcomes because more successful funds tend to liquidate earlier than less successful ones.

- *The choice of fund performance measure matters.* Researchers can report fund performance in terms of the public market equivalent, the internal rate of return, or the investment multiple. The IRR and TPVI are absolute measures of returns and do not take into consideration that investors have other alternatives and would invest in other assets if they did not invest in private equity. The IRR suffers from the serious drawbacks described earlier in this chapter. Comparison of the IRR with the performance of the stock market is possible, but suffers from any weaknesses in its calculation. The PME is generally used in academic research to measure PE performance relative to the performance of the stock market. Jenkinson, Harris, and Kaplan use the PME to examine the performance of PE funds compared with the stock market over the life of the fund.[47] However, they use the IRRs of private equity and stock market indexes to compare annual performance of the two asset classes.

- *The choice of a benchmark matters.* Since the question in these studies is whether investments in private equity buyout funds outperform investments in public equities, researchers need to choose a stock market index against which to benchmark PE performance. The usual choice is the S&P 500 index, which tracks companies with a minimum equity value of $5 billion—far larger than the equity value of the vast majority of the companies acquired by PE funds. Some studies benchmark against stock market indexes that more closely match the investments available to PE funds, which reduces the performance of PE funds relative to the stock market. Any strong conclusion about whether the U.S. buyout industry has outperformed the stock market, as Higson and Stucke acknowledge, "requires further research on the appropriate benchmark."[48]

- *Perhaps most importantly, none of these studies makes an adjustment for the greater risk associated with investments in private, as compared with public, equities.* Investments in private equity entail more risk than do investments in shares of publicly traded companies. First, PE investments entail "commitment risk": unlike investments in publicly traded companies, which are executed at the time the commitment to invest is made, PE investments are often made months or years after investors have made a commitment of capital to the PE fund. The investor has no control over the timing of the PE fund's investments and cannot alter the investment decision in line with changing conditions in financial markets. Second, compared to publicly traded companies, PE-owned companies carry far higher debt loads, which can lead to a higher risk of financial distress or bankruptcy. Finally, investments in PE funds are illiquid—they cannot be exited quickly. Although limited partners can sell their PE commitment to another party on the "secondaries" market, they are likely to have to sell at a steep discount—if they can find a buyer at all. As Harris, Jenkinson, and Kaplan note, "Investing in a portfolio of private equity funds . . . inevitably involves uncertainties and potential costs related to the long-term commitment of capital, uncertainty of cash flows and the liquidity of holdings that differ from those in public markets. . . . Further research is required to calibrate the extent of the premia investors require to bear these risks."[49] As we saw earlier, Florida's State Board Administration, which oversees the state's public pension plan, expects its PE investments to outperform the stock market benchmark by three percentage points to compensate for the greater lack of liquidity and greater riskiness of these investments. And the managers of Harvard University's endowment want a 4 percent outperformance for their PE investments.

Recent Studies of Private Equity
Fund Performance

Robert Harris, Tim Jenkinson, and Steven Kaplan, "Private Equity Performance: What Do We Know?" (2013) In this study, Harris, Jenkinson, and Kaplan revisit the methodology of the study undertaken earlier by Kaplan and Schoar, using data derived from over two hundred institutional investors (limited partners) in private equity buyout funds that use the Burgiss system for record-keeping and performance monitoring.[50] About 60 percent of the LPs in their sample are public or private pension funds and over 20 percent are foundations or endowments. A total of 598 buyout funds formed between 1984 and 2008 are included in the analysis, but relatively few funds are from vintages earlier than 1993. Two-thirds of the funds began operations between 2000 and 2008; these necessarily include unrealized investments for which NAVs had to be estimated. The analysis uses the "stated values" of NAVs for investments that have not been exited.[51] Unrealized investments for which NAVs had to be estimated are 3 percent or less of invested capital for the median fund in pre-1999 vintages, but nearly 40 percent for the 2000 vintage, 70 percent for 2003, and about 90 percent for 2005 to 2008. Only 2 percent of investments in the median 2007 vintage fund had been realized at the time of the analysis.

The analysis uses the public market equivalent to compare investments in private equity funds to equivalently timed investments in the stock market. The researchers use data through March 2011. PE cash flows are net of fees and carried interest. Using the S&P 500 as the benchmark, the researchers found that, "ignoring vintage year, the average fund in the entire sample has an average PME of 1.20 and a median PME of 1.11."[52] That is, the authors report that the average fund in their sample outperformed the stock market by 20 percent over the life of the fund. Weighting fund returns to account for differences in the amount of capital committed to the fund, the researchers found a weighted average PME of 1.27—or an outperformance of 27 percent over the life of the fund.[53] The large difference between the average and median outperformance indicates that the outperformance is driven by top-performing funds. Using ten years as the life span of the fund, the 20 percent higher level of performance of the average fund implies an annual outperformance on average of less than 2 percent, while the weighted performance of 27 percent implies an annual outperformance of just over 2.4 percent.

For the median or typical private equity fund, the 11 percent higher performance of the median fund implies an annual outperformance of just over 1 percent a year. This study finds a far better record of PE performance than in the Kaplan and Schoar study, where the median fund underperformed the stock market.[54] The median rate may be the most relevant measure of PE performance for most investors, who cannot be certain they are investing in a top-quartile fund. Half the funds in the sample had annual returns less than this. It is unlikely that annual outperformance of this magnitude is sufficient to compensate for the greater riskiness of PE investments compared to investing in publicly traded stocks. Many limited partners view an annual outperformance of 3 to 4 percent as the return necessary to compensate for the increased risk and illiquidity of PE investments.[55]

Harris, Jenkinson, and Kaplan make the claim that "the buyout funds have significantly outperformed public markets—by around 20% over the life of the fund, or 3–4% per annum."[56] This would be a significant annual outperformance, but how do the researchers obtain it? They chose not to calculate the annual outperformance of PE funds from their analysis of the public market equivalent—their preferred measure of PE performance. Instead, they used an alternative method to separately calculate annual outperformance. This alternative methodology implies that the effective life of a PE fund is five years on average—shorter than its legal life of ten years.[57] This is problematic. The statement that funds are effectively liquidated after five years is contradicted by their own data.[58] Note that while private equity funds often expect to exit an investment in a particular portfolio company within five years after acquiring it, the fund typically still has unsold companies in its portfolio over a much longer period.

In 2011 the median percentage of unrealized investments for ten-year-old vintage 2001 funds in the data set utilized by Harris, Jenkinson, and Kaplan was a surprisingly high 42.5 percent; for five-year-old vintage 2006 funds, it was 89.2 percent. By comparison, for twelve-year-old vintage 1999 funds, which clearly had reached the end of their life span, it was just 10 percent. A life span of ten years for a PE buyout fund seems like a more reasonable estimate than five to six years. Other researchers consider ten years (or more) to be the typical life span of a PE fund. Higson and Stucke, for example, note that "the returns from a private equity fund can only be measured with certainty when the fund is fully liquidated, which is usually well beyond the nominal 10-year fund life." They further remark that, "in practice, it would be rare for a private equity fund to have zero cash flow activity between its 5th to 8th anniversary, or to be even liquidated that early."[59] In their own data set, Higson and Stucke report that just 2 percent of 2004 and 2005 vintage funds were liquidated by 2010—that is, five or six years after they were launched.[60]

The difference in performance between the average and the median funds in the Harris, Jenkinson, and Kaplan analysis—the median fund did only half as well as the average fund—suggests that the outperformance of PE funds is driven by top performers. Unlike Kaplan and Schoar, however, Harris, Jenkinson, and Kaplan do not report the performance of funds at the twenty-fifth and seventy-fifth percentiles, so it is not possible to draw precise conclusions about investments in top-performing and in low-performing funds relative to the stock market. The Harris, Jenkinson, and Kaplan study does find better fund performance than the earlier study: the median fund in Kaplan and Schoar's study under-performed the S&P 500, while the median fund in Harris, Jenkinson, and Kaplan's study outperformed this benchmark. The difference may be due to the fact that the Burgiss data are of higher quality than the TVE data used in the earlier analysis. It is also possible that the results of Harris, Jenkinson, and Kaplan's 2013 study were influenced by the inclusion of funds (more than 80 percent of the Burgiss sample) that began operations between 2000 and 2008. Between 38 and 98 percent of investments by the median fund in those vintages had not yet been realized in 2011, and cash flows for those investments necessarily included estimates of NAVs. It will be another five years or so until the great majority of these funds have been liquidated and this ambiguity can be resolved.

Harris, Jenkinson, and Kaplan examine the sensitivity of their results to the choice of stock market benchmark.[61] They repeat their analysis using the Russell 3000 index of small and midsize publicly traded companies, the Russell 2000 index of small publicly traded companies, and the Russell 2000 value index, which is a subset of the Russell 2000. The sample average PME using the S&P 500 was 1.20. This falls to 1.18 using the Russell 3000 as the benchmark, to 1.11 using the Russell 2000, and to 1.07 using the Russell 2000 value index. At the median, the PME using the S&P 500 was 1.11. It falls to 1.09 using the Russell 3000, to 1.02 using the Russell 2000, and to 0.99 using the Russell 2000 value index. Average PE fund out-performance declines markedly in comparison with indexes of shares of publicly traded companies that more closely resemble the companies that PE funds acquire for their portfolios. If the Russell 2000 is the appropriate index, these results show that investors in half the funds in the sample would have been better off investing in an index fund of companies in that index. The results of this analysis do not appear to support the authors' conclusion that the outperformance of PE buyout funds appears "to be relatively insensitive to assumptions about benchmark indices."[62]

David Robinson and Berk Sensoy, "Cyclicality, Performance Measurement, and Cash Flow Liquidity in Private Equity" (2011) Robinson and Sensoy's study begins with the observation that PE fund performance is cyclical. Funds launched in boom periods perform poorly in absolute terms. That is, the absolute performance of buyout funds raised during boom periods in fund-raising, measured by the internal rate of return, is significantly worse than the performance of funds raised during fund-raising bust periods. There is often more fund-raising activity when interest rates are low and easy access to credit encourages general partners to pay high prices for attractive target companies. Then, as interest rates rise, the debt struc-ture of the portfolio companies may appear unattractive and companies bought at high prices may be difficult to exit at a profit. Fund distributions are likely to suffer, as is performance. However, these cycles in PE fund-raising follow similar boom-and bust-periods in the stock market. Distributions from the sale of portfolio companies and net cash flows to funds tend to be low when valuations of publicly traded companies are low. There is a tendency for PE performance and stock market performance to follow similar patterns. Thus, it is unclear whether the poor absolute performance of PE buyout funds following booms in fund-raising translates into poor performance relative to the stock market as well.[63]

To examine this question, the researchers adopt and expand the methodology in Kaplan and Schoar's 2005 study. They use a proprietary database of quarterly cash flows provided by a large, anonymous limited partner that includes information on a large sample of PE funds raised after 1995. The funds are mainly U.S. funds and span the vintage years 1984 to 2009. However, the LP investor shifted away from investments in private equity after 2001; as a consequence, coverage of buyout funds is especially good in the 1994 to 2001 period, but falls after that as this investor cut back on investments in later PE funds. As the researchers acknowledge, the fact that the data come from a single limited partner raises questions about the representativeness of the sample.[64] These questions cannot be resolved (and apply more generally to every study of PE performance), as there is no data set that includes the universe of PE funds to which the sample can be compared. The quarterly data used in the analysis extend to the second quarter of 2010. There are 542 buyout funds in the sample, and the U.S. buyout funds represent 56 percent of total capital committed to U.S. buyout funds. Funds with recent vintage years are still active. However, the researchers want to base their performance analysis on actual cash flows. Hence, much of the analysis focuses on a subsample of 368 funds, from vintage years 2005 or earlier, that had been officially liquidated by June 30, 2010, or had no cash flow for the last six quarters up to that date.

Because results using the full sample do not differ from those using the liquidated subsample, Robinson and Sensoy conclude that there is no evidence that stated NAVs are a biased estimate of market values for unsold companies in fund portfolios in this sample of PE funds.[65] This finding contrasts with the results of a study by Jenkins, Sousa, and Stucke, who examined whether fund valuations are fair and accurate.[66] They examined quarterly fund valuations using data on 761 investments made by the California public pension fund CalPERS. Analyzing quarterly variations in fund valuations of PE buyout funds, they examined these specifically in relation to efforts to raise follow-on funds. These researchers find that valuations for active funds generally tend to be conservative and substantially understate the value of subsequent distributions.[67] Valuations in their sample of funds jump in the fourth quarter, when funds are usually audited. They also find, however, that fund valuations are inflated in periods when new funds are being raised, with fund valuations gradually reversed after fund-raising for the follow-on fund has been completed. For liquidated funds, cash has been returned to investors and final performance measures can be calculated without this ambiguity. But since GPs can manage fund valuations for active funds, interim performance measures for active funds, which are based on stated net asset values, "have limited power to predict ultimate returns."[68] This is especially true of internal rates of return. Interim public market equivalents are better predictors of final performance once the fund-raising for follow-on funds has been completed.[69] The researchers "find a distinctive pattern of abnormal valuations which matches quite closely the period up to the first close of the follow on fund. It is hard to rationalize the pattern we observe, except as a positive bias in valuation (of remaining portfolio companies) during fundraising."[70]

Robinson and Sensoy analyze PE buyout fund performance relative to the S&P 500 index and then extend the analysis by replacing the S&P 500 benchmark "with narrower indexes more closely tailored to a particular fund's investment strategy."[71] Based on the strong correlation between the size of a buyout fund and the size of the companies it acquires for its portfolio, and the relationship between the size of PE funds and average returns, the researchers use benchmarks tailored to the funds in their sample. PE cash flows are net of fees and carried interest.

The results of Robinson and Sensoy's analysis of PE fund performance relative to the S&P 500 closely mirror those of Harris, Jenkinson, and Kaplan. Robinson and Sensoy find that the PME for the average fund in the liquidated subsample using the S&P 500 index is 1.18 and the median is 1.09.[72] Thus, the average fund outperforms the S&P 500 by 18 percent over its life span, while the median fund outperforms it by 9 percent.[73] If PE funds have a life span of ten years, then annual outperformance is less than 1 percent at the median and less than 2 percent for the average PE firm. The strong average PE performance is driven by the performance of top-quartile funds, which outperformed the S&P 500 index by 46 percent over the life of the fund, or 4 percent per year. The PME for the bottom quartile of funds was 0.82. These funds underperformed the S&P 500 index by a wide margin, earning only 82 percent of what would have been earned from a similar investment in shares of companies in this stock market index.

Measuring private equity performance relative to stock market indexes more closely tailored to the PE funds in the sample yields results that are distinctly inferior to those of Harris, Jenkinson, and Kaplan. Robinson and Sensoy find that the apparent outperformance of investments in private equity relative to investments in the stock market decreased substantially when more appropriate benchmarks were used. In this case, they find that the average tailored PME is 1.10, the median tailored PME is

1.00, and the tailored PME is 1.37 at the seventy-fifth percentile and 0.77 at the twenty-fifth percentile.[74] The average fund outperforms the stock market by less than 1 percent a year. At the median, PE performance just matches the performance of the relevant stock market index; there is no outperformance at all. Half of all PE funds in this data set do better than the stock market, and half do worse.

Top-quartile funds in this sample outperform the relevant stock market index by a little over 3 percent a year—a respectable return. Bottom-quartile funds earn only about three-quarters of what they would have earned over the life of the fund by investing in the stock market, trailing behind passive investment in a stock market index fund by 2 percent a year.

Higson and Stucke, "The Performance of Private Equity" (2012) Chris Higson and Rüdiger Stucke were the first researchers to be granted access to the PE fund cash flow database of Cambridge Associates, a PE advisory firm with over nine hundred LP clients, broad coverage of the industry, and a long history; the database includes 556 funds for the vintage years 1986 to 2008. Nevertheless, this database is incomplete. LP Source, according to Higson and Stucke, counts 1,500 funds. The researchers supplement data from Cambridge Associates with data for an additional 613 U.S. buyout funds collected from self-reports from a number of single LPs. According to the researchers, the full sample consists of 1,169 funds and covers almost 85 percent of the LP Source universe of U.S. private equity (buyout) funds by value.

Higson and Stucke use a number of different methodologies to calculate private equity fund performance and its comparison to the stock market, including internal rates of return, total value to paid-in capital, yield spreads (the difference between the IRRs of private equity and stock market investments), and the public market equivalent. They begin by reporting absolute measures (IRR and TVPI) of PE fund performance. Several interesting results emerge from their analysis of absolute PE fund performance. The vintage years 1980 to 1985 were "golden (vintage) years for buyout performance, though they involved few funds and relatively little capital."[75] Based on returns in these golden years, "IRRs of above 25% and TVPIs of above 2.5 achieved by many funds in the first half of the 1980s became the unofficial return goal of the buyout industry: 'returns of 25 and 2.5.'"[76] Returns of vintages from the second half of the 1980s were very disappointing, however, as highly leveraged portfolio companies did poorly in the economic downturn following the end of that decade. As the researchers clearly show, PE returns are highly cyclical.[77] Moreover, they exhibit a strong downward trend over time. Over all the years in their full sample of PE buyout funds, the IRR achieved by PE funds was far below the "25 and 2.5" goal. The overall IRR was

8.6 percent, and the TVPI was 1.41. Looking at the absolute performance of the full sample by decade, IRR fell from 16.5 percent for vintages from the full 1980s decade to 11.4 percent for 1990s vintages, and 7.2 percent for 2000 to 2008 vintages. The corresponding TVPIs went from 2.34 to 1.61 to 1.28. Median IRRs fell from 14.2 percent for 1980s vintages to 9.9 percent for the 1990s vintages and 6.5 percent for the 2000 to 2008 vintages; median TVPIs decreased from 2.05 to 1.51 to 1.16.[78]

Higson and Stucke construct a comparison of PE fund IRRs with the S&P 500 stock market index using the following approach: They hypothetically invest equally in the stock market index whenever a PE fund calls capital from its LP investors to make an investment. Changes in the value of the capital invested in the stock market index correspond to increases or decreases in the index. They divest an equal amount from the index whenever a PE fund distributes capital back to LPs. The researchers then calculate the IRR of these hypothetical cash flows and compare this with the IRR calculated from the annually pooled cash flows of the PE funds in their data set. The difference between the two IRRs is the "IRR spread." Turning to the performance of PE funds relative to the stock market, Higson and Stucke—in line with the other studies reviewed here—find that "in most vintage years the average outperformance is above the median, often significantly, indicating that the substantial excess returns are largely driven by positive outliers."[79] Comparing IRRs to stock market returns to derive "IRR spreads," they found that U.S. private equity funds from the 1980s delivered an average yield spread of 2.44 percent a year. For the 1990s, the average spread was 4.70 percent, and for 2000 to 2008 the average spread was 5.88 percent.

We earlier discussed the potential problems with IRR as a measure of fund performance and will not repeat those points here. We note that Jenkinson, Sousa, and Stucke analyzed the entire history of quarterly NAVs and cash flows for investments made by CalPERS in PE buyout funds. They found that interim IRRs have "limited power to predict ultimate returns."[80] Interim PMEs are better predictors of the final performance of PE buyout funds.[81]

For comparability with other studies of private equity performance, Higson and Stucke also use the methodology from Kaplan and Schoar's 2005 study to calculate the public market equivalent using both the S&P 500 index of very large companies and the S&P 600 index of companies more comparable to the companies acquired by PE funds. Companies in the S&P 600 index have an equity value of $200 million to $1 billion, which mirrors the size range of most PE buyout transactions. Higson and Stucke refer to the PME as the "adjusted TVPI." They analyze PE cash flows over the entire sample, including funds that are still active, relying on stated NAVs for companies still held in PE fund portfolios.[82] Using the S&P 500 index as the benchmark, they find an average PME of 1.23

over all funds and all years, and a median PME of 1.13. (These results are very close to those of Harris, Jenkinson, and Kaplan, who also analyzed a sample that included both active and liquidated funds and who found an average PME of 1.20 and a median PME of 1.11.) Over the typical ten-year life span of PE funds, the Higson and Stucke results imply an average outperformance by PE funds of 2 percent a year and a median outperformance of 1.3 percent a year.

Higson and Stucke also examine the PME using the S&P 600 index of companies with valuations closer to those of companies in PE fund port-folios as the benchmark. The results are much more modest. The average PME over all funds and all years relative to this benchmark is 1.09 and the median is 1.03. This implies that average outperformance per year is less than 1 percent and that median outperformance is less than half a percent (about 0.3 percent) a year.

Results of analyses using the public market equivalent suggest that discussions of the outperformance of investments in private equity have focused too heavily on top-performing funds and placed too much emphasis on comparisons with the S&P 500. As Higson and Stucke put it, "The cross-sectional variation is considerable with just over 60% of all funds doing better than the S&P, and excess returns being driven by top-decile rather than top-quartile funds."[83] Focusing on the performance of the median fund and using arguably more appropriate stock market benchmarks suggests that for many LPs in PE funds the rewards may not be sufficient to compensate for the added risk and lack of liquidity these investments entail.

Conclusion

Only the top-performing PE funds—the top 25 percent, or perhaps the top 10 percent—outperform the stock market by a reasonable margin. Unfortunately, not every limited partner can be an investor in one or more of these funds. In general, it is the largest LPs and those that invested early in private equity—LPs such as CalPERS, the Oregon Public Employees System, or the Yale endowment—that have access to these funds. Median fund performance relative to the stock market is more relevant for most LP investors. And it would be helpful for these investors to know relative performance at the twenty-fifth percentile (the bottom quarter of funds) and at the seventy-fifth percentile (the top quarter of funds), which not all studies report.

Excess returns to private equity investments relative to what could be earned by investing in the stock market appear to be greatest when measured using the internal rate of return to compute yield spreads. But even using this measure, Higson and Stucke found that over all the years of their data 37 percent of PE funds underperformed the stock market, and that by decade the proportion of funds that underperformed the S&P 500 ranged from 51 to 34 percent.[84] Comparing the IRR of PE funds with an IRR computed for the stock market remains controversial among researchers, with most preferring the use of the public market equivalent.

For studies using the PME method, whether and to what extent PE funds outperform the stock market over the life span of the fund depends on the stock index chosen as the benchmark. Nearly all funds have a legal life span of ten to thirteen years. Data in the three articles on PE fund performance reviewed here suggest that most funds still have significant cash flows in years five to eight after their start date, and relatively few have been liquidated at that point. Taking ten years as the life span of a PE fund, average annual outperformance compared to the S&P 500 index is about 2 percent or a little higher a year, and median outperformance is 1 percent a year or less. The choice of a stock market index as the benchmark against which to measure PE fund performance makes a very large difference. The study that used the most complete sample of PE funds (Robinson and Sensoy's) and used stock market indexes more closely tailored to the PE funds in the sample found that the median PE fund did not outperform the stock market at all. Top-quartile funds in this sample outperformed the relevant stock market index by a little over 3 percent a year—a return in line with what many LPs believe is a reasonable premium for the lack of liquidity when funds are tied up for ten years. Bottom-quartile funds earn only about three-quarters of what they would have earned over the life of the fund by investing in the stock market, underperforming passive investment in a stock market index fund by 2 percent a year.

Whichever benchmark is used, the relatively small annual outperformance by PE funds on average and at the median is not likely to be what LPs were expecting. For most investors, the return on PE investments probably does not provide enough of a premium to justify the additional risk.

This may prove to be especially problematic for pension funds, which are major investors in PE funds. CalPERS provided Jenkinson, Sousa, and Stucke with data on 291 investments in private equity buyout funds made through 2011. Of these, 130 investments (45 percent of the total) occurred in the peak PE fund-raising vintage years 2005 to 2008. In past cycles, funds launched during boom fund-raising periods performed more poorly than other funds. Funds with vintages in the first half of the 1980s had spectacular returns on portfolio companies sold early, but the decade did not end so well for PE investors. Funds launched in the early 2000s that exited portfolio companies in the boom years 2005 to 2007 also racked up exceptional gains. How these funds perform over their life span, however, depends on the prices at which they are able to exit their remaining investments.

Funds launched in the peak fund-raising years of the boom period have been struggling to successfully exit their investments in the post-crisis period. As Higson and Stucke note, "Perhaps the biggest question is the outturn (outperformance) of the funds raised since the mid-2000s in the lead up to the recession. A reliable judgment on this needs data that will take years to emerge."[85] This is precisely the question facing pension fund trustees. Pension funds are the stewards of the deferred compensation (retirement income) of millions of ordinary workers; they have a special obligation to evaluate the risk-return trade-off carefully when investing in private equity.

═ Chapter 7 ═

Private Equity's Effects
on Jobs and Labor

Earlier chapters examined the private equity business model, how PE makes money, and how different types of PE firms influence the management of organizations across a wide spectrum of industries and markets. We have argued that the classic private equity model is different from that of public corporations in its debt-heavy capital structure, light legal oversight, lack of transparency and accountability, and higher risk-taking. We have also shown that the PE market is segmented, with buyouts of small and midsize companies offering less collateral for leveraging debt and more opportunities for operational improvements than larger companies with values of $500 million and above. These differences suggest that buyouts of small and midsize companies offer more opportunities for job growth than buyouts of large corporations, where use of leverage, financial engineering, and downsizing are more likely.

With such a varied landscape, what conclusions can we draw about the net effect of private equity on the quality of jobs, employment levels, and labor relations? That is the question we tackle in this chapter. It is a difficult one to assess because portfolio companies that are taken private offer little publicly available information, and private equity firms consider proprietary the strategies they use to manage their workforces and internal operations. The research record on this topic is thin, and the data typically come from the interested parties—the PE owners themselves. Nonetheless, there are a small number of rigorous econometric studies on the overall impact of PE investment on employment, productivity, and wages in the United States, and we carefully review these studies in the next section. In addition, we draw on a series of original case studies in private equity–owned companies to examine the process and impact of takeovers on the quality of jobs and pay as well as labor relations in union-represented workplaces.

In general, the most rigorous econometric studies show that job destruction is greater than job creation in PE-owned companies compared to their publicly traded counterparts. Moreover, job destruction is particularly steep for buyouts of public corporations that are taken private. These findings are contrary to the claims of private equity advocates that PE firms often buy up financially distressed companies, turn them around, and are an important source of job growth for the U.S. economy. In fact, the econometric evidence shows that compared to comparable public companies, those acquired by private equity have higher employment growth in the five years prior to acquisition and the acquisition year. And as noted earlier in our book, prior to the 2008 financial crisis, distressed investing accounted for only about 2 percent of PE acquisitions. As in the leveraged buyouts of the 1980s, private equity today targets companies with strong fundamentals. The quantitative research also shows that PE-owned companies have higher productivity than comparable public companies in the acquisition year, and increase productivity primarily through downsizing, plant closings, divestitures and acquisitions, and production shifts to consolidated units—not to improvements in productivity in existing or "brownfield" sites. Finally, compared to companies not taken over by private equity, wages are higher in the acquisition year in companies purchased by private equity, but post-buyout, wages fall. Thus, the productivity-wage gap increases after private equity acquires a company.

These findings of higher job and income loss for employees in PE-owned companies indicate that private equity contributes in important ways to the growing inequality in the U.S. economy. Private equity depresses the wages of employed workers, and those who are laid off—particularly blue-collar workers—typically do not find new employment with wages and benefits as high as their prior jobs. But PE partners make outsized returns from these strategies.

No quantitative data exist to trace the impact of private equity on work intensification and labor relations, so it is not possible to summarize a "net effect" of private equity in these areas. But similar to the patterns of job growth and destruction in PE companies, our case studies show a range of different labor strategies used by PE firms.[1] We found little evidence that private equity owners are generally more hostile to labor unions and collective bargaining than managers in publicly traded corporations. There are examples of both small and large PE firms that have negotiated contracts in good faith with unions[2]; in other cases, a private equity firm's anti-union animus has led to serious labor law violations. American and foreign-owned publicly traded companies across the board take advantage of the lax labor laws in the United States that give wide girth to managerial prerogative in the hiring, firing, and management of labor. In contrast to their counterparts in Europe, where a thicker web of labor institutions shapes labor-management relations and curbs some excesses, PE owners in the United States face few institutional constraints on their behavior.[3] U.S. unions lack the legal support of codetermination or the works council laws that require new owners in the European context to consult or negotiate with unions over restructuring and the transfer-of-ownership laws that require new owners to abide by prior labor contracts.

The variety of cases in this chapter reflects this thin institutional landscape—from instances in which new private equity owners exhibit a high level of hostility toward unions to instances in which they have an explicit commitment to peaceful labor relations as a strategy to make money. The attitudes of private equity investors towards labor vary from hostile to pragmatic to indifferent. Their labor strategies depend in part on the philosophies or strategic assumptions of the PE firm's leaders. In some cases, new PE owners have had the advantage of building a labor relationship from scratch—in contrast to prior owners mired in a deep legacy of union mistrust and conflict. As our study of the steel industry demonstrates, the new PE owner Wilbur Ross negotiated directly with the steelworkers union on more pragmatic grounds than did the managers of the publicly traded steel companies that preceded him. In this and other cases, PE owners exhibited no particular position on labor: as long as they made their targeted returns, they were agnostic about whether a union was present or not. In the case of Wilbur Ross, his three year investment netted him $4.5 billion—just equal to what retirees lost in their health and pension plans.

But this is where private equity owners, because they promise to extract higher-than-average returns in a short time frame, appear to diverge from their public company counterparts. As most union workplaces offer higher wages and benefits than their non-union counterparts, PE owners have sought substantial cuts in jobs, wage levels, benefits, and, especially, pensions—even in companies that were financially healthy when they were taken over. The need to service the debt drives job cuts and an increase in workloads for remaining workers. In sum, the available case record shows that whether private equity firms negotiate or not with unions, the earnings of PE owners often come at the expense of workers' jobs, income, and retirement savings.

The Impact of Private Equity on Employment, Productivity, and Wages

The most comprehensive and rigorous analyses of the employment, earnings, and productivity effects of private equity in the U.S. have drawn on industry data on PE transactions from the Capital IQ database and have combined this with the U.S. Census Bureau data. Employment and earnings data are drawn from the Longitudinal Business Database (LBD), which covers job creation and destruction for the entire non-farm private sector. Productivity data is available for manufacturing enterprises only, based on the Annual Survey of Manufactures (ASM) and Census of Manufactures (CM). The longitudinal data and analyses are complicated and impressive, linking changes in PE ownership to changes in employment, productivity, and earnings between 1980 and 2005.

The results of data analyses are spelled out in a series of sophisticated econometric papers by Steven Davis and his colleagues.[4] While the findings in each paper differ somewhat based on different specifications and sub-samples, the overall results tell a consistent story. The 2008 and 2011 papers by Davis and colleagues focus on employment outcomes alone. The 2009 paper focuses on productivity and wages, while the 2013 paper brings all of these issues together, largely replicating the 2011 employment findings and expanding the 2009 analyses of wages and productivity.

In the 2008 employment paper, the data consisted of 5,000 U.S. target companies and about 300,000 target establishments in these companies, acquired in private equity transactions from 1980 to 2005. An establishment refers to an actual work site—for example, a single store, warehouse, office, or corporate headquarters. A firm may be a single establishment or it may have multiple establishments. In the 2011 and 2013 papers, the sample is reduced to a much smaller number of private equity-owned companies and establishments—3,200 U.S. companies and 150,000 establishments—acquired from 1980 to 2005. In all of these studies, control groups were constructed by matching PE-owned establishments (or companies) to other establishments (or companies) that were comparable in terms of industry, age, size, and single/multi-establishment status (i.e., whether they were independent or part of a larger organization). Employment and earnings outcomes were analyzed by tracking them at PE-acquired *establishments* for five years before and after the PE transaction and for two years post-buyout for target *companies*, and then comparing these with outcomes at control establishments and companies. Productivity in manufacturing plants was tracked for five years prior to acquisition and two years post buyout.

The descriptive statistics tell an important story, confirming the observation that private equity firms target better-performing companies. The selection effects of PE are noteworthy. Prior to the buyout, employment growth in the PE target companies is higher—about 2 percent in the five years prior to the buyout plus 2 percent in the acquisition year.[5] Earnings per worker are also higher: "1.1 percent greater than continuing establishments at comparable firms, at the time of private equity transactions"; and labor productivity in manufacturing plants at the time of acquisition is "3.8 percent higher on average at continuing establishments of target firm than at continuing establishments of comparable firms in the same industry and of similar size and age."[6] This is consistent with the findings in Becker and Pollet that greater profitability is a significant predictor that a public company will be taken private.[7]

The econometric analyses (discussed below) show that two years after acquisition, employment and earnings in the target firms have fallen relative to controls, while productivity in the manufacturing plants has grown. These effects are primarily due to greater job creation and destruction, greater downsizing and divestiture of establishments, and greater entry and acquisition of new establishments. It is due to the reallocation of labor across sites within target firms—or organizational restructuring—rather than investments in continuing or existing plants.

The 2008 analysis found that the average cumulative two-year employment difference at PE-owned establishments was 6.7 percent in favor of controls.[8] Results from the 2013 analysis of the smaller subsample of PE-owned companies and establishments are more favorable to private equity, but still show that there was greater job loss in PE-acquired companies and establishments compared to controls.[9] At the establishment level, the researchers found a greater risk of job loss following a PE buyout, with about half of this greater risk being due to a higher probability that the establishment would be shut down following a PE buyout.[10] At the firm level, they found that PE-owned companies were more likely to create new greenfield establishments. Summarizing their findings, Davis and colleagues reported that "employment shrinks more rapidly, on average, at target establishments than at controls after private equity transactions. The average cumulative difference in favor of controls is about 3 percent of initial employment over two years and 6 percent over five years."[11] Not only does net employment in PE-acquired establishments shrink relative to net employment in control establishments, but "[g]ross job destruction at these target establishments outpaces destruction at controls by a cumulative 10 percentage points over five years post buyout. These results say that pre-existing employment positions are at greater risk of loss in the wake of private equity buyouts."[12] Manufacturing, retail, and services are the industry sectors in which private equity was most active in the 1980 to 2001 period.[13] The five-year cumulative effect on employment in establishments in these sectors was negative in all three industry sectors, and most strongly negative in the retail sector.[14]

Despite these findings regarding job destruction in establishments, Davis and his colleagues concluded that employment growth in PE target companies is only slightly less than in controls. They reported that "employment shrinks by less than 1 percent at target companies relative to controls in the first two years after private equity buyouts."[15] To reach this conclusion, they first added together the numbers of jobs gained and lost at continuing establishments, jobs lost at establishments that shut down, and jobs gained at greenfield establishments.[16] Job loss at target companies relative to controls over the two-year time horizon on this basis was 3.62 percentage points,[17] rather than the 6.7 percentage points found in the 2008 study. To reach the conclusion in the 2013 study that job losses were less than 1 percent at PE-owned companies relative to controls, the researchers also included the effects of *acquisitions and divestitures* of establishments on job creation. Since PE-owned firms acquire more establishments than do publicly-owned companies, this calculation reduced the employment differences between the two types of companies. "Acquired" jobs, however, are not created by private equity, but simply "inherited." Jobs are transferred from the payroll of one company to another, with no net job creation in the economy as a whole.

One further finding warranting attention concerns a subset of companies in the sample that focuses only on public companies that are bought out and taken private. Including acquisitions and divestitures, the researchers found that in these buyouts, "target employment contracts by more than 10 percent relative to controls" in the first two years post-buyout.[18] Looking more narrowly at job creation and destruction in public-to-private PE transactions, the analysis showed that while employment growth in continuing establishments of target companies modestly exceeded that in control companies, the deaths of establishments in target companies greatly exceeded those in control companies and the births of establishments (new greenfield establishments) in target companies lagged substantially behind those in control companies.[19] This suggests that if the acquisition and divestiture of establishments were not included, the employment contraction at PE target companies in public-to-private buyouts relative to control companies would be even steeper.

The researchers report a striking contrast in private equity buyouts of privately held (that is, independent) companies, with employment at targets apparently growing 10 percent relative to controls in the first two years post buyout. But here, nearly all of the positive job "creation" is the result of far greater acquisition of existing establishments by PE targets than by controls.[20] Employment growth in the continuing establishments of target companies modestly exceeded that of control companies; deaths of establishments in targets modestly exceeded those in controls; and establishment births (new greenfield establishments) in targets lagged slightly behind those in controls. This suggests that, without the inclusion of acquisition and divestiture of establishments, the effect of PE buyouts of privately held companies on employment relative to controls would be a wash.

With respect to productivity growth among U.S. manufacturing companies, Davis and his colleagues found that the labor productivity gap between targets and controls grows from 3.8 percent at the time of acquisition to 5.1 percent two years later.[21] The 2013 analyses show a 2.14 log point gain for total factor productivity (TFP) at the targets over the two-year period, with entry and exit effects accounting for 74 percent of the higher growth at the target firms.[22] Among continuing establishments, PE target companies were much more likely to close those plants with lower productivity than were the control companies. Thus downsizing and plant closings were an important source of productivity growth. The authors note that, "If private equity buyouts improve relative TFP in continuing plants, the effects are either too small to reliably discern in our sample, or the gains mount too slowly to capture in our two-year tracking interval."[23]

These quantitative results leave some questions unanswered. Recall first that the sample was restricted to companies that can be tracked for two years after the PE investment and omits companies that disappear entirely, which may, of course, have been poor performers with low productivity growth. For those companies in the sample, however, it is clear that much of the apparent improvement in productivity was simply a composition effect due to the closing of some plants and shifting of work to the more productive ones. It is not possible with this type of aggregate data to evaluate whether the more productive plants benefited from investments made by the prior owners or the new PE owners. In particular, we cannot tell whether the higher productivity plants benefited from new investments in employee skills, technology, and work organization or from the use of temporary or "flexible" workers[24] and workers going along with a new management strategy of work intensification out of concern that their work site would be downsized or closed.[25]

The impact of private equity on wage levels is particularly noteworthy. Overall, earnings per worker (EPW) at the target firms, which were 1.1 percent higher than controls in the acquisition year, fell by 4 log points in the two years post-buyout.[26] Additional analyses show that earnings per worker particularly fell in wholesale, retail, and services (by 6 to 8 log points)—sectors that disproportionately employ less skilled and low-wage workers. But wages increased by 9 log points in PE firms in financial services, insurance, and real estate—industries that disproportionately hire skilled and higher paid workers. Employee wages also fell dramatically in public-to-private deals (7 log points) and by 2 points in private-to-private deals. In manufacturing, employment fell markedly while productivity rose and wages were stagnant.[27]

The findings also suggest that private equity restructuring strategies increase wage inequality through several different mechanisms. First, they depress wages in already lower wage industries and raise wages in already higher wage industries. Second, workers employed in private equity buyouts are more likely to lose their jobs, and the best econometric studies of job loss show that when unemployed workers find new jobs, they typically earn lower wages and benefits and have lower wage-earnings profiles over their lifetimes.[28]

Davis and his colleagues also conclude that ". . . private equity firms are increasing the gap between productivity and earnings per worker."[29] That is, private equity firms raise productivity while lowering employment and earnings of employees, thereby shifting the distribution of performance gains from workers to themselves. These findings are consistent with the shareholder theory of the firm, promoted from the 1970s on, in which a larger share of the wealth from productive activities is shifted from other stakeholders to shareholders.

The fact that employment and productivity effects largely occur through job reallocation across plants provides some insights into private equity operational strategies. As Davis and his colleagues note, "The job reallocation rate at target firms exceeds that of controls by 14 percentage points over two years post buyout. About 45 percent of the extra job reallocation reflects a more rapid pace of organic employment adjustments [within target firms], and the rest reflects acquisitions and divestitures."[30] While the authors do not decompose the relative contributions to productivity of existing establishments versus acquisitions and divestitures, it is likely that they follow the pattern of job reallocation. That is, more productivity improvements appear to come from buying and selling plants. This type of "creative destruction" strategy raises the question: Would productivity gains have been higher if private equity had invested the same resources in continuing plants where skilled labor already existed, rather than recruiting and training new workers at newer sites? The reallocation strategy seems consistent with private equity's overall preference for buying and selling—companies and pieces of companies—rather than reinvesting in existing ones, perhaps because this better meets their shorter time horizon.

The downside of the reallocation strategy is that it creates higher levels of churn—not only labor displacement but also the relocation of families who need to follow jobs—for example, from the rustbelt to the sunbelt. Closing factories rather than investing in them destabilizes communities that are left with fewer jobs and with shuttered buildings whose maintenance or rebuilding costs the communities must bear. Reallocation also facilitates de-unionization as older union sites are closed and non-union sites are opened elsewhere. This process is illustrated in three of our cases that follow—US Foods, Archway & Mother's Cookies, and Stella D'oro.

It is not possible to untangle what proportion of wealth extraction for private equity comes from productivity improvements versus financial engineering or tax advantages. But clearly, the econometric evidence shows that PE general partners, on average, make quite different strategic calculations regarding the companies they own—compared to public corporations—and that they are able to manage and control the operations and employment decisions of portfolio companies sufficiently to produce substantially different results. As investors, they clearly take charge: They manage the companies they own and determine the employment security and wages of employees in their portfolio companies. In sum, the econometric findings for employment, productivity, and employee wage levels appear broadly consistent with the case study literature, which we turn to now.

Case Studies of Labor-Management Relations

The quantitative evidence suggests that private equity ownership, on average, lowers employment levels and the earnings of workers while improving productivity. The aggregate data do not, however, shed light on the mechanisms through which these effects occur, nor on the range of variation in the management and labor strategies of PE firms compared to their publicly owned counterparts. Productivity improvements may occur through investments in new technologies and workforce skills and organization that increase output for a given staffing level, or through work intensification and layoffs that simply reduce the denominator without increasing production.

Case studies provide the opportunity to interpret quantitative trends, with real stories of how new private equity owners influence workplace processes and negotiate or not with unions around jobs, wages, and benefits. Although private equity typically targets healthy companies, our cases also include the acquisition of companies that were facing financial distress or bankruptcy. The cases cover a wide range of industries, from aerospace, auto supply, and steel to food processing and distribution, hospitality, health care, and energy production and distribution. They include large PE buyout houses like KKR, Blackstone, and Bain Capital as well as midsize or small firms like Catterton Partners and Brynwood Partners and specialized firms like Onex Partners.

We begin by discussing the more constructive instances in which private equity negotiated in good faith with unions and worked to preserve employment, wage, and benefit levels, given the economic context they faced. We then turn to more destructive cases in which private equity focused more on financial engineering than on investing in operational improvements, resulting in a loss in jobs, wages, and/or benefits for employees and, at times, putting the entire enterprise in financial distress. A third category of cases are those in which labor relations begin with high levels of conflict, but union militancy is able to convince the new PE owners to negotiate with labor. Finally, we end with more complex cases in which private equity firms have negotiated in good faith with unions, but the outcomes of the PE buyout are uncertain because of the high levels of debt incurred or the financial engineering undertaken. The appendix to this chapter provides a summary of these cases.

Constructive Approaches to Labor-Management Relations

A small number of private equity firms have made a strategic decision to work constructively with labor—either for philosophical reasons or because it makes good business sense. The founder of Yucaipa, Ron

Burkle, for example, has received a number of awards from labor organizations, including the AFL-CIO and the Los Angeles Labor Federation, for his commitment to enhancing community economic development and labor relations.[31] Another boutique firm, BlueWolf Capital Partners, highlights on its website its constructive relationships with labor unions as a source of added value.[32] Similarly, KPS Partners states that its "ability to work constructively with major unions in North America and increasingly in Western Europe has resulted in the creation of enterprises that are profitable and positioned for success over the long term."[33] In a 2013 acquisition of Wausau Paper, it negotiated a collective bargaining agreement with the unions as a condition for acquiring the company and agreed to assume liability for defined-benefit-pension and other post-retirement-benefit obligations.[34] The largest Canadian private equity firm, Onex Partners, which we feature in the following case study, has a strong track record of working successfully with unions. Often, however, a constructive approach to unions is based on pure pragmatism—as we show in the case of Wilbur Ross and the steelworkers union—in that the skilled workers represented by the union were critical to the financial success of the enterprise. In the case of the acquisition of Dana Corporation, the lead negotiator at Centerbridge Partners, a relatively new PE firm, was philosophically committed to working with the union and saving the company.

Spirit AeroSystems: Labor Management Engagement in Aerospace Spirit AeroSystems represents a relatively successful case of constructive union-management negotiations in a large private equity buyout. The new PE owners succeeded in gaining union contract concessions, but labor-management relations generally have been productive and have provided the basis for the enterprise remaining successful and for the workforce sharing in that success. The company was formed in 2005 when Onex Private Equity Partners purchased Boeing's Wichita aircraft division. The division was the largest manufacturer of Tier 1 aero structures in the world, producing products and services such as fuselage systems, propulsion systems, and wing systems for aircraft original equipment manufacturers and other operators in North America and Europe. Boeing wanted to outsource manufacturing and get rid of what it called "under-performing assets," but others argue that this move was part of a larger Boeing strategy to outsource parts and create cost competition between Boeing plants and outside suppliers. Boeing also complained about high union wages and inflexible work rules, and the company had a legacy of negative relations with the International Association of Machinists and Aerospace Workers (IAM). The professional-technical and engineering workforce is represented by the Society of Professional Engineering Employees in Aerospace (SPEEA). At the time of the Onex acquisition, the division had a workforce of over 12,000, with over 6,000 represented by IAM and 4,600 by SPEEA.[35]

The spin-off of the Boeing aircraft division was a risky proposition in the eyes of many union leaders and employees. They believed that the success of aerospace manufacturing depended on an integrated approach in which divisions coordinated with one another to produce the final product, and companies have more leverage to induce or demand coordination across units than do independent companies across a supply chain. Once the Wichita plant was outsourced as an independent company, it no longer faced internal pressures for coordination. Instead, it faced external pressures from the private equity owners to maximize shareholder value, regardless of whether the results were the best in terms of the quality of the aircraft that Boeing was assembling. Some critics argue that this type of outsourcing led to the problems that Boeing faced with its 787 Dreamliner.[36] Specifically, the Wichita plant produced high-value-added systems that required precision engineering and a highly skilled workforce. Other companies to which work was outsourced by Boeing did not necessarily meet these standards. In addition, Boeing insisted that the new company would need to develop other customers—a difficult task in a market where the entire customer base consisted of perhaps five large aircraft manufacturers.[37] Onex would need to develop a diversified customer base for Spirit to be successful. Initially, Spirit was able to negotiate long-term exclusive supply agreements with Boeing for all products and services previously supplied for the 737, 747, 767, 777, and new 787 platforms. Subsequently, it diversified by acquiring the aerostructures unit of BAE Systems in the United Kingdom in 2006, thus adding Airbus as a significant new customer.[38]

For Onex, the role of the unions in the deal was critical because they represented the highly skilled workforce needed to run the plant. The machinists union had maintained a strong position against changes in wages and work rules that management viewed as uncompetitive. Onex felt that it especially needed assurances from the IAM that it would get job cuts and wage and work rule concessions before the deal could be signed. When Onex did not get those assurances, it nonetheless took the risk and acquired the aircraft division. Onex reportedly put up $464 million of the $1.5 billion purchase price—or 31 percent of the total.[39]

To engage with the IAM, Onex immediately hired an outside labor consulting group, the Gephardt Group, which had substantial credibility among unions. Spirit also retained Jeff Turner, a former Boeing management executive, who also had trust and credibility with workers and worked well with the head of the IAM, Tom Buffenbarger. Spirit and the IAM negotiated a concessionary contract in 2005 with the combined effort of top management and union leadership and the Gephardt Group. Workers initially turned down the contract, but later passed a version with minor changes, under persuasion from the labor-management leadership team. The five-year contract included job cuts of roughly 15 percent of the workforce, wage reductions of 10 percent, and minor work rule changes. A certain number of laid-off employees, whom management considered "poor performers," were not included on the recall list. In exchange, union members who were "first day" hires (but not new hires) would receive stock and cash payouts when the company went public. The contract maintained a defined-benefit pension plan.[40]

The technical, professional, and engineering employees took a different approach. They refused to accept wage cuts in exchange for participation in the proceeds of an initial public offering in 2006. Instead, they maintained their wage rates and also negotiated an innovative job security plan that replaced the conventional layoff system with a "shortweek" system in the event of economic difficulties. They used this provision during a Boeing strike: employees worked a three-day week, supplemented by unemployment benefits, and did not lose health or other company benefits. However, concessions in the medical retiree program increased the early retirement age from fifty-five to sixty-two and increased premium contributions. The SPEEA workforce also was reduced by 6 percent. To get the contract passed, SPEEA required the chief company negotiator to present the contract to the members and explain the logic of the concessions.[41]

These cost-cutting measures, coupled with a dramatic increase in demand for aircraft, led to a major turnaround for Spirit that far exceeded expectations. Spirit's revenues climbed from $3.2 billion in 2006 to $4.1 billion in 2007. The company went public in November 2006 and raised $1.4 billion in the IPO (more than enough to repay Onex's initial investment), and machinist members received $61,000 each in cash and stock—double what they had expected. The SPEEA members were initially disgruntled at not receiving a payout from the IPO until the union was able to show them that by maintaining their wage rates they more than made up the difference. At the time of the IPO, the company reported that it employed 11,600 workers.

The 2010 IAM negotiations focused on job security. The IAM had previously offered Boeing a ten-year contract, but Boeing turned it down. Onex and the IAM at Spirit took up the idea and negotiated a controversial ten-year agreement that required CEO Turner, IAM president Buffenbarger, and representatives of the Gephardt Group to engage in workshops with frontline employees, line managers, and stewards to listen to their concerns and explain the benefits of a contract that aligned the interests of management and employees. The final contract granted workers ten years of job security at the Wichita plant in exchange for pay flexibility through some additional gain-sharing and profit-sharing programs. The contract made few changes in the health care plan and also locked in the current defined-benefit plan.[42]

Job security has not been a major issue for the SPEEA workforce, and in fact, the company has had to raise base salary rates above the contract minimum for engineers in order to retain them. The SPEEA contracts were negotiated for engineers in 2009 (for three years) and 2012 (for six years) and for the professional-technical unit in 2011 (for nine and a half years). In both second contracts, the union negotiated strong contracts, but also a performance bonus plan that has had disappointing payouts.[43]

The leadership of both unions has characterized their relationship with Onex as positive and that with the former Boeing management still at Spirit as much improved. This is not to suggest that contract negotiations have been easy or that disagreements do not surface, but both unions say that their relationship with management has become more productive and that it allows them to discuss problems openly when conflicts emerge. In 2013, SPEEA represented approximately 3,170 professional, technical, and engineering employees, while the machinists had over 6,000 members at Wichita. In addition, in April 2012, the IAM organized 126 workers at a newly opened facility in Kingston, North Carolina, which Spirit built to design and manufacture major parts for Airbus aircraft.[44] In December 2012, the IAM and management negotiated a twelve-year contract, approved by the membership, which continues unless either party wishes to reopen negotiations. A joint partnership committee will oversees the agreement.[45]

Onex and its Onex Partners I Fund have realized outsized investment returns from Spirit, which had reached $2.5 billion as of 2011.[46] Following the 2007 IPO, the company issued two additional IPO offerings: one in May 2007 for $1.05 billion, and one in April 2011 for $245 million. Onex is still the majority owner.[47] These gains did not come at the expense of Spirit's financial condition, which remained strong through 2011, despite the fact that projects involving new customers met with many challenges and led to millions of dollars in losses until the company had had enough experience to be able to build the new products and cost the contracts appropriately. Total annual revenues were $3.2 billion at the time of the 2006 IPO, $4.86 billion at the 2011 IPO, and $5.19 billion as of September 2012. The company reported that it employed 12,000 workers in 2012.[48] Total assets were $5.37 billion in January 2013, compared to $3.1 billion in 2006.

Despite these successes, however, the Dreamliner debacle caused the company to take a write-down of $184 million in 2012 as well as cut costs.[49] The CEO who led the company in its constructive relations with its unions, Jeff Turner, retired in November 2012.[50] And union relations in 2013 were scarred by a sudden decision by the company to fire thirty-seven engineering employees, drawing attention to the fragile nature of these labor-management partnerships.[51]

Distressed Investing: Saving the U.S. Steel Industry After the decimation of much of the steel industry in the 1980s—when U.S. steel employment fell from 399,000 in 1980 to 204,000 in 1990[52]—the industry enjoyed a brief period of recovery in the early to mid-1990s. To improve productivity, some major integrated mills began to restructure and adopt work organization strategies more common in the successful mini-mills.[53] In the context of growing worldwide demand for steel in the mid-1990s, productivity improved and employment loss slowed. However, the 1997 East Asian economic crisis led to a wave of cheap steel imports as countries dumped steel in the American market. China's entry into the World Trade Organization in 2001 hit U.S. steel markets even harder, and by 2001 global overcapacity in the industry was estimated at about 300 million tons.[54] Steel prices plummeted, and between 1998 and 2003, forty-five steel companies declared bankruptcy, eighteen mills were shut down, and 55,000 steelworkers lost their jobs. The steel industry lost $12 billion between the fourth quarters of 2000 and 2003. Sixteen pension plans covering over 250,000 employees, with $10 billion in underfunded benefits, were terminated and turned over to the Pension Benefit Guaranty Corporation. And over 210,000 retirees and their dependents lost their retiree health care benefits.[55]

It was in this context that Wilbur Ross, an investment banker with twenty-five years' experience, made a deal with the steelworkers union. His experience as an adviser to shareholders in bankruptcy restructuring cases at Rothschild, Inc., had given him the know-how to assess the value of distressed industries and make money by restructuring them. He had established the WL Ross & Co. investment firm in 2000 and attracted institutional investors such as CalPERS, GE Capital, and Goldman Sachs.[56] In 2002 he formed the International Steel Group (ISG) to serve as a platform for buying four LTV Steel facilities, and in 2003 he acquired a US Steel plate mill and Bethlehem Steel Corporation's liquidated plants. Taken together, Ross had acquired a 20 percent ownership stake in the industry.[57] In 2004 Ross completed his acquisitions in steel with Georgetown Steel, Weirton Steel, and facilities in Trinidad and Tobago owned by HBI.

The key to turning around the steel plants and making a profit was to buy the mills out of bankruptcy—to gain clout, get the assets at a bargain, and rid the company of its legacy health care and pension liabilities. Ross bought the Cleveland steel mills and other assets of LTV out of bankruptcy for $90 million in cash, plus $235 million in assumed liabilities—or just over 25 percent cash and the remainder in debt.[58] Ross typically bought about one-third of the debt of a bankrupt company he intended to bid on and then turned it into equity later in order to gain leverage in the bankruptcy proceedings.[59] The cash payment made by his firm and its limited partner investors equaled 3.6 percent of the $2.5 billion value of the assets on the books.

Timing and political support also mattered. Ross was aware that President George W. Bush was contemplating the imposition of tariffs on imported steel to offset illegal dumping by foreign steelmakers. While other steel manufacturers were campaigning against tariffs on steel, Ross embraced them as a means for the U.S. industry to recover. On October 23, 2001, the U.S. International Trade Commission concluded that twelve out of thirty-three types of steel products had been adversely affected by the dumping of imports. On March 5, 2002, a month after Ross purchased LTV, Bush imposed a 30 percent temporary tariff on fourteen of the categories of steel. The tariffs continued until December 4, 2003—a critical eighteen months in the restructuring of LTV, Acme, and Bethlehem Steel. The tariffs enabled the U.S. steel industry to recover sufficiently to take advantage of rising steel prices, demand spurred by China's explosive growth, and a 0 percent financing scheme for car buyers from the U.S. auto industry.[60]

Ross had begun negotiating with the steelworkers union in 2001, prior to purchasing LTV. Ron Bloom, then special assistant to the USWA president Leo Gerard, played a critical role, as he was able to draw on his prior experience in turnaround and restructuring cases at Lazard Frères & Co. and his own investment banking firm, Keilin and Bloom. The union had been in a protracted twelve-month fight with LTV during its bankruptcy, with LTV demanding $1.3 billion in concessions in wages, benefits, overtime pay, and job security, as well as other nonmonetary contract provisions. The union agreed to a modified labor agreement (MLA) approved by the federal bankruptcy court to keep the plants open, but LTV demanded further concessions and moved ahead with liquidation, which the court approved in December 2001.[61] Wilbur Ross, by contrast, did not carry the kind of animosity toward the union that the legacy companies did. As Tom Conway, an international vice president of the steelworkers union who was involved in the negotiations, notes, "The difference with these private equity guys is that they are who they are—a degree of honesty about them—I'm looking to make money, I'm not your friend." The union shared Ross's pragmatic approach. It had no particular position toward private equity, but rather wanted to work with someone who was willing to sit down and bargain directly to keep the businesses going.

The steelworkers union, which had been doing its own research into the economics of the industry, recognized the need for restructuring and work reorganization. The cost structure of the integrated mills was much higher than the mini-mills, owing to high levels of management overhead, inefficient work organization and technology, and retiree health and pension costs. Retiree costs in the top seven integrated mills equaled 12 percent of the weighted average price per ton of steel; while the top mini-mills had an operating surplus of $30 per ton in 2000, the top integrated mills were losing $41 per ton.[62] While managers in the integrated mills thought that they could retreat to the high end of the steel market and leave the low end to the mini-mills, the union saw it differently. The industry was fragmented and in need of consolidation, and it probably had room for two major integrated mill players. The union had developed a plan to work with the integrated mills to improve operations. According to Tom Conway, who played a major role in the restructuring process, "We concluded that if we didn't come to operate like mini-mills, then we could make concessions and give up health care and pensions and the integrated mills still would not be able to compete."[63] The legacy of poor labor relations and mistrust, however, made it almost impossible to develop this kind of joint productivity pact, and each company rejected the union plan out of hand.

"It was Wilbur who got it," says Conway. "He took the USW work plan and implemented it. He had the capital, could talk to labor, and avoided the drama. He originally took LTV, then others. He took our work plan and said, 'I don't know anything about making steel.'"[64] The agreement with Ross was made with a handshake, and the steelworkers worked without a full contract until December 2002. The work plan included looser work rules, cuts in benefits, and union layoffs in exchange for management layoffs and the union's major role in managing the plants. Ross reopened the LTV operations with about three thousand workers and a new management team from Nucor Steel.[65] The union accepted workforce reductions of 20 percent, mainly among the oldest workers, and management's ranks declined by 40 percent.[66] Ross consulted with the union in deciding which managers to let go.

Productivity improvements were immense. ISG was able to reduce man-hours of labor per ton from two and a half to one, resulting in a cost of $250 per ton (half the cost of production under LTV and Bethlehem) when steel was selling for $300 per ton.[67] The union's work reorganization plan played a major role in the turnaround. Under the prior "Taylorist" system of job structures, work was divided into thirty-six narrowly defined jobs with little differentiation in pay (about ten cents per hour), so workers had little incentive to learn new jobs or train replacements. Under the new plan, according to Tom Conway, "we took six broad categories and slotted about six old jobs into each. Then we had to retrain everyone to learn the new jobs. Old mill management was saying, 'This can't work.' PE said, 'Looks like it can.' It took fine-tuning over a couple of years, but we got through it, and the structure is now used throughout industry. Then we negotiated about a $1.25 an hour differential between grades to give incentives to gain skills. We restructured work in the integrated mills along the lines of the mini mills."[68]

The six-year bargaining agreement with ISG, signed in December 2002, became the model for a 2003 integrated steel agreement covering all workers in former LTV, Acme, and Bethlehem operations. It set base wages at $15 to $20.50 per hour, plus an incentive bonus plan and profit-sharing; provided for health care coverage, full-time work hours, overtime pay, and seniority; and included important nonmonetary clauses, such as the maintenance of standard contract protections, a neutrality clause, and limits on pay for top managers. It also established an expanded role for the union in running the plants, including implementation of the work redesign plan, an extensive training program, health and safety committees, a "lay-off minimization plan," and a union nominee to the ISG board of directors. Active union members were folded into the Steelworkers Pension Trust, a multi-employer defined-benefit pension plan.[69]

The members hardest hit by the restructuring of the mills were older workers who were targeted for layoffs and retirees, who under the bankruptcy rulings lost their health care coverage and saw their pensions diminished under the PBGC insurance plan. The union openly said that workers over fifty-five would not be retrained for the redesigned jobs, and it negotiated a transition assistance program (TAP), which gave laid-off workers up to $50,000 in severance and one year of health care coverage. To cover retiree health care costs beyond the initial year, the union negotiated to establish a voluntary employees' beneficiary association (VEBA), with contributions contingent on corporate profitability.[70] Given the context and the opportunity to save the industry, most union members understood that these difficult choices were necessary.

By April 2005, Ross had sold ISG to Mittal Steel for $4.5 billion in cash and stock, making an estimated fourteen times his investment in less than two years.[71] Although the deal between Ross and the steelworkers union saved the industry, the bittersweet pill for the union was that Ross's profits almost exactly equaled the losses sustained in the pension and health care programs for retirees. In 2006 Mittal merged with Arcelor Steel, based in Belgium, to become the world's largest steel producer. The ISG mills continue to operate competitively, and the next round of collective bargaining negotiations occurred in 2012.

Distressed Investing and Union Negotiations in Auto Supply Wilbur Ross's foray into distressed steel is one of the most dramatic instances of private equity labor-management cooperation, driven in this case by Ross's need for skilled labor to restart the mills and by the steelworkers' desire to save the industry and jobs. Centerbridge Capital Partners is another PE firm that worked with the steelworkers and autoworkers unions, this time to bring Dana Corporation out of bankruptcy with a new contract.

Dana Corporation, a major supplier of core parts to the auto industry, had generated more than $2 billion in losses in five years, owing to overleverage (an aggressive expansion campaign in the early 2000s), an overly complex global footprint as a result of the expansion, and declining revenues from the auto industry.[72] It filed for Chapter 11 bankruptcy in March 2006.[73] It had had a contentious relationship with the USWA and the United Auto Workers (UAW); in the context of the bankruptcy, it took an aggressive stance toward the unions and would only bargain separately with them. When the parties could not reach an agreement, Dana asked the bankruptcy court to void the labor agreement in early 2007. Ron Bloom approached Centerbridge as a potential investor, and the USWA retained Centerbridge as an adviser.[74] The newly formed PE firm Centerbridge Partners had just raised its first PE fund and was looking for its initial investment. Its auto industry expert, Steve Girsky, had joined Centerbridge after serving as special adviser to the former GM CEO Rick Wagoner. (Girsky would become GM's vice chairman of corporate strategy and business development in 2010.) Bloom and Girsky provided the kind of experience and trust that could bring the parties together. Centerbridge was critical in convincing Dana Corporation to negotiate jointly with the two unions, and it sat on the unions' side of the table.[75]

In bankruptcy court, the company sought to completely void its obligations to retirees,[76] which totaled $1.1 billion for union retirees, but in negotiations it agreed to establish a VEBA to cover retiree health and long-term disability and to contribute $700 million in cash to the fund, plus approximately $80 million in common stock of the reorganized company. The USWA and UAW pension plans were frozen, but the company retained pension liabilities, and the new contract folded active members into the multi-employer plan of the Steelworkers Pension Trust. Dana also won a two-tier wage structure for selected plants, reduced disability benefits, and a freeze on the accrual of credited service and benefits under the pension plans for current employees. The company estimated that it would save $100 million annually as a result of the negotiations.

Central to the court's acceptance of the reorganization plan was Centerbridge's agreement to invest $500 million in cash for convertible preferred stock (estimated to be worth up to 25 percent of the diluted common stock of the new company) and to facilitate the investment of up to $250 million by other investors. Other cost savings came from renegotiated contracts with customers (an estimated $180 million annually), cuts in non-union employee benefits (approximately equal in value to the union cuts), and reductions in overhead ($40 million to $50 million annually).[77] When the company emerged from bankruptcy in January 2008, Centerbridge played a central role in implementing the reorganization plan and appointed three of the seven directors in the reorganized company.[78]

The unions made important gains as well for the 4,300 workers covered by the contract. In an unusual development, the key elements of the reorganization plan were included in the contract, with the unions having the right to strike if the company made changes to the plan. The contract also stipulated a limit on debt liabilities of $1.5 billion and a target liquidity cushion of a minimum of $1 billion—which later saved the company from bankruptcy during the financial crisis in 2008 and 2009. The company has been profitable since then. Dana also agreed to neutrality provisions, and the unions eventually organized almost all of the company's unorganized plants. Constructive labor relations continued through the decade, and the parties worked out a positive agreement in 2011.[79]

Financial Engineering and Financial Distress: Lost Jobs and Employee Welfare

The approaches taken by Onex Partners, Wilbur Ross, and Centerbridge stand as unusual examples of private equity's willingness to deal pragmatically with American labor in the restructuring of manufacturing plants. These cases demonstrate the fact that PE owners can make their targeted returns while still negotiating agreements with unions that provide workers with at least some level of job security and decent wages and benefits, as well as a voice in ongoing decisions over operations. The next set of cases show the opposite—PE owners focusing on financial engineering and the extraction of wealth at the expense of employees and, in some cases, the sustainability of the enterprise. Delphi Automotive and Hawker Beechcraft represent large leveraged buyouts, while Archway & Mother's Cookies Company and Stella D'oro Biscuit Company were both small niche companies that ended in bankruptcy after a PE buyout.

Financial Engineering and Outsourcing in Auto Supply The restructuring of Delphi Automotive Corporation, following the financial crash, provides an example in which not only employees but also taxpayers subsidized the outsized returns of the private equity and hedge fund owners of Delphi while these owners restructured the company, closed all but four of its twenty-nine operating plants in the United States, and sent all of the twenty-five thousand union jobs to China. Other buyers who lost the bid would have saved American jobs.

Delphi, a critical parts internal supplier to GM, was spun off from GM in 1999 as its own independent company. After Delphi declared bankruptcy in 2005, several private equity firms and hedge funds started buying up its distressed debt at bargain prices—some at 20 cents on the dollar—including Elliott Management, a PE and hedge fund firm; the PE firm Third Point Partners; and the hedge funds Silver Point Capital and John Paulson & Company. The auto industry task force, headed by Steven Rattner, began its work in February 2009 to negotiate a deal between auto industry companies and their creditors to save the industry. GM and the U.S. Treasury had been working with the United Auto Workers to develop a joint venture with Platinum Equity, a buyout firm owned by Michigan native Tom Gores, whose firm had worked with Delphi for years, who understood the auto parts business, and who felt loyal to Delphi and GM. The plan would have returned key Delphi operations to GM, closed fourteen plants, and kept the remaining union plants open.[80]

Delphi had reached an agreement to sell most of its global operations to Platinum Equity for $3.6 billion. General Motors would have provided $250 million to finance Delphi's operations until it exited bankruptcy and would have provided more than $2.5 billion of the $3.6 billion that Platinum Equity bid for control of the company. GM would have acquired some of Delphi's plants and its global steering division. The new Delphi would have assumed the majority ($2.1 billion) of pension liabilities. Negotiations were under way with GM about the possibility of it assuming the remaining assets and liabilities of Delphi's hourly pension plan.[81]

Delphi's PE and hedge fund creditors, however, rejected the deal and demanded twice as much for the bonds they held as the deal could pay. In the meantime, Elliott Management tripled its acquisition of Delphi bonds—paying 20 percent of their face value—and joined with Paulson, Silver Point, and Third Point to control Delphi. Delphi offered to forgo the Platinum plan if the PE firms and hedge funds would agree to a plan that would save as many jobs as possible. But the PE and hedge fund creditors said no. Instead, they persuaded the bankruptcy judge to hold an auction for all of Delphi's stock.[82] On July 28, 2009, Platinum Equity lost the auction for the company. The creditors' group outbid Platinum Equity, paying 67 cents per share. On August 3, 2009, Delphi won court approval to sell its steering business and four plants to GM, with the remaining businesses going to the creditors, who sent the work and twenty-five thousand union jobs to China. The company is now incorporated overseas.[83]

Two years later, in November 2011, Delphi's new owners—the consortium of creditors that won the auction for the company—took Delphi public. Shorn of its health care and pension liabilities, and with its debt burden substantially reduced, Delphi commanded a price of $22 per share at its IPO, earning a profit of more than 3,000 percent for the PE firms and hedge funds that owned it. Since then, the company's share price has increased substantially.[84] It stood at $30 a share in November 2012 and almost $60 a share in December 2013.

These gains could not have been made without taxpayer subsidies. In a March 2009 meeting between the Treasury, GM, and the consortium of creditors, the consortium demanded that the Treasury give it $350 million or it would shut Delphi down. Delphi held inventory that was absolutely critical to the survival of GM, and the consortium got its money. At the same time, claiming cash shortage, it eliminated health insurance for its non-union pensioners; the Treasury task force later found that millions of dollars had been withheld by debt-holders from Delphi accounts. Then, in July 2009, the consortium of creditors that took over Delphi refused to pay any U.S. worker pensions, forcing a government agency, the Pension Benefit Guaranty Corporation, to take over the Delphi pension system. By its own rules, the PBGC had no choice and had to cut the pension benefits of higher-paid, mainly salaried workers; twenty thousand workers were forced to accept substantially reduced pensions.[85]

In addition to the losses in jobs and retirement security for twenty-five thousand autoworkers, taxpayers subsidized Delphi for a total of $12.9 billion. The cost to the government agency of taking over the Delphi pension payments was $5.6 billion. GM also forgave money owed it by Delphi. In reality, this money was in fact owed to the U.S. Treasury (and thus to the American people), as the Treasury was the majority owner of GM at the time. GM forgave $2.5 billion in debt owed to it by Delphi and $2 billion that the creditors' consortium owed to it upon Delphi's exit from Chapter 11 bankruptcy. In addition, Delphi received $2.8 billion in funds from the Troubled Asset Relief Program (TARP) to keep it operating.[86] In a recent assessment of the Delphi Corporation, one of the PE owners, Third Point's Daniel Loeb, reportedly told his investors that Delphi was an exceptional investment because "it has 'virtually no North American unionized labor' and, thanks to U.S. taxpayers, 'significantly smaller pension liabilities than almost all of its peers.'"[87]

Overleverage at Hawker Beechcraft Aerospace The aerospace corporation Hawker Beechcraft provides an example of an overleveraged and overpriced private equity investment that turned into a disaster for the company, employees, creditors, and investors when the financial crisis hit in 2008. On March 26, 2007, GS Capital (the PE arm of Goldman Sachs) and Onex Partners (the largest Canadian PE firm) purchased the Hawker and Beechcraft aerospace divisions of Raytheon for approximately $3.3 billion—paid largely with debt—and renamed it Hawker Beechcraft.[88] It was the largest PE acquisition in the industry, out of a total of eighty-five acquisitions made between 2004 and 2009.[89] The company designed, marketed, and provided support services for business and specialty aircraft for government, military, corporate, and individual customers.[90] Roughly 30 percent of its business came from government contracts.[91] Its manufacturing workforce is represented by the International Association of Machinists.

At the time of the acquisition, the company was in strong financial condition. By May 3, 2012, however, Hawker Beechcraft had filed for bankruptcy protection. At the time, its debt obligations—principal and accrued interest—were $2.6 billion.[92] In 2008 the financial crisis caused a severe downturn in the demand for business jets (a major line of business for Hawker Beechcraft). All of the major competitors serving this market segment—including Cessna, Learjet, Gulfstream Aerospace, Textron, and Embraer—suffered. Only Hawker Beechcraft, however, laid off thousands and went bankrupt. Both industry analysts and the company's own executives and bankruptcy documents attribute the bankruptcy to the combination of the market downturn and an unmanageable debt load from the PE acquisition.[93] In the months before bankruptcy, the company's CEO, Steve Miller, stated that while the company had made efforts to improve its operations, the debt load weighed down its ability to make a turnaround.[94]

The company's labor strategy probably contributed to its poor performance. According to union leaders, the lead private equity partner, GS Capital, did little to build employee commitment or foster a constructive relationship with the union—unlike Onex Corporation in its labor relations strategy at Spirit AeroSystems. The company immediately began production in Mexico, opening its first manufacturing plant in Chihuahua in October 2007 and a second soon thereafter. It claimed that the Mexican facilities would help alleviate space constraints in U.S. operations and establish the company's footprint in Mexico. It anticipated a workforce of roughly nine hundred in Mexico in the next five years.[95]

Union representatives, however, tell a different story—that GS Capital had no commitment to the Wichita plant and was intent on moving production to Mexico as well as Louisiana, where they hoped to take advantage of Hurricane Katrina–linked government subsidies. In addition, parts coming back from Mexican plants were of low quality and had to be reworked. In the first round of contract negotiations, the IAM struck for three weeks when the owners demanded concessions based on the threat of moving jobs to Louisiana. Onex stepped in to broker a deal. The company kept the plant in Wichita by getting the local government to match the subsidies offered by Louisiana.[96] The company subsequently received $45 million in incentives from the state and local governments on condition that it keep at least 4,000 employees in Wichita over ten years.[97] GS Capital has not met that obligation.

In 2008, Hawker Beechcraft employed about 9,800 people, including 7,000 at its Wichita plant and the remainder at operations in Salina, Kansas; Little Rock, Arkansas; Mexico; and the United Kingdom.[98] By late 2008, however, the company started laying off workers, and as of September 2009, 3,553 U.S. workers had lost their jobs—roughly 36 percent of the October 2008 workforce.[99] At the time it sought bankruptcy protection, Hawker Beechcraft employed approximately 5,420 employees, 45 percent of whom (2,430 workers) were covered by the IAM union contract in Wichita.[100]

To stabilize operations over the 2009 to 2012 period, the private equity owners negotiated with lenders, amended various loan agreements to provide additional liquidity, and amended covenants on the loans to avoid default. To reduce the debt load, they bought back some of the company's debt at a discount, at creditors' expense. In October 2010, the company terminated approximately 8 percent of its salaried workforce, closed several facilities in Wichita, outsourced additional operations, and negotiated what the company described as "an innovative and favorable collective bargaining agreement with the IAM and its members." The company also made changes in senior leadership, hiring a new chief financial officer in September 2011 and a new CEO in February 2012.[101]

The union contract, negotiated in August 2011 and approved by 69 percent of the members, exchanged pay and job security for concessions in health care and pensions. The five-year contract included pay raises of 1 percent in each year beginning in 2013, a joint partnership for retraining at the plant, and a job security pledge: "For the term of this agreement, the company will maintain an aircraft manufacturing presence in Wichita, Kansas for composites, assembly, test, paint, inspection, planning, and aircraft completion and delivery."[102] In exchange, workers would shift to a company health care plan and their share of premium payments would increase to 15 percent in 2012, 20 percent in 2013, 25 percent in 2014, and 30 percent in 2015 and 2016. The agreement retained in place the pensions provided in the union's defined-benefit pension plan for vested hourly employees and retirees, but froze any further accruals as of December 31, 2011. It created a new retirement savings plan and retained a 401(k) plan for all workers in which the company matched 50 percent of the employees' first 4 percent contribution.[103] As of January 1, 2011, the union pension plan covered 2,841 active employees, 3,006 employees who were vested but no longer employed at Hawker Beechcraft, and 2,564 retirees.[104]

Despite layoffs, union concessions, and extensions on loans, Hawker filed for Chapter 11 bankruptcy protection on May 3, 2012, to write off $2.6 billion in debt and $1.25 million in annual interest charges.[105] Prior to filing for bankruptcy, the company obtained agreement from a significant majority of its secured lenders and senior bondholders for its proposed financial restructuring—the "Restructuring Support Agreement."[106] Those senior lenders included the hedge funds Centerbridge Partners, Angelo, Gordon & Co., Sankaty Advisors LLC, and Capital Research & Management. In a debt-for-equity swap, they expected to get 89 percent of the equity in the reorganized Hawker, with unsecured creditors getting the remaining 11 percent.[107]

The company's initial request for bankruptcy protection did not include an explicit provision to end its three defined-benefit pension plans. The plans for salaried and non-union hourly workers were closed to new hires as of January 2007, with defined-contribution plans instead covering all new hires.[108] In 2011 the company was able to get an exclusion of new hires from the defined-benefit plan in its negotiations with the union. At the time of the bankruptcy filing, the pensions were underfunded at $600 million, making the Pension Benefit Guaranty Corporation the company's largest creditor.[109] Negotiations through the second half of 2012 ended with a settlement, approved by the bankruptcy court in December. The PBGC took over the plans for the salaried and non-union hourly workers. These workers and retirees will only receive their retirement benefits up to the PBGC maximum guarantee. The PBGC will receive $11 million for the release of liens and an unsecured claim of $419.5 million paid in new stock.[110] Under the union plan, negotiated and approved by the membership in August 2012, the company will retain responsibility for the plan, and union members will receive the full benefits they accrued under the defined-benefit plan plus any new contributions under the defined-contribution plan.[111]

In their attempt to find a buyer for the company, Hawker Beechcraft first chose Superior Aviation Beijing and gained approval in July 2012 from the bankruptcy court to have an exclusive negotiations agreement. The $1.8 billion deal, however, failed. As of December 2012, Hawker Beechcraft's plan to liquidate its jet inventory had been approved, along with its bankruptcy reorganization plan, which included renaming the company Beechcraft Corporation and focusing on a narrower set of products (turboprop, piston, special mission, and trainer/attack aircraft). Interested buyers include Textron, the parent company of Cessna, and Embraer.[112]

In the end, who benefited and who lost from this private equity deal? The bankruptcy lawyers received $10.7 million in fees and $642,000 in expenses for their services to Hawker Beechcraft.[113] The PE owners received undisclosed amounts in fees. The company tried to pay eight senior executives a total of $5.33 million in bonuses in 2012, but the effort was rejected by the bankruptcy court judge, who said the reward was unjustified.[114] Hawker Beechcraft will emerge from bankruptcy as a fraction of the company it was. Thousands of workers lost their jobs, although, fortunately, many did not lose the pensions they had accrued. The union estimates that the Wichita plant will eventually employ about 1,500 machinists—about one-third of the pre-buyout workforce.[115] The losers also include creditors who bought the company's debt and pension funds and other limited partner investors whose investment in the company was nearly wiped out. Within two years of the LBO, Goldman Sachs had written down the value of the company by 85 percent.[116]

Private Equity and Plant Closings in Food Processing Archway & Mother's Cookies, based in Ashland, Ohio, was founded by a husband-and-wife team in Battle Creek, Michigan, in 1936. It specialized in "home-style cookies" and played an important role as an anchor factory in the Ashland area, with a population of 22,000. The factory employed about 275 workers who were represented by the Bakery, Confectionery, Tobacco Workers and Grain Millers International Union (BCTGM). The company underwent two private equity acquisitions in the 2000s that left it in bankruptcy. In 2000, Parmalat Financziaria, an Italian PE investor, purchased

Archway & Mother's for $250 million, but by 2003 the investment company filed for bankruptcy under the weight of $18.2 billion in debt in one of the largest financial scandals in Europe (unrelated to Archway). The Catterton Partners private equity firm picked up the company for an undisclosed amount in January 2005.[117]

Catterton, known for buying and fixing up midmarket consumer products companies, promised to improve Archway & Mother's Cookies' sales and competitive position. It put three of its partners on the company's board of directors, and unlike other PE firms, it hired an outside management company, Insight Holdings, to run daily production operations. Rather than investing in products and promotions to improve sales, however, management immediately started cutting costs; product quality plummeted. Employees reported that the company began using cheaper ingredients, while distributors reported that they received packages that were not properly sealed. In addition, Catterton's shutdown of a long-standing bakery and distribution plant in Oakland, California, not only eliminated 230 jobs but led to delays between when cookies were baked and when they reached stores.[118]

More importantly, management began engaging in fraudulent accounting practices to maintain its line of credit with Wachovia Bank, its primary creditor. Wachovia required that certain financial targets be met in order to keep open the lines of credit to Archway. Keith Roberts, who became the company's director of finance in October 2007, found that Archway & Mother's was booking nonexistent sales. One distributor, for example, reported that he would receive $4,000 worth of product, but the baking company was charging him for $14,000 worth of cookies. It was also sending erroneous sales data to Wachovia in 2007 and 2008 to justify how much it could borrow. When Roberts reported these problems to his superiors, he was told that this accounting approach had to continue in order to get Archway through a credit crunch. Frustrated with the continued fraudulent behavior, Roberts resigned in the summer of 2008.[119]

On October 3, 2008, Catterton announced that it was shutting down the Archway factory. Two hundred and seventy-eight union workers lost their jobs; they later found out that the company had stopped paying their health care insurance premiums months earlier. Catterton filed for bankruptcy on October 6. The closure was also a blow to the economic stability of the small town where it was located. The mayor of Ashland immediately organized thirty support agencies to help the unemployed workers. He then worked to get the factory reopened by mobilizing political support from state politicians, the governor, U.S. senator Sherrod Brown, and others. The mayor also made presentations to the bankruptcy court to urge the judge to choose a buyer who would keep the business whole—including the brand and intellectual property—and not break it up and sell off the assets.[120]

In December 2008, the bankruptcy judge chose Lance, Inc., to buy the entire Ashland factory intact for $30 million. He chose Kellogg North America to acquire the Mother's Cookies side of the business for $12 million. Lance announced that it would soon reopen the plant for production, begin by rehiring sixty workers, and rehire others as demand grew. In a December 9 meeting with employees, Lance gave every worker a $1,500 debit card to help them through their period of unemployment and to signal that Lance would be committed to the community. Ashland's mayor viewed this $420,000 infusion of outside money as an economic development grant—a boon to the local economy, particularly as the Christmas shopping season unfolded. Workers received their prior salary (reportedly about $15 per hour); however, the plant opened as a non-union shop.[121]

In the meantime, Catterton faced several lawsuits. In August 2009, the workers filed a class-action lawsuit, alleging that Catterton Partners violated the Worker Adjustment and Retraining Notification Act (WARN) by not giving them sixty days' advance notice when it closed the Ashland plant in 2008. They sought full payment of wages and benefits that would have been accrued during the sixty-day period. They argued that Catterton was the "employer" for the purposes of the WARN Act and should be held liable for failure to provide workers with advance notice of the shutdown and their employment termination. In an important ruling, the court concluded that Catterton and the cookie company should be considered a "single employer." It held that Catterton was liable for damages because it was the "de facto" decision-maker responsible for the actions leading up to the lawsuit—in this case, the shutdown of the plant and termination of employees without notice.[122] An important criterion in the federal regulations for deciding who is liable for damages is whether "the parent company exercises de facto control over the subsidiary."[123] Subsequently, the suit was settled.[124]

Creditors also sued Catterton for widespread accounting fraud. In its bankruptcy filing, Archway reported that it owed $27.3 million to its thirty largest creditors.[125] The lawsuit claimed that Catterton and inside management had engaged in a prolonged period of accounting fraud in order to secure loans from Wachovia and that their actions brought about the company's collapse.[126] Subsequently, Wachovia recovered most of the money it lent to Archway, but Catterton and its limited partners lost their investment.[127]

Like Archway & Mother's, Stella D'oro Biscuit Company was a small cookie factory with a niche market that played an anchor role in its community and provided jobs. Founded in 1932 in the Bronx by Joseph and Angela Kresevich, it was a historic Italian-style bakery that made breadsticks, biscotti, egg biscuits, margherites, and other Italian-style cookies. The company was well known among New Yorkers and had a large

Orthodox Jewish following because it made some of its cookies without dairy products (pareve). The family sold the company to Nabisco in 1992 because the heir apparent was killed in the 1989 San Francisco earthquake; Nabisco sold it to Kraft in 2000.[128] Nabisco, and then Kraft, neglected the small biscuit company, began using cheaper ingredients, and eliminated the popular pareve cookies. Revenues fell from $65 million in 1992 to $30 million in 2006, and hundreds of workers were laid off. Kraft sold the company to the PE firm Brynwood Partners in 2006 for $17.5 million.[129]

The company was viewed as a community institution and had a "quintessentially American" immigrant workforce.[130] It also was one of the only remaining anchor factories in the Bronx, where the loss of good blue-collar jobs had led to high rates of poverty. Most workers had years of tenure with the company and had negotiated decent wages and benefits through their union, the BCTGM Local 50. Although labor relations historically had been positive, Brynwood Partners immediately demanded large cuts in union wages and benefits. In the first contract negotiations, Brynwood demanded a $1-per-hour wage cut per year for five years, as well as cuts in vacation and sick days, pensions, and health care benefits.[131] Workers were making between $18 and $23 per hour—$36,000 to $46,000 a year.[132] After failed negotiations in August 2008, the 134 workers struck for eleven months—none crossed the picket line—and the company hired replacement workers.

In June 2009, however, an administrative judge ruled that the firm had engaged in unfair labor practices because it refused to turn over the company's audited financial statement, unilaterally declared an impasse in negotiations, and illegally locked out the workers when they offered to go back in May 2009. Federal labor law requires companies to provide the union with financial information if the company claims it is financially unable to meet union demands. The ruling was upheld by a National Labor Relations Board (NLRB) panel, and the company was ordered to pay back wages with interest and benefits—estimated at between $3 million and $4 million—for a two-month period after the union offered to return to work in May 2009.[133] As of 2012, the ruling was still being appealed.[134]

The victory was bittersweet, however. Brynwood Partners responded by putting the company up for sale in August and shuttering the factory in October 2009.[135] It was purchased by Lance, Inc., the Charlotte, North Carolina, company that purchased Archway Cookies and that has a reputation for being anti-union. Lance paid much less for the company than did Brynwood (which had purchased it for $17.5 million).[136] Lance then moved all of the Stella D'oro production to the Archway Cookies plant in Ashland, Ohio. The plant, which reopened with about sixty former Archway workers in December 2008, grew to about two hundred with the integration of the Stella D'oro production, but none of the former Stella D'oro workers were offered jobs.[137]

To add insult to injury, the National Labor Relations Board's decision that the company owed back pay and interest to the workers was overturned in March 2013 by the U.S. Court of Appeals for the Second Circuit.[138] Finding that Stella D'oro was not guilty of violating any federal labor law, the court nullified the NLRB's order.

From Conflict to Constructive Engagement

Many unions do not have the power or organizational capability to take on private equity owners. In some cases, however, unions have successfully engaged in militant mobilization and "educated" PE owners about their need to engage in collective bargaining. Two cases—one involving the Steelworkers at Ormet Aluminum, and the other the Teamsters at US Foods—are representative of unions' ability to change PE owners' attitudes toward unions and turn conflictual labor-management relationships into more constructive ones based on negotiated settlements.

Ormet Aluminum: Anti-Union Animus and Union Militancy Ormet Aluminum represents a case in which the Steelworkers faced fierce anti-union animus from private equity owners, but nonetheless prevailed in winning a strong contract through sustained union mobilization. In 2004 Ormet Aluminum, headed by the fiercely anti-union CEO Emmett Boyle, filed for bankruptcy. Faced with falling aluminum prices and rising energy costs, the company filed a reorganization plan with the bankruptcy court, backed by $30 million in financing from the private equity firm MatlinPatterson. The PE firm, which focused on distressed investing, had increased the amount of Ormet's debt it held during the bankruptcy proceedings in order to increase its leverage, and it emerged as the largest holder of secured debt, which gave it more leverage in the proceedings.

After the company and the union failed to reach agreement over a concessionary contract, the bankruptcy court ruled in November 2004 that the company could void its labor contract. Thirteen hundred union members at the Ohio plant went on strike in response. The union also filed unfair labor practice charges for the company's unilateral implementation of changes in the labor contract,[139] and it engaged the support of four pension funds that were limited partners in the MatlinPatterson PE fund.[140] Ormet emerged from bankruptcy in May 2005. The union's protracted corporate campaign continued against Ormet and MatlinPatterson for nineteen months and included ongoing protest rallies around the country and at corporate headquarters, massive placarding in Manhattan against the PE firm, and "road warrior teams" that showed up at the residences and events of corporate and PE principals. Finally, MatlinPatterson retired Emmett Boyle as CEO and started negotiating with the union.[141] The parties reached a tentative contract on June 30, 2006, covering fifteen hundred workers in three plants in Ohio and Louisiana.[142] Since then, labor-management relations have been generally constructive at the highest levels.

In February 2013, however, the company again filed for Chapter 11 bankruptcy, citing falling aluminum prices and rising electricity costs. It received $60 million in debtor in possession (DIP) financing from Wells Fargo and $30 million from the PE firm Wayzata Investment Partners, which became the stalking-horse bidder. In June 2013, a Delaware bankruptcy court approved the sale of assets to Wayzata for $130 million plus the assumption of certain debt liabilities. It also approved the transfer of unfunded pension liabilities totaling $260 million to the PBGC.[143]

US Foods and the Teamsters The case of US Foods (formerly known as US Foodservice) provides a good example of private equity's use of work intensification and anti-union strategies to increase returns on its investments. Through a series of mobilizations, however, the union was able to win organizing drives and contract strikes that have led to negotiated settlements and recent efforts to establish more constructive relationships.

US Foods is the second-largest U.S. distributor of food and beverage products to small groceries, restaurants, hospitals, hospitality companies, prisons, military bases, and schools through regional supermarket chains. Royal Ahold, the Dutch supermarket operator, acquired the company in 2000 for $3.6 billion and then purchased Alliant Exchange (Alliant Foodservice) for another $2.2 billion, which together generated annual revenues of $14 billion. In July 2007, Royal Ahold spun off the company to the PE firms Clayton, Dubilier, & Rice (CD&R), Kohlberg Kravis Roberts (KKR), and National City Equity Partners for $7.1 billion.[144] The PE firms put up approximately 32 percent of the purchase prices, with the remainder funded through debt assumed by US Foods. The company employed about twenty-five thousand workers at the time of the PE transaction. The International Brotherhood of Teamsters (IBT) represented four thousand workers at about twenty-five of the company's warehouses.[145] The company is about half the size of its main competitor, SYSCO, and other competitors include ARAMARK, Keystone Foods, MAINES, MBM, and Performance Food.

According to the Teamsters, the union immediately sought to work out a cooperative agreement with the new owners to improve efficiencies and rationalize the labor process in exchange for a company pledge not to engage in anti-union activities. The Teamsters hired an outside labor consultant to help out and offered the expertise of senior union members with deep industry expertise who could suggest cost-saving process changes—for example, improvements in delivery times through changes in routing deliveries to cope with local traffic patterns—without adversely affecting the quality of jobs. The company was not interested in pursuing this approach, however, and instead used consultants to introduce computer-driven processes and electronic monitoring that intensified and dehumanized work, according to union members.[146]

Labor relations, which had been reasonably positive under Ahold, became extremely contentious. The new owners immediately fired the existing management and hired anti-union consultants, which in one organizing campaign in Phoenix, Arizona, led to over two hundred violations of the National Labor Relations Act. The company's behavior was so egregious that the NLRB took the extraordinary step of ordering it to recognize the union and negotiate a contract for the 250 workers. The settlement also included reinstatement and back pay for employees terminated during the campaign.[147] In another organizing campaign in Ohio, the company's anti-union activity led to an election rerun.[148]

Contrary to its stated goal of improving efficiency, US Foods systematically shifted work from its unionized facilities to more distant, non-union work sites in the same region. In Philadelphia, local customers with long-term relationships of trust with the union truckers complained of poor service and signed petitions in support of the union's efforts to move the work back to the warehouse just outside of Philadelphia and closer to the customers' premises. The effort was successful, and the Philadelphia local signed a two-year contract that protected the jobs of workers at this facility. In St. Louis, the union was not successful in preventing the movement of work to two non-union facilities 150 miles or more away from the city. Despite the high number of customers in the St. Louis area, the unionized distribution center lost more than half of its workforce; workers still fear that the company may close the facility.[149] In 2011 the company closed a Paducah, Kentucky, distribution center, and 240 workers lost their jobs.[150]

In November 2011, the company and union again faced a standoff when the union accused the company of failing to negotiate in good faith and filed unfair labor practice charges against the company. The facility in Streator, Illinois, disciplined a worker for being absent while he was in contract negotiations. The conflict led to sympathy strikes throughout the United States at US Foods facilities in Colorado, Indiana, Minnesota, Missouri, New Jersey, New York, and Washington.[151] The company and the union settled the contract and all outstanding issues on December 5, 2011.[152]

The returns to private equity investors are not known. US Foods leased rather than owned its warehouses at the time it was acquired by private equity, so the sale of property assets was not an option for returns to investors. In addition, industry analysts at the time estimated that the PE owners overpaid for the company by some $2 billion (it was valued at between $5.1 billion and $5.7 billion and purchased for $7.1 billion).[153] The PE owners have pursued a growth strategy through add-ons of smaller food distributors and related companies. Between 2010 and 2012, they acquired nine smaller food distributors, including Nino's Wholesale, Midway Produce, WVO Industries, Great Western Meats, Vesuvio Foods, and Cerniglia Products (distributors of Italian foods), Ritter Food Service (a distributor of poultry, meats, and seafood), Hawkeye Foodservice Distribution, and Glover Wholesale, based in Americus, Georgia.

With annual revenues of $20 billion and a workforce of twenty-five thousand in 2012, the company was ranked the eleventh-largest private company by *Forbes* magazine. However, a continuing debt burden remains a problem after seven years of private equity ownership. The company refinanced $700 million in debt on November 30, 2012, in order to retire a $700 million senior secured loan due in 2014.[154] As of January 2013, the company had debt obligations of $4.6 billion, and Standard & Poor's assessed its risk profile as "'highly leveraged' for the foreseeable future . . . based on our opinion that the company has a very aggressive financial policy and significant debt burden."[155]

Despite US Foods' high debt load, its main competitor and largest U.S. food distributor, SYSCO Corporation, announced in December 2013 that it would buy out US Foods for $3.5 billion and assume its debt, in a deal valued at $8.2 billion. Clayton Dubilier & Rice LLC and KKR, which bought US Foods in 2007 for $7.1 billion, including debt, will take away about $1.25 billion, or a 55 percent gain on their $2.25 billion equity investment in the company. They also took away an estimated 160 percent profit on the $375 million in notes they paid for US Foods' debt, which was refinanced in 2013. With the acquisition, SYSCO will control over 25 percent of the North American market, up from 18 percent before the sale.[156]

Mixed Blessings: Negotiated Contracts, Uncertain Outcomes

We end with two cases that illustrate the problems inherent in the private equity business model, even when the PE owners negotiate in good faith with unions and other stakeholder groups. In the case of Energy Future Holdings (EFH), formerly Texas Utilities Corporation, the consortium of PE firms that purchased the company in 2007 engaged with the union, the International Brotherhood of Electrical Workers (IBEW), and other community and environmental stakeholders to make sure that it developed a constructive relationship with each party that dealt with their objections to the sale. Although the union continues to have a constructive relationship with the PE owners, and the union contract has provided good jobs and benefits, the debt overhang from the highly leveraged buyout and poor market conditions has put the corporation in serious financial distress, and its future is uncertain. In the case of Hospital

Corporation of America (HCA), the company has similarly negotiated in good faith with its unions, the National Nurses Union (NNU) and the Service Employees International Union (SEIU). Again, however, the debt overhang from the leveraged buyout, coupled with financial engineering strategies, has raised serious questions about how the company can service the debt, maintain profitability, and provide quality patient care in the content of declining Medicare reimbursements and the demands of the Affordable Care Act.

Energy Future Holdings: The Future of Texas Utilities The largest leveraged buyout in the history of private equity deals occurred in October 2007 when KKR & Co., the Texas Pacific Group (TPG), and the PE arm of Goldman Sachs acquired Texas Utilities Corporation (TXU), valued at $48.1 billion. Texas Utilities was the fifth-largest utility in the United States, employing some 7,262 workers and serving over 2 million customers, primarily in northern Texas. The consortium invested $8.3 billion of equity and leveraged the remaining 82 percent, borrowing $39.8 billion.[157]

The deal was controversial, not only because of its size, but because many stakeholder groups had interests in the success of the enterprise. The announcement of the prior CEO of TXU, C. John Wilder, that he would build eleven new coal-fueled power plants mobilized a broad cross-section of groups against him—from environmentalists to local and state legislators, community groups, and even businesses. Wilder also had plans to create a new company and contract out the work to that entity, leading the unions to mobilize and oppose the plan before the Public Utility Commission and the State Legislature. Finally, he alienated consumers and politicians when he refused to lower electricity prices when they rose after hurricanes.

The PE consortium examined the situation and adopted strategies to appease these stakeholder groups. It proposed to build three rather than eleven coal-powered plants, and it received the blessing of the Natural Resources Defense Council and the Environmental Defense Fund. It hired high-profile politicians such as James Baker III as advisers or lobbyists and spent some $17 million on lobbying to minimize legislative opposition and regulatory oversight of the project.[158]

It also hired a consultant, Richard Gephardt, former U.S. congressman and CEO of the Gephardt Group, to intervene with the union—the International Brotherhood of Electrical Workers. The PE consortium agreed to keep all work in-house and to negotiate in good faith with the union. The 2007 contract included an agreement that staff would not be reduced in any of the businesses, a neutrality clause, and commitments to terminate outsourcing and bargain in good faith with newly organized IBEW members. The consortium also agreed to invest in TXU divisions Oncor and Luminant Energy, hold quarterly meetings with the IBEW, and more generally support job growth and economic development in Texas. Along with quarterly meetings with the IBEW, TXU's private equity owners also set up the Sustainable Energy Advisory Board, which includes representatives from environmental groups, labor, and the community.[159]

The PE consortium restructured the former TXU (now EFH) into a holding company and three operating companies: TXU (the unregulated customer service and sales company), Luminant (the unregulated power generation company), and Oncor (the regulated transmission company). Most of the union members work for Oncor. The union has worked closely with the PE consortium and believes that the company has been well run. It has allowed the managers who know the business to run the three companies and has encouraged a focus on efficient, dependable service. It has developed innovative products—new applications for phones, Internet billing access, free night service, and so on—to compete with the unusually stiff competition in Texas. (There are some two hundred service and sales providers in Texas compared to handfuls in other states.) It has maintained its no-layoff pledge and hired some 1,600 workers (mainly retiree replacements) since 2007.[160] Between 2007 and 2012, overall employment grew by about 25 percent, to 9,300.[161]

But despite their financial expertise and innovative management and labor relations strategies, the private equity partners did not anticipate the downturns in energy prices that made the highly risky, overleveraged deal an economic albatross. Wholesale power prices are tied to natural gas prices. The PE investors bet that natural gas prices would continue rising, but they did not. The financial crisis hit, demand fell, and supply grew through the discovery of new reserves and fracking exploration in North America and Europe. In addition, unlike other states with regulations that guarantee a certain level of profits, energy generation (but not transmission) markets in Texas are completely unregulated.[162]

As the company's revenues fell, it undertook a series of "distressed exchanges," or efforts to refinance its debt by amending and extending its debt obligations. Moody's reduced the ratings of EFH's debt in these instances when the company offered to exchange debt for pennies on the dollar.[163] When EFH announced a debt exchange in October 2009 for up to $4 billion in new senior secured notes at a 9.75 percent interest rate to cover notes coming due in 2014 to 2034, only $357.7 million of debt was exchanged. It received $500 million in debt financing in January 2010 from Citigroup, Credit Suisse, Goldman Sachs, and JPMorgan.[164] In 2011 the company gained some breathing room when lenders agreed to extend the due dates on $22 billion in loans to key subsidiaries from 2013 and 2014 to 2016 and 2017. The extension will cost the company about $850 million.[165]

In 2011, however, the company suffered losses of $1.9 billion,[166] and had lost some 17 percent of its customers to lower-cost competitors.[167]

The company's debt load in 2011 was about $40.7 billion, approximately equal to its load at acquisition in 2007, and its leverage was 9.3 times EBITDA in 2011, compared to 8.4 in 2007.[168] KKR carried its investment in the company on its books at 10 cents on the dollar, and Warren Buffett called his $2 billion investment in the bonds of the company "a big mistake." By the beginning of 2012, the company's bonds that were due in 2015 were trading at the deep discount of 28 cents on the dollar—a 60 percent yield.[169] Moreover, credit default swap traders were betting 91 percent odds that the company would default in the next three years.[170]

In January 2012, Moody's dropped its rating for EFH and its subsidiaries (with one exception) from stable to negative—to a Caa2 Corporate Family Rating (CFR), a Caa3 Probability of Default Rating, and a SGL-4 Speculative Grade Liquidity Rating—all indicators of financial distress. The downgrades affected approximately $37 billion in debt securities. Moody's cited the company's weak liquidity reserves and its unsustainable business model based on an overly complex capital structure.[171] Notably, the lower ratings were primarily due to the poor performance of the subsidiary that generates and markets electricity and is the principal source of the company's revenues. Oncor, by contrast, EFH's 80 percent–owned subsidiary for electric transmission and distribution, is still regulated by the Texas State Public Utility Commission, and its ratings remained stable.[172] As a regulated entity, Oncor's debt is "ring-fenced" from the holding company.

Analysts viewed the company's strategy of "amending and extending" its debt obligations as a temporary solution that would not allow it to survive. As of June 30, 2012, the company had total liabilities of $52.2 billion, compared with total assets of $44.1 billion, according to data compiled by Bloomberg.[173] In August 2012, the company was raising $750 million in debt financing from undisclosed lenders, part of which would go to pay a January 2013 dividend.[174]

The company's long-term survival, however, depends on its ability to pay the interest on its bonds, which in turn depends on a rise in the price of natural gas, a low probability. Prices for natural gas were $7.00 to $8.00 per million British thermal units in 2007, $4.00 in 2011, $2.32 in early 2012, and just over $4.00 in mid-2013. The industry analyst Andrew DeVries at CreditSights estimates that prices need to reach $6.15 for the company to break even after paying interest and other expenses, but long-term forecasts put the price at $4.50 to $5.00.[175]

Despite the financial distress of Energy Future Holdings and the frustrations of investors who have seen few returns, TPG and the other private equity partners have taken $528 million in fees. According to Energy Future's regulatory filings, the company has paid $300 million for PE consulting on the buyout, $171 million in annual management fees, and $57.3 million for advice on debt deals.[176]

In November 2012, the PE partners also gained a $450 million windfall in a debt exchange at the expense of bondholders. A regulatory filing on October 30 had raised the possibility that the company's troubles might lead it to default on its debts. That led to a decline in the price of the bonds held by its creditors. In this situation, the creditors were willing to accept a debt exchange that reduced EFH's outstanding debt by $450 million in exchange for new debt that carried a much higher 12 percent interest rate. The creditors lost $450 million in this debt exchange.[177]

Limited partner investors in the TPG fund that bought EFH also have not fared so well. According to *Fortune's* Dan Primack, "TPG readily admits to investors that its fifth fund was a mess, with massive craters like TXU. . . . TXU is being carried at just around five cents on the dollar. . . . In other words, [for investors] things can't get any worse."[178] Major public pension funds in the United States were big investors in the PE funds that sponsored the TXU deal, including the California State Teachers' Retirement System (CalSTRS), the Washington State Investment Board, the Oregon Public Employees' Retirement System, the New Jersey Division of Investment, and the Pennsylvania State Employees' Retirement System.[179]

From the perspective of the union, it is notable that the PE consortium did not resort to cost-cutting and downsizing, but it is unlikely that they could have cut their way out of their debt problem given its size. Despite the consortium's constructive dealings with the union, its high-leverage business model has left 9,300 workers uncertain about their future. The company lost $1.91 billion in 2011 and $3.36 billion in 2012, according to Bloomberg.[180]

Under a proposed prepackaged bankruptcy filed with the SEC in April 2013 for the unregulated side of the business only, senior creditors, or first-lien holders, would wipe out $25 billion in debt in exchange for an 85 percent ownership in the company plus $5 billion in cash or new long-term debt. The PE owners would retain a 15 percent ownership. The company would get $3 billion in credit and $5 billion in new long-term debt. The PE owners, however, face a number of activist hedge funds that have bought up EFH debt and hope to force a bankruptcy. Saddled with $44 billion in debt in November 2013, the company was able to meet interest payments, but it failed to reach agreement with creditors on a restructuring plan. Analysts estimate that the company will be out of cash by early 2014. In the meantime, EFH also owns 80 percent of the regulated utility Oncor, which is viewed as a safe cash cow. It is worth roughly $7 billion, but has only $7 billion in debt because state regulations limit the size of its debt. Ironically, then, it may be the staid regulated utility that provides owners with some return on their investment.[181]

Financial Engineering at Hospital Corporation of America HCA Holdings, Inc., the largest for-profit health care entity in the United States, provides roughly 4 to 5 percent of all hospital services in the country.[182] With total revenues of $36.8 billion in 2013, it ranks number 82 in the Fortune 500.[183] It employs 199,000 and provides services to more than 20,000 patients each day, on average, in 165 hospitals and 115 freestanding surgery centers with approximately 41,000 beds in 20 states in the United States as well as in England.[184] In 2006, HCA was the subject of one of the largest leveraged buyouts in U.S. history when a consortium of private equity investors acquired it for $21 billion and took the company private. The key investors were Bain Capital Partners, Kohlberg Kravis Roberts, Merrill Lynch Global Private Equity, Citigroup, Bank of America, and HCA CEO Dr. Thomas F. Frist Jr. [185] In total, the group paid $4.5 billion in return for 100 percent of the post-buyout equity in HCA, while raising the remaining 80 percent of the purchase price (about $17 billion) through the issuance of debt. At the time, HCA had an enterprise value (outstanding equity and debt) of $33 billion.[186] A small minority of employees were represented by the Service Employees International Union (SEIU) and the California Nurses Association (now NNU, the National Nurses Union).

The health care sector has attracted considerable private equity investment because it is growing (and continued to grow during the recession) and receives a steady flow of cash from Medicare and Medicaid. In 2006 the HCA PE owners would have anticipated above-market returns on their investment within a three- to five-year period through a variety of mechanisms: selling off assets, reducing costs, improving operations, or waiting for the stock market to rise and selling the company at a higher price. But as of 2008, the recession had limited or eliminated these strategies, leaving the new owners with fewer options and lower returns than they expected. The inherent challenge in LBOs, especially those of significant size, is weathering cyclical changes in market conditions after taking on so much debt. HCA's financial well-being was particularly strong in 2005 before the buyout, then fell sharply from 2006 to 2008 before returning to 2006 levels in 2009.

By 2010, the PE consortium had attempted to secure returns on their investment by going public and selling off one-fifth of the company via shares valued at $4.6 billion. This would have allowed the PE investors to recoup 75 percent of their original investment while retaining an 80 percent share in the company.[187] Like many attempts by private equity to take portfolio companies public in recent years, however, the bid stalled. The company then turned to dividend recapitalizations. During 2010, HCA paid its PE owners $4.25 billion in dividends, which virtually covered their original investment. The dividends were paid out in three tranches—$1.75 billion in January, $500 million in May (a time when the company itself admitted that its "substantial debt" could limit its growth[188]), and $2.1 billion in November. The third tranche was partially financed by junk bonds issued by the new holding company, HCA Holdings, because debt issued by subsidiaries had reached limits set by existing debt covenants.[189] According to Standard & Poor's, HCA's payout was the largest PE dividend since 2005.[190]

HCA justified its move based on improved earnings and debt ratios, but one bond analyst said that those were onetime improvements due to changes in accounting methodology.[191] HCA debt received a Caa1 rating from Moody's, seven levels into speculative, or "junk," status. This type of debt is highly risky for investors because it is issued by a holding company (HCA Holdings) that has no assets, is unsecured by collateral from operating subsidiaries, is subordinate to the existing debt of those subsidiaries, and contains no negative pledge covenants against the issuance of future debt or dividends.[192]

At the end of 2010, HCA's owners filed for an IPO, valued at $4.6 billion. Potential investors would need to consider whether HCA had made sufficient operating improvements and profits to offset the risks of high leverage in a competitive and uncertain market. As of December 31, 2010, HCA's debt level was $28.2 billion—or almost ten times its cash flow from operations for that year. This high leverage made the company more vulnerable to further economic downturns and might negatively affect its future ability to raise additional capital or refinance debt obligations. Since 2008, HCA had managed its debt obligations by refinancing at higher interest rates or "amending and extending" loans.[193] The Patient Protection and Affordable Care Act of 2010 also added uncertainty to future revenues: it would increase revenues by covering uninsured individuals but would also reduce the growth of Medicare payments and decrease the share of Medicare and Medicaid payments going to hospitals. Those two programs made up 40.7 percent of HCA's 2010 revenue.[194] Potential investors also would need to be comfortable with the lead underwriters, who had a conflict of interest.[195] Despite these concerns, HCA successfully went public on March 9, 2011, raising $3.79 billion and selling 126 million shares at $30 a share.[196] The market favored this IPO because unlike most sectors of the economy, health care emerged from the financial crisis in relatively good shape, and HCA "throws off a lot of cash."[197]

The private equity owners—KKR, Bain Capital, and North Cove Partners (formerly Merrill Lynch Private Equity)—gained substantially from the IPO, while each retained a 24.6 percent equity interest in the company.[198] For example, after the payment of the hurdle rate to the limited partners (typically 8 percent), Bain would have received 30 percent of the carry from the sale, while it contributed only about $64 million to the $1.02 billion Bain PE fund that invested in the 2006 HCA buyout. In addition, Bain had received $76 million in management fees charged to investors, $62 million in management fees charged to HCA, and a $58 million transaction fee.[199] Post-IPO, however, the company's debt stood at $26 billion ($12 billion more than the company's assets).[200]

The IPO was particularly lucrative because the private equity consortium had initially purchased the company at a below-market share price, allegedly through collusion with other PE firms. This information emerged from a 2011 class-action lawsuit by shareholders, alleging that the HCA PE consortium had conspired to keep the HCA stock price low by asking the other interested PE firms to "step down on HCA," or not compete.[201] The lawsuit alleges that other private equity firms agreed to this in exchange for the HCA PE owners not competing on the buyouts of other private equity firms—the most immediate being the buyout of Freescale by a PE group led by Blackstone. While the PE consortium paid $51 per share for HCA stock in 2006, industry estimates valued the stock at well over that price, with an estimated loss to HCA shareholders of $1 billion.[202]

In 2011 and 2012, the private equity consortium continued to engage in financial engineering. In a move to boost stock prices, HCA repurchased 80 million shares of common stock for $1.5 billion in September 2011. Despite the fact that the company reported in its December 2010 SEC filing that it did not intend to issue any more dividends "for the foreseeable future," it issued two additional dividend recapitalizations in 2012—$1 billion in February and $1.15 billion in November—and it announced a third dividend recap for $1.15 billion in December.[203] The dividends benefit HCA's largest shareholders—Bain Capital and KKR, each of which currently owns about 20 percent of the company. Moody's estimated that HCA had paid out a total of $6.7 billion in dividends and share repurchases after the February 2012 tranche, which together with the November 2012 dividend would bring payouts to some $9 billion since 2006. The company's stock price reacted negatively to the November and December announcements.[204] In December, the PE owners also announced they would issue a second IPO for $1.86 billion.[205]

This track record of gains by private equity owners, along with the original owners and top managers of HCA, stands in stark contrast to agency theory that PE ownership leads to more efficient allocation of resources and limits opportunities for managerial opportunism at the expense of shareholders. In this case, PE owners and the company's top managers made oversized returns on investment primarily through financial engineering and allegedly by colluding to eliminate competitors and reduce the share price before taking the company private, to the detriment of existing shareholders.

What implications does this kind of financial engineering have for employees, patients, and the sustainability of HCA as an organization? This question is difficult to answer given the lack of publicly available information. After 2006, the HCA private equity owners improved the company's profitability in part by cutting costs and improving the cash flow—raising the cash flow margin from an average of 5 percent in 2006 to 7 percent in the 2007 to 2010 period.[206] A recent academic study of

HCA performance before and after the buyout is suggestive. Using data from the Medicare Hospital Cost Report Information System for 130 HCA hospitals and 490 comparison hospitals, the authors found that HCA had lower expenses and lower full-time-equivalent staff than did comparable public hospitals. HCA hospitals also showed a significant decrease in capital investments in fixed assets between 2006 and 2009, and their cash-flow margin ratio was substantially higher than local counterparts throughout that period.[207]

These quantitative results resonate with the anecdotal evidence of serious understaffing at HCA hospitals from nurses at unionized HCA hospitals as well as lawsuits filed by patients. Understaffing and patient care have been central issues in union organizing campaigns, contract negotiations, and policy initiatives before state legislatures. In October 2010, nurses from SEIU Local 121RN, employed at Riverside Community Hospital in southern California, testified before the State Senate Health Committee oversight hearing on their HCA-owned hospital's failure to comply with state-mandated nurse-to-patient ratios. The California Department of Public Health Services substantiated the complaints of noncompliance in every month of 2010 through October.[208]

Moreover, at the same time that HCA had announced its $2 billion dividend to private owners at the end of 2010, its negotiations with nurses at two of its California hospitals (West Hills and Riverside Community) had stalled over the issue of staffing levels, along with guaranteed time for rest and meals. The nurses stated that the hospitals' policy of "staffing by numbers," based on standardized nurse-to-patient ratios, ignored the variation in acuity of patients, leading to understaffing for the patients most in need of care. At the same time, nurses had been involuntarily sent home and lost pay when the hospitals determined that nurse-to-patient ratios were too high. To call attention to their concerns, the nurses called a five-day "permitted" strike on December 23, 2010, which concluded on December 28 without incidents or danger to patients. The nurses had the full backing of other unions, the Los Angeles Federation of Labor, and major state political leaders, including California assemblyman Bob Blumenfield, California state senator Fran Pavley, and California governor-elect Jerry Brown.[209]

The issue of understaffing has surfaced in a number of lawsuits. In July 2000, HCA paid $2.7 million in a malpractice settlement through its Wesley Hospital.[210] In 2006 a class-action lawsuit over nurse staffing was filed in Kansas when a patient claimed that her husband died owing to a lack of postoperative care that was not given to him because hospital nurses were already spread too thin.[211] In June 2010, two nurses from Texas and Kansas filed individual lawsuits against HCA for violations of federal wage and hour laws. They charged that HCA routinely required them to work during their lunch breaks, despite the fact that the hospital's computer system automatically deducted that time from their work schedules. The lawsuits sought national class-action status and collective-action status to represent nonexempt HCA employees in the two states.[212]

In November 2009, a former nurse who was a payroll administrator and later finance coordinator at HCA's London hospitals sued the company for scheduling and compensation violations at its six hospitals, charging that the company wrongly logged up to 120,000 nurse shifts, leading to underpayment of wages. The SEC is investigating these charges. Analysts at Gimme Credit, an independent research service, noted that these charges dovetail with concerns they had raised earlier that improvements in operating earnings reported by HCA could be due to changes in its billing procedures in emergency departments.[213] More recently, HCA is under investigation for Medicare fraud—billing for unnecessary and costly interventional cardiology procedures that raise profits and can endanger patient health. Prior to PE ownership, HCA had settled the largest Medicare fraud case in history ($1.7 billion) with the Justice Department in 2000. The current investigation raises serious questions about the failure of HCA under PE ownership to rein in these kinds of practices.[214]

Despite this record on patient care and understaffing, the private equity owners have negotiated quite positive contracts with their unions, including the incorporation of neutrality language for union organizing in a selected set of hospitals. As a result, in 2010 and 2011 the NNU and its organizing arm (the National Nurses Organizing Committee) organized approximately 6,500 new members at HCA hospitals in right-to-work states (Texas, Florida, Missouri, and Nevada), where organizing is particularly difficult. Similarly, SEIU organized 15,000 workers at HCA and Tenet Hospitals in those states.[215] NNU and SEIU each also won neutrality rights in negotiations with Tenet Hospital, where NNU now represents 1,700 nurses in Florida and Texas and SEIU represents additional nurses in Florida.

In sum, the track record of HCA raises serious questions about its ability to provide adequate patient care while also meeting the expectations of its shareholders. Through financial engineering, the private equity owners have extracted at least $10 billion in shareholder returns—the overwhelming bulk of which has gone to the PE firms and the Frist family. This raises a series of questions about the impact on patient care and the future sustainability of the corporation. How does HCA's debt load and financial engineering affect its health care operations? What are the sources of outsized returns for the investors, and how sustainable is the debt load that has been amended and extended on a number of occasions? If the $10 billion in shareholder returns had been used for improving the quality of care, what difference would that have made for patients at HCA hospitals?

Conclusion

In this chapter, we have tried to make sense of the quantitative and qualitative evidence on the impact of private equity on employment and labor relations in the portfolio companies they own. The available quantitative evidence shows that PE-owned companies, on average, have had lower net employment growth post-buyout than comparable publicly traded companies, despite the fact that the PE acquisitions had higher employment growth pre-buyout. In research on manufacturing plants alone, where productivity data are available, PE-owned companies outperformed comparable publicly traded companies, owing largely to plant shutdowns and the shift in work from less-productive to more-productive establishments within the PE-owned companies. In the PE-owned plants post-buyout, higher productivity was accompanied by lower employment growth and wage reductions, thereby contributing to an increase in the productivity-wage gap and to patterns of inequality more generally. The source of higher productivity is unclear: it could have come from investments in new technologies and work processes that the prior owners made and that the PE owners took advantage of by shifting more production to those plants; or the new owners could have made those investments; or they could have focused on downsizing and work intensification; or higher productivity may have resulted from some combination of these strategies.

The qualitative case studies offer some insights into these aggregate trends. In each case, it is clear that private equity ownership brought about major changes for workers and their unions. PE owners acted as employers in bargaining collectively with their unions. The main point of consistency across the PE-owned companies was that, with few exceptions, and no matter what the attitudes of private equity toward labor, employees experienced losses in jobs and/or wages and benefits. This was true for the more constructive cases—such as Spirit AeroSystems, the steel industry, and Dana Corporation—as well as the more conflictual ones, including Delphi, Hawker Beechcraft, Archway & Mother's Cookies, Stella D'oro, Ormet Aluminum, and US Foods. In the most positive case, Spirit AeroSystems owners achieved enormous and disproportionate returns of some $2.5 billion after only five years, in part by obtaining important union concessions in terms of cuts in jobs, wages, and benefits. Likewise in the steel industry, Wilbur Ross walked away with $4.5 billion—about the same amount of money as the retired workers lost in health care and pension benefits.

Beyond these consistencies, however, the differences in private equity's approach toward labor often made a big difference in how workers fared. In the case of Spirit AeroSystems and the cases of distressed investing in the steel industry and Dana Corporation, workers fared far better than they would have under prior ownership, where a history of labor-management antagonism thwarted constructive negotiations. The new PE owners took a pragmatic approach that allowed labor to accept concessions in exchange for job stability, modified but decent benefits, a voice in ongoing operations, and the ability to organize new members. Moreover, in these cases, the fact that workers shared in the gains in productivity did not erode the returns to the PE owners. Rather, as workers had a stake in the enterprise, they contributed to its ongoing competitiveness. At Energy Future Holdings, where the combination of high leverage and a downturn in the price of natural gas has undermined the returns for investors, the fact that the owners took a constructive approach to labor has not only provided good jobs but also has sustained the productive capacity of the enterprise, at least until now. At Hawker Beechcraft, the high degree of leverage in the buyout contributed in large part to the company's bankruptcy and the loss of thousands of jobs, but the company's willingness to at least negotiate with the union and save the employee pension funds stands in stark contrast to the Delphi case.

The hostile approach of private equity and hedge fund owners at Delphi Corporation led to the loss of twenty-five thousand decent-paying manufacturing jobs to China, while the owners made billions. An alternative plan that had been negotiated by the union and another bidder would have made the company profitable by making necessary cuts while still preserving at least half of the jobs that were sent to China. In the cases of Archway & Mother's Cookies and Stella D'oro, PE mismanagement (and managerial fraud) and the inability or unwillingness to work with labor led to plant closings and job losses that had spillover effects in the small communities where they were located; when the two companies were purchased by a new owner and combined into one operation, they reopened as a non-union facility. These differences in the strategies used by PE owners clearly made a large difference for the welfare of workers.

Appendix

See Table 7A.1.

Table 7A.1   Case Summaries of Private Equity Labor Relations Strategies and Outcomes

PE-Owned Company	PE Owners	Unions	Company Economic Condition	Equity Invested	Deal Value	Deal Year	Labor Relations	PE Outcomes, Returns	Company and Labor Outcomes
Spirit AeroSystems (Aerospace)	Onex Partners	IAM, SPEEA	Strong	$464	$1,500	2005	Constructive	2007, 2001 IPOs yield $2.5 billion in returns; Onex still majority owner	2005–2012: Unions accept cuts in jobs wages and retiree benefits; company IPO in 2006 yields large cuts bonuses for workers; strong company performance; job growth; stable union relations
Five US Steel Legacy Companies (20 percent of industry)	Wilbur Ross & Co.	USWA	Bankrupt	$321	$1,285	2001–2003	Constructive	Sold to Mittal Steel for $4.5 billion	Union drives work reorganization and accepts wage and job cuts with contract protections; large cuts in managerial workforce; productivity gains immense; major cuts in retiree pensions of $4.5 billion, equal to private equity returns

(*Appendix continues on p. 236.*)

Table 7A.1 *Continued*

PE-Owned Company	PE Owners	Unions	Company Economic Condition	Equity Invested	Deal Value	Deal Year	Labor Relations	PE Outcomes, Returns	Company and Labor Outcomes
Dana Corporation (Auto supply)	Centerbridge	UAW, USWA	Bankrupt	$500	Undisclosed	2008	Constructive	2008; Company emerges from bankruptcy and remains profitable thereafter	Union contract stipulates limits on debt liabilities to $1.5 billion, which saves company during recession; union agrees to reduced wages and benefits; retirees covered by new health and retirement fund
Delphi Corporation (Auto supply)	John Paulson & Co., Silver Point Capital	UAW	Bankrupt	Undisclosed	Undisclosed	2009	Strongly anti-union	2011 IPO yields profit of 3,000 percent	25 of 29 plants shut down; 25,000 union jobs offshored; taxpayers pay $12.9 billion in subsidies
Hawker Beechcraft (Aerospace)	Goldman Sachs Capital, Onex Partners	IAM	Strong	Undisclosed	$3,300	2007	Union marginalization	2012: Goldman Sachs writes down the company's value by 85 percent	3,500 workers (36 percent of total) lose jobs; union negotiates wage and benefit concessions; 2012 bankruptcy, with $2.6 billion debt; PBGC takes over pension plans

Company	PE Firm	Union			Year	Union stance			
Archway & Mother's Cookies (Food processing)	Catterton Partners	ICBWU	Bankrupt	Undisclosed	2005	Strongly anti-union	Undisclosed	Management engages in fraud; company acquired by strategic investor Lance, Inc. for $30 million	Substantial cost-cutting; product quality declines; 2008 bankruptcy; plants shutdown, 400 workers lose jobs; workers file lawsuit for violation of WARN Act; new owner re-opens as non-union plant with 60 workers.
Stella D'oro (Food processing)	Brynwood Partners	ICBWU	Moderate	Undisclosed	2006	Strongly anti-union	$17.5	Company acquired by strategic investor Lance, Inc. for $17.5 million	Brynwood found guilty of unfair labor practices in contract negotiations, shuts down plant in 2009; 134 workers lose jobs
Ormet Aluminum	Matlin Patterson	USWA	Bankrupt	Undisclosed	2004	Anti-union to constructive	$30.0	2005 out of bankruptcy; 2013 back in bankruptcy; sold to Wayzata for $130 million	19-month union campaign leads to 2006 labor contract with decent wages and benefits for 1,500 workers; PGBC assumes $260 million in unfunded pension liabilities
US Foods (Food distribution)	Clayton, Dubilier, Rice; KKR; National City Equity Partners	Teamsters	Strong	Undisclosed	2007	Anti-union to constructive	$7,100	2013: High debt of $4.6 billion viewed as high risk profile by S&P	Work intensification, job loss in union sites; expansion in non-union facilities

(Appendix continues on p. 238.)

Table 7A.1 *Continued*

PE-Owned Company	PE Owners	Unions	Company Economic Condition	Equity Invested	Deal Value	Deal Year	Labor Relations	PE Outcomes, Returns	Company and Labor Outcomes
Energy Futures Holding (Utilities)	TPG, Carlyle	IBEW	Strong	$8,300	$48,100	2007	Constructive	2007–2012: Profit losses; no returns for investors; Carlyle writes off investment; PE gets $171 million in annual fees	2007–2012: 25% job growth; Positive labor relations; but $44 billion in debt 2013 leads analysts to predict bankruptcy
Hospital Corporation of America (Health care providers)	Bain, KKR, Merrill Lynch, Frist	SEIU, NNU	Strong	$4,500	$21,000	2006	Constructive	2010–2011: PE recoups two times its investment—$9 billion through dividend recaps and IPO	2012: Employment relatively stable but on-going union complaints of understaffing; PE negotiates neutrality agreements that bring in over 20,000 new union members; debt remains at $26 billion over assets of $14 billion

═ Chapter 8 ═

Dilemmas for Pension Funds
as Limited Partners

Public and private employee pension funds—so-called workers'
capital—contribute over one-third of all money committed to private equity for investment. As such, these limited partners deserve
careful attention. They particularly deserve attention because they face
unique dilemmas in their roles as limited partners in PE funds. Managers
of pension funds have the fiduciary responsibility to act in the best interests of their members. That is, they need to make investments that ensure
the long-term stability of the fund as well as its short-term ability to
meet payment obligations to members who are retirees. Allocations to
higher-risk alternative investments, such as private equity, have been
attractive when funds need to be shored up or meet retiree payments.
At the same time, however, fund beneficiaries have identities and interests as workers—or former workers—who may not want to benefit from
short-term strategies if they undermine the jobs and well-being of other
workers. U.S. private-sector unions that participate in union or multi-
employer pension funds have an even more direct dilemma. They represent retirees' pension funds while also representing active workers whose
workplace may be taken over by a PE firm that is engaged in cost-cutting
and downsizing. These dueling roles of representing the interests of
workers as retirees and the interests of workers as active employees are
not present for European unions, whose pensions are typically funded at
the national level.

U.S. public pension funds represent the largest block of investors in
private equity—some 25 percent of commitments to all international funds
that closed between 2009 and 2011. They were followed in rank order by
fund-of-fund managers (those managing a portfolio of investment funds),
private-sector pension funds, insurance companies, high-net-worth individuals, banks and investment companies, family offices, foundations,
endowment plans, corporate investors, and others.[1] Private-sector pension
funds committed 10 percent of all investments in that period.[2]

The evidence regarding the impact of private equity on limited partner returns as well as its net negative effect on jobs in the economy raises fundamental questions about why pension funds should be committing billions of dollars to this model of investment activity. From the perspective of employee pension security, we saw in chapter 6 that finance economists have thrown cold water on the idea that private equity regularly delivers outsized returns on its investments. Reports of outsized returns regularly reported by the industry use the internal rate of return (IRR) to evaluate performance. But finance academics have shown that this measure is deeply flawed, both because it gives misleading results and because it does not compare PE investments to alternative investments that might have yielded higher returns. By contrast, credible academic econometric studies have compared PE returns to those of the public market, such as the S&P 500 or comparable indices. By this measure, PE returns barely match the market—only the top quartile of funds surpass it. Similarly, as outlined in chapter 7, the best empirical research by labor economists shows that private equity's impact on job creation has also been negative, as PE-owned companies destroy more jobs than they create via downsizing, outsourcing, and plant closures. And bankruptcy rates are double those of comparable public companies.

Given the questionable level of returns of private equity to pension funds and the negative effects on employment and company sustainability, why do union and public pension funds continue to invest in private equity? And why, in some cases, are they raising the proportion of their funds committed to private equity and other alternative investments?

In this chapter, we analyze the complex relationship between the general partners (GPs) of private equity funds and their limited partners (LPs), with particular attention to pension funds as LPs. This relationship is complex for several reasons. First, the rules of the deal for limited partners to invest in PE funds put them in an asymmetric or unequal relationship with general partners, who make and manage all of the investment decisions and receive a relatively greater proportion of the returns compared to the money that they put at risk. This arrangement, in which LPs are passive investors, dates to the early funds raised by KKR and used to buy out the Houdaille Corporation in 1979.[3] As detailed in chapter 3, LPs typically make a ten-year commitment to the PE fund and must make funds available when the commitments are called by the GP for investment. Under the "2 and 20" model, LPs pay a 2 percent annual fee to GPs over the ten-year life of a fund, regardless of whether all of the committed funds are invested or the fund is making any money. And while GPs provide only 1 or 2 percent of the equity in a private equity fund, they receive 20 percent of the returns once a hurdle rate has been reached.

Public and union pension plans that invest in private equity funds face additional dilemmas. Pension fund managers have a strict fiduciary duty to make decisions in the best interest of current and future beneficiaries. Although they can delegate responsibility for financial accounting or investment management to service providers, they must do sufficient due diligence to make sure that the actions of the service providers are in the best interests of their members. They must also monitor the actions of their service providers to ensure conformance with the LP agreements they make with private equity. But the actions of PE partners are not transparent, nor are the data and assumptions used to evaluate fund performance. Thus, pension funds have the difficult challenge of meeting their fiduciary responsibilities to members when they may lack the information needed to do so.

This arrangement raises several questions. Why are limited partners willing to go along with what appears to be such an unequal relationship? How can LPs evaluate the performance of PE funds when much of the information on their investments, including the valuation of portfolio companies, is not transparent? What measures do LPs use to assess whether the opportunity costs of their PE investments outweigh the benefits? To what extent have LPs undertaken reforms to improve their bargaining power with GPs and the contractual agreements that govern LP investments?

Pension fund managers also need to assess whether PE strategies that maximize short-term gains are at odds with the long-term stability of the pension fund—an issue particularly salient in the postcrisis period, when returns to megadeals made in the bubble economy crashed. Many argue that the current norm, based on twentieth-century conventions, does not fit the reality of the twenty-first century, particularly in the aftermath of the financial crisis. John Adler and Jay Youngdahl write that labor unions have failed to use the power of their pension funds to improve the functioning of capital markets and the sustainability of companies, despite the fact that this issue has been on union agendas for over three decades.[4] This raises a broader question of whether private equity investments are consistent with the broader interests and values of PE fund participants.

The questions raised by the Great Recession have heated up the debate around these issues and led to a series of efforts by limited partners to reform their contracts with private equity and better align the interests and activities of general partners with their own. This approach to reform appears to have made modest improvements in the agreements that LPs negotiate with PE partners, but the larger issue of their commitment to the PE business model is yet to be tackled.

The Scale and Scope of Pension Fund Investments

Public pension funds invested over $250 billion in U.S. private equity funds between 2000 and 2012, according to data collected by PitchBook. This figure does not include commitments from private-sector pension

Figure 8.1   U.S. Public Pension Commitments to Private Equity, 2000 to 2012

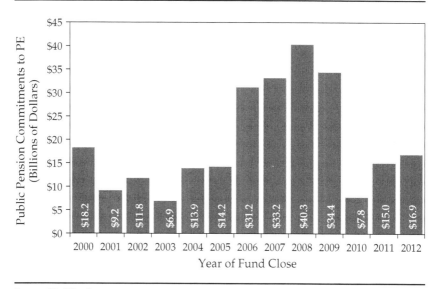

Source: PitchBook.

funds, as the data for these pension funds are less reliable; but these are estimated to add $100 billion to the total of U.S. pension fund commitments to U.S. PE funds in this period. Although pension fund commitments tended to follow the more general boom-bust pattern of investment in private equity in this decade, public pension funds continued to make large commitments even after the crisis hit in 2007 and 2008. Figure 8.1 shows that pension fund investments were modest in the early 2000s, accelerated dramatically in the boom years of 2006 and 2007, and continued to be large in 2008 and 2009, before dropping off to preboom levels thereafter. Notably, commitments to funds that closed in 2011 and 2012 were *higher* than commitments in any year from 2001 to 2005.

This substantial commitment to risky investments reflects several factors: the changing regulatory environment that has freed up pension fund managers to invest in a wider range of financial products and the increased availability of those products; decreasing Treasury yields; the changing guidelines for the Employee Retirement Income Security Act (ERISA) that have encouraged riskier investments; and the increasing demands for payouts of benefits to an aging membership. We discuss these patterns in more detail in the following section.

Estimates regarding the proportion of private equity funds that come from public pensions vary depending on the source of data and whether

Figure 8.2   Public Pension Funds as a Percentage of Private Equity Fund-Raising, 2000 to 2012

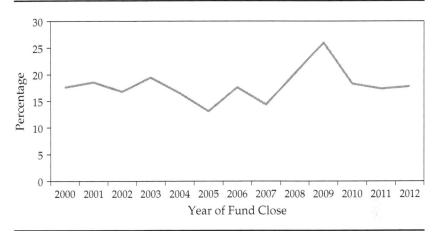

Source: PitchBook.

national or international funds are considered. PitchBook estimates that U.S. public pension fund commitments to U.S. PE funds as a share of all committed funds averaged 18 percent annually from 2000 to 2012, with little variation except in 2009, when they averaged 26 percent (figure 8.2). With respect to global fund-raising, a 2013 Bain Capital report using Preqin data estimated that public pension funds contributed about 25 percent of all capital committed to U.S. and international PE funds that closed in the 2009 to 2011 period.[5] The different estimates may reflect the fact that the PitchBook data only cover U.S. PE funds whereas the Bain report covers international funds as well.

Recall that any individual private equity firm does not raise funds every year, but rather opens a new fund every several years (typically three to five years), undertakes fund-raising, and closes the fund when the target amount for the fund has been reached. Similarly, pension funds do not typically make a commitment to a fund every year; each commitment is for a ten-year period. Whether a public pension fund is able to invest in a new PE fund depends on how quickly it realizes returns from prior PE investments. Figure 8.3 shows the number of pension funds in each year from 2000 to 2012 that had committed to a PE fund that closed in the prior year, the prior three years, the prior five years, or the prior ten years. For the entire period, the number of funds that had invested in private equity in the prior ten years grew from 86 in 2000 to 126 in 2012—a 47 percent increase.

Figure 8.3   Public Pension Funds with Commitments to Private Equity, 2000 to 2012

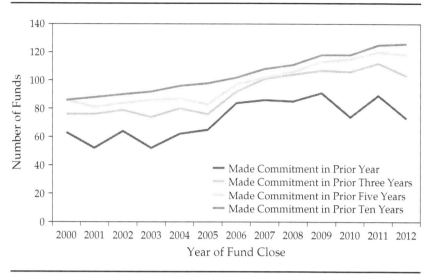

Source: PitchBook.

Other measures of the relative importance of private equity to pension funds are the *amount* of total commitments to private equity and the *proportion* of total investments allocated to private equity. The pension funds with the largest amount of capital committed to private equity are shown in table 8.1. CalPERS is by far the largest contributor to PE investments, with almost twice the size of commitments by CalSTRS (the California State Teachers' Retirement System). The states of Washington, New York, Oregon, and Texas are the next-largest contributors.

The states with the largest proportion of funds allocated to private equity are not necessarily the largest. Aggregate data on this measure are more difficult to come by, but according to one study by Wilshire Trust Universe Comparison Service, pensions with assets over $5 billion had an average allocation to private equity of 13 percent as of June 30, 2012, up from 9.5 percent in 2011.[6] PitchBook data provide a more conservative estimate of 8 percent for the fifty funds with assets over $5 billion for which data are available. For all eighty funds in the PitchBook database with at least 1 percent invested in private equity, the average and median percentage of PE investment is also 8 percent; the weighted average is 9.9 percent.[7] According to PitchBook, at the end of 2013 the top ten funds with PE investments had an average allocation of 19 percent.[8]

Table 8.1   Public Pension Funds with the Largest Commitments
to Private Equity, 2013

Limited Partner	Private Equity Allocation (Millions of Dollars)	Private Equity (Percentage)	Assets Under Management (Millions of Dollars)
California Public Employees' Retirement System (CalPERS)	$42,000	16%	$269,100
California State Teachers' Retirement System (CalSTRS)	21,759	13	170,000
Washington State Investment Board	16,170	18	91,360
New York State Common Retirement Fund	14,926	9	160,400
Oregon Investment Council	14,900	18	81,000
Oregon Public Employees' Retirement System	13,550	21	63,240
Teacher Retirement System of Texas	13,145	10	134,454
Ontario Municipal Employees' Retirement System	10,257	12	84,769
Pennsylvania Public School Employees' Retirement System	8,040	22	50,500
New York State Teachers' Retirement System	7,400	8	95,100
Florida State Board of Administration	6,500	5	169,200
Florida Retirement System	6,476	5	168,100
New York City Employees' Retirement System	5,925	6	46,389
Massachusetts Pension Reserves Investment Trust	5,917	12	54,400
Ohio Public Employees' Retirement System	5,271	6	82,600
Virginia Retirement System	5,000	9	58,300
Teachers' Retirement System of the State of Illinois	4,600	12	40,200
State Teachers' Retirement System of Ohio	4,386	7	68,000
New York City Retirement Systems	4,157	4	139,200

(Table continues on p. 246.)

Table 8.1   *Continued*

Limited Partner	Private Equity Allocation (Millions of Dollars)	Private Equity (Percentage)	Assets Under Management (Millions of Dollars)
Los Angeles County Employees' Retirement Association	3,831	9	42,000
Indiana Public Retirement System	3,400	12	28,300
North Carolina Retirement Systems	2,960	4	81,100
Iowa Public Employees' Retirement System	2,871	11	25,100
Maryland State Retirement Pension System	2,500	6	40,620
State of Connecticut Retirement and Trust Funds	2,265	9	26,600
Teachers' Retirement System of the City of New York	2,100	6	32,775
Public School Retirement System of Missouri	1,943	6	34,600
Kentucky Retirement Systems	1,796	12	14,600
Arizona State Retirement System	1,754	6	28,400

Source: PitchBook, authors' calculations.

Pension Fund Fiduciary Duty and Private Equity Investments

Developments in law and economics since the 1970s have played a central role in shaping the allocation strategies of limited partners in general, and pension funds more specifically. As Steve Lydenberg, a top scholar on fiduciary responsibility, notes, "The concept of fiduciary duty sits at the confluence of two powerful streams of Western intellectual thought, the legal and the economic: the legal because fiduciaries are managing the assets of others whose interests the law seeks to protect; the economic because fiduciaries assume the role of investors in the marketplace in managing these assets."[9]

These developments in law and economics have affected economic behavior at two interconnected levels: at the level of productive enterprises and at the level of institutional investors. At both levels, the assumptions of agency theory and modern portfolio theory have redefined how managerial responsibilities are to be executed—at the firm level between managers and shareholders, and at the institutional investor level between pension fund managers and beneficiaries. When private equity enters as an actor, it is at the center of these relationships—as an investor that disciplines corporate managers on behalf of shareholders and as a PE general partner responsible for investing capital committed by pension funds, which must comply with the fiduciary duty to act in the best interests of pension fund beneficiaries. This complex legal and economic role is open to agency problems and conflicts of interest.

The assumptions of agency theory have affected economic behavior at the level of the firm, as we argued in chapter 2. We described how this theory addresses the issue of the alignment of interests between shareholders and managers: managers' responsibility to shareholders is to maximize their returns regardless of the impact of these decisions on other stakeholders or on the long-term sustainability of the business. Private equity buyouts represent one of the most extreme examples of the enactment of agency theory: a small group of investors is able to control enterprise-level decision-making so as to extract maximum returns for themselves over a relatively short period of time by selling off assets, requiring payment of dividend recapitalizations, and making excessive use of leverage.

Corporate law came to embrace the maximization of shareholder returns as a standard for corporate fiduciary responsibility. This dominant view, however, came under increasing attack by critical legal scholars, who argued that in fact there is little in business and corporate law, or in the court's interpretation of these bodies of law, to justify a focus on shareholder value as the singular measure of a company's fulfillment of its fiduciary duties.[10]

A similar debate has occurred at the level of institutional investors. For pension funds the central question is: What is the fiduciary responsibility of pension fund trustees, and how is this defined? To what extent, for example, must pension funds maximize the short-term returns to the fund?

Pension funds are based in trust law and have a fiduciary duty that is higher than that imposed on corporations—"something stricter than the morals of the market place," according to the American jurist Benjamin Cardoso.[11] The law requires strict adherence to principles of loyalty and impartiality in acting in the best interests of current and future beneficiaries. This entails the avoidance of self-interested behavior and conflicts of interest and the full and truthful disclosure of information on fund activities to beneficiaries. The legal language that historically governed the actions of pension fund managers states that these fiduciaries must use "the entirety of their skill, care, and diligence" when exercising their authority, and that they must use their discretion in deciding whether or not to delegate authority and to whom.[12]

Legal scholars, however, have noted that while the legal standard for fiduciary duty has not changed, expectations for achieving that duty have: "The definitional content of the investment function of this duty has been in constant evolution," according to Jay Youngdahl,[13] and its interpretation is "dynamic," note James Hawley and his colleagues.[14] Through most of the twentieth century, the courts interpreted the content of that duty to be that of investing in only the safest assets, such as government bonds. This approach was modified in the "Second Restatement of the Law of Trusts," issued by the American Law Institute's 1959 convention of legal experts. It adopted the "prudent man rule," characterized as "how men of prudence, discretion and intelligence manage their own affairs, not in regard to speculation, but in regard to the permanent disposition of their funds."[15] Nonetheless, certain investments continued to be ruled out as improper, including those in speculative securities, purchase of securities in new enterprises, and purchase of land for resale.[16] Thereafter, adherence to this standard collapsed in the face of ongoing changes in the economy and innovations in the financial industry that offered a much broader array of investment vehicles with potentially higher rates of return.

Recognizing these changes, the 1974 ERISA created a national framework for pension standards and set only a general standard, the "prudent man rule," to describe the standard that should be used to judge whether a pension fund is meeting its fiduciary duties. This language offered pension trustees latitude to use their best "reasonable" judgment in the allocation of pension assets in a broad range of investment vehicles, including the stock market, speculative securities, and junk bonds. While ERISA covers only private-sector pension plans, most public pension funds have followed its precepts as well as the guidelines issued by the Employee Benefit Security Administration of the U.S. Department of Labor, which oversees the act.[17]

In this context, debate focused on how to define "reasonable." In his award-winning article on this topic, Lydenberg explains that historically legal interpretations drew on notions of good judgment and discretion in managing one's own needs, which were viewed as encompassing not only individual needs but also those of family, community, and society. Economists, by contrast, defined "reasonable" in terms of "rational," individual, self-interested behavior.[18] Rational economic investment behavior came increasingly to be defined in terms of modern portfolio theory, which assumes that markets are efficient, information is symmetric and able to correct temporary market imbalances, investors are risk-averse, and risks can be minimized through diversification, securitization, and hedging to maximize rewards at the level of the portfolio.[19] A significant contribution of modern portfolio theory was to conceptualize risk at the level of a portfolio of assets, rather than examining the risk associated with each individual investment, as had historically been the norm. Returns could be increased by investing in riskier assets, and these risks could be managed in a carefully chosen portfolio of such assets. Risk could be reduced by diversification at the portfolio level.[20] Pension managers could also use securitization, which in theory reduces risk by bundling and reselling a set of assets that have different levels of risk. And they could hedge against future risks by using derivatives and futures options based on sophisticated mathematical modeling.[21] Thus, modern portfolio theory encouraged investors to enhance returns by taking on more risk.[22]

The important point for this discussion is that modern portfolio theory became the dominant approach for allocating pension fund assets. It encouraged pension fund managers to invest in riskier individual financial products (which would provide higher returns) because they could manage these risks at the portfolio level. As Lydenberg notes, modern portfolio theory "crowded out the more reason-based thinking" that allowed fiduciaries to define prudence and loyalty more broadly.[23] This economic theory transformed the legal framework in which fund managers operated.

By 1992, when the American Law Institute revisited the law of trusts and issued the "Third Restatement of the Law of Trust," it embraced the idea that fund trustees should be given leeway in investment decisions and adopted the assumptions of modern portfolio theory by substituting the language of the "prudent investor rule" for the "prudent man rule." The duty of loyalty became defined narrowly in terms of a fiduciary's duty to assess risk and return and diversify investments to limit losses.[24] The 1997 Uniform Prudent Investor Act reaffirmed these standards, allowing for investments in a wide range of risky products and for delegation of responsibilities to expert service providers. It prescribed that trustees must focus on the portfolio-level risk-return trade-off and use diversification to minimize risk.[25]

Similarly, in its 1994 ERISA guidelines, the Employee Benefit Security Administration defined fiduciary duty strictly in terms of minimizing risk and maximizing returns. Its 2008 guidelines strengthened the prohibition against selecting investments on any basis other than the economic interests of the plan, with specific reference to the tools of modern portfolio theory analysis: "In evaluating the plan portfolio, as well as portions of the portfolio, the fiduciary is required to examine the level of diversification, degree of liquidity, and the potential risk/return in comparison with available alternative investments."[26] And further, if fiduciaries do rely on factors outside the interests of the plan and are challenged, they "will rarely be able to demonstrate compliance with ERISA absent a written record demonstrating that a contemporaneous economic analysis showed that the investment alternatives were of equal value."[27] The directive goes on to use the example of a pension fund's investment in a limited partnership that plans to invest in a company that competes with the plan's sponsor. That fact alone would not be grounds for disallowing the investment.[28]

Critics have identified several problems with modern portfolio theory that undermine its scientific authority as a basis for investment decisions. Behavioral economists have shown that its assumptions of self-interested rationality are flawed because the decisions of real market actors reflect a much wider set of "irrational" factors. Finance economists have argued that the economic definition of risk does not capture the full level of uncertainty or ambiguity in real markets, so that relying on this definition of risk does not produce accurate forecasts of returns. In an award-winning paper, for example, Menachem Brenner and Yehuda Izhakian demonstrated this point by modeling the impact of risk as well as a measure of ambiguity on returns, and found that while the former had significant positive effects on returns, the latter had significant negative effects.[29]

Moreover, modern portfolio theory assumes that the risk management strategies adopted by portfolio managers do not affect the amount of risk in financial markets as a whole. The financial crisis exploded this assumption. Because investors are risk-averse and can be held personally liable for the underperformance of their funds, they tend to follow the same practices as their peers, leading to what Keith Johnson and Frank Jan de Graff call copycat or "herding behavior."[30] Thus, when all investors follow the precepts of modern portfolio theory, their collective behavior can have a major impact on financial markets. In the 2000s, institutional investors chased risky investments to increase their short-term returns, with confidence that their risks were diversified away; in doing so, they contributed to heightened systemic risk. As Lydenberg aptly states, "Instead of being disconnected from the systemic risks of the market, they increase it by increasing systemic risk through the increase of the supply of, and demand for, risky products"—leading to heightened volatility and boom-bust cycles that undermine the stability of the economy.[31] And systemic risk that affects the entire market cannot be diversified away.[32]

Given their investment in risky assets and their economic power to influence global financial markets, pension funds are implicated in the financial crisis. The average pension assets-to-GDP ratio for countries in the Organisation for Economic Cooperation and Development (OECD) was 76 percent in 2007.[33] The crisis cost pension funds dearly, with a loss in 2008 alone of some $5.4 trillion (20 percent) of global pension assets, undermining the long-term security of millions of beneficiaries.[34] The lesson from the financial crisis is that the value and sustainability of pension funds depend on the long-term sustainability of corporations and growth in the American economy.[35] And the collective focus on short-term profits leads to "the unintended consequences of destroying long-term value, decreasing market efficiency, reducing investment returns, and impeding efforts to strengthen corporate governance."[36] This was the conclusion of a panel of experts—corporate leaders, asset and hedge fund managers, and institutional investors—brought together *before* the financial crisis by the Business Roundtable Institute for Corporate Ethics, which represents CEOs from over 160 global corporations, and the CFA Centre for Financial Market Integrity, which is the industry voice for financial market ethics.[37]

The heavy reliance on modern portfolio theory in defining the judicial duty of loyalty also had the effect of marginalizing the importance of the second duty under the "prudent man rule"—that of impartiality, which requires trustees to consider the needs of future as well as current beneficiaries. Ed Waitzer and his colleagues argue persuasively that the duty of loyalty and impartiality needs to be rebalanced to avoid a repeat of the kind of losses experienced in the financial crisis.[38] This rebalancing would require a change in focus toward long-term wealth creation, which "requires consideration of a wide range of governance, systemic, and intangible factors that extend beyond short-term financial or other performance metrics."[39]

In line with modern portfolio theory, pension funds have sought higher returns through investments in private equity funds even when the returns are the result of the significant downsizing, destabilization, and, in the extreme, even bankruptcy of U.S. corporations. Many pension funds continue to invest in private equity, and as we saw earlier in this chapter, the number of funds investing in private equity has increased since the financial crisis. Arguably, pension funds are under greater pressure than ever to enhance returns after the losses of the economic crisis and to cover current retirement outlays without increasing beneficiary or taxpayer contributions. Many pension fund trustees and managers remain convinced of the soundness of current financial thinking and of the ability of PE funds to deliver returns that "beat the market." And to the extent that PE investments do beat the market, the "prudent investor" rule can be interpreted as requiring fund managers to continue to invest in these funds. The impact of the financial crisis, however, has alerted some pension fund managers and trustees to the need to reexamine their own PE investments and to consider whether they are at odds with the long-term sustainability goals of their pension funds.

Another challenge to pension funds' ability to fulfill their fiduciary duty is the heightened complexity of the service-provider supply chain. With the rise of complex financial instruments and alternative investment strategies, pension funds have come to rely more and more on expert service providers. ERISA allows trustees and fund managers to delegate some of their investment authority to these providers, but if they do, they must ensure that their delegates conform to the high standards of ERISA—to act only in the best interests of fund participants and beneficiaries. Johnson and de Graff point out the potential for the misalignment of interests. The beneficiaries themselves have little or no control over how pension funds are invested, trustees typically serve a limited time and may lack the requisite skills or knowledge to effectively assess investment decisions, and the compensation of investment managers often includes bonuses that depend on the short-term performance of the assets they manage.[40]

In private equity deals, particularly large ones, these supply-chain complexities and potential conflicts of interest are exacerbated. The supply chain may involve a consortium of different PE firms with different approaches, a large number of lenders that provide substantial loans, a number of service providers that do the underwriting, lawyers for all of these parties, and others. Yet under the current norms of PE partnerships, pension fund trustees and managers typically do not have access to the kind of information that would permit them to determine whether PE general partners, or the service providers they contract with, are acting in the best long-term interests of fund beneficiaries.

Aligning the Interests of the Limited and General Partners

Agency theory provides the basis for private equity's claim that it is a more efficient form of corporate governance that better aligns the interests of the shareholders (in this case the limited partners and general partners) and a company's top management so that the shareholders are able to maximize their returns on investment. The interests of the LPs and GPs are aligned to the extent that they both depend on the dividends and profits from owning and selling a portfolio company. Agency theory does not anticipate, however, the many ways in which the interests of LPs and GPs may be misaligned, depending on how the LP agreement is structured. The problems of alignment particularly emerged in the postcrisis years.

Excessive or unwarranted management fees were at the top of limited partners' complaints to the general partners of funds. According to a 2011 Preqin study based on detailed interviews with fifty leading institutional investors, 50 percent felt that excessive management fees were a key problem.[41] In the classic "2 and 20" model, LPs pay a 2 percent annual management fee to the GPs to manage the fund. GPs receive 20 percent of profits from investments (so-called carried interest) over a given hurdle rate. For a $100 million LP investment in a ten-year fund, LPs are paid $2 million annually, or $20 million over ten years.

In addition, as we have noted, the empirical evidence that private equity investments actually beat the market needs careful scrutiny. Moreover, in

Figure 8.4   Contributions from and Distributions to Limited Partners, 2000 to 2012

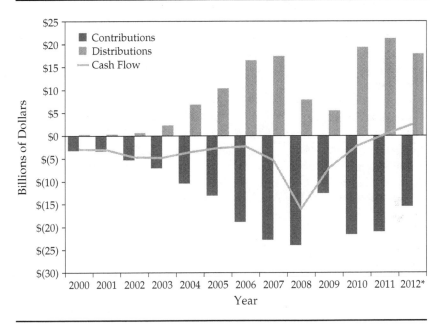

Source: PitchBook.
Note: 2012 figures as of September 30, 2012.

the postcrisis period in particular, the returns on investment promised by PE funds often failed to meet expectations or to materialize at all because private equity could not exit portfolio companies, nor could GPs invest all of the money from a given fund, because opportunities for good investments had fallen. Thus, LPs felt that they were overpaying on management fees when GPs were not able to use all of the funds they had committed or when GPs were not able to exit investments and return distributions to them in a timely fashion. Some PE managers accept the LP position. In the "SuperReturn 2012" conference in Boston, for example, Cerberus Capital Management cofounder and CEO Steve Feinberg admitted, "General partners make absurd amounts of money. We're all overpaid. LPs asking for fee discounts are completely justified."[42]

A comparison of limited partner contributions to private equity funds and distributions from those funds illustrates this point. As figure 8.4 shows, LP contributions have exceeded distributions in most years since 2000, but distributions particularly fell off during the crisis years of 2007 to 2009. They began to break even in the period 2010 to 2012, largely because PE firms increased their use of dividend recapitalizations—putting more debt on portfolio companies in order to pay dividends to themselves and their limited partners.

Limited partners have sought to reduce the absolute size and relative weight of management fees in the compensation of PE general partners. Not only are management fees costly, but it is carried interest (that is, returns on investments) that is expected to align the interests of LPs and GPs, not management fees. The incentives for GPs are the opposite—over time they have become more dependent on management fees compared to carried interest.

The carry components of GP compensation have shifted to fixed income components for several reasons. The conventional understanding is that general partners have earned about two-thirds of their compensation from carried interest and one-third from fixed components such as fees. At some point that relationship changed. One econometric study of 144 buyout funds raised between 1993 and 2006 found that almost two-thirds of the revenue of PE firms came from fixed components, but this study did not show how or when the proportion of fixed-to-carry changed over this time period.[43] It did document that the proportion of GP revenues from fees relative to carry increased with the size of the fund in successive rounds of fund-raising during the period under study, prior to the financial crisis. General partners in these larger funds earned more even though the funds returned lower revenues per dollar of committed funds.[44] After the crisis, the relative importance of management fees rose because investment returns were lower, spurring PE firms to look for other ways to make money, including diversification into managing other asset classes, such as hedge funds, which depend more on management fees than private equity. LPs worry that, as PE funds diversify and grow larger, they lose their focus on their "core" buyout business. A third factor pertains to those PE firms that have gone public—such as Blackstone, KKR, and Apollo—and now need to produce regular returns and pay dividends to their own shareholders.

The most extreme case is Blackstone, where, in 2010, fees from managing assets and advisory services accounted for 63 percent of dividend payouts, and for 82 percent in 2011. Private equity now accounts for only 25 percent of Blackstone's business.[45] PE firms can make money by maximizing assets under management, in the interest of their own shareholders, or maximizing returns on portfolio investments, in the interest of limited partners. According to Feinberg of Cerberus, "I do think there's an issue here in funds that are too large and funds that have acquired too many assets under management. . . . If your goal is to maximize your returns as opposed to assets under management, I think you can be most effective with a big company infrastructure and a little bit smaller fund size."[46] Similarly, according to a 2012 report by the PE consultant

StepStone Group LLC, recent activities such as "asset aggregation and going public or selling stakes to third parties" have reduced the alignment between LPs and some of the larger PE firms.[47] In sum, the interests of the limited partners of PE funds may be at odds with the interests of the shareholders of those firms.

Recommendations of the Institutional Limited Partners Association

This question of misalignment returns us to the earlier discussion in this chapter of how pension fund trustees and managers, as well as other fund trustees, ensure that they are meeting their fiduciary duties when they outsource investment decisions to suppliers such as private equity firms. How do they ensure that the PE general partners are acting in the best interests of fund beneficiaries when pension funds have little input into decision-making and little access to transparent information on fund performance?

There was enough concern over the misalignment of LP and GP interests after the financial crisis to cause the Institutional Limited Partners Association (ILPA) to issue a set of principles for private equity partnerships in September 2009.[48] ILPA, which started out as an informal networking association among LPs investing in private equity, was founded in 2002. It includes pension funds, endowments, insurance companies, and foundations that invest in private equity, and it now represents over 250 LPs with over $1 trillion in PE assets.[49] The introduction to the report notes that while the partnership structure historically has been successful in aligning LP and GP interests, "certain terms and conditions that have gradually evolved should receive renewed attention," including the alignment between GPs and LPs, fund governance, and transparency.[50] The ILPA accepted input from GPs, LPs, and others after the principles were issued, and in January 2011 it released "Version 2.0" of the report, which had a somewhat more conciliatory tone.[51]

The 2011 report reiterated the concern of limited partners over the alignment of interests, noting that "GP wealth creation from excessive management, transaction or other fees and income sources, reduces alignment of interest," and that "a GP's own capital at risk serves as the greatest incentive for alignment of interests."[52] LPs believe that this kind of "skin in the game" is needed because over the course of the ten-year PE fund, GPs make many decisions that are not observable; given this lack of transparency, the LP agreement must be structured to align GP and LP interests. A 2010 Preqin survey found that at least two-thirds of GPs contributed less than 3.5 percent—the minimum that the ILPA recommends is needed for alignment of interests.[53] GPs and LPs also disagree on how those contributions should be made: GPs prefer to simply waive management fees and raise the amount of carried interest they receive (which has tax advantages), while the ILPA recommends that GPs should make cash contributions as a stronger signal of their commitment to the fund's success.

A second issue raised in the ILPA report is whether limited partner agreements (LPAs) are based on a "deal-by-deal" distribution-of-carry model (the common U.S. approach) or a "whole fund waterfall" structure (the common European approach). In the deal-by-deal model, the general partner receives profits, or carry, for each investment once the LPs' capital for that investment is returned, plus their share of the profits for that investment. Thus, GPs may receive carry throughout the ten-year period of the fund. LPs worry that this may leave them exposed to losses if future deals do not perform well. Thus, deal-by-deal agreements typically include a "clawback" provision so that if there is overpayment of carried interest, GPs must return funds to the investors.[54] Clawback provisions depend, however, on the creditworthiness of the GP and may require litigation to enforce. The "back-ended carry" or the "whole fund approach," endorsed by the ILPA, calculates carried interest on the performance of the entire fund; this approach simplifies accounting and reduces the likelihood of GP-LP conflict. The ILPA also insists that carried interest should be based on net rather than gross profits, and on an after-tax basis.[55]

Deal-by-deal models continued to prevail in almost half of the U.S. funds closed in 2009 and 2010, according to a 2010 Preqin survey, while that model applied to only 11 percent of European and Asian funds.[56] The ILPA recommends that where deal-by-deal models continue, LPs should insist on a set of detailed clawback protections, including the return of all fees and expenses to date (rather than on a pro-rata basis); the requirement for a carry escrow account with reserves of at least 30 percent of carry distributions plus additional funds to cover clawbacks; joint and several liability of individual GP members; and "robust enforcement powers" for LPs, including the direct ability to enforce the clawback.[57]

The ILPA principles are also a response to the heightened disputes over management fees that occurred in the postcrisis period. The principles call on PE funds to disclose a fee model based on a budget to cover "reasonable" expenses and salaries for professionals and staff and other operating and administrative costs, such as rent, overhead, and deal sourcing. Fees should be reduced toward the end of an investment period or in the formation of follow-on funds. Moreover, all monitoring, transaction, advisory, or exit fees should go 100 percent to the benefit of the fund to reduce any conflict inherent in the manager working for the company in which the partnership has an investment.[58] In the past, these fees were split fifty-fifty between the GPs and the LPs.[59]

"Zombie funds" have also undermined the rates of return that limited partners realize, and they became a particular source of contention in the postcrisis period when private equity funds were less able to exit their investments. Zombie funds occur when returns from investments in portfolio companies fail to materialize after many years—often defined as the fund's predetermined life span plus two years. TorreyCove Capital Partners, a consulting firm, classified about two hundred private equity funds worth some $100 billion as zombie funds in 2012.[60] Preqin reported a higher number: 1,200 zombie funds worth $116 billion in global assets.[61] Many limited partners continue to pay management fees on these funds despite the fact that they have little chance of recouping their investment. The state of Illinois, for example, spent $580,000 on fees for zombie funds in 2010. Subsequently, it was able to negotiate down the percentage of fees paid, but the fees were not eliminated.[62] Many GPs simply hang on to these investments, hoping that at some point better options for exit may materialize. In the meantime, LPs have few options: "It's quite difficult for investors in zombie funds to do anything other than wait for their release," according to Christopher McDermott, marketing chief at Coller Capital Inc.[63] Under the ILPA principles, GPs would need the approval of the Limited Partner Advisory Council (LPAC), which oversees a PE fund, to gain a one-year extension; otherwise, they would have to liquidate the fund within one year of its expiration.[64]

Limited partners in general also worry about the increased use of co-investment strategies in the aftermath of the crisis. In this approach, an LP negotiates an agreement with a PE fund in order to invest directly in a portfolio company along with the GP of the fund, gain a decision-making role in investment strategies, and have more access to information. Co-investment agreements have become popular because some LPs (typically the very large funds) can use them as a strategy to increase their weight in decision-making and control over PE funds, while GPs view them as a means of keeping their investment in portfolio companies below an 80 percent threshold to avoid legal liabilities for pension funds in the case of a company's bankruptcy. For the LPs who are not co-investors, however, these more privileged partnerships raise the specter that the alignment of GPs and the remaining LPs will be thrown off. The ILPA addressed this issue by stating that the GP should only be allowed to invest in a pooled fund vehicle and not co-invest in a select number of underlying deals. LPs also are concerned that GPs may use other vehicles to invest in opportunities that would otherwise be appropriate for the fund they have committed to; the ILPA principles state that these arrangements must be disclosed prior to the close of the fund.[65]

Standards of governance in PE funds have also drawn serious attention because GPs have sole discretion over investment decisions during the long period in which LPs hold illiquid commitments to the fund. Fund agreements often have only minimal requirements that GPs acknowledge conflicts of interest in their annual report, rather than notify LPs and gain their consent on a course of action prior to a conflict occurring.[66] The ILPA principles require that all conflicts of interest and all self-dealing be disclosed and approved by the LPAC ahead of time. The principles also outline a series of procedures to protect and remedy LP interests in the event of unforeseen conflicts of interest, changes in the fund's investment strategy or key members of the GP team, or breeches of the partnership agreement or fiduciary duties. For example, a significant change in the management team should trigger an automatic suspension of the investment period, which might become permanent unless reinstated by a supermajority vote of LPs. Managers may leave, for example, if a fund is not performing well. Moreover, the principles call for a simple majority of LPs to be able to terminate a fund or remove a GP for cause.[67] The current standard typically requires a supermajority of 85 to 95 percent to terminate a manager for cause.[68] Finally, the principles encourage the enhanced role of LPACs in audit review, monitoring of GP activities and expense allocation, approval of valuation methodologies, and new business initiatives, and they provide an exhaustive protocol for LPAC best-practice approaches.[69]

Concerns over transparency are related to governance issues, as LPs need accurate information to monitor and evaluate the performance of the GPs, their observance of standards of judiciary responsibility, and their adherence to the LP agreement over its long duration. But LPAs typically do not provide extensive rights to information.[70] The ILPA principles explicitly identify the need for regular disclosure of all fees (including financing, monitoring, transactions, redemption, or those charged to the fund by an affiliate of the GP), capital calls and distributions, and material risks and how they will be managed. They also provide detailed requirements for the quarterly and annual financial reports on the fund and portfolio companies.[71]

Some have argued that LP discontent over management fees and fund performance and the release of the ILPA principles in the post-crisis period have led to a shift in the balance of power between LPs and GPs. One legal writer, for example, starkly asserted that "the balance of power has shifted from the investment managers who create private equity funds to the pension plans and other folks with money that invest in the private equity asset class."[72] Similarly, Altius Associates, a global PE firm, stated in its annual report that major changes are occurring in GP-LP relations around the world. According to its head of investor relations, Eric Warner, "Most major GPs are now meeting with significant LPS on a quarterly basis, with full portfolio reviews, including all major changes, cash flow statements and details of drawdowns, distributions and any valuation changes."[73] He went on to note that these changes have

required PE firms to add staff; the ILPA has gained members and credibility over these issues; and this trend is likely to continue given ongoing
changes in regulations. Also supporting this view, a 2011 Preqin study
of fifty major institutional investors found that 69 percent of LPs would
potentially forgo investment in a fund if it did not conform to ILPA principles. Preqin concluded that it is becoming increasingly difficult for GPs
to justify partnership agreements that fail to take seriously the ILPA's
guidelines for terms and conditions.[74]

Yet the same study by Preqin noted that little change has occurred in
such fundamental areas as the deal-to-deal distribution model or carry or
the level of contributions that GPs make to private equity funds. Warner's
comments pertained to the "significant" limited partners. And while the
media has frequently alluded to the idea that management fees are moving from a 2 percent level to 1.5 percent, the evidence is mixed. Mercer's
"2012 Global Asset Manager Fee Survey" said that U.S. alternative asset
managers are moving toward a "1.5 and 20" standard.[75] But Preqin examined management fees collected in 2011 and found that they continued
to average 2 percent, except for funds over $1 billion, for which it was
1.71 percent.[76] In sum, the relative balance of power between LPs and GPs
may have shifted for some of the most visible and largest institutional
investors, but change for the limited partners as a whole appears to be
moving quite slowly.

New Approaches to Alternative Investments

While the ILPA outlined a series of reforms that would better align the
interests of general partners and limited partners, those principles are
currently viewed as aspirational, with real behavioral change slow to
materialize. Within LP organizations, such as pension funds and foundations, whether and how much to invest in private equity has been a
hotly contested issue. While some advocate the complete disinvestment
of funds in private equity, others argue for investments to expand to
almost 50 percent of the portfolio. According to a recent survey by Collier
Capital of 140 limited partners who invest in private equity, many said
that members of their organizations were quite hostile to investing in private equity. Among LPs of pension plans, 37 percent said that colleagues
wanted their organization to reduce or eliminate completely their investment in private equity. Among LPs of foundations and endowments, the
percentage was 43 percent.[77]

Some large pension funds have simply sold off their investments in PE
funds, an approach that has given rise to a so-called secondaries market
for PE investments. Among the first to take this step was the California
Public Employees' Retirement System, the country's largest, which sold
off $2 billion in PE commitments in 2007.[78] In 2012 both the Wisconsin

Investment Board and the New York City pension fund completed sales of PE investments worth about $1 billion each. The Wisconsin board ostensibly sold off commitments to Blackstone, the Carlyle Group, and KKR because it could not be certain that the three publicly traded firms would put the interests of fund beneficiaries first.[79] Others, however, are increasing their allocation to private equity; the North Carolina state senate approved legislation, for instance, that would allow up to 40 percent of the state pension fund to be invested in alternative assets (private equity, hedge funds, and the like)—up from its current 34 percent.[80]

A handful of powerful institutional investors and general partners have experimented with alternative ownership and governance structures, including separate LP accounts, co-investment, and direct investment approaches. Separate LP accounts are structured so that the GP will manage a special account for a limited partner for a reduced fee, with the LP offered first access to deals in exchange for a longer investment time horizon than the typical five- to seven-year framework. The GP gains a more substantial and stable capital commitment. Although LPs' use of co-investment funds has increased in recent years, this strategy remains too new to evaluate; however, large investments in individual portfolio companies lack even the limited diversification of a PE fund with multiple portfolio companies and may prove risky.

Co-investment strategies may be one way for LPs to gain a larger decision-making role in PE fund investment decisions. But PE firms view co-investment strategies as a way to protect themselves from the pension liabilities of bankrupt portfolio firms. Under ERISA, the legal standard is that owners are liable for pensions if they control at least 80 percent of the company (the "common control group liability" benchmark). PE funds can avoid that 80 percent standard by co-investing with other PE firms or LPs. The issue became more salient in 2012, when the Teamsters sued Sun Capital, claiming it was liable for the pensions of workers in the bankrupt company that it owned, Scott Brass. As we discuss in more detail in chapter 9, the Massachusetts District Court sided with Sun Capital, but the appellate court sided with the union and sent the case back to the lower court for further review. Ira Bogner, a partner at the law firm Proskauer, summarized the strategy succinctly in an interview with *Private Equity Manager:* "You could give a limited number of investors the ability to take a slice of the investment to get you under the 80 percent, and this means you don't have the same investor base, and you have the same argument that those entities shouldn't be aggregated [under common control] as well."[81] The Massachusetts District Court decision has shown that some courts can be receptive to the argument that splitting an investment across multiple funds or partners is a legitimate way of spreading risk. That opens the door for co-investments (a legitimate risk diversification strategy) to double as a shield against pension liabilities when enough side-investors dip the fund below an 80 percent stake in any given portfolio company.[82]

Direct investment approaches provide pension funds with the greatest independence to pursue strategies in the interests of their beneficiaries without concern for conflicts of interest with general partners. They simply involve investing directly in the buyout of portfolio companies. Canadian funds have been the most aggressive in pursuing direct investment, often through the establishment of their own PE funds rather than investments in funds sponsored by PE firms. Successful examples come from the Ontario Teachers' Pension Plan and the Canada Pension Plan. The Ontario Teachers' Pension Plan has invested $12 billion in private equity of its roughly $100 billion asset base.[83] The Canada Plan is a major player in PE deal-making and has closed some of the largest deals in the postcrisis period—including a $4 billion acquisition with TPG of a major health care data provider, IMS Health, and a $5 billion joint investment with Onex Partners in 2010.[84]

Among these approaches, only the last seems to offer pension funds an avenue for using the private equity business model while retaining control over key investment decisions and portfolio company strategies. But this approach does not address the fundamental critique of modern portfolio theory and the problems of short-term investment horizons raised by legal scholars. Similarly, the principles articulated by the Institutional Limited Partners Association spell out a series of important reforms that would improve the balance of power for limited partners in terms of management fees, the distribution of carried interest, governance structures, and transparency, but without altering the fundamental premises of investment decisions—those based on short-term returns and the diversification of risk through portfolio management, securitization, and hedging. Pension funds might get a somewhat better deal with the general partners, but without questioning what types and mixes of investments are in the long-term interests of the fund and its beneficiaries. Here Edward Waitzer states that pension fund trustees must take the lead in order "to aggressively advance the process of developing models that are not solely about rules and reporting or compliance, but rather, involve thinking more deeply about what motivates good behavior and informed judgment."[85] More broadly, pension funds are called on to incorporate standards of environmental, social, and corporate governance metrics into their investment decisions.

Conclusion

The limited partners in private equity funds face a series of legal, economic, and political dilemmas in managing their unequal relationship with the general partners of those funds. In particular, the largest block of PE investors—pension funds—are held to a very high standard of fiduciary duty to act in the best interest of their current and future beneficiaries. Lack of transparency itself is particularly problematic when pension fund trustees are held legally accountable for investment decisions that are completely under the control of GPs and their supply chain of service providers.

Since the passage of ERISA in the 1970s, the legal duty to act in beneficiaries' best interest increasingly became defined in economic terms, based on modern portfolio theory. Returns to investment could be maximized by managing risk at the portfolio level—and minimized through diversification, securitization, and hedging. With the assurance that this approach minimized their exposure to risk, pension fund trustees were encouraged to invest in riskier assets, such as PE funds, in order to enlarge short-term returns. Investing in private equity, with its promise to deliver outsized returns in a five-year window, was viewed as consistent with acting in the best interests of beneficiaries. As pension funds increasingly allocated billions of dollars to high-risk, high-return investments, they contributed importantly to systemic risk and the financial crisis, which in turn undermined the long-term stability of pension funds. Thus, by pursuing their economic strategy to maximize short-term value for current beneficiaries, trustees perhaps failed, ironically, in their duty to protect the interests of long-term beneficiaries and the fund itself.

In the postcrisis period, some limited partners have recognized the problematic nature of the LP-GP relationship and have used the Institutional Limited Partners Association to push for reforms in LP agreements with private equity funds. Some reforms attack the outsized management fees that general partners charge and the relative distribution of returns to LPs and GPs, particularly in light of the low yields, failures to exit portfolio companies, and zombie funds that have been written off altogether in the period since the crisis. LPs seek to better align the interests of GPs with their own by shifting the relative proportion of GP pay that comes from profits (carried interest) as opposed to management fees. And they have sought to shift the balance of power in decision-making by creating an active role for limited partner advisory committees in the monitoring and oversight of portfolio companies, in the transparency of information they receive, and in their ability to terminate fund commitments or GP contracts. They have also sought alternative arrangements for investing, including co-investment, having separate accounts, and direct investment in the portfolio companies themselves.

The reforms themselves, however, as well as their limited adoption, do not address the fundamental contradiction faced by pension funds—that adherence to an economic standard of maximizing short-term returns may be at odds with the fiduciary duty to act in the best interest of long-term beneficiaries and the sustainability of the funds. Such adherence may also be in conflict with the moral obligations and values of beneficiaries who, as workers, may not wish to benefit from short-term strategies that undermine the jobs and well-being of other workers or the stability of the economy as a whole. To meet this challenge, then, pension funds need to reassess their standards and consider a broader range of criteria as the basis for allocating their investments.

= Chapter 9 =

Regulating Private Equity

A s we saw in earlier chapters, private equity firms recruit investors—pension funds, hedge funds, sovereign wealth funds, endowments, wealthy individuals—and accumulate large private pools of capital. They use these funds in leveraged buyouts, at undisclosed prices, of operating companies that they acquire for their portfolios, typically taking control of them. Private equity is a financial intermediary that allocates the savings of its limited partners to financial investments. It is part of the so-called shadow finance sector and provides an alternative financing mechanism to the more highly regulated and transparent traditional financial system.[1]

Among the new financial intermediaries that have emerged as major players in the last four decades, private equity most directly takes control of the management of, and employment relations in, operating companies that produce goods and services and employ millions of U.S. workers. The number of companies that passed through a period of ownership and governance by private equity increased rapidly in the 2000s. The pace of expansion slowed in the postcrisis period, but remained strong. Between 2000 and 2012, PE firms invested over $3.4 trillion in about 18,300 leveraged buyouts, of which two-thirds (about 11,500) were publicly traded companies or divisions of corporations or were independently owned. The remaining one-third were companies purchased by one PE firm from another. The Private Equity Growth Capital Council (PEGCC), the private equity industry association, estimates that between 2000 and 2010 some 7.5 million workers worked or were currently employed in PE-owned companies. As a result, the imprint of PE ownership and control of Main Street companies extends broadly into the U.S. economy. The rules that govern PE ownership and control of companies affect a large cross-section of Americans.

Decades of research have identified critical management strategies that sustain companies for the long term. These include building trust with stakeholders—suppliers, vendors, creditors, workers, and customers—as well as investing in worker skills, engaging frontline employees in problem-solving, and enabling employees to share in the success of the enterprise.[2] Some private equity firms—especially those that take over small or midmarket companies with enterprise values below $300 million—may adopt these practices as a means of adding value to the acquired company.

However, the evidence we have provided in this book, from SEC filings, bankruptcy records, original case studies, and a review of the research in finance economics, shows that all too often private equity owners have engaged in financial engineering—high leverage, the sale of assets, tax arbitrage, dividend recapitalizations, bankruptcy proceedings—to maximize their own returns while putting operating companies and their stakeholders in jeopardy. The use of financial incentives and close monitoring, hiring, and firing of top executives aligns these managers' interests with those of the company's PE owners—its shareholders—who take over the strategic management of the company and measure success in terms of short-term financial performance. The impact on other stakeholders and on the company's long-term competitiveness and sustainability beyond the period in which it is held by private equity becomes a secondary consideration. The research evidence also shows that taxpayers often subsidize PE returns and that PE firms find ways to skirt pension liabilities and shift them to the Pension Benefits Guaranty Corporation.

Outcomes for Stakeholders and Company Sustainability

The strategic decisions of private equity owners may have negative consequences not only for a company's current employees but also for a wide range of stakeholders—from suppliers, bondholders, other creditors, and retirees to customers, the broader community, and the taxpaying public. Private equity may boost profits by reneging on implicit contracts with suppliers and vendors. Customers may be ill served if customer service is outsourced to low-cost subcontractors. Long-standing implicit agreements with employees regarding pay, pensions, working conditions, and labor relations—and sometimes even explicit agreements—may be violated. Rising disparities in pay and employment security destroy the "share the gain, share the pain" ethos that underlies effective teamwork and promotes a company's organic growth. Aggressive use of tax avoidance strategies enriches PE owners at the expense of other taxpayers and of the common good. A lack of transparency and the use of flawed measures of fund performance may mislead limited partners who invest in PE funds and lead to disappointing investment returns for pension funds in periods when PE firms cannot rely on a bubble economy to deliver outsized returns.

The private equity business model builds in incentives for the risky behavior and high use of leverage that increase the probability of financial distress in portfolio companies. The "2 and 20" model—which results in excessive compensation for partners in PE firms, even when some of the portfolio companies they acquire perform poorly—may encourage them to engage in reckless behavior in pursuit of a big win. Earnings that formerly would have been retained by the company and used to invest in research and innovation may be used instead to pay large dividends to the company's PE owners, squeezing the development of the process and product technologies vital to the company's long-term success and the economy's growth. The high use of debt boosts profits for the acquired company's PE owners in good economic times but spells trouble for workers and other stakeholders in bad times. Even a well-managed company, through no fault of its own, may experience financial difficulties in an economic downturn. But highly leveraged companies face much higher risks of default, as the research evidence shows. Without an adequate equity cushion, many companies' debt burdens became unsustainable in the postcrisis years.

Asset stripping and dividend recapitalizations transfer resources from the portfolio company to its PE owners, undermining managers' ability to improve portfolio company operations. Dividend recapitalizations that load the acquired company with even more debt, usually in the form of junk bonds, particularly exacerbate the risks of default that operating companies face in an economic downturn. Even a temporary decline in sales that reduces revenue below expectations leads to downsizing, layoffs, and cuts in worker pay and benefits as operating companies seek to service their debts. Workers, suppliers, and customers are not, however, the only losers. Financial difficulties often result in the portfolio company's bonds trading at pennies on the dollar, creating serious losses for its bondholders. Creditors often try to avert outright default on bonds and loans and to salvage the situation with "amend and extend" agreements that give the operating company time to recover. But highly leveraged companies may nevertheless default on their debts and enter bankruptcy—with high costs for creditors, for workers' jobs and pensions, for vendors, and for the communities in which the bankrupt company has operated. In the extreme, the company may be unable to emerge from bankruptcy and is liquidated.

Still pending are a series of leveraged buyouts from the 2005 to 2007 period that have huge debt loads, much of which private equity has been able to refinance through amend-and-extend agreements. Many PE firms with debt scheduled for repayment in the next few years used the low-interest-rate environment in 2012 to extend maturities and, especially, to take profits out of these companies by issuing new debt and paying themselves and their limited partners dividend recapitalizations. But slow economic growth persists, and the future of companies acquired at high prices at the height of the economic boom remains uncertain.

Yet, as we have also seen, pools of private capital raised by private equity firms can play a constructive role in the economy. Most PE firms are structured as limited partnerships and, as a consequence, are able to facilitate investments that in the current institutional environment may not otherwise receive needed financing. Private equity plays a role in financing high-risk turnarounds for companies in financial distress or bankruptcy. The United States might not have a competitive steel industry today if private equity had not bought up a number of failing integrated steel mills in 2003. Publicly traded companies that are profitable but lag the industry's leaders can benefit from access to the management know-how as well as the capital that PE funds can provide.

Private equity firms also assist small companies in an environment in which the consolidation of the banking system and the declining numbers of local community banks have reduced the ability of small and midsize companies to access financing for investment and expansion. Midmarket PE deals have helped some small and midsize companies, especially those owned by the founding family, to innovate and expand by bringing them access to professional management, strategic decision-making, and financial capital. PE firms may "add value" by developing and implementing a business strategy that takes an operating company to the next level and promotes improvements in operations (supply-chain management, modernization of equipment and technology, process improvements, worker engagement). Even in these instances, however, financial engineering plays an important role in enhancing returns to private equity, though the use of debt financing and dividend recapitalizations is considerably lower.

The goal of public policy should not be to eliminate private equity's use of private pools of capital to finance strategic improvements, but to rein in the excesses of PE firms and the funds they sponsor and to ensure transparency and legal accountability. Public policy needs to reduce the incentives that promote the excessive use of debt and financial engineering and to encourage greater use of operational improvements to achieve superior outcomes for portfolio companies, shareholders, other stakeholders, and the economy. As we discussed in chapter 3, the distinction is the PE's profit-seeking activities that increase the size of the economic pie and its rent-seeking activities designed to redistribute income and wealth from other stakeholders to PE firms and partners.

We begin by briefly reviewing the perverse incentives that prevail in the private equity model and then turn to a discussion of policy measures that can address these incentives and promote value creation by PE firms, mitigate the adverse effects of rent-seeking behavior on other stakeholders and the economy, and hold private equity accountable for its actions in the same way as other employers.

Debt, Moral Hazard, and Perverse Incentives

Debt is the lifeblood of the private equity industry, but its effects are perverse. In good economic times, debt is an important source of high returns for PE investors. But high levels of leverage increase the risk that the portfolio company will fail. The upside gains, which in good times are substantial, accrue to the PE firm and its investors; the losses on the downside fall overwhelmingly on the portfolio company's other stakeholders.

This is a classic example of moral hazard. The private equity firms that make the decisions about the amount of debt to load on a portfolio company are wagering that things will go well while their fund owns the company. Debt magnifies private equity's winnings if the wager pays off. The losses, should the debt load prove too heavy a burden and the portfolio company become bankrupt, are borne by the portfolio company's stakeholders, its bondholders and other creditors, and its employees and retirees. As in any case of moral hazard, these incentives lead PE firms to engage in risky behavior—in this case, to make excessive use of debt. Moreover, private equity's voracious appetite for debt helped fuel the growth of the shadow banking system. To meet this growing demand for loans, banks sought sources of funds other than customer deposits. They turned to off-balance-sheet activities such as the securitization of commercial mortgages and the use of collateralized debt obligations and credit default swaps. These off-balance-sheet activities enabled banks to get around the regulations that ensured the safety of the U.S. financial system and to fund risky investments in highly leveraged companies.[3]

Top executives in acquired companies that have been loaded up with too much debt face a situation with its own perverse incentives. Private equity funds, as we saw in chapter 6, mainly acquire healthy companies that are growing more quickly than other similar establishments in their industry sector; investing in distressed companies is a small sliver of PE activity. Executives in companies acquired in a leveraged buyout are then handed a debt structure by their PE owners and a management plan to service the debt and deliver the high returns these investors expect. The PE owners have the power to hire and fire them and to structure their compensation packages. The promise to this small group of senior managers is this: if they can meet the PE owners' performance targets, they will be richer than they ever dreamed possible once the company is sold; if they fail to deliver, they will be dismissed. This arrangement turns the portfolio company's top managers into the PE owners' "agents": the executives' individual self-interests are now in sync with those of the new owners. As one knowledgeable observer has noted, "The corollary is that [these incentives] may detach the senior team from employees, managers and other groups with whom they had implicit contracts and relationships based on trust."[4]

Like the private equity owners, these senior executives can expect to cash out in three to five years. What happens to the operating company after that is of no concern to the PE firm and its investors—or to the company's top management. Executives in companies whose debt burden precludes them from investing in new technology, employee skills, or organizational improvements have a strong incentive to downsize jobs. Over private equity's time horizon of a few years, this may boost profit margins, improve productivity via work intensification, and make the company appear attractive to prospective buyers. Downsizing is facilitated by the fact that companies in the United States are not required to provide severance payments based on years of service to employees who are let go. Employees who have invested ten or twenty years of their lives helping a company grow and making it an attractive target for acquisition by a PE firm can be fired with little or no notice—and without a severance package that recognizes their investments in valuable firm-specific skills. Firing these employees is a tempting option for managers under pressure to show quick improvement in the bottom line. Executives, by contrast, regardless of their years of tenure, expect a generous severance package; there is no requirement for similar treatment of other employees. Downsizing is costless to the company in the short term. Here again, the incentives favor short-term behavior that benefits private equity but has negative effects on other actors and on the economy.

Curb Private Equity Compensation to Reduce Moral Hazard and Risky Behavior

The "2 and 20" compensation formula described in chapter 3—the PE firm receives an annual payment of 2 percent of committed funds from the limited partners plus 20 percent of the profit (carried interest) on the fund's investments—has yielded huge pay packages for PE firm partners. And notably, while the general partners of PE funds receive 20 percent of the profit after achieving a hurdle rate and make all the investment decisions, they invest only $1 to $2 for every $100 invested by the limited partners in the PE fund and the companies it acquires, with debt used to cover the majority of the purchase price.

The "2 and 20" compensation formula, by providing 20 percent of the profits to general partners who have put up only 1 to 2 percent of the equity, creates perverse incentives for the GPs and encourages them to take on excessive risk—more risk than is socially optimal. With little of their own funds at risk, they are largely insulated from losses if a portfolio company fails. As a result, they can focus on the gains from a risky strategy and ignore the possibility of losses, creating a classic moral hazard situation. As Private Equity International put it: "Bigger returns mean bigger carried interest payouts for the GPs . . . GPs get into the private equity business with the hope of building fortunes through carried interest. If things don't work out well, the other fees associated with private equity fund management are nice consolation prizes, but not overly exciting to ambitious GPs."[5]

A few leading private equity firms are publicly traded and required to report the earnings of their top executives. Perhaps the most highly paid PE executive in 2012 was Stephen Schwarzman, who, as cofounder and chief executive officer of Blackstone Group, received $350,000 in salary and $8.1 million from his share of the firm's carried interest. Tony James, Blackstone's president and chief operating officer, received $350,000 in salary, a $30.1 million bonus, and $2.8 million in carried interest. Not far behind Schwarzman were Henry Kravis and George Roberts, KKR & Co.'s cofounders and co-CEOs, who each received $300,000 in salary and $34.7 million in carried interest. The median pay (base pay, bonus, and carried interest) in 2012 of senior deal-makers in PE firms, while not quite at these levels, was a still rich $1 million.[6]

Incentives that encourage excessively risky behavior are an important contributor to systemic risk. A major aim of the 2010 Dodd-Frank Act passed in the aftermath of the 2008 financial crisis was to reduce systemic risk. To this end, the act explicitly sought to curb excessive executive compensation packages in order to reduce the danger of moral hazard. Section 956 of the act provides broad authorization for regulators to limit excessive compensation at "covered" financial institutions—broadly, any financial institution, including private equity firms, with consolidated assets of $1 billion or more. The rules adopted by regulators to implement this provision require an annual report that "describes the structure of the covered financial institution's incentive-based compensation arrangements . . . that is sufficient to allow an assessment of whether the structure or features of those arrangements provide or are likely to provide excessive compensation, fees, or benefits to covered persons or could lead to material financial loss to the covered financial institution."[7]

As John Coffee observes, these rules are very general and abstract and, except in the case of an institution designated by the authorities as a "too big to fail" institution with over $50 billion in consolidated assets, do not require the reporting of any quantitative data. Instead, these rules require only a narrative description, which, as Coffee observes, is likely to produce "long-winded boilerplate from securities lawyers adept at covering the waterfront in opaque prose."[8]

In the aftermath of the financial crisis and the excessive risk-taking that helped bring it on, Congress attempted to address the role of moral hazard and incentive-based compensation, such as carried interest, in providing incentives for such risky behavior. But the rules adopted by regulators for implementing curbs on the compensation of executives of firms—including the partners in private equity firms—fall far short of that goal and are likely to have a negligible effect on the behavior of general partners in PE funds. Congress should revisit this issue and provide legislation with real teeth that can reduce the incentives for excessive risk-taking by financial institutions, including PE firms.

End Preferential Tax Treatment of Carried Interest

Congress urgently needs to eliminate the carried interest loophole in the tax code and tax carried interest as ordinary income, as is the case with all other forms of performance-based pay. In 2013 the tax rate on carried interest was increased to 20 percent. Taxing it as ordinary income would increase the rate at which this income is taxed and raise nearly $12 billion from 2014 to 2018, and $16 billion from 2014 to 2023.[9]

Many private equity executives admit privately that this tax loophole is indefensible and should be eliminated.[10] The carried interest loophole treats the 20 percent share of a PE fund's profits as if it were investment income and thus taxes it at the lower capital gains rate. In reality, carried interest is income that derives from the effort and skill of the general partners and from the service they provide to the funds' limited partners by managing their investments.[11] For the most part, carried interest does not represent a return on capital that GPs have invested because nearly all of the capital is put up by the fund's LPs. Given that the GPs put up only 1 to 2 percent of the capital invested by the fund, they should be entitled to 1 to 2 percent—not 20 percent—of the fund's profit. This disparity between GPs' investments and returns led the industry publication *Private Equity Manager* to conclude that GPs' disproportionate share of a PE fund's gains is "more akin to a performance bonus than a capital gain" and to agree with the view "that a GP's share of profits made on investor capital should be taxed as income, not capital gains."[12]

Although this type of incentive-based pay has an element of risk for the general partners, it is no different in this respect than other performance-based pay arrangements, such as sales commissions, tips, gain-sharing, or profit-sharing bonuses.[13] Indeed, the existence of this tax loophole has led some PE fund managers—notably at funds sponsored by the PE firms Bain and Apollo—to "waive" the 2 percent fee charged to limited partners that is taxed as ordinary income in exchange for additional carried interest taxed at the lower capital gains rate. This move may be legally dubious and is under examination by the IRS.[14] The IRS has put the fee waiver topic in its "Guidance Plan" (a list of items to examine) for fiscal year 2014.

The most common argument in favor of treating carried interest as a capital gain is that this income is deferred until the portfolio companies are sold. The analogy is to an entrepreneur or inventor who invests "sweat equity" into a business he or she starts, drawing little or no pay for the effort and skill provided while building the business into a going concern.[15] When the business is sold, the profit from the sale of the business is considered a capital gain. Carried interest is the reward for the sweat equity invested by the PE fund's general partner, according to the video on this topic from PEGCC.[16]

The presumed tax advantage for sweat equity is described by a skeptical tax expert as follows:

> This analogue tax advantage is thought to be available to a self-employed individual who devotes skill and effort to building her own business. The business owner may currently forgo fully compensating herself for her labor contribution and instead take the compensation later when she sells all or part of her business for a greater profit. By doing so, she delays and potentially converts what is really income from labor into long-term capital gains. A shop owner, for example, who works day and night to build a business with a loyal customer base, and who is compensated for that effort largely in the form of proceeds from the eventual sale of her business's going-concern value, a capital asset, sees those labor-produced gains taxed at long-term capital gains rates.[17]

In the PEGCC video, the entrepreneur is a baker who builds up her bakery business and then sells it at a profit. The ordinary business of the baker is baking. But PE firms are not bakers or entrepreneurs. Rather, they are more analogous to real estate developers, who are not allowed to treat the real estate they acquire and hold for eventual sale as a capital asset. Similarly, PE funds should not be able to treat the portfolio companies they acquire and hold for eventual sale as capital assets.

There are other obvious differences between the young baker starting her own business and the general partner in a private equity fund. The baker is building a start-up into a successful business, but PE funds overwhelmingly acquire ongoing successful businesses for their portfolios. She is collecting little or no salary while pouring skill and effort into building the bakery, while PE general partners collect large annual management fees from the limited partners and, often, the portfolio companies as well.[18]

Proponents of taxing carried interest as a capital gain, however, have a ready response to these objections. They reject the idea that there is a difference in kind between starting a business and building it into a successful company, on the one hand, and turning around a failing business or increasing the enterprise value of a successful business, on the other. Both, they argue, require entrepreneurial skill and effort. They argue further that the PE fund general partner may be extremely well paid, but nevertheless is earning less than he is contributing to increasing the value of the fund's portfolio of companies. Thus, like the entrepreneur who starts his or her own business, he is contributing sweat equity. This may seem like a dubious defense of the analogy between a struggling individual entrepreneur starting a business and the handsomely paid general partner of a PE fund, but even if we were willing to accept these arguments, a further problem with this analogy arises.

Unlike an enterprise built by a single entrepreneur, the companies in the portfolio of a PE fund are owned by a group of people—the fund's general partner and the limited partner investors, and GPs and LPs are treated very differently in the tax code. This difference makes the general partner very different from the individual entrepreneur.

Consider the situation of the individual entrepreneur. The labor expenses incurred in running a business are expenses that are deductible against business profits when calculating the business's tax liabilities. As Chris Sanchirico observes, when the individual entrepreneur supplies skill and effort without being fully compensated, he or she is trading a tax advantage in the present for a tax advantage in the future.[19] The higher business taxes paid during the years of building up the business, as a result of the entrepreneur's decision to forgo pay during those years, are paid by the same person who gets the tax advantage when the business is sold and the deferred labor income is transformed into capital income.

The situation is very different in the case of a private equity fund.[20] If the general partner of the fund forgoes a salary commensurate with the skill and effort applied to improving the businesses in the fund's portfolio and is compensated for this work later in the form of carried interest, two things happen. First, the general partner receives a significant tax advantage, as the compensation for these services will be taxed at the lower capital gains rate. Second, because this compensation is not received in the form of salary paid to the GP, it cannot be deducted from the profits of the PE fund. Deferring the compensation of the GP and treating it as a capital gain raises the amount of profit earned by the limited partners in the PE fund. For those LPs whose income is taxable, this raises the amount of taxes they have to pay. The gains of the GP in this case would come at the expense of these LPs.

Why then, do the limited partners go along with this arrangement rather than paying the general partner a higher salary or management fee that fully compensates them and provides them with a tax deduction? The answer to this riddle is that most LPs in PE funds are tax-exempt—for example, they are university foundations, nonprofit foundations, or union pension plans.[21] Because of their tax-exempt status, they do not suffer from higher taxes when the GP forgoes salary in favor of deferred compensation. As a result, the tax-exempt LPs—who presumably gain an advantage, perhaps in the form of lower management fees than would otherwise prevail—do not raise objections to this arrangement. As Sanchirico observes, the joint taxation of general and limited partners is lower than it would be if the compensation of GPs took the form of salary payments and was subject to the income tax on ordinary income. This arrangement leaves room for GPs to engage in side deals with LPs that allow both to come out ahead. The difference in tax rates between the GP and the tax-exempt LPs leads them to engage in joint tax arbitrage to avoid paying taxes—a possibility not open to the individual entrepreneur and business owner.[22]

Whatever similarities can be adduced between an individual entrepreneur and the general partner in a private equity fund, the analogy ultimately fails because of the fundamental difference between the two cases in the tax implications of deferring labor income until the sale of a business and converting it to capital income.

Some observers have gone further, questioning not only the taxation of carried interest as a capital gain but asking whether, under current law, even the profits received by the private equity fund's limited partners (to the extent that this income is taxable) should qualify for preferential capital gains treatment. Steven Rosenthal uses the analogy to real estate developers, who in the ordinary course of their business often take many years to buy, develop, and resell real estate at a profit. During that time, the real estate is treated for tax purposes as if it is being held for sale to customers. Similarly, PE funds in the ordinary course of their business buy, develop, and resell corporations to customers at a profit as remuneration for their work to improve them. Tax law is clear that the real estate held by real estate developers is not a capital asset, and similarly, corporations held by PE funds should not be treated as a capital asset by the IRS. Moreover, while all fund managers—hedge funds, mutual funds, private equity funds—provide "managerial attention" to buying, tracking, and selling their stocks, only PE fund managers take an active role in managing the companies whose stock they own. Thus, Rosenthal concludes, the profits of a PE fund from the sale of a portfolio company arise from the everyday operation of the fund and are the type of profits that Congress sought to exclude from preferential capital gains treatment.[23]

Reduce Incentives to Load Portfolio Companies with Excessive Debt

The use of debt, as we saw in chapter 3, is a core element of the private equity business model. It boosts the returns of a PE fund without exposing the PE firm that sponsors the fund to a heightened risk of bankruptcy—a classic case of moral hazard.

The extensive use of leverage has three advantages for private equity firms. First, because responsibility for repaying the debt falls on the company that was acquired, the only money the PE firm and its investors have at risk is the initial equity they put up as a down payment.[24] Second, the greater use of leverage magnifies the returns to private equity from its successful investments while minimizing the losses from its unsuccessful efforts. And third, the U.S. tax code treats debt more favorably than equity since interest on debt, unlike dividends paid to shareholders, can be deducted from corporate income in calculating tax liabilities. The tax deductibility of debt is designed to promote behavior that benefits the U.S. economy, as in the deduction of interest on mortgages to promote homeownership. But it is unclear why the government would want to provide a tax break for debt financing to encourage companies to use debt rather than equity for capital investments.

The tax advantages of debt amount to a subsidy from taxpayers to companies that make use of debt in financing transactions. For PE funds that use high levels of leverage—much in excess of what most publicly traded companies consider prudent—this tax subsidy contributes substantially to the funds' returns. Nicholas Donato, writing in *PE Manager*, noted that "the interest write-off has been a key component of the private equity model, allowing dealmakers to supplement their capital firepower with tax advantageous leverage on target companies."[25] In what might be called taxpayer-financed capitalism, the reduced taxes from the higher interest deduction increase the portfolio company's enterprise value and the returns to the PE investors without creating new wealth for the economy—essentially a transfer of wealth from taxpayers to PE firms and their investors. The lost tax revenue comes at the expense of the general public, who must either pay higher taxes or face cuts in public services. Limiting the amount of debt used in transactions would diminish the likelihood of financial distress and bankruptcy and reduce the taxpayer subsidy of PE returns.

The use of debt to finance leveraged buyouts by private equity funds increased during the boom years. PE-sponsored leveraged loan volume peaked in 2007 before declining precipitously in 2008 and 2009 as lenders tightened standards following the onset of the financial crisis. PE transactions made greater use of equity and less use of debt. Leveraged loan volume began to recover in 2010, but remained far below its peak. The volume of such loans doubled between 2010 and 2012 before really taking off again in 2013. Debt financing of leveraged buyouts has risen strongly and begun to approach levels last seen in the boom years. The share of covenant-lite loans—loans that fail to provide lenders with control over further borrowing by the loan recipient and fail to require regular reviews of the borrower's operating performance—increased dramatically beginning in 2011.[26]

Limit Debt

Can the tendency of private equity to make excessive use of debt financing be curbed? The experience of the Dana Corporation is suggestive. As we saw in chapter 7, negotiations between the Dana Corporation and the unions representing its workers (the steelworkers and autoworkers unions) to reduce costs and improve competitiveness included a stipulation that limited the company's debt liabilities to $1.5 billion and required a target liquidity cushion of a minimum of $1 billion. These requirements later saved the company from financial distress during the 2008–2009 crisis. Such negotiated requirements for capital adequacy are rare, but suggest that establishing limits on leverage can be effective in saving companies from financial distress.

Limits on leverage ordinarily must be established by legislation. There are three general approaches for accomplishing this: placing a cap on the amount of debt that can be used to acquire a portfolio company; eliminating the tax deductibility of interest; and establishing rules designed to limit risky behavior. Capping the amount of debt that can be used to acquire an asset is not unheard of in the United States. The SEC's Regulation T, established during the Depression, limits the amount of debt an individual can run up in his or her brokerage account when buying shares of stock. Regulation T currently allows an individual to borrow up to 50 percent of the initial purchase price of a qualified security.

There is no economic case for a government subsidy to business to encourage companies to use debt rather than equity, and it is unclear why taxpayers should be asked to subsidize borrowing by corporations. If interest on debt were no longer tax-deductible, private equity firms could still decide to use as much or as little debt as they wanted in acquiring a portfolio company. Eliminating the tax deductibility of interest payments on debt would not directly limit the amount of debt that PE firms are able to leverage on portfolio companies. It would, however, remove a major incentive for loading these companies up with such high levels of debt relative to the value of the enterprise.

The third approach—requiring private equity to explicitly take risk into account in deciding how much debt to use—is the approach taken by the European Parliament in its Alternative Investment Fund Manager Directive.[27] Of the various approaches to limiting debt, this is likely to be the most acceptable to the industry, as it takes into account the differences in size and strategy among PE funds as well as the variation in portfolio companies' assets and ability to amortize debt. Of course, such prescriptive rules have the disadvantage in that PE lawyers can be expected to go to great lengths to figure out ways to skirt the regulations.

In addition to requiring a risk assessment for the use of debt, the AIFMD requires alternative investment fund (AIF) managers who use leverage as part of their investment strategy to set maximum leverage limits and to carry out related risk and liquidity management activities. While the directive does not limit the investments or strategies that an AIF can use, it does require the AIF manager to set a maximum leverage limit, taking into account the investment strategy of the fund, the sources of leverage, and the nature of the collateral. The AIF manager must disclose the total amount of leverage to investors and regulators on a regular basis, and regulators may impose limits on the level of leverage based on concerns about systemic risk.[28] EU member states were required to enact national legislation by July 2013 to implement the directive, which covers both EU and non-EU funds and their managers.[29]

Like their European counterparts, U.S. regulators became alarmed by the return of the type of aggressive use of debt that had occurred during the boom.[30] The Federal Reserve, the Federal Deposit Insurance Company (FDIC), and the Office of the Comptroller of the Currency (OCC) have been concerned about the rising levels of leverage and deteriorating underwriting standards by banks making such loans. Guidelines in place since 2001 proved too weak to rein in the use of debt during the boom, and stronger supervisory guidelines—the Interagency Guidance on Leveraged Lending—were issued in late March 2013.[31] The regulators backed off from their initial approach—a clear rule that would have required banks to examine a company's ability to amortize senior secured debt or repay 50 percent of total debt in a five- to seven-year period. Instead, they now simply require clear, written, and measurable underwriting standards that take into account the borrower's ability to pay off senior secured debt or repay a substantial portion of total debt over the medium term. The guidelines define transactions in which the borrower's total debt exceeds four times its earnings (EBITDA) or senior secured debt exceeds three times earnings as leveraged loans, and they note that a leverage level after planned asset sales greater than six times earnings is a cause for concern.[32]

The guidelines, which apply only to bank lending, had a compliance date of May 21, 2013, and later that summer, a dozen big banks got letters from regulators asking them to comply with the guidelines. Several of these banks have decided against financing PE buyouts of corporations that are too burdened with debt. Banks that fail to conform to the guidelines will not be breaking a law, but they do face the possibility of greater regulatory scrutiny. The effectiveness of this threat will depend on whether the Fed is willing to issue formal enforcement orders—which banking regulators failed to do before the 2008 financial crisis.[33] A return to the simple rule originally proposed by regulators to limit the level of leverage would eliminate ambiguity and reduce the ability of banks to flout the guidelines; legally binding regulations would be a more effective enforcement mechanism than guidelines.

Since it is banks and not private equity funds that are affected by these guidelines, PE firms may simply turn to the shadow banking system to finance their leveraged buyouts of portfolio companies—a trend already well under way prior to the financial crisis. One way of addressing private equity's ability to use excessive amounts of leverage would be for the SEC to adopt an approach similar to the European AIFMD. The general partner in a PE fund could be required to set a maximum amount of leverage that can be used to purchase portfolio companies based on the fund's investment strategy, the size of the companies it takes over, the type of collateral available in such companies, and the sources of the borrowed funds. This maximum level of leverage on individual portfolio companies as well as the total amount of debt used in acquiring the fund's portfolio companies would have to be reported to the SEC on a regular basis; the SEC would review both the maximum level of leverage on a company and the aggregate level of debt used in the fund's transaction and would be able to place limits on each of these based on its assessment of the risks associated with the PE fund's use of debt. Individual PE funds are not large enough to create systemic risk, although, as we argue in the next section, the industry as a whole indirectly played a role in the 2008–2009 financial crisis by contributing to the growth of the shadow banking system.

The Dodd-Frank Act already requires the general partners of PE funds to report much of this information to the SEC. Adopting requirements similar to those in the AIFMD would reduce the excessive use of debt and ensure that debt levels were reasonable based on the characteristics of a fund's portfolio companies and on the ability of these companies to amortize the debt over a reasonable period of time.

Private Equity's Contribution to the Growth of the Shadow Banking System

Private equity industry leaders maintain that their activities did not contribute to the 2008 financial crisis and that they should therefore not be regulated. However, lax financial regulation aided the development of new financial instruments, including collateralized loan obligations (CLOs), that were widely used by banks (or "syndicates," groups of banks) that make leveraged loans to businesses. In the case of private equity, CLOs are used to securitize the debt that PE funds lever on the firms they acquire. Modeled on mortgage-backed securities, CLOs combine multiple leveraged loans and slice them into "tranches," or classes of debt with different risk characteristics. CLOs made up of riskier tranches pay a higher interest rate than those that consist of less risky tranches. Banks and bank syndicates that make leveraged loans to PE firms or other businesses package these loans into CLOs that, under normal business conditions, can be quickly sold to other institutional investors. The banks earn fees on these transactions and, except in periods of economic crisis, experience relatively little risk from underwriting leveraged loans.

This ability of banks that make leveraged loans to securitize the debt dramatically increased private equity's access to credit and expanded the amount of capital available for investment by PE funds. With debt accounting for up to three-quarters of the purchase price of portfolio companies during the 2003 to 2007 period, leveraged debt issued by PE-owned portfolio companies and resold as CLOs by lenders increased dramatically. The response of banks to private equity's demand for leveraged loans effectively contributed to the growth of the shadow banking system.[34] Tempted by the lucrative fees to be earned on the sale of CLOs and reassured by their ability to securitize this debt and sell it on, banks were willing to engage in such lending.

The private equity segment of the financial services industry is too small to trigger a financial crisis on its own. But that does not mean that the leveraged loans issued by portfolio companies of PE funds did not contribute to increased financial risk. As *Fortune* commentator Dan Primack observed: "From 2005 to 2008, private equity loaded copious amounts of debt onto thousands of new acquisitions, without regard to how even a mild economic downturn could make it nearly impossible for those companies to repay their loans."[35] The industry was saved, in Primack's view, by policies of the U.S. central bank (the Federal Reserve System) that kept interest rates close to zero.

The low-interest-rate environment facilitated amend-and-extend agreements in which debt-holders, seeing few investment alternatives, preferred to extend the original loan—usually extracting a higher rate of interest—rather than force the PE-owned borrowers into default. Starting in 2011 and accelerating in 2013, investors seeking yield were again willing to buy leveraged loan securities, thus enabling the portfolio companies to refinance their outstanding debts at favorable rates.[36]

Banks that make leveraged loans rely on an "originate to distribute" model in which a bank or a bank syndicate arranges and underwrites the loan and then distributes most of the loan by selling it to other institutions rather than holding it on its own balance sheets. During the boom, banks held 10 percent or less of each of the leveraged loans they originated.[37] Banks sell leveraged loans to bank and nonbank institutions, including hedge funds, high-yield bond funds, pension funds, insurance companies, and other institutional investors seeking higher-yield investments, usually as "collateralized loan obligations"—securities backed by payments on the underlying loans made by portfolio companies.

Between 2005 and 2007, banks provided around $1.1 trillion in leveraged loans in the U.S. market to private equity funds. The PE funds used $634 billion to finance a total of 956 leveraged buyouts and the remainder for other purposes, such as the refinancing of companies in fund portfolios or dividend recapitalizations. Just ten commercial and investment banks arranged and underwrote nearly $489 billion, or 77 percent of the U.S. syndicated leveraged buyout loans.[38]

Selling these risky leveraged loans rather than holding them on their own balance sheets enabled banks to circumvent the capital adequacy and risk management requirements to which they were subject. Banks sold CLOs through "off-balance-sheet financial entities," part of the shadow banking system that the banks themselves established for this purpose. "In a typical transaction, the sponsoring banking organization transfers the loans and other assets to a bankruptcy-remote special purpose vehicle, which then issues asset-backed securities consisting of one or more classes of debt."[39] These securities were sold to bank and nonbank institutions, with riskier tranches of loans—those with longer maturities and slower amortization rates—going to nonbank institutions.

The originate-to-distribute model increased the difficulty for regulators in evaluating the exposure of the financial system to leveraged loans. Federal bank regulators are able to determine the concentrated leveraged debt exposures of supervised banks, but lack data to assess such exposures by nonbank investors. Such data are difficult for regulators to collect and track.[40] The rapid growth of private equity transactions and PE-generated debt in the years prior to the financial crisis contributed to the growth of securitization and the shadow banking system. The lack of transparency surrounding the buildup of this PE-generated debt magnified the dangers.

The volume of CLO issuance rose rapidly beginning in the first quarter of 2005 and peaked in the second quarter of 2007. The volume of CLOs declined abruptly—nearly disappearing in the years following the onset of the economic crisis—before beginning to rebound in late 2011.[41] By the first quarter of 2013, the volume of CLOs had recovered to precrisis levels. CLO issuance in 2013 was driven by the resurgence in PE-sponsored leveraged loans, with eight portfolio companies of PE-sponsored funds borrowing $2 billion or more and another eight borrowing between $1 billion and $2 billion in the leveraged loan market.[42]

Private equity funds are among the least transparent financial entities because, until the recent enactment of reforms, exclusions in the Investment Company Act of 1940 enabled most of these funds to avoid registering with the SEC and meeting the SEC's reporting requirements. Prior to passage of the 2010 Dodd-Frank Act, this exclusion applied to any fund that did not make and did not propose to make a public offering of its securities and either had outstanding securities that were owned by no more than one hundred persons, or had outstanding securities that were owned exclusively by qualified purchasers.[43]

Section 404 of the Dodd-Frank Act proposed to remedy this lack of transparency and reduce the excessive exposure of the financial system to risk. It requires advisers to private equity (and hedge) funds with more than $150 million in assets to register with the SEC and report basic organizational and operational information about the funds. Reporting requirements and frequency of filing reports depend on the size and type of fund. Information that is reported includes total assets under management, types of services, clients, employees, and potential conflicts of interest. For large funds (over $1 billion in assets under management), the section requires the identification of positions greater than 5 percent of net asset value (NAV), the use of leverage, the weighted average debt-to-equity ratio of portfolio companies, and the institutions providing bridge financing and the amount thereof; information about portfolio company debt and any defaults is also required. On October 31, 2011, the SEC adopted final rules for reporting requirements; initial forms were required to be filed by August 29, 2012. The information collected is not publicly available. It is intended to help the SEC and the Financial Stability Oversight Council (FSOC) monitor systemic risk.[44] Unfortunately, a Congressional budget deal in January 2014 failed to fund additional inspectors for the SEC, reducing the chance of an audit to 1 in 17.

Reporting is a step in the right direction, but does little to actually reduce the amount of debt used by PE funds in acquiring companies. That will require a legal framework that establishes limits on the use of leverage, subject to review by regulators.

Reduce Incentives for Asset Stripping

Private equity funds often purchase portfolio companies with extensive real estate holdings, sell off the real estate, and use the proceeds to repay the initial equity investment of the funds' partners—including in some cases a substantial return to these PE investors. Selling off these assets and requiring the portfolio company to lease back the properties it once owned may leave the company without a buffer to handle economic downturns, as occurred in the case of the Mervyn's store chain (chapter 3) and some of the restaurant cases we reviewed. While workers, vendors, creditors, and companies lost jobs, income, or solvency, the PE owners walked away virtually unscathed.

In general, U.S. corporate law recognizes corporations as legal entities separate from their shareholders, officers, and directors. Corporate obligations are the liability of the corporation, not of the shareholders who own the corporation. These individuals have broad protection from being held personally responsible for the debts and liabilities of the corporation. Thus, the corporate form of business organization shields or insulates shareholders from liability for wrongdoing or debts incurred by the corporation. This "corporate veil," as it is sometimes called, is what is meant by the limited liability of shareholders, officers, and directors of a corporation.[45]

Limited liability plays a positive economic role by making it possible for publicly traded corporations to raise large amounts of capital by aggregating investments from numerous small investors. If liability were not limited, these small shareholders could find themselves liable for a substantial corporate obligation if the company got into difficulty. They might well be unwilling to take the risk and invest, making the development of large, modern corporations impossible. But limited liability also creates opportunities for opportunistic behavior by shareholders that would not exist if the shareholders were directly responsible for the corporation's obligations. This is especially true in companies with a small number of shareholders who effectively control decision-making. Limited liability protection may sometimes provide shareholders with an incentive to loot a company of its assets without regard for the effect on the company's ability to pay its creditors. Shareholders, however, do not always get away with this kind of behavior. They are not protected under law in cases where a corporation's shareholders act with reckless disregard for creditors' claims—knowingly taking actions that benefit them and that undermine the corporation's ability to meet its obligations to its creditors. Courts can pierce the corporate veil and make shareholders responsible for paying what is owed to creditors, and they do so especially if shareholders have used the corporate entity for criminal or fraudulent purposes. The court "pierces the corporate veil" in order to prevent shareholders from using the limited liability afforded to them by the corporation in a way that is unjust and unfair to creditors.[46]

When a corporation goes bankrupt, creditors can try to recover from shareholders what the company owes them. Bankruptcy courts typically use some combination of the following criteria to determine whether the behavior of shareholders warrants piercing the corporate veil:

- Grossly inadequate capitalization and too much debt (though this is not a sufficient factor to justify piercing the corporate veil)
- The siphoning off of assets (as in the Mervyn's case)
- The comingling of assets (shifting assets from one subsidiary to another, as alleged in the Clear Channel case)
- Misrepresentation or fraud (a sufficient reason to pierce the corporate veil)
- Absence of corporate formality (for example, inadequate board meetings or failure to keep adequate accounting records)[47]

In general, creditors must demonstrate that several of these criteria hold and that there is an element of injustice and basic unfairness in order for the court to be willing to pierce the corporate veil.

There is a general reluctance on the part of Congress to roll back the limited liability protections afforded by the corporate form. In the case of publicly traded companies with many small investors, piercing the corporate veil would expose large numbers of small shareholders to the risk of huge liability. A further objection to restricting limited liability protections is that vendors are already free to bargain in advance for shareholder liability for the corporation's debts. Freedom of contract already provides vendors with the ability to bargain in advance for shareholders to assume personal liability if they have concerns about the corporation's solvency. In the Mervyn's case, a major lender did ask Sun Capital, one of the private equity owners, for such a guarantee. When Sun Capital refused, the lender declined to make the loan. As a result, Mervyn's was unable to stock its stores for the important back-to-school buying season—which led to the department store chain's bankruptcy and demise.

The freedom-to-contract argument assumes that the true condition of the corporation can be discerned by those who are extending credit. When shareholders or officers knowingly strip the corporation of assets needed for the business's long-term stability and its ability to repay its debts, they may also take steps to conceal the company's true financial situation. A vendor or lender may not be able to discern whether those who control the corporation are engaging in actions intended to benefit themselves at the expense of creditors.

Limited liability provides important protections for shareholders in companies that experience large losses or default on loans despite the best efforts of management to avoid such an outcome. Problems beyond the company's control may undermine the viability of even well-run companies. Limited liability protection should continue to prevail in these cases. But limited liability should not be extended to shareholders in cases where the company's financial distress is the result of deliberate actions by shareholders for their own benefit. In particular, limited liability protections should not be extended in cases of asset stripping that benefit a company's shareholders and are followed within a few years by the bankruptcy of the company. As David Millon observes:

> If limited liability is not tailored so as to exclude losses resulting from shareholder opportunism, it will protect shareholders whose corporations default because of their own opportunism as well as those whose corporations are unable to pay their debts despite the shareholders' good faith efforts to manage the business responsibly.[48]

Corporations acquired by private equity funds in leveraged buyouts differ in important respects from other corporations because the debt incurred to acquire the company is borne by the company, not by its PE owners. In addition, the proportion of debt-to-equity financing is higher, and the resulting higher-risk loan carries a higher interest rate. In many cases, the PE owners install a CEO or other top manager whom they have employed in the past and whose loyalty is to the PE firm, not the company. Also, unlike publicly traded companies, PE-owned companies have a concentrated ownership structure that permits the company's shareholders to control appointments to its board of directors and to closely monitor and manage the company's strategic direction and operations. Finally, both the PE owners and the corporation's top managers expect to cash out in a period of just a few years and may have little concern for how the company performs in the years after they exit the investment. This structure provides both the opportunity and the incentive for PE owners to engage in opportunistic behavior to enrich themselves at others' expense. It permits PE owners to carry out actions, hidden from public view, that undermine the corporation's solvency without regard for the claims of its vendors and creditors or the welfare of the corporation's employees and the general public.

The differences between publicly traded and PE-owned corporations suggest that it should be possible to treat opportunistic asset stripping as an exception to limited liability protections. Although it may be beneficial in general, limited liability should not be so broadly construed that it protects illegitimate actions by shareholders or shields them from responsibility for dubious actions undertaken by the corporation at their bidding.

This situation can be addressed by requiring a type of "prenuptial" agreement when a private equity fund acquires a company for its portfolio. Such an agreement would require PE owners to take personal responsibility for negative outcomes that arise as a result of their sale of company assets. Typically, a portfolio company's real estate or similar assets are used as collateral for the secured creditors who provide the loans that finance the initial acquisition of the company. When these assets are sold, the loans are repaid; typically, the PE investors turn a handsome profit on the sale. As in the Mervyn's and Friendly's cases examined in earlier chapters, the portfolio company is then forced to lease back its former assets, which are vital to its operations and the conduct of its business.[49] The primary purpose of a prenuptial agreement would be to protect the company's unsecured creditors.

If the sale of the portfolio company's assets does not undermine the ability of the company to function, to meet its debt payments, and to pay its unsecured creditors, then there would be no negative consequences for the company's private equity shareholders. If, however, during the term of the agreement (a period perhaps of ten years after the assets are sold) the company is unable to pay its debts and meet its obligations, then the company's PE owners, including the PE firm that sponsored the fund, would be required to relinquish their limited liability protections and to be individually and collectively responsible for paying what the company owed its creditors. This would include obligations to vendors, to workers for unpaid wages and severance pay, and to employee pension and health and welfare funds.

An agreement that removes the limited liability protections of private equity shareholders in cases where the assets of a newly acquired portfolio company are sold off would reduce the incentives to engage in such behavior when it is contrary to the company's interest. PE shareholders engaged in financially responsible management practices would suffer no ill consequences from such a statutory requirement.

Prohibit Dividend Payments to Private Equity Investors in the First Two Years

Dividend payments to private equity investors in advance of an exit from a portfolio company are another form of asset stripping in that they transfer resources that should be used to "add value" to the company from the company to its shareholders. Corporate law already places some limits on the payment of dividends to shareholders. Shareholders must leave sufficient equity in the company to ensure that assets are not less than liabilities and that the company is able to pay its bills. Taking out dividends that cause the company to subsequently default on its loans is a breach of fiduciary duty, and directors are personally liable if they declare dividends that make the company insolvent.[50]

But even a dividend distribution that does not drive a portfolio company into bankruptcy effectively transfers resources from the company to its private equity shareholders. Most egregious, in this regard, is the use of dividend recapitalizations. Hospital Corporation of America (HCA), for example, delayed its IPO from 2010 to 2011 because of uncertainty about its ability to achieve its target share price. Nevertheless, the PE owners of HCA were able to recover nearly all of their initial investment in 2010 because HCA issued additional debt that year, including junk bonds, and issued three dividend recapitalizations worth a total of $4.25 billion.[51]

The volume of dividend recapitalizations increased following the 2003 reduction in the tax rate on dividends to 15 percent. Dividend recapitalizations in the three years following the tax change totaled $71 billion, an average of about $24 billion a year, compared to a $10 billion total over the previous six years.[52] The tax treatment of dividends made this method of extracting value from a portfolio company tax-efficient for its PE owners but reduced federal and state tax receipts. The volume of dividend recaps declined during the economic crisis but jumped dramatically in 2012, owing to low interest rates, an increase in the tax rate on dividends anticipated at that time, and continued difficulty in exiting investments.[53] According to Dealogic, the number of dividend recapitalizations by private equity firms increased from fifty-five in 2011 to seventy-seven in 2012, with the value of these dividend recapitalizations doubling from $17.7 billion to $33.4 billion in the same period.[54] Dividend recapitalizations reached a record high even in the middle market.[55]

Dividend recapitalizations are often carried out shortly after a portfolio company is acquired. Only six months after Hertz Car and Equipment Rental Company was acquired by Carlyle, Clayton, Dubilier, & Rice, and Merrill Lynch, they loaded the company with $1 billion in order to pay themselves a dividend recapitalization.[56] Harry & David was acquired by Wasserstein & Co. and Highfields Capital Management in 2004; a year later, they took a dividend of $82.6 million and then two more dividends totaling $19 million. These dividends guaranteed the PE investors in Harry & David a 23 percent return no matter what happened to the company—which later declared bankruptcy.[57] Moody's Investor Service singled out PE firms TH Lee and Apollo for drawing dividends from one-third of their portfolio companies in the first year following the leveraged buyout. By 2008, a relatively high proportion of companies acquired by these two PE firms had experienced financial distress in meeting their debt obligations.[58]

Limited liability facilitates this type of opportunism as well. Private equity shareholders can use their ability to control the actions of the portfolio company to require the company's directors to pay out dividends. This may make it more difficult for the portfolio company to make payments to its creditors and so increases the risk of default.[59] Directors can be held personally liable if the company becomes insolvent because of the dividends they have declared, as this would be a breach of their fiduciary duty to the company. But it is often difficult for creditors to prove this claim.

Whether financed by issuing junk bonds that raise the debt burden of the portfolio company or are simply paid out of the company's cash flow, these dividend payments divert resources to private equity investors and away from the portfolio company. Dividend payments reduce the capacity of the company to increase the value of the enterprise through investments in product or process technologies, professionalization of management practices, and improvements in employee skills and capabilities. This is in direct contradiction to the claims of PE firms that their outsized returns are the result of the improvements they make in portfolio company strategy and operations and the value they add to the companies they acquire. Fortune's Dan Primack puts it this way: "They [dividend recapitalizations] can skew alignment of interests, imperil otherwise-healthy companies and make a mockery of private equity's 'value creation' claims. Moreover, they can provide limited partners with short-term cover at the expense of long-term gains."[60]

Specific regulations that prevent portfolio companies from paying dividends to PE investors for a period of twenty-four months after the acquisition would curb the most reckless use of dividend payments to PE shareholders. The European Union's Alternative Investment Fund Manager Directive, for example, rules out the payment of dividend recapitalizations in the European Union in the first twenty-four months after a portfolio company is acquired. That is, a PE fund cannot add extra debt onto a portfolio company or have it buy back shares for a two-year period after the fund acquires control. Smaller EU portfolio companies—those with fewer than 250 employees and annual revenue less than €50 million—are exempt, but these companies rarely pay dividend recaps to their PE owners in any case.[61]

Increase Transparency

Private equity is famously private. The Dodd-Frank Act tried to change that by requiring PE funds to file regular reports with the SEC. Unlike publicly traded companies, these accounts can be narrative rather than quantitative and are not available for public inspection. Moreover, even since implementation of the Dodd-Frank reporting requirements in August 2012, PE funds have not been required to publicly disclose which companies they own, the incomes earned by senior managers and partners in the PE firm that sponsors the fund, or the financial statements of their portfolio companies. Yet creditors, vendors, suppliers, managers, workers, and unions need this information in order to make informed decisions about their interactions with PE-owned companies. Workers and their unions are often unaware that the company where they are employed is owned by a PE fund—especially when PE investors acquire the company through holding companies located offshore. The right of stakeholders to this information, and of workers to know who their employer is, has long been recognized in the case of publicly traded companies.[62]

The lack of transparency in private equity reporting can be especially costly to investors in PE funds, who can find PE performance difficult to measure and comparisons across funds hard to carry out. The internal rate of return (IRR) is widely used as a measure of absolute performance by PE funds, the PEGCC, and in-house LP investment managers and external consultants. But as we saw in chapter 6, many finance experts agree that the IRR is not a good measure of the returns that LPs actually receive from investments in private equity. It is sensitive to the timing of distributions. Exiting a successful investment in a portfolio company in the first few years of a fund's existence boosts the fund's IRR, regardless of whether doing so makes economic sense or leads to the highest payoff to LPs. A dividend recapitalization at an early stage, even if it weakens the portfolio company's subsequent performance, likewise provides a bump to a fund's IRR. Averaging across funds or reporting returns from a sequence of three ten-year funds sponsored by a PE firm as if it were a single thirty-year fund can raise the IRR substantially and mask the declining performance of subsequent funds. The absence of publicly available information on PE funds makes it difficult to check the accuracy of the IRRs reported by PE firms or how well *reported* IRRs predict the *actual* returns received by LPs when the fund reaches the end of its life span and is liquidated.

Moreover, a fund's IRR is an absolute measure of its performance. It does not take into account other uses of the committed capital that could have brought higher returns. In boom periods, IRRs tend to rise, but so does the stock market. A high or rising IRR does not, by itself, indicate that the decision to invest in private equity makes good economic sense. Investing in the stock market is generally viewed as the alternative to investing in private equity. While the industry and its practitioners focus on the IRR, finance scholars measure the performance of PE funds by comparing their returns with what an investor could have earned from equivalent investments in the stock market. The preferred measure used by most researchers is the public market equivalent (PME), which benchmarks the performance of PE investments against a particular stock market index. The relative returns of PE funds across all funds are far more modest than those based on the internal rate of return.

All measures of PE performance face the challenge that a fund's true performance cannot be known until all distributions to limited partners have been made and the fund is liquidated, usually ten years after the fund was launched. In the interim, while the fund is active, the value of the companies still in the fund's portfolio and the fund's net asset value must be estimated. The introduction of fair value accounting has improved estimates of the value of portfolio companies and of the NAV of a fund's portfolio. But the fund's general partner, who is responsible for estimating the NAV, still has considerable room to maneuver, and some evidence suggests that GPs inflate the value of a fund when they are fund-raising for a subsequent fund and lower it when fund-raising is complete. This significantly affects the size of the interim IRRs that are reported in fund-raising documents, but these effects quickly reverse. As a result, interim IRRs have very limited power to predict the ultimate performance of a fund: "Investors should put little, or no, weight on the IRRs that they read in marketing documents when deciding whether to invest in a follow-on fund."[63] PMEs, which measure the performance of a fund relative to the stock market, also make use of NAVs for active funds, but this measure is less affected by the pattern of inflation and reversal of NAVs. The researchers conclude that interim PMEs are good predictors of final payouts to limited partners. Investors would be better informed about the performance of a PE fund if it reported the PME measure rather than IRRs on a quarterly basis.[64]

Understanding the performance of private equity as an asset class is hampered, as we saw in chapter 6, by the fact that there is no comprehensive, unbiased, and widely available data set that can be used to evaluate PE performance. Research is currently carried out on data sets that have been made available to individual researchers and that suffer from "selection bias." They do not encompass the universe of PE funds or a random sample drawn from such a universe. The extent to which the funds included in any research sample are representative of the universe of PE funds cannot be determined. The data sets used in recent studies that show that PE investments outperform the stock market are incomplete or have unknown biases, and it remains impossible to persuasively demonstrate either significantly superior or significantly inferior performance of investment in PE funds relative to investments in the shares of publicly traded companies. As Phalippou concludes, "The only way to put these issues to rest is with comprehensive, accurate and open data access. . . . Most if not all of these questions could be tackled if the data were comprehensive, unbiased and more widely available."[65] Now that the Dodd-Frank Act requires most PE funds to register with the SEC, and the SEC has shown a willingness to investigate conflicts of interest and misrepresentations by general partners,[66] the opportunity may exist for the creation of such a data set.

A truism of private equity performance, as David Snow observed, "is that, in the end, the only thing that matters is how much money you got back compared with how much you put in."[67] These net returns are not fully known, however, until all of the investments in the fund have been sold, the fund has been liquidated, and the cash has been distributed to the limited partners. Interim IRRs, as we have seen, do not predict the ultimate performance of a fund. However, using interim values of the PME significantly increases the predictive accuracy of final PME values, and indeed, these are calculated privately by more sophisticated pension fund managers for funds in their portfolios. It is surprising, therefore, that this superior measure of fund performance is not in general use.

The problem for industry participants is that the public market equivalent standard shows that private equity funds do not perform as well as they say they do. With fund-raising for subsequent funds and bonuses throughout the industry tied to fund performance, general partners and investment professionals have a shared interest in presenting fund performance in the best possible light. Perhaps that explains the continued use of IRRs as the performance measure reported by industry participants.

Whatever the reason, using IRR as a measure of fund performance may not be in the best interest of LP investors or pension fund beneficiaries, who may be misled by exaggerated reports of current fund performance to invest in subsequent funds sponsored by the same PE firm. Tim Jenkinson, Miguel Sousa, and Rüdiger Stucke conclude that the use of IRRs "may also go some way to explain one of the major puzzles associated with private equity—why the highest level of persistence in returns across funds is in the bottom quartile."[68]

It is surprising (or perhaps not) that the Institutional Limited Partners Association, the professional association of in-house professionals and external consultants who advise LPs on investment decisions, endorses the use of IRR as a measure of fund performance. Best practice in financial accounting should require the use of PMEs when PE funds report returns to investors and to the public. The ILPA principles should propose that PE funds report quarterly, using final PME values as a more accurate guide to fund performance.

Update the WARN Act to Recognize the Role of Private Equity Owners as Employers

On Saturday, January 5, 2013, the plant manager at the Golden Guernsey Dairy in Waukesha, Wisconsin, told workers that he had received an email from the plant's private equity owner, Los Angeles–based OpenGate Capital, informing him that the eighty-year-old dairy was to be closed down immediately. Employees were told to gather their belongings and leave; those not at work were told not to return. A few days later, OpenGate announced that Golden Guernsey had filed for Chapter 7 bankruptcy, a move signaling that the PE firm planned to liquidate the milk-processing business. As we saw in chapter 5, the abrupt and unexpected closing of the dairy just fifteen months after its acquisition by OpenGate left the 112 employees of the milk bottling and distribution facility—seventy of them represented by the Teamsters union—without jobs and facing an uncertain future. The unexpected closure also left family-owned dairy farmers scrambling to find other bottling facilities to take their milk, schools and grocery stores looking for new sources of supply, and dairy haulers who delivered Golden Guernsey milk to groceries from Milwaukee to Chicago wondering if their milk distribution businesses could survive. The closing of the milk-processing facility affected the entire upper Midwest dairy industry.[69]

The motive for shutting down the dairy with no advance notice to workers, their union, or workforce officials remains murky; OpenGate provided no reason for its action. It appears, however, that under federal and state statutes that govern plant closings, OpenGate may have been responsible for providing sixty days' pay and benefits to Golden Guernsey employees. The federal WARN (Worker Adjustment and Retraining Notification) Act requires an employer with one hundred employees or more (or an employer shutting down a plant with fifty employees or more) to provide advance notice that employment will be terminated sixty days prior to a plant closing or mass layoff that results in employment loss. The Wisconsin Business Closing Law (WBCL) is similar to the federal WARN Act, but applies to employers with fifty workers or plant closings affecting twenty-five workers or more. Under the WBCL, the employer is required to provide notice to employees, the collective bargaining representative, local elected officials, and the state dislocated workers unit sixty days in advance of the closing. Under both federal and state statutes, employees who do not receive such notification are eligible to collect pay and benefits for each day the notice was not provided, up to sixty days. The closing of the Golden Guernsey Dairy meets both the federal and state requirements for notice. Workers at the dairy have filed WARN Act and WBCL Act complaints seeking redress.[70]

Can OpenGate Capital be held liable for the back pay and benefits due the Golden Guernsey Dairy workers? In general, there are substantial obstacles in common law to holding remote ownership entities such as private equity firms responsible for the actions of their subsidiaries. In other contexts—liability for workers' defined-benefit pensions or retiree health benefits when a portfolio company enters bankruptcy, for example—PE firms have successfully fought the notion that they are employers of workers in the portfolio companies they control. But the WARN Act may be different, and the case of Archway & Mother's Cookies, Inc., described in chapter 5, is instructive.

PE firm Catterton Partners bought struggling Archway & Mother's Cookies out of bankruptcy in January 2005 from another PE company but failed to turn the company around. In 2008 it closed Archway's factories and laid off hundreds of workers without notice. Later that year, Archway filed for bankruptcy protection. Former Archway employees filed a WARN Act complaint against Catterton Partners in August 2009, arguing that Catterton was an "employer" for WARN Act purposes and was liable for failing to provide workers with the required sixty days' notice. On February 17, 2010, the U.S. District Court for Connecticut ruled that the PE firm and the bankrupt cookie company could be considered a "single employer" for WARN Act purposes. Since Catterton made the decision to shut down the bakeries and dismiss the employees, the court concluded, there was no question about its control over Archway. The court denied Catterton Partners' motion to dismiss and allowed the litigation to go forward.[71]

The Archway case is only one of a number of recent cases in which the courts have recognized remote entities as "employers" for WARN Act purposes. The Archway case has not yet been decided, but it is nevertheless significant that the court has allowed it to go forward; common law theories about piercing the corporate veil did not provide an automatic shield against WARN Act liability for these remote ownership entities.[72] The Connecticut court's ruling means that Catterton may be liable for sixty days' pay and benefits for six hundred to seven hundred employees.[73]

Twenty-five years ago, in 1988, Congress passed the WARN Act because it recognized that employees and their communities bear a disproportionate burden when an employer shuts down a facility without warning. By requiring employers to provide notice to employees in advance of closing a plant, the WARN Act protects workers, their families, and their communities and mitigates the high price imposed by such shutdowns.[74] The abrupt closing of Golden Guernsey Dairy by OpenGate Capital disrupted the livelihoods of dairy farmers, milk haulers, and grocers from Wisconsin to Illinois, and its reverberations affected the dairy industry of the entire upper Midwest. OpenGate is the entity that made the decision to shut down the milk-processing facility; as such, it should be held liable for the pay and benefits owed the dairy's workers under the WARN Act. Today thousands of operating companies employing several million U.S. workers are owned by private equity firms that exercise de facto control over decisions regarding mass layoffs and facility closings. While the courts have begun to recognize that PE firms are "employers" for WARN Act purposes, amending the act to specifically recognize the liability of PE owners in these situations would assure workers and communities of the protections that Congress intended when it required employers to provide sixty days' advance notice of shutdowns.

Hold Private Equity Owners Accountable for Portfolio Companies' Pension Liabilities

The bankruptcies of numerous portfolio companies while in private equity hands—including such well-known companies as Hostess, Friendly's restaurants, the auto parts maker Delphi, and the retailer Eddie Bauer, among many others—raises the concern that some sophisticated PE investors may be using the bankruptcy courts to rid themselves of the pension obligations they assumed when they acquired these companies. The overall increase in companies that declared bankruptcy between 2009 and 2012 and shifted workers' pension payments to the Pension Benefit Guaranty Corporation contributed to a record-high deficit at that agency and raised the prospect that the PBGC might need to be bailed out by taxpayers.[75] Against this backdrop, both the Employment Retirement Income Security Act (ERISA) and certain provisions of the bankruptcy code need to be updated for the twenty-first century in order to protect the deferred income that workers earn during their working years and receive when they retire.

Update ERISA

While the District Court of Connecticut found that the private equity owners of Archway & Mother's Cookies met the definition of an "employer" for WARN Act purposes, the situation with respect to PE owners' liability for employee pensions is less clear. A ruling by the District Court of Massachusetts in October 2012 found that two PE funds sponsored by Sun Capital Partners, which together owned 100 percent of Scott Brass, Inc., and held a controlling interest in the company, were not responsible for Scott Brass's unfunded pension liabilities when the company declared bankruptcy.[76] This ruling was overturned on appeal by the First U.S. Circuit Court of Appeals in Boston in July 2013.[77] A month later, in August, Sun Capital Partners returned to the appeals court to request that it reconsider its ruling.[78]

In the Sun Capital case, a multi-employer pension plan—the New England Teamsters and Trucking Industry Pension Fund—claimed that private equity funds sponsored and managed by Sun Capital were responsible for payment to the pension fund of "withdrawal liability" in connection with the bankruptcy of Scott Brass. When an employer withdraws from a multi-employer pension plan, that employer is required to pay the pension plan "a sum sufficient to cover the employer's fair share of the pension's unfunded liabilities."[79] This is what is meant by withdrawal liability. Title IV of ERISA requires that any parent or subsidiary that is a "trade or business" and that has an 80 percent or greater ownership stake in a company that contributes to a multi-employer pension plan is jointly and separately liable for paying the withdrawal liability. The Teamsters pension plan, arguing that the two Sun Capital funds that together owned 100 percent of Scott Brass were its parent company for purposes of ERISA, sought to recover the approximately $4.5 million in withdrawal liability owed by Scott Brass when it went bankrupt and withdrew from the pension plan.

Sun Capital had acquired Scott Brass, a fully integrated mill producing high-quality brass and copper strip, in 2006. Sun Fund IV acquired 70 percent of Scott Brass, and Sun Fund III acquired the remaining 30 percent from the Golden family, which had founded the company in 1956. Scott Brass was acquired for $7.8 million, $3 million in cash (exchanged for $1 million in stock and $2 million in debt) and an additional $4.8 million in debt.[80] Scott Brass withdrew from the pension plan in October 2008, and in November the company declared bankruptcy. In December, the Teamsters pension fund demanded that Scott Brass pay the withdrawal liability it owed and also demanded payment from the Sun Funds. It argued that the Sun Funds and Scott Brass constituted a "controlled group" and could be considered to be a single entity for ERISA purposes; the Sun Funds were therefore legally responsible for paying the withdrawal liability.[81] A controlled group is a family of related entities where one parent trade or business owns at least 80 percent of one or more other trades or businesses. Under ERISA, members of a common controlled group "are jointly and severally liable for the pension liabilities of each other member of the controlled group."[82] Congress established controlled group liability primarily to prevent situations in which employers could avoid their obligations under ERISA by operating through separate entities. The goal was to protect the solvency of pension funds and of the PBGC.

In demanding that the Sun Funds pay the withdrawal liability, the Teamsters pension fund was relying on a 2007 opinion from the PBGC that held that for purposes of Title IV of ERISA, a private equity fund similar to the Sun Funds was engaged in a "trade or business" and was liable for the withdrawal liability. The Supreme Court had previously developed a test that could be used to establish whether an activity constitutes a trade or business, and the PBGC concluded that PE owners met that test. Relying on that precedent, which had been upheld by bankruptcy courts in numerous cases, the Teamsters pension fund argued that the Sun Funds qualified as a trade or business because they took over a majority of board-of-director positions; they played a role in the day-to-day operations of Scott Brass; they were entitled to receive dividends, capital gains, and interest from Scott Brass; and their general partners received management fees. The Teamsters pension fund argued further that a main purpose for the seventy-thirty ownership of the two funds was to split their investment in Scott Brass and avoid exceeding the 80 percent threshold, thus also avoiding potential future withdrawal liability.

In June 2010, the Sun Funds filed a lawsuit in the District Court of Massachusetts seeking a declaratory judgment from the court that they were not "trades or businesses" under ERISA; that their investment transactions were not structured with the primary purpose of "evading or avoiding" withdrawal liability; that the funds and their portfolio companies did not constitute a single "controlled group" for purposes of ERISA; and that they were not required to make payment to the Teamsters pension fund.

In its October 2012 opinion, the district court found that the Sun Funds did not qualify as a trade or business because they did not have employees, own any office space, or make or sell goods. Moreover, while the Sun Funds' general partners received fees, the court based its decision largely on tax returns for the funds themselves, which showed only investment income (dividends and capital gains), and on tax cases that narrowly construed the meaning of "trade or business" to prevent income tax avoidance.[83] The Sun Funds admitted that one purpose of the seventy-thirty ownership split was to limit the potential that they would face withdrawal liability in case Scott Brass declared bankruptcy. But the district court found that this was not the major goal of the seventy-thirty structure and that the structure was not aimed at avoiding a pending or known liability, only an uncertain future potential liability. The Sun Funds did not, therefore, meet the criterion to be considered a controlled group.

The Massachusetts District Court's decision was widely applauded in the private equity community. The law firm Debevoise & Plimpton heralded the court's rejection of ERISA liability for a PE fund as a "Ray of Light."[84] Edward Wildman's client advisory was headlined, "Potential ERISA Title IV Liabilities of Private Equity Firms—Eliminated by the *Sun Capital* Decision?"[85] *Private Equity Manager* provided commentary that suggested that PE firms might offer limited partners in its funds opportunities to invest alongside the PE firm (so-called co-investment opportunities) "to double as a shield against pension liabilities" and "to dip the fund's investment below an 80 percent stake in any given portfolio company."[86] Debevoise & Plimpton concluded that ERISA risks should be viewed as "high-priority items" and that private equity sponsors "may wish to consider structural risk-reductions mechanisms such as were used by Sun Capital."[87]

General partners in PE funds have begun eagerly offering co-investment opportunities to limited partners. In part this greater interest in attracting co-investments may reflect a desire by GPs to shield their funds from pension plan liabilities of a bankrupt portfolio company. The Massachusetts District Court decision would appear to provide GPs with a fiduciary duty to recruit co-investors to keep the fund's ownership stake in a portfolio company it controls below the 80 percent threshold. The view among law firms advising PE sponsors is that "the district court's decision represents a significant victory for private equity firms."[88]

The Teamsters pension fund appealed the bankruptcy court's ruling, and the PBGC filed an amicus brief in the appeal.[89] On July 24, the First U.S. Circuit Court of Appeals in Boston ruled that one of Sun Capital's private equity funds could be held liable for Scott Brass's ERISA pension obligations. The significance of this ruling was explained by Victor Fleischer, a leading expert on the taxation of private equity.[90] The court found that the PE fund was not just a passive investor in Scott Brass, but was also actively engaged in managing the company. As we saw earlier in this book, it is the general partner of a PE fund who makes decisions for the fund and oversees the management of the fund's portfolio companies—in the Scott Brass case, with the assistance of a management company affiliated with Sun Capital. The management company took an active role in managing Scott Brass, getting involved in decisions regarding investment strategy and the hiring or termination of employees.[91] But what about the limited partners? Are they merely passive investors in the portfolio companies so that the fund is not engaged in a trade or business? In the Scott Brass case, the appeals court ruled that the limited partners received an economic benefit from their relationship with the general partner and the management company that ordinary passive investors would not receive and therefore that the fund was engaged in a trade or business for ERISA purposes. The appeals court did not rule on whether the seventy-thirty ownership split between two Sun funds counts as an 80 percent ownership stake in Scott Brass and has sent this question back to the lower court for a decision on this issue and on whether Sun Capital is liable for Scott Brass's pension liabilities. The appeals court also denied Sun Capital's request for a rehearing.

The appeals court's decision that the PE fund is engaged in a trade or business is significant, in Fleischer's view, because it collapses a legal structure intended to keep separate the activities of the general partner and the limited partners in a fund and establishes that PE funds are not necessarily passive investors and may actively control the companies they buy.[92] In reversing the Massachusetts court's decision, the First Circuit Court adopted an "investment plus" test to determine whether a PE fund constitutes a trade or business and to distinguish a PE fund that constitutes a trade or business from a passive investor.[93]

The decision of the First Circuit Court of Appeals, the first to hold that a PE fund can be a trade or business for ERISA purposes, is not binding on courts in other circuits, which may take another view of the matter. Moreover, in August 2013, Sun Capital Partners asked the appeals court to reconsider its ruling. The PBGC, which has argued since 2007 that PE funds are trades or businesses for ERISA purposes, welcomed the ruling.[94] It is not clear, however, that this ruling is sufficient to protect the retirement benefits in defined-benefit pension plans for workers in companies acquired by PE funds.

Pensions are deferred compensation earned by workers for work performed today—income they will receive in the future instead of higher wages today. ERISA, passed in 1974 and amended six years later in 1980, was designed to ensure that private-sector workers receive the pensions due them when they retire. In particular, the interests of all workers in a multi-employer pension fund are protected by the requirement that employers that withdraw from the plan pay their fair share of the pension plan's unfunded liabilities. In 2010 (the last year for which data are available) there were nearly 1,300 multi-employer defined-contribution pension plans that held about $105 billion in assets on behalf of approximately 4 million participants.[95] The bankruptcy of a participating company is a common reason for withdrawal.

Recognizing this fact and intending to protect the retirement income earned by workers, Congress made parent companies and subsidiary companies—all companies that are "under common control," that is, members of a common controlled group—equally liable to pay the bankrupt company's fair share of the pension fund's unfunded liabilities upon withdrawal from the pension plan. The 1980 amendment states that "all employees of trades or businesses (whether or not incorporated) which are under common control shall be treated as employed by a single employer and all such trades and businesses as a single employer."[96] The intent of Congress was to protect the pensions of working people so that employers cannot escape their responsibilities by adopting organizational structures that obscure ownership and control.

Congress should act to remove any doubt about the obligations of private equity funds for employee pensions. It should define a PE fund as a trade or business for the purposes of ERISA; it should simplify the rules governing what constitutes an 80 percent stake in an operating company to reduce opportunities for skirting this requirement; and it should explicitly recognize that the general partners of a PE fund control the decisions made by the fund and its co-investors. Inviting co-investments to increase the capital available to the GPs of a fund for investment can make economic sense, but this strategy should not be available as a means to evade the 80 percent threshold. Amending ERISA to take account of developments in the ownership, governance, and management of portfolio companies would restore the protections for workers' pensions that the ERISA legislation was designed to address. It would also resolve any conflict between the moral responsibilities and fiduciary responsibilities of a PE fund's general partners.

Update the Bankruptcy Code

The purpose of Chapter 11 bankruptcies, as commonly understood, is to protect a struggling company from the demands of its creditors while it reorganizes its operations and finances so that it can emerge from bankruptcy as a viable, ongoing business with a sustainable level of debt. The bankruptcy court oversees the establishment of a plan that provides for the successful reorganization of the company and the equitable satisfaction of creditors' claims. This includes the claims of employees, retirees, and other unsecured creditors as well as those of the company's secured creditors. The 1978 amendments to the bankruptcy code included provisions for a streamlined sale of a company's assets provided that the bankruptcy court approves the quick sale. These are so-called 363 cases, named after Section 363 of the amended bankruptcy code that permits these sales. This provision was intended to be used infrequently, and only in those cases where the delays inherent in restructuring a company so it can emerge from bankruptcy protection pose a serious threat to the value of the company's assets, and where value for stakeholders is best preserved by selling off all or substantially all of the company's assets piecemeal to the highest bidder in a competitive auction.

In the early 1990s, 363 sales were quite rare; only 4 percent (9 of 244 cases) of bankruptcies of large, publicly traded companies, for example, resulted in 363 sales. Since 2000, however, more than one-fifth of such bankruptcy cases (125 of 608 cases, or 21 percent) have been disposed of in this way.[97] Not only has there been a dramatic increase in the number of bankruptcy cases resolved through streamlined sales of the company's assets, but increasingly the courts have allowed the sale of the entire company shortly after bankruptcy is declared. Such 363 sales occur without the company and its creditors first putting in place a plan for distributing the proceeds among the various stakeholders.[98] It is becoming increasingly common for sophisticated financial investors that sell or buy companies out of bankruptcy—notably, private equity firms—to structure the transaction as a 363 sale. Such sales avoid the safeguards for unsecured creditors that are present when a bankrupt company develops a plan of reorganization for emerging from bankruptcy. In particular, 363 sales avoid the need to renegotiate contracts, including pension obligations. In 363 sales, secured creditors are paid out of the proceeds of the sale while unsecured claims get short shrift. In particular, pension benefit payments are usually shifted to the Pension Benefit Guaranty Corporation, and PBGC termination premiums are not paid. The PBGC estimates that in the decade from 2003 through 2012, employees and retirees lost more than $650 million in 363 sales of bankrupt companies owned or controlled by PE firms. This has exacerbated the severe financial stress that the PBGC has been put under in recent years.[99]

Using 363 sales to avoid pension obligations is especially egregious when a bankrupt portfolio company owned by one affiliate of a private equity firm is sold to another of the firm's affiliates, often with no other bidders competing for it. We saw this earlier in this book in the case of Friendly's. The ice cream restaurant chain went bankrupt while in the hands of a PE fund sponsored by Sun Capital and was sold in a 363 sale to another Sun Capital affiliate, but with its pension obligations offloaded onto the PBGC. At the end of the day, Sun Capital had retained its financial interest in Friendly's, but neither the PE firm nor any of its affiliates had any responsibility for the restaurant chain's pension obligations to Friendly's employees and retirees. Friendly's is far from the only example. Oxford Automotive and Relizon, among other companies that went bankrupt while in PE hands, were also sold from one affiliate of a PE firm to another affiliate.[100]

This situation is exacerbated by the escalating use of a practice known as "credit-bidding." As we saw in the Friendly's bankruptcy case, credit-bidding allows a secured creditor to obtain possession of a bankrupt company at auction simply by agreeing to forgive the debt that the company owes it rather than paying cash for the company. No money needs to change hands. Credit-bidding has become increasingly common, especially in section 363 sales. Section 363 of the bankruptcy code allows a secured creditor to "credit-bid" to purchase a bankrupt company at auction. The bankruptcy court ruling in such sales typically frees the buyer from any liability to other creditors, including vendors, pension plans, and other unsecured creditors. Loans made to the bankrupt company in its better days typically are worth only a fraction of their face value once the company goes bankrupt. If creditors tried to sell a loan of, say, $100 million, they would get far less than $100 million for it. The loan might be worth just half its face value, say $50 million.[101] However, when such creditors offer to acquire the company by forgiving the debt, the debt is valued at its face value (also called its par value)—that is, at the full $100 million, rather than at its true value of only $50 million. At the auction where the company is to be sold, an independent third party would have to bid more than the $100 million credit-bid in order to outbid these creditors and acquire the company. The secured creditors will be able to credit-bid to become the owners of a company worth $100 million by forgiving a debt that is now really worth only $50 million.

Even if an independent analysis showed that the bankrupt company was worth $100 million, no other buyer will show up at the auction to bid on the company because the credit-bidder can top a cash bid of $100 million with a credit-bid of $100 million and a cash bid of $1. A credit-bidder always has a huge advantage over a cash-bidder. There can be no competitive bidding process in such a situation.

A 363 sale is extremely advantageous to the major secured creditor or creditors in a bankruptcy case. In the case of a bankruptcy that is resolved through a plan of reorganization, the secured lenders must typically agree to some distribution for the unsecured creditors, who receive a share of the proceeds from the sale of the bankrupt company in order for the court to approve the plan. The pension plan is frequently the largest unsecured creditor in a bankruptcy case. When a bankruptcy is resolved through a reorganization plan, financial analysts at the PBGC can present evidence on behalf of the bankrupt company's workers and retirees regarding whether the company can afford its pension plan and whether freezing the plan is a better alternative than terminating it. In the case of a 363 sale, no such forum exists in which evidence can be presented to the bankruptcy court; the new owners typically emerge from the auction free of the company's pension obligations.

Not surprisingly, there has been a widespread shift to 363 sale cases from plan cases in Chapter 11 bankruptcy proceedings. This shift has favored the interests of secured creditors over those of employees, retirees, vendors, and other unsecured creditors and has undermined the fairness of the bankruptcy process in ways not anticipated in 1978. The development of new financial institutions not envisioned by Congress in 1978 has undermined the ability of bankruptcy courts to ensure that other stakeholders are fairly treated.

In light of these developments, we propose that Congress should revisit the 1978 reforms of the bankruptcy code and restore a fair and equitable balance among the competing interests of a bankrupt company's secured and unsecured creditors. At a minimum, restoring fairness in bankruptcy proceedings would seem to require a buyer in a 363 sale, like a buyer in a traditional Chapter 11 bankruptcy, to assume the company's pension obligations unless it can demonstrate to the bankruptcy court that it cannot afford to do so.

Require Severance Pay for Employees Linked to Years of Service

The decision to lay off experienced workers who have helped to build a business is one of the most difficult decisions that corporate managers may be called on to make. It particularly violates norms of fairness and equity when the layoffs are caused by the strategies of private equity owners to boost their own profits. In the United States, where fewer than 7 percent of private-sector workers are represented by a union, the decision to close a facility or lay off workers is virtually costless to employers. Where employers contribute to workers' pension or retirement savings plans, reducing the workforce via offshoring or subcontracting the work reduces not only payroll costs but the company's pension liabilities as well.

When private equity acquires a company in a leveraged buyout, the interests of former shareholders are generally well protected because private equity pays them a premium above the current stock price for their shares in the company. But shareholders do not single-handedly create the value that makes a company an attractive takeover target. Enterprise value in modern companies is built through the combined efforts of financial investors (shareholders and creditors) and human capital investors (executives and employees) who invest skills and effort.[102] Human capital—which can be thought of as the knowledge, skills, ideas, and commitment of employees—plays a critical role in creating companies that are attractive targets for acquisition by private equity. These successful companies have typically elicited effort and commitment from their employees via both formal contracts that define wages, benefits, and deferred compensation and implicit contracts that, while legally unenforceable, promise employees that their effort and loyalty will be repaid. Employees, as Lynn Stout observes, often believe

> that if they stay with the firm, perform well, and the firm prospers, they will receive in the future not just the benefits they are entitled to under their explicit employment contracts (when these exist) but also raises, promotions, and some job security. What's more, firms often encourage such beliefs. By signaling to their hires that if they remain loyal and do a good job they will receive discretionary future rewards beyond those mandated by the firm's explicit contracts, firms can inspire employees from the shop floor to the executive suite to work harder and to invest more in firm-specific human capital—knowledge, skills, and relationships that are valuable to the firm, but worthless to any other potential employer.[103]

Managers and shareholders committed to the long-term sustainability and success of the enterprise benefit, as do employees, from the extra effort and investment in skills that such implicit contracts elicit.

But what happens to these implicit contracts if the company is subsequently acquired by a private equity fund that hopes to exit the investment in three to five years? As Andrei Shleifer and Lawrence Summers argued in the context of the leveraged buyouts of the 1980s, there may be a strong temptation in this case for the new owners to renege on these implicit understandings.[104] Consider the following simple example.[105]

Suppose for simplicity that a company succeeds in getting its employees and managers to invest more effort and acquire more firm-specific skills than required and rewarded by their formal contracts. It does this through an informal understanding with employees that in the future they will share in the success of the company through job security and higher pay. Years later, with experienced employees paid the promised higher wages, the company's employee-related expenses are $100 million. If it has sales revenue of $110 million and no other expenses, the company's annual profit is $10 million. Now suppose that this company is acquired by a private equity fund interested only in maximizing the company's profit over the next few years. The new PE owners may decide to ignore the past investments that employees have made in firm-specific skills and the fact that they were not paid at that time for making these investments. Observing that this company is paying above-market wages, the new owners may choose to renege on workers' implicit contract with the company and reduce payroll costs by laying off workers or cutting pay and benefits. If payroll costs are reduced by 5 percent, from $100 million to $95 million, the new owners will see the company's annual profit increase from $10 million to $15 million—a 50 percent increase. Product quality or customer service may suffer as a result of understaffing or reductions in workers' efforts, and this may hurt the long-term competitiveness of the company. But the new owners may believe that such negative consequences will take years to make themselves felt and will be negligible during the relatively short time they intend to hold the company.

Our argument is that employees make investments in the companies that employ them via their investments in firm-specific skills in the course of their job tenure and through the provision of discretionary effort to resolve problems and make incremental improvements in production processes.[106] In the case of a takeover of the company by a financial firm that plans to exit the investment in just a few years, the return to employee investments in skills and problem-solving, as the example demonstrates, is vulnerable to expropriation by the new owners and by executives whose interests are aligned with these owners. As Katherine Stone notes, "Employees do not have effective means under existing labor, contract, or corporate law to protect these investments [in firm-specific skills]."[107] Unions, when present, can provide some weak enforcement of implicit contracts through formal contract provisions requiring just cause to fire workers. But unions represent just a small fraction of private-sector workers.

A conceptually clear way to address this issue and protect employees' investments in skills is to require private equity firms to pay severance packages related to employees' length of service in the event that they are laid off without just cause following the takeover of a financially sound company. Analogous to the "golden parachutes" that companies negotiate and typically provide to executives, such severance packages would give lower-level employees comparable protection against the negative effects of job dislocation. Such a requirement would discourage reckless and disruptive actions when a company is acquired that cause lost jobs, destroy established supplier and customer relations, and impose costs on the communities in which the target companies are located. A nationally legislated minimum severance package related to length of tenure would make layoffs of experienced workers whose investments created value for the company a last resort. This is especially important in the case of publicly traded companies or divisions of such companies that are taken private, as job losses in the years following these types of takeovers are common and typically occur in the first year or two after the LBO.

Conclusion

Private equity is a relatively new financial player that emerged nearly forty years ago and grew to maturity in a period of extensive financial deregulation. It has thrived in the shadows of the regulated financial system, growing into a significant new form of ownership and governance of operating companies that employ several million U.S. workers. Its virtues can be seen in its willingness and ability to invest in distressed businesses and industries and turn them around and in its capacity for helping successful small companies to grow to scale. This book has highlighted many such instances. Private equity's excesses have also become clear, framed by the notable failures in the aftermath of the 2008 to 2009 recession of several iconic companies. This chapter has located the source of moral hazard at the core of the PE business model. As then Federal Reserve chairman Ben Bernanke observed, "The problem of moral hazard has no perfect solutions, but steps can be taken to limit it." As he noted, regulatory reforms and restrictions on certain activities "can directly limit risk-taking." We have proposed policies that limit moral hazard and rein in the most egregious excesses of the PE business model and that will hold private equity accountable for those actions that undermine the welfare of employees and other stakeholders.

The proposed policies will improve the sustainability of operating companies taken over in leveraged buyouts. They will provide a more equitable balance among the interests of all of a company's stakeholders and will restore to workers in PE-owned companies the same protections against mass dismissal and safeguards for their retirement pensions that Congress intended. They will increase transparency and reduce the riskiness of PE investments for pension funds and other limited partners and will provide LPs with information that can bring expectations of returns into line with reality. Partners in PE firms that make their money, as advertised by the Private Equity Growth Capital Council and other industry advocates, by adding value to the portfolio companies they acquire will see little difference as a result of these policies. For partners in PE firms that make their money through financial engineering in the myriad ways documented in this book, these policies will bring an end to the rent-seeking and risk-shifting behavior that has increased their slice of the economic pie without actually helping the pie to grow and that has made their careers in private equity so extremely lucrative.

It will be challenging to achieve these policy reforms. The financial services industry exercises significant influence in Washington. In recent years, the financial sector was the largest source of contributions to national political campaigns and engaged in extensive lobbying, employing three thousand lobbyists in 2007.[108] In 1999 investment banks, commercial banks, securities firms, and insurance companies—which previously had competing interests—came together to support passage of the Financial Services Modernization Act (the Graham-Leach-Bliley Act). This legislation repealed part of the law passed during the Great Depression that separated banks, securities companies, and insurance companies and prevented them from consolidating their activities. With passage of the Graham-Leach-Bliley Act in 1999, the largest financial institutions now shared common interests. These firms have successfully joined together to protect their common business interests and oppose regulations that they view as inimical to their growth.

Arthur E. Wilmarth argues that, in addition to the high level of spending on campaign contributions and lobbying, there are three additional factors that help explain the finance industry's outsized influence on the political process.[109] First, the patchwork of regulatory agencies and the competition among financial regulators to be the main agency in charge of supervising particular types of financial institutions have created opportunities for "regulatory arbitrage"—that is, seeking to be regulated by the most lenient agency. Second, politicians and regulators can expect strong pushback from the industry when they oppose what it sees as its interests as well as a loss of lucrative opportunities for subsequent employment in the financial services industry. And third, this "revolving door" in which regulators move back and forth between private-sector employment in financial services firms and public-sector employment in regulatory agencies leads to "cognitive capture" of regulators who tend to see things from the perspective of industry players rather than that of the public.

Still, the finance industry is not all-powerful. The Dodd-Frank Act passed despite massive resistance from Wall Street. Even acknowledging the industry's subsequent success in weakening the act's provisions, this was a formidable accomplishment. President Barack Obama defeated Mitt Romney, Wall Street's favored candidate in the 2012 presidential election and recipient of the lion's share of the industry's political contributions in that race. A determined electorate can successfully call for important reforms, including those that rein in the excesses documented in this book.

═ Notes ═

Chapter 2

1. Fligstein (1990) and Davis (2009).
2. Chandler (1954).
3. Berle and Means (1932) and Dodd (1932).
4. Stout (2012), 17–18.
5. Chandler (1977) and Lazonick (1992).
6. Doeringer and Piore (1971).
7. Osterman (1984).
8. Donaldson (1984), 3.
9. Chandler (1977) and Lazonick (1992).
10. Palley (2007).
11. Kochan, Katz, and McKersie (1986).
12. Appelbaum and Schettkat (1995).
13. Chandler (1994), Davis (2009), and Lazonick (1992).
14. Fligstein (1990) and Lazonick (1992).
15. Baker and Smith (1998), 13.
16. Davis, Diekmann, and Tinsley (1994) and Fligstein (1990).
17. Lazonick (1992), 175.
18. Ibid., 177.
19. Hayes and Abernathy (1980).
20. Fligstein (1990) and Zorn (2004).
21. Jensen and Meckling (1976).
22. Stout (2012).
23. Jensen and Meckling (1976) and Jensen (1986).
24. See Lazonick and O'Sullivan (2000), 13–35.
25. Kaufman and Englander (1993).
26. Fama and Jensen (1983).
27. Jensen (1986), 325.
28. Lazonick (1992), 175.
29. Lowenstein (2004).
30. Zorn et al. (2005).
31. Prahalad and Hamel (1990).
32. Zuckerman (2000).

33. Lydenberg (2012). See chapter 7 for a fuller account of the influence of modern portfolio theory on ERISA regulations.
34. Useem (1996).
35. Gompers and Metrick (2001) and Zorn et al. (2005), 274.
36. Baker and Smith (1998), 80.
37. Donaldson (1994).
38. Zuckerman (2000).
39. Zorn et al. (2005), 276.
40. Jarrell (1983).
41. Baker and Smith (1998), 18.
42. Akerlof and Romer (1993).
43. Ibid.
44. Ibid.
45. Ibid.
46. Prof. William Black, litigation director of the Federal Home Loan Bank board at the time, communication with the authors, November 15, 2011.
47. Baker and Smith (1998) and Anders (2002).
48. Baker and Smith (1998), 27.
49. Ibid., 51–52.
50. Lowenstein (2004), 6–7.
51. Jensen (1986), 328.
52. Lazonick (1992), 167–68.
53. Baker and Smith (1998), 65ff.
54. Ibid., 95–123.
55. Anders (2002), Baker and Smith (1998), Carey and Morris (2010), and Holland (1989).
56. Anders (2002).
57. Ibid.; see also Holland (1989).
58. Holland (1989).
59. Baker and Smith (1998), appendix.
60. Holland (1989), 226 ff.
61. Baker and Smith (1998), 26.
62. Ibid., 171.
63. Ibid., 99.
64. Ibid., 85.
65. Ibid., 23.
66. Mitchell and Mulherin (1996).
67. Davis and Stout (1992), 624–25.
68. Davis et al. (1994), 554–61.
69. Kochan et al. (1986).
70. Hammer and Stern (1986).
71. Katz (1995).
72. Bureau of Labor Statistics, "Union Members—2012" (press release), January 23, 2013, available at: http://www.bls.gov/news.release/pdf/union2.pdf (accessed January 23, 2013).
73. Oi (1962).
74. Becker (1964).
75. Cappelli (1999).
76. Holmstrom and Kaplan (2001), 125.

77. Zorn et al. (2005), 275.
78. Kaplan (1997).
79. Holmstrom and Kaplan (2001), 132–34.
80. Donaldson (1994).
81. Lowenstein (2004), 17–19.
82. Hall and Liebman (1998).
83. Lazonick (2011).
84. Jung and Dobbin (2012), 65–86.
85. Lowenstein (2004).
86. Loomis (2005).
87. Baker and Smith (1998), 192.
88. Ibid., 194.
89. Goldberg et al. (2010).
90. "Exemptions for Advisers to Venture Capital Funds, Private Fund Advisers with Less Than $150 Million in Assets Under Management, and Foreign Private Advisers," in "Rules and Regulations," *Federal Register* 76(129, July 6, 2011); PriceWaterhouseCoopers, LLC, "A Closer Look: The Dodd-Frank Wall Street Reform and Consumer Protection Act," 2011, available at: http://www.pwc.com/us/en/financial-services/regulatory-services/publications/dodd-frank-closer-look.jhtml (accessed February 13, 2014).
91. Fleischer (2008); Government Accountability Office (2008), 72; and Marples (2008).
92. Jickling and Marples (2007), 6.
93. MacGilis (2011) and Rubin et al. (2011).
94. Europa (2010) and European Union (2011).
95. Gospel, Pendleton, and Vitols (2014).
96. Eder, Steve, Gregory Zuckerman, and Michael Corkery. "Pensions Leap Back to Hedge Funds," *Wall Street Journal.* May 27, 2011, available at: http://online.wsj.com/news/articles/SB10000142405270230365480457634776 2838825864 (accessed February 10, 2014); PitchBook data, 2013, authors' calculations, 2013.
97. Batt and Appelbaum (2012).
98. Data from Private Equity Growth Capital Council, "PE by the Numbers," 2011, available at: http://www.pegcc.org/education/pe-by-the-numbers/ (accessed December 30, 2011).
99. Private Equity Analyst (2008). 2007 Review and 2008 Outlook. NY. Dow Jones, cited in Kaplan and Strömberg (2009).
100. Data on private equity transactions in this book refer to leveraged buyouts of companies located in the United States and come from PitchBook, an independent research firm specializing in PE data and analysis. We report LBO transactions, including general leveraged buyouts, management buyouts, management buy-ins, add-ons, secondary buyouts, public-to-private buyouts, leveraged recapitalization, and corporate divestitures. In consultation with the research team at PitchBook, we use a slightly different definition of PE investments in leveraged buyouts than we used in figure 1 of Appelbaum and Batt (2012a) and Appelbaum and Batt (2012b).
101. See, for example, Strömberg (2008) and Kaplan and Strömberg (2009).
102. PEGCC (2013). Data from PEGCC, available at: www.pegcc.org/education/pe-by-the-numbers/ (accessed December 26, 2013).

103. Wharton on Private Equity, Wharton School, University of Pennsylvania, "2011 Wharton Private Equity Review: Gradually Regaining Ground," June 28, 2011, available at: http://kw.wharton.upenn.edu/private-equity/pe-review/2011-wharton-private-equity-review-gradually-regaining-ground/(accessed December 30, 2011).
104. Authors' calculations based on PitchBook data.
105. The regions are defined as follows: *Midwest*—North Dakota, South Dakota, Nebraska, Kansas, Iowa, and Missouri; *Mountain*—Montana, Idaho, Wyoming, Nevada, Arizona, Colorado, Utah, and New Mexico; *South*—Texas, Oklahoma, Arkansas, Louisiana, Kentucky, and Tennessee; *Southeast*—Mississippi, Alabama, Georgia, Florida, South Carolina, and North Carolina; *West Coast*—Alaska, Hawaii, Washington, Oregon, and California; *Great Lakes*—Minnesota, Wisconsin, Illinois, Indiana, Michigan, and Ohio; *Mid-Atlantic*—Virginia, West Virginia, Washington, D.C., Maryland, Delaware, Pennsylvania, New York, and New Jersey; and *New England*—Maine, Vermont, New Hampshire, Massachusetts, Connecticut, and Rhode Island.

Chapter 3

1. Froud et al. (2008), 2.
2. Ibid., 8.
3. Kaplan and Strömberg (2009).
4. Froud et al. (2008).
5. See chapter 1 for the organizational chart of the private equity firm business model.
6. Temple (1999).
7. Baker and Smith (1998), 165ff.
8. Charles V. Bagli, "Buying Landmarks? Easy. Keeping Them? Maybe Not," *New York Times,* January 16, 2010; Charles V. Bagli, "Stuyvesant Town's Lenders Take over Property," *New York Times,* October 26, 2010; Oshrat Carmiel, "Ackman's Group Exits Stuyvesant Town Investment with $45 Million Intact," *Bloomberg News,* October 27, 2010.
9. Iliana Jonas, "Stuyvesant Town/Peter Cooper Owner, Tenants Settle Suit," Reuters, November 30, 2012.
10. Kevin Roose, "Private Equity Giants Use Size to Lean on Suppliers," *New York Times,* DealBook, July 7, 2012.
11. Singh (2008). Available at http://dealbook.nytimes.com/2012/07/11/16-million-reams-of-paper-please/.
12. Axelson et al. (2008) and Strömberg (2008).
13. Chakraborty, Weisbach, and Zhou (2009), 7.
14. Platt (2009) and Senbet and Wang (2012).
15. Kaplan and Strömberg (2009).
16. Strömberg (2008).
17. Ibid., 8.
18. Mara Lemos Stein, "Moody's Says LBO Default Recoveries Match Non-LBOs," *Daily Bankruptcy Review,* June 4, 2012, available at: http://bankruptcynews.dowjones.com/article?an=DJFDBR0020120604e864p2k8b&from=NL&pid=10 (accessed June 5, 2012).

19. Ibid.
20. Ibid.
21. Kevin Lavin, "Corporate Defaults Go Their Own Way," *Daily Bankruptcy Review*, February 22, 2012, available at: http://bankruptcynews.dowjones. com/Article?an=DJFDBR0020120222e82me7f39&ReturnUrl=http%3a%2f% 2fbankruptcynews.dowjones.com%2fArticle%3fan%3dDJFDBR0020120222 e82me7f39 (accessed February 13, 2014).
22. Mark Maremont, "Romney at Bain: Big Gains, Some Busts," *Wall Street Journal*, January 9, 2012.
23. Global Credit Research, "Moody's: Lackluster Performance for Bubble-Era Buyouts," December 7, 2011, available at: http://www.moodys.com/ research/Moodys-Lackluster-Performance-for-Bubble-Era-Leveraged-Buyouts—PR_232792 (accessed January 14, 2011).
24. Tom Hals, Sue Zeidler, and Caroline Humer, "Insight: New Bankruptcy Ripples May Emerge," Reuters, October 11, 2011.
25. Tiffany Kary and Sophia Pearson, "NewPage, Cerberus-Owned Papermaker, Files for Bankruptcy," *Bloomberg Businessweek*, September 7, 2011, available at: http://www.businessweek.com/news/2011-09-07/newpage-cerberus-owned-papermaker-files-for-bankruptcy.html (accessed June 6, 2012).
26. Hotchkiss, Smith, and Strömberg (2012).
27. GAO (2008), 46.
28. Ibid., 52.
29. Froud et al. (2008) and Froud and Williams (2007).
30. Metrick and Yasuda (2009/2011), 10.
31. Ibid., 16.
32. "Spotlight Compensation," *PE Manager Yearbook 2012*, 27, available at: www. privateequitymanager.com/Article.aspx?article=71006 (accessed March 3, 2013).
33. Metrick and Yasuda (2009/2011), 29.
34. Ibid., 7.
35. Ibid., 37.
36. Michael Luo and Julie Creswell. "Companies Ills Did Not Harm Romney's Firm," *New York Times*, June 22, 2012, available at: http://www.nytimes. com/2012/06/23/us/politics/companies-ills-did-not-harm-romneys-firm.html?_r=0 (accessed March 12, 2013); Joseph Lichterman, "Romney's Role at Failed Bain-Owned Supplier Challenged," *Automotive News*, May 26, 2012, available at: http://www.autonews.com/article/20120526/ OEM10/120529930/1424#axzz2ns174J9x (accessed March 12, 2013).
37. Eric Wieffering, "Buffets Inc.: Revisiting a Deal Gone Wrong," *Star Tribune*, January 25, 2012; Jake Anderson, "Suit: Former Buffets Owners, CEO Bilked Millions," *Twin Cities Business*, April 12, 2010, available at: http://tcbmag. blogs.com/daily_developments/2010/04/lawsuit-owner-bilked-millions-from-buffets-inc.html.
38. For a full discussion, see Peter Morris (2011), "Portfolio Company Fees—Some Empirical Evidence and Recommendations," *The Review of Private Equity*, 1–33, available at: http://papers.ssrn.com/sol3/papers.cfm?abstract_ id=2370462 (accessed December 23, 2013).

39. Metrick and Yasuda (2010).
40. Morris, "Portfolio Company Fees."
41. Ibid.
42. Dan Primack, "Term Sheet," *Fortune,* June 25, 2012.
43. Jenkinson, Sousa, and Stucke (2013) and Phalippou (2008).
44. Valuation Research Corporation, "Fair Value Rules Impact Private Equity World" (VRC alert), February 2007, available at: www.valuationresearch. com (accessed March 12, 2013); Douglas Peterson, "SEC Increases Its Scrutiny of PE Valuations," Reuters, PEHub, December 17, 2012, available at: http:// www.pehub.com/177727/sec-increases-its-scrutiny-of-pe-valuations% E2%80%A8.../ (accessed March 12, 2013).
45. Jenkinson et al. (2013).
46. Metrick and Yasuda (2010) and Robinson and Sensoy (2011).
47. Harris, Jenkinson, and Kaplan (2013).
48. Acharya, Hahn, and Kehoe (2009).
49. Ibid., 33, and table 10.
50. Emily Thornton, "Perform or Perish," *Bloomberg Businessweek,* November 4, 2007, 38–45.
51. Metrick and Yasuda (2010).
52. Folkman et al. (2009).
53. Hoskisson et al. (2013).
54. In chapter 5, we adopt the definition of market segments used by PitchBook, among others. The small-market segment refers to companies with an enterprise value under $25 million; the lower middle market includes companies with an enterprise value of $25 million to $100 million; enterprise values in the "core" middle market range from $100 million to $500 million; the large middle market has enterprise values from $500 million to $1 billion; and the "mega" market comprises companies with enterprise values of more than $1 billion.
55. Buchanan (1980), 4.
56. "Twelve Leading For-Profit Acute-Care Hospital Companies," *Becker's Hospital Review,* September 4, 2009, available at: http://www.beckershospital review.com/lists-and-statistics/12-leading-for-profit-acute-care-hospital-companies.html (accessed July 3, 2011).
57. The largest PE-owned hospital chain is Hospital Corporation of America (HCA), which we discuss in chapter 5.
58. Robert Weisman, "Equity Firm Set to Buy Caritas," *Boston Globe,* March 25, 2010.
59. Advisen, "Private Equity and Hospitals: Providence or Problem?" May 11, 2011, available at: topical_report_private_equity_hospitals-1.pdf (accessed June 29, 2012).
60. *PitchBook News,* June 21, 2012.
61. "U.S. Healthcare: Mixed Diagnosis," *Financial Times,* Lex Column, June 27, 2012.
62. Jay Hancock, "Hospital Stocks Soar as Court Upholds Health Act," Capsules, Kaiser Health News, June 28, 2012, available at: http://capsules.kaiser healthnews.org/index.php/2012/06/hospital-stocks-soar-as-court-upholds-health-act/ (accessed December 19, 2013).

63. Former CFO of a large not-for-profit hospital chain, interview with the authors, February 17, 2012.
64. Louise Radnofsky and Christopher Weaver, "Health Law Battle Enters Round 2," *Wall Street Journal,* July 1, 2012.
65. Kaplan and Strömberg (2009).
66. PitchBook, "Axle Tech Company Profile," 2008.
67. Private Equity Growth Capital Council, "New PEGCC Video Chronicles the Transformation of Axle Tech from a Regional Manufacturer to a Global Industry Leader," 2012, available at: http://www.pegcc.org/newsroom/in-the-news/new-pegcc-video-chronicles-the-transformation-of-axletech-from-a-regional-manufacturer-to-a-global-industry-leader/(accessed June 13, 2012).
68. Carlyle Group, "Case Study: Axle Tech International," available at: www.carlyle.com/investor-relations/case-studies/axletech-international (accessed July 17, 2012).
69. Thornton, "Perform or Perish."
70. Ibid.
71. Wynnchurch Capital, Case Studies: Axle Tech International, "Helping a Corporate Orphan Realize Its Full Potential," no date, available at: http://www.autonews.com/article/20120526/OEM10/120529930/1424#axzz2ns174J9x (accessed June 13, 2012).; PitchBook, "Axle Tech Company Profile," 2008.
72. Cited by University of Wisconsin–Oshkosh professor Tony Palmeri, "Palmeri's Oshkosh Newsmakers of 2003," December 24, 2003, available at: http://www.uwosh.edu/faculty_staff/palmeri/commentary/newsmakers2003.htm (accessed July 28, 2012).
73. Wynnchurch Capital, Case Studies: Axle Tech International.
74. Ibid.
75. Water sports executives, interview with the authors, May 12, 2012; PitchBook, "Watermark Paddlesports Water Sport Division Company Profile," 2013; PitchBook, "Confluence Company Profile," 2013.
76. NRS executives, interview with the authors, May 12, 2012.
77. PitchBook, July 2, 2012.
78. Folkman et al. (2009).
79. Government Accountability Office (2009).
80. PitchBook, "Awarix Company Profile, 2012"; PE firm partner, interview with the authors, August 2, 2012.
81. Carolyn Pritchard, "McKesson Agrees to Buy Awarix," *Wall Street Journal,* MarketWatch, July 16, 2007, available at: http://articles.marketwatch.com/2007-07-16/news/30738967_1_mckesson-patient-flow-largest-prescription-drug-distributor (accessed February 13, 2014).
82. ComFrame, Awarix case study, available at: http://www.pdf-repo.com/pdf_1a/160g1o81m951b799a.1html (accessed December 19, 2013).
83. PE firm partner, interview with the authors, August 2, 2012.
84. Ibid.
85. Luke Johnson, "Private Equity to Presidency Is a Leap," *Financial Times,* July 24, 2012.

86. Smith, Peter. 2006. "S&P Says Rise in Leveraged Recaps Could Increase Defaults." Financial Times, August 14, 2006, available at: http://www.ft.com/intl/cms/s/0/3680c5e0-2b31-11db-b77c-0000779e2340.html#axzz2ty4UQRqS (accessed February 21, 2014)

87. Wieffering, "Buffets Inc.: Revisiting a Deal Gone Wrong"; PitchBook, "Buffets Holdings 2008 Company Profile."

88. Appelbaum, Batt, and Clark (2013); Dan Primack, "Term Sheet," *Fortune,* December 7, 2011; "The Year in 2008 PE-Backed Bankruptcies," *Wall Street Journal,* MoneyBeat (formerly DealBook), December 29, 2008.

89. PitchBook, "Urban Brands Company Profile," 2013.

90. PitchBook, "Harry & David Holdings Company Profile," 2011.

91. See the PBGC website at: http://www.pbgc.gov/wr/trusteed/plans/plan21857600.html.

92. Lynn Cowan and Peter Lattman, "HCA Files for $4.6 billion IPO," *Wall Street Journal,* May 8, 2010, available at http://online.wsj.com/news/articles/SB10001424052748703338004575230060296275590 (accessed December 19, 2013).

93. Carrick Mollenkamp, "HCA Pays Owners $2 Billion," *Wall Street Journal,* November 10, 2010.

94. Carrick Mollenkamp, "HCA Pays Big Dividend to Its Owners," *Wall Street Journal,* November 10, 2010; Michael Aneiro, "HCA to Sell $1.5bn in Junk Bonds to Par Private Equity Dividend," *eFinancial News,* November 10, 2010, available at: www.efinancialnews.com/story/2010-11-10/hca-pays-third-dividend.

95. U.S. Securities and Exchange Commission, "HCA Holdings, Inc.: Form S-1: Registration Statement Under the Securities Act of 1933," December 22, 2010, available at: http://www.sec.gov/Archives/edgar/data/860730/000095012310115879/y83802asv1.htm#10.

96. Ken Terry, "Big IPO for HCA Hospital Chain, but Buyers' Remorse Remains a Distinct Possibility," CBS, MoneyWatch, March 14, 2011, available at: http://www.bnet.com/blog/healthcare-business/big-ipo-for-hca-hospital-chain-but-buyers-8217-remorse-remains-a-distinct-possibility/2687 (accessed July 13, 2012).

97. Ryan Dezember, "The Many Ways Blackstone Made Money on SeaWorld's IPO," *Wall Street Journal,* MoneyBeat, April 22, 2013; PitchBook, "Seaworld Entertainment Company Profile," 2013.

98. Dezember, "The Many Ways Blackstone Made Money on SeaWorld's IPO."

99. Joseph E. Casson and Julia McMillen 2003. "Protecting Nursing Home Companies: limiting liability through corporate restructuring." *Journal of Health Law* 36(4): 577–613.

100. Davis et al. (2011).

101. Davis, Middleton, and Spitzer (2007).

102. See Kirkland and Ellis LLP website at: http://www.kirkland.com/sitecontent.cfm?contentID=220&itemID=8139 (accessed July 12, 2012).

103. Kaplan and Strömberg (2009).

104. Government Accountability Office (2008) and Luehrman and Scott (2007).

105. PitchBook, "Hertz Company Profile," 2011.

106. Luehrman and Scott (2007).

107. Government Accountability Office (2008) and Luehrman and Scott (2007).

108. Government Accountability Office (2008); PitchBook, "Hertz Company Profile," 2011.
109. Andrew Ross Sorkin, "Is Private Equity Giving Hertz a Boost?" *New York Times,* September 23, 2007.
110. Ibid.
111. PitchBook, "Hertz Company Profile," 2011.
112. Yahoo Finance, "Hertz Global Holdings, Inc. (HTZ)," July 17, 2012, available at: http://finance.yahoo.com/q/ks?s=HTZ+Key+Statistics (accessed July 17, 2012).
113. Government Accountability Office (2008).
114. Ibid.
115. "Hertz Will Eliminate a Further 1,350 Jobs," *New York Times,* Associated Press, March 1, 2007.
116. Government Accountability Office (2008).
117. Ibid.
118. "Hertz to Lay Off 4,000," *New York Daily News,* News Wire Services, January 16, 2009; "Hertz Rental Car Plans to Cut 4,000 Jobs," *New York Times, Bloomberg News,* January 17, 2009.
119. Dan Primack, "Term Sheet," *Fortune,* May 7, 2013.
120. Kaplan and Strömberg (2009).
121. Badertscher, Katz, and Rego (2012).
122. De Mooij (2011).
123. Axelson et al. (2008).
124. Chakraborty et al. (2009).
125. Kaplan (1989) and Kaplan and Strömberg (2009).
126. Jeff Gerth and Allan Sloan, "Five Ways GE Plays the Tax Game," ProPublica, April 4, 2011, available at: http://www.propublica.org/article/5-ways-ge-plays-the-tax-game# (accessed March 22, 2012); David Kochieniewski, "GE's Strategy Lets It Avoid Taxes Altogether," *New York Times,* March 24, 2011; Todd Bishop, "WA Seeks New Tax Revenue from Software, But Not From Microsoft," Tech Flash, *Puget Sound Business Journal,* March 26, 2010. Available at: http://www.bizjournals.com/seattle/blog/techflash/2010/03/wash_tax_plan_shakes_small_software_makers_skips_microsoft.html?page=all (accessed December 19, 2013).
127. Badertscher et al. (2011).
128. McGladrey, "Private Equity Tax Solutions: Case Study," April 9, 2012, available at: http://mcgladrey.com/content/mcgladrey/en_US/what-we-do/industries/private-equity/case-studies/private-equity-tax-solutions.html (accessed December 19, 2013).
129. Fleischer (2010).
130. Ibid.
131. Badertscher et al. (2011).
132. Michael Luo and Mike McIntyre, "Offshore Tactics Helped Increase Romneys' Wealth," *New York Times,* October 1, 2012.
133. Ibid.
134. Serena Ng, "Firms Move to Scoop Up Own Debt," *Wall Street Journal,* August 24, 2009.
135. Cited in Christopher Palmeri, "Harrah's Gets Some Debt Relief," *Bloomberg Businessweek,* April 22, 2009.

136. Will Deener, "Chip Maker Freescale Semiconductor's Taken Drastic Steps to Make a Dent in Its Debt," *Dallas Morning News,* August 22, 2010.
137. Palmeri, "Harrah's Gets Some Debt Relief."
138. Austin Smith, "Apollo's Leon Black Shows Debt Dexterity in Down Market," *New York Post,* July 8, 2010; "Harrah's Getting Ready to Cut Debt, Report Says," *New York Times,* DealBook, March 2, 2009.
139. Peter Morris, correspondence with the authors, August 9, 2011.
140. Ibid.
141. Ibid.
142. Akerlof and Romer (1993).
143. Ibid.
144. Strömberg, Hotchkiss, and Smith (2011), 4.
145. Mike Spector, "Two Hats a Fit for Friendly's Owner," *Wall Street Journal,* July 27, 2012.
146. Peg Brickley, "Sun Capital to Recapture Friendly's with 'Credit Bid,' " *Wall Street Journal,* December 30, 2011.
147. U.S. Bankruptcy Court for the District of Delaware, "Declaration of Steven C. Sanchioni of Friendly Ice Cream Corporation in Support of Debtors' Chapter 11 Petitions and First Day Motions," in the U.S. Bankruptcy Court for the District of Delaware, *In re: Friendly's Ice Cream Corporation, et al., Debtors, Chapter 11, Case 11-13167, 2011;* Jenn Abelson, "U.S. Alleges Fraud in Friendly's Case," *Boston Globe,* December 13, 2011.
148. PitchBook, "Stant Company Profile," 2013.
149. Spector, "Two Hats a Fit for Friendly's Owner."
150. Shleifer and Summers (1988).
151. Metrick and Yasuda (2010), 5.
152. Jung (2011).
153. Appelbaum, Batt, and Clark (2013).
154. Beck (2010), Clark (2009), Folkman et al. (2009), Thompson (2003), and Wood and Wright (2010).
155. Fligstein (2001).
156. Leslie Earnest, "Investors Cheer as Target Weighs Shedding Chains," *Los Angeles Times,* March 12, 2004.
157. Julie Tamaki, "Target Set to Sell Mervyn's Chain," *Los Angeles Times,* July 30, 2004; Emily Thornton, "How Private Equity Strangled Mervyn's," *Bloomberg Businessweek,* November 25, 2008, available at: www.businessweek.com/magazine/content/08_49/b4111040876189.htm; Elaine Misonzhnik, "Private Equity Racks Up Checkered Record in Retail Buyouts," National Real Estate Investor, June 29, 2009, available at: http://retailtrafficmag.com/retailing/operations/private-equity-retail-buyout-record-0629/index2.html.
158. Misonzhnik, "Private Equity Racks Up Checkered Record in Retail Buyouts."
159. Cleary Gottlieb Steen & Hamilton LLP, "Delaware Bankruptcy Court Allows Debtor's Suit Against Seller in LBO to Proceed" (Cleary Gottlieb alert memo), March 29, 2010.
160. Levenfeld Pearlstein, "Real Estate Case Study 1," 2011, available at: http://www.lplegal.com/about-lp/success-stories/real-estate-case-study-1. Levenfeld Pearlstein provided MDS Realty with counsel and assistance in the sale of the real estate assets.

161. Corporate executive, interview with the authors, June 10, 2011.

162. Thornton, "How Private Equity Strangled Mervyn's."

163. Former high-level manager at Mervyn's headquarters, interview with the authors, June 30, 2011.

164. Corporate executive, interview with the authors, interview June 10, 2011.

165. Former high-level manager at Mervyn's headquarters, interview with the authors, June 30, 2011.

166. Ibid.

167. Thornton, "How Private Equity Strangled Mervyn's"; Rachel Dodes and Jeffrey McCracken, "Mervyn's Is Close to Bankruptcy Filing," *Wall Street Journal*, July 29, 2008.

168. U.S. Bankruptcy Court for the District of Delaware, "Affidavit of Charles R. Kurth, Executive Vice President and Chief Financial and Administrative Officer of the Debtors, in Support of First Day Motions," in the U.S. Bankruptcy Court for the District of Delaware, *Chapter 11, Case 08-11586 (KG), Jointly Administered, In re: Mervyn's Holdings, LLC, et al., Debtors, State of California, County of Alameda, July 29, 2008.*

169. Shleifer and Summers (1988), 38.

170. Thornton, "How Private Equity Strangled Mervyn's."

171. Dodes and McCracken, "Mervyn's Is Close to Bankruptcy Filing."

172. U.S. Bankruptcy Court for the District of Delaware, "Affidavit of Charles R. Kurth, . . . First Day Motions."

173. Lawyer knowledgeable about the Mervyn's case, interview with the authors, May 19, 2011.

174. U.S. Bankruptcy Court for the District of Delaware, "List of Creditors Holding the Thirty Largest Unsecured Claims," in the U.S. Bankruptcy Court for the District of Delaware, *Chapter 11, Case 08-11586 (KG), Jointly Administered, In re: Mervyn's Holdings, LLC, Debtor, A Delaware Limited Liability Company, July 29, 2008.*

175. Peter Lattman, "Mervyn's Fights to Keep Its Store Doors Open," *Wall Street Journal*, July 21, 2008.

176. U.S. Bankruptcy Court for the District of Delaware, "Order Denying Motion to Dismiss," in the U.S. Bankruptcy Court for the District of Delaware, *Chapter 11, Case 08-11586 (KG), Adv. Proc. 08-51402 (KG), Re Dkt 43, In re: Mervyn's LLC, Plaintiff v. Lubert-Adler Group IV, LLC, et al., Defendants, March 17, 2010.*

177. Froud et al. (2008), 8.

Chapter 4

1. Gordon Green and John Coder, "Changes in Household Income During the Economic Recovery: June 2009 to June 2012," Sentier Research, LLC, 2012, available at: www.sentierresearch.com (accessed August 3, 2012).

2. For a review of theory and data, see Kaplan and Strömberg (2009), 137–43.

3. Ibid.

4. Dan Primack, "Term Sheet," *Fortune*, November 23, 2011.

5. David Bogoslaw, "Private Equity's Year from Hell," *Bloomberg Businessweek*, December 4, 2008.

6. "The Final List: 49 PE-Backed Bankruptcies in 2008," Reuters, PEHub, January 5, 2009.

7. In 2013 increased scrutiny by regulators and limited partners led some PE firms to agree to lower the management fees paid by limited partners to general partners and to eliminate the monitoring fees paid by newly acquired portfolio companies. See PitchBook, "Deal Multiples and Trends Report: 3Q 2013." In early 2013, the SEC received a complaint from a whistleblower claiming that PE firms that collect transaction fees from their portfolio companies have been violating securities laws by charging these fees without first registering as broker-dealers. In April, an SEC attorney argued publicly that PE firms that receive transaction fees should have to register as broker-dealers and be subject to the more stringent regulations in this regard that apply to investment banks. See Dan Primack, "Private Equity Has a Whistleblower Problem," *Fortune*, December 2, 2013, available at: http://finance.fortune.cnn.com/2013/12/02/private-equity-whistleblower/(accessed December 29, 2013).

8. Bogoslaw, "Private Equity's Year from Hell."

9. FMag, "PE-Backed Bankruptcies," FashionMag.com, August 18, 2008, available at: http://us.fashionmag.com/news-43007-PE-backed-bankruptcies (accessed August 3, 2012).

10. "Sorting Through the Aftermath of Private Equity Deals," *New York Times*, DealBook, February 29, 2012.

11. Arnold M. Knightly, "Harrah's Entertainment Plans to Lay Off More Workers," *Las Vegas Review-Journal*, October 4, 2008; Michael Sheffield, "Harrah's to Lay Off 200 Tunica Workers," *Memphis Business Journal*, November 3, 2010; Tom Wilemon, "Harrah's Lays Off Tunica Employees," *Memphis Daily News*, November 5, 2010.

12. DealBook, "Sorting Through the Aftermath of Private Equity Deals"; Dan Primack, "Caesar's Entertainment: Don't Get Too Excited by Caeser's," *Fortune*, February 8, 2012; AltAssets, "Apollo, TPG-Backed Caesars Entertainment Files for IPO," November 16, 2011, available at: http://www.altassets.net/private-equity-news/by-news-type/deal-news/apollo-tpg-backed-caesars-files-for-ipo.html (accessed February 9, 2012).

13. PitchBook, "Clear Channel Communication Company Profile," 2011.

14. DealBook, "Sorting Through the Aftermath of Private Equity Deal."

15. Gregory Zuckerman, "Add Gabelli to List Upset with Transfers at Clear Channel," *Wall Street Journal*, March 8, 2012; "Update 1—Clear Channel, Bain Sued over Cheap Loan," Reuters, March 8, 2012.

16. PitchBook, "Clear Channel Communication Company Profile," 2011.

17. Thornton McEnery, "The Biggest Private Equity Buyouts in History," *Business Insider*, April 18, 2011, available at: http://www.businessinsider.com/the-biggest-private-equity-deals-in-history-2011-4?op=1 (accessed August 29, 2012).

18. DealBook, "Sorting Through the Aftermath of Private Equity Deals"; Shira Ovide, "Biggest Private Equity Losers," *Wall Street Journal*, Deal Journal, May 27, 2011.

19. Jeffrey McCracken, "By the Numbers: Linens 'n Things Bankruptcy Filing," *Wall Street Journal*, Deal Journal, May 2, 2008.

20. FMag, "PE-Backed Bankruptcies"; Emily Thornton, "How Private Equity Strangled Mervyn's," *Bloomberg Businessweek,* November 25, 2008; PitchBook, company profiles.
21. "The Year in PE Bankruptcies," *The Deal Magazine,* April 13, 2012.
22. Ibid.
23. Shira Ovide and Mike Spector, "Chapter 11 Is Next Page for Reader's Digest," *Wall Street Journal,* August 18, 2009.
24. Tiffany Kary and Sophia Pearson, "NewPage, Cerberus-Owned Papermaker, Files for Bankruptcy," *Bloomberg Businessweek,* September 7, 2011.
25. Jonathan Stempel, "Tour Bus Operator Coach America Files Bankruptcy," Reuters, January 3, 2012.
26. Hotchkiss, Smith, and Strömberg (2012), 2.
27. Ibid., 10.
28. LeveragedLoan.com (2013). Standard & Poor's Financial Services LLC (S&P), Leveraged Loan Primer, 2013, available at: http://www.leveraged loan.com/primer/ (accessed December 23, 2013).
29. Hotchkiss, Smith, and Strömberg (2012).
30. Mara Lemos Stein, "Moody's Says LBO Default Recoveries Match Non-LBOs," *Bankruptcy News,* June 4, 2012, available at: http://bankruptcynews. dowjones.com/article?an=DJFDBR0020120604e864p2k8b&from=NL& pid=10 (accessed June 5, 2012).
31. Ibid.
32. Ibid.
33. Michael J. de la Merced, "Wall of Junk Debt Maturities Looms, Moody's Says," *New York Times,* DealBook, February 1, 2010.
34. Kevin Lavin, "Corporate Defaults Go Their Own Way," *Bankruptcy News,* February 22, 2012, available at: http://bankruptcynews.dowjones.com/article? an=DJFDBR0020120222e82me7f39 (accessed June 5, 2012).
35. PitchBook, "Deal Multiples and Trends Report: 3Q 2013," 6.
36. Preqin, "Deals and Exits Overview," *Preqin Quarterly Private Equity* (April 2012), 18; Arleen Jacobius, "Easy Credit Could Prompt Some Setbacks for PE Firms in New Year," *Pension&Investments,* January 7, 2013, available at: http://www.pionline.com/article/20130107/PRINTSUB/301079977/ easy-credit-could-prompt-some-setbacks-for-pe-firms-in-new-year (accessed January 8, 2013).
37. Preqin, "Secondary Buyouts," *Private Equity Spotlight* 7(11, November 2011): 5.
38. Bain & Company, Inc., *Global Private Equity Report 2012,* 5.
39. PitchBook, "Private Equity Fundraising and Capital Overhang Report: 2H 2013."
40. Henry Sender, "Centerbridge to Return $500M to Investors," *Financial Times,* September 30, 2012.
41. Henry Sender, "TPG Co-Founder Warns on Returns," *Financial Times,* September 30, 2012.
42. Authors' analysis of the PE data reported in figure 1.2.
43. Dan Primack, "Private Equity's 'Golden' Hangover: Where Are the Mega-IPOs?" *Fortune,* October 5, 2012.
44. PitchBook/Merrill Datasite, "Private Equity Exits Report: 2H 2013," 9.
45. Bain & Company, Inc., *Global Private Equity Report 2013,* 47.

46. Peter Lattman, "Buyout-Shop Swap Multiplan in $3.1 Billion LBO," *Wall Street Journal*, July 9, 2010.

47. *PitchBook News,* August 1, 2012.

48. Preqin, "Secondary Buyouts," *Private Equity Spotlight* 7(11, November 2011): 3; Bain & Company, Inc., *Global Private Equity Report 2011,* 13.

49. PitchBook, "Private Equity Exits Report: 1H 2013," 7.

50. Alan Wagner, "Secondary Buyouts Make 3Q Comeback, PitchBook Data Show," *PitchBook Blog,* September 30, 2013, available at: http://blog. pitchbook.com/secondary-buyouts-make-comeback-in-3q-new-pitch-book-data-show-2/(accessed December 23, 2013).

51. PitchBook/Merrill Datasite, "Private Equity Breakdown: 4Q 2013," 13.

52. Preqin, "Secondary Buyouts," *Private Equity Spotlight* 7(11), November 2011: 3; Bain & Company, Inc., *Global Private Equity Report 2011,* 44.

53. PE firm managing director, interview with the authors, August 6, 2012.

54. PitchBook/RR Donnelly, "Fundraising Report: 2H 2012."

55. Bain & Company, Inc., *Global Private Equity Report 2011,* 14; Bain & Company, Inc., *Global Private Equity Report 2012,* 16–19.

56. Bain & Company, Inc., *Global Private Equity Report 2012.*

57. Peter Lattman, "Swashbucklers Transformed, and Now Much Tamer," *New York Times,* December 11, 2012.

58. Bain & Company, Inc., *Global Private Equity Report 2012.*

59. PitchBook/RR Donnelly, "Fundraising Report: 2H 2012."

60. PitchBook, "Private Equity Fundraising and Capital Overhang Report: 2H 2013."

61. PitchBook, *PitchBook PE News,* October 13, 2013; Preqin, "Private Equity Fundraising in 2013 YTD Up 20% on Same Period in 2012" (press release), October 1, 2013, available at: https://www.preqin.com/docs/press/Private_Equity_Q3_13.pdf.

62. Preqin, "Private Equity Fundraising in 2013 YTD Up 20% on Same Period in 2012."

63. Vivianne Rodrigues, "U.S. Companies Return to Dividend Recaps," *Financial Times,* October 19, 2012.

64. Ibid.; Bryant Ruiz Switzky, "$1B Booz Allen Dividend Would Bring Carlyle Group Dividend," *Washington Business Journal,* July 11, 2012, available at: http://www.bizjournals.com/washington/blog/2012/07/booz-allen-dividend-would-bring.html?page=all (accessed October 19, 2012).

65. Rodrigues, "U.S. Companies Return to Dividend Recaps."

66. PitchBook/RR Donnelly, "Fundraising Report: 2H 2012."

67. Ibid.

68. Chad Eric Watt, "Gaining Insight While Most Are Pulling Back," *Dallas Business Journal,* November 7–13, 2008; Plante & Moran, "Private Equity Firms Provide Opportunity for Middle Market Companies," July 15, 2009, available at: www.plantemoran.com/perspectives/articles/pages/private-equity-firms-provide-opportunity-for-middle-market-companies.aspx (accessed November 2, 2010); American Executive, "Insight for Success," May 2010.

69. Jeff Bounds, "National Envelope Corp. Bought Out of Ch. 11," *Dallas Business Journal,* September 17, 2010, available at: http://dallas.bizjournals.com/

dallas/stories/2010/09/20/story1.html; Michael Volpe, "Claim Jumper Files Bankruptcy, Sells Assets to Private Equity Firm," *Orange County Business Journal,* September 10, 2010, available at: http://www.ocbj.com/news/2010/sep/10/claim-jumper-files-bankruptcy-sells-assets-private/ (accessed October 29, 2010).

70. Extended Stay America, "About Extended Stay America," available at: http://www.extendedstayhotels.com/About/Default.html; see also Extended Stay America, "Announcements," available at: http://www.extendedstayhotels.com/about/announcements.html (both accessed October 2, 2012).

71. Ralph R. Mabey, quoted in U.S. Bankruptcy Court for the Southern District of New York, "Report of Ralph R. Mabey, as Examiner," *In re: Extended Stay, Inc., et al., Debtors, Chapter 11, Case 09-13764 (JMP), April 8, 2010,* 19.

72. Ibid., 59.

73. Ibid., 19, 47.

74. Ibid., 60, exhibit IV-B-4.

75. Lingling Wei and Mike Spector, "Blackstone Group LP Is Going Back to the Future in the Distressed Hotel Industry," *Wall Street Journal,* April 22, 2010.

76. "Extended Stay Hotels Seeks Bankruptcy Protection," *New York Times, Bloomberg News,* June 16, 2009.

77. Mabey, "Report of Ralph R. Mabey," 150, 60, 100.

78. Xiang Ji, "Distressed-Debt Investing Shows Great Promise," Institutional Investor, September 20, 2010, available at: http://www.institutionalinvestor.com/Popups/PrintArticle.aspx?ArticleID=2673738 (accessed October 11, 2010); Lingling Wei and Mike Spector, "Blackstone Joins Extended Stay Bid," *Wall Street Journal,* April 22, 2010.

79. "Extended Stay Hotels Exits Chapter 11 with Strengthened Balance Sheet and Renewed Outlook for the Future," PR Newswire, October 8, 2010, available at: http://www.prnewswire.com/news-releases/extended-stay-hotels-exits-chapter-11-with-strengthened-balance-sheet-and-renewed-outlook-for-the-future-104597569.html; K. MacBeth, "Extended Stay Hotels Exit Chapter 11," *Daily Bankruptcy Review,* October 11, 2010.

80. Andrew Ross Sorkin, "Extended Stay Exits Chapter 11 After $3.9 Billion Buyout," *New York Times,* DealBook, October 11, 2010.

81. Lingling Wei and Kris Hudson, "Key Investor Stands in Hotel Rubble," *Wall Street Journal,* June 16, 2009.

82. Mabey, "Report of Ralph R. Mabey," 411.

83. Jacqueline Palank, "Extended Stay Trustee Sues over 'Tainted' $8 Billion 2007 Buyout," *Daily Bankruptcy Review,* June 15, 2011, available at: http://bankruptcynews.dowjones.com/Article?an=DJFDBR0020110615e76f0002t (accessed July 15, 2011).

84. "Update 6—Blackstone Sued for $8 Bln over Extended Stay Role," Reuters, June 15, 2011.

85. PitchBook, "Extended Stay Hotels Company Profile," 2013.

86. "Blackstone Settles Extended Stay Lawsuit for $10 Million," Reuters, June 20, 2013.

87. Mark Heschmeyer, "Blackstone Does It Again: Extended Stay Hotels Regain Luster After Surprise Twist," CoStar Group, January 30, 2013,

available at: http://www.costar.com/News/Article/Blackstone-Does-It-Again-Extended-Stay-Hotels-Regain-Luster-After-Surprise-Twist/145213 (accessed October 8, 2013).

88. Neil Callanan and Elizabeth Dexheimer, "Extended Stay Hotel Chain Seeks Up to $500 Million in IPO," *Bloomberg News,* October 8, 2013; "Hotel Chain Extended Stay Files for $100 Million IPO," Reuters, July 22, 2013.

89. PitchBook, "National Envelope Company Profile," 2013.

90. Andrew Ross Sorkin, "H.I.G. Capital to Finance Shapes Bankruptcy," *New York Times,* DealBook, May 12, 2008.

91. Glenn Siegel and Davin Hall, "Investor Strategies to Realize Returns in Troubled Situations," *Preqin Quarterly,* Q2, 2010.

92. PitchBook, "Stant Company Profile," 2013.

93. S. D. Murray, "To Make a Deal, Fortunoff Checks into Chapter 11," *New York Times,* Dealbook, February 5, 2008; Rachel Feintzeig, "Fortunoff Looks to Re-launch Jewelry Business," *Wall Street Journal,* Bankruptcy Beat, August 10, 2010.

94. "Clinton on Romney: 'Business Experience Does Not Guarantee Success' as President," PBS *NewsHour,* "Newsmaker Interview," June 5, 2012, available at: http://www.pbs.org/newshour/bb/politics/jan-june12/clinton_06-05.html.

95. Harner (2008), 706.

96. Ji, "Distressed-Debt Investing Shows Great Promise."

97. Appelbaum, Gittell, and Leana (2011).

98. Matt Wirz, "Debt Loads Climb in Buyout Deals," *Wall Street Journal,* December 16, 2012.

99. Ibid.

100. PitchBook, "Deal Multiples and Trend Report: 3Q 2013," 3.

101. Wirz, "Debt Loads Climb in Buyout Deals."

102. Matt Wirz, "Debt Makes Comeback in Buyouts," *Wall Street Journal,* June 13, 2013.

103. Alex Lykken, "Buyouts? No, Thanks: PE Firms Focus on New Strategies," *PitchBook PE News,* October 21, 2013.

104. David Carey, "The Great Private Equity Shakeout," *The Deal Magazine,* October 15, 2010; David Carey, "Reinventing the Dealmakers," *The Deal Magazine,* October 25, 2010.

105. Lattman, "Swashbucklers Transformed, and Now Much Tamer."

106. Lykken, "Buyouts? No, Thanks."

107. Economy Watch. "U.S.-Linked Yuan-Based Private Equity Funds Exploding," September 11, 2010, available at: www.economywatch.com/in-the-news/U.S.-linked-yuan-based-private-equity-funds-exploding-11-09.html (accessed November 2, 2010).

108. Ibid.; Christine Idzelis, "KKR's Profit Falls," The Deal Pipeline, November 4, 2010; Mike Lucas, "The Morning Leverage: Why China Is the Place to Be for PE," *Wall Street Journal,* September 30, 2010; Henry Sanderson, "Silver Lake Seeks China Technology Companies as Yuan Private Equity Grows," *Bloomberg News,* September 16, 2010; Samuel Shen and Jacqueline Wong, "Carlyle Fundraising for Beijing Fund Nearly Done," Reuters, July 30, 2010; Gregory Zuckerman, "Wall Street Warms to China Story," *Wall Street Journal,* January 2, 2011.

109. Neil Gough, "Private Equity in China: Which Way Out?" *New York Times,* DealBook, January 10, 2013.

110. Ibid.

111. Manjeet Kripalani, "Private Equity Pours into India," *Bloomberg Businessweek,* June 20, 2005, available at: www.businessweek.com/magazine/content/ 05_25/b3938158_mz035.htm (accessed November 4, 2010); Yassir A. Pitawalla, "India Is Awash in Private Equity," CNNMoney, *Fortune,* January 11, 2007, available at: http://money.cnn.com/magazines/fortune/fortune_ archive/2007/01/22/8398211/index.htm (accessed November 4, 2010); Vikas Bajaj, "Financier Invests Cautiously in India," *New York Times,* April 27, 2009.

112. Avneet S. Kochar, "Indian Private Equity: The Case for Optimism," *Wall Street Journal,* October 2, 2013.

113. Guillermo Parra-Bernal, "Big Private Equity Eyes Brazil for Tasty Deals," Reuters, December 16, 2009; Spencer Ante, "Brazil: The Next Hotbed of Venture Capital and Private Equity," *Bloomberg Businessweek,* The Tech Beat, June 26, 2009, available at: www.businessweek.com/the_thread/techbeat/ archives/2009/06/brazil_the_next_hotbed_of_venture_capital_and_private_ equity.html (accessed November 2, 2010); Bain & Company, Inc., *Global Private Equity Report 2011,* 45–46.

114. Vincent Bevins, "Blackstone Joins the Private Equity Surge in Brazil," *Financial Times,* September 30, 2010; AltAssets, "Warburg Pincus Leads $201 million Investment in Brazilian Hydro Company," *AltAssets: Private Equity News,* September 22, 2010, available at: www.altassets.com/private-equity-news/ article/nz19292.html (accessed November 4, 2010); Ante, "Brazil: The Next Hotbed of Venture Capital and Private Equity."

115. Luciana Magalhaes, "Brazil's Former Central Banker Says Economic Woes Are Home Grown," *Wall Street Journal,* August 5, 2013; Jonathan Shieber, "Unrest in Brazil Could Bring Long-Term Benefits for Investors," *Wall Street Journal,* August 5, 2013.

Chapter 5

1. Hoskisson et al. (2013), 26; Wright (2013). This may also explain why some studies report more positive operational and HR practices for European PE-owned enterprises, as they tend to be smaller in size, use less leverage, and are more constrained by labor institutions and union contracts (Bacon et al. 2004).

2. Kanter (1989).

3. Latham & Watkins, *The 2012 Middle Market Report: PitchBook Data.*

4. *Preqin Quarterly: Private Equity: Q1 2012* (April), 8.

5. Berger and Udell (1998, 2002).

6. Berger and Udell (2002).

7. Ibid.

8. Berger, Goldberg, and White (2001).

9. See the review in ibid.

10. Paglia and Harjoto (2012).

11. Ibid., panel A of tables 4 and 6.

12. Note that, like the numbers presented in other chapters, these data represent leveraged buyouts of companies located in the United States and come from PitchBook. LBO transactions include general leveraged buyouts, management buyouts, management buy-ins, add-ons, secondary buyouts, public-to-private buyouts, leveraged recapitalization, and corporate divestitures.

13. Latham & Watkins, *The 2012 Middle Market Report: PitchBook Data.*

14. PitchBook/Merrill Datasite, "Private Equity Breakdown: 4Q 2013," 8, 9.

15. The analysis of exits by market segment is based on data available for 53 percent of all exits in the PitchBook database.

16. PitchBook/Merrill Datasite, "Private Equity Breakdown: 4Q 2013," 8.

17. Interview with Private Equity Partner, July 18, 2012.

18. Calculations based on PitchBook data, 2000 to 2012.

19. PitchBook, "InterMedia Outdoors Company Profile," 2012; PitchBook, "Barrett Productions Company Profile," 2012.

20. Berkshire Partners, "The History of Carter's Inc.," available at: filebox.vt.edu/y/yuqi/berkshire.ppt (accessed March 3, 2013).

21. Ibid.; Lisa Ward, "Berkshire Partners: Invested in the Long Term," *The Deal Magazine,* August 31, 2012, available at: http://www.thedeal.com/magazine/ID/049175/2012/sept-3-2012/berkshire-partners-invested-in-the-long-term.php (accessed March 3, 2013).

22. Berkshire Partners, "Berkshire Partners Announces a Distribution of Carter's Common Stock," November 9, 2005.

23. Ward, "Berkshire Partners."

24. Managing partners at three PE firms engaged in these deals, interviews with the authors, January 17, 2012, July 18, 2012, and August 6, 2012.

25. PitchBook, "The Riverside Company Profile," 2013.

26. Riverside, "About," available at: http://www.riversidecompany.com/About.aspx (accessed March 3, 2013).

27. Paglia and Harjoto (2012), 46, table 6.

28. Ibid., 14.

29. Ibid., 15.

30. Ibid., 45, table 5, panel A.

31. PitchBook, "Aidells Sausage Company Profile," 2012.

32. PitchBook, "PitchBook Deal Terms and Multiples Survey: 3Q 2012," 4.

33. Encore Consumer Capital, "Investment Strategy: Criteria," 2013, available at: http://www.encoreconsumercapital.com/strategy_criteria.html (accessed April 15, 2013).

34. PitchBook, "Aidells Sausage Company Profile," 2012.

35. Sara Lee, *The Way Forward: 2011 Annual Report,* 2012, available at: http://www.annualreportowl.com/Sara%20Lee/2011/Annual%20Report.

36. PitchBook, "Aidells Sausage Company Profile," 2012.

37. On June 6, 2012, Aaron Money, managing partner at FFL, and Scott Gill, CEO of Chief Manufacturing (later Milestone AV Technologies), presented a case study of this midmarket company at "SuperReturn 2012" in Boston. Except where indicated, information on this case comes from their presentation and PowerPoint.

38. PitchBook, "Friedman, Fleischer, and Lowe Company Profile," 2013.

39. Twice, "Mount Makers Chief, Sanus Merge Companies," October 22, 2004, available at: www.twice.com/article/236312-Mount_Makers_Chief_Sanus_Merge_Companies.php (accessed June 20, 2012).

40. PitchBook, "Milestone AV Technologies Company Profile," 2012.

41. Ibid.

42. Ibid.

43. "Study: PE Lacks Operational Savoir-faire," *PE Manager: PEI Alternative Insights* 103 (March 2013): 6.

44. Natalie Alcala, "Juicy Couture Sold to Marilyn Monroe's Brand Rep for $195M," Racked LA, October 8, 2013, available at: http://la.racked.com/archives/2013/10/08/juicy_couture_sold_to_marilyn_monroes_brand_rep_for_195mm.php (accessed October 12, 2013).

45. Karlee Weinmann, "Juicy Couture Sells for $195M as Retail Buyouts Sizzle," Law360, October 7, 2013, available at: http://www.law360.com/articles/478511/juicy-couture-sells-for-195m-as-retail-buyouts-sizzle.

46. John Gordon, interview with the authors, March 13, 2013.

47. John Gordon, "Private Equity and Restaurants—The Good, Bad and the Ugly." Franchise-Info (International Association of Franchisees and Dealers), November 7, 2011, available at: http://www.franchise-info.ca/supply_chain/2011/11/private-equity-and-restaurants-2011-update.html (accessed March 16, 2013).

48. Ibid., 1.

49. Tiffany Hsu, "Carl's Jr. Owner CKE Delays IPO: Analysts Say Investors Balked at the Firm's Debt Load and Poor Growth Prospects," *Los Angeles Times,* August 11, 2012.

50. Demetri Diakantonis, "PE's Dining Casualties," *The Deal,* April 13, 2012, 1. http://pipline.thedeal.com/tdd/ViewBlog.dl?id=45959#ixzz201BoR4xv

51. PitchBook, "Ignite Restaurant Company Profile," 2013.

52. Thomas Content, "Waukesha Dairy Plant Golden Guernsey Suddenly Closes," *Milwaukee Journal Sentinel,* January 5, 2013.

53. Ibid.; Wagner, "Holder Teams with Van Hollen to Kill 100 Wisconsin Jobs"; Sarah Millard, "Update: Golden Guernsey Dairy Closes Its Doors," WaukeshaPatch, January 5, 2013, available at: http://waukesha.patch.com/articles/is-golden-guernsey-dairy-closed-for-good (accessed January 13, 2013).

54. Rick Barrett, "Hope Persists for Golden Guernsey Plant's Future," *Milwaukee Journal Sentinel,* January 12, 2013.

55. Wagner, "Holder Teams with Van Hollen to Kill 100 Wisconsin Jobs."

56. Ibid.

57. Sarah Millard, "Golden Guernsey Purchase Now Complete," WaukeshaPatch, September 12, 2011, available at: http://waukesha.patch.com/golden-guernsey-purchase-now-complete (accessed January 13, 2013).

58. OpenGate Capital, "Andrew Nikou," available at: http://www.opengate-capital.com/about-us/meet-the-team/andrew-nikou/ (accessed February 7, 2013).

59. Luisa Beltran, "Strike a Pose: Andrew Nikou OpenGate CEO in Reality Show Talks," Reuters, PEHub, August 16, 2011, available at: http://www.pehub.com/115745/strike-a-pose-andrew-nikou-opengate-ceo-in-reality-show-talks (accessed February 7, 2013).

60. Barrett, "Hope Persists for Golden Guernsey Plant's Future."
61. Ibid.; Rick Barrett and Erin Richards, "Despite Dairy Closing, Milwaukee-Area Milk Deliveries Continue," *Milwaukee Journal Sentinel*, January 7, 2013.
62. Jeff Engel, "Golden Guernsey Union Disputes OpenGate Claim of Lack of Cooperation," *Milwaukee Business Journal*, January 10, 2013.
63. Quoted in Barrett, "Hope Persists for Golden Guernsey Plant's Future."
64. Ben Handelman, "OpenGate CEO Discusses Closure of Golden Guernsey Dairy," Fox 6 News, January 9, 2013, available at: http://fox6now.com/2013/01/09/opengate-capital-ceo-discusses-closure-of-golden-guernsey-dairy/(accessed February 10, 2013).
65. Engel, "Golden Guernsey Union Disputes OpenGate Claim of Lack of Cooperation."
66. Barrett, "Hope Persists for Golden Guernsey Plant's Future."
67. Engel, "Golden Guernsey Union Disputes OpenGate Claim of Lack of Cooperation"; "Golden Guernsey Union Denies Company Allegations," BizTimes.com, January 11, 2013, available at: www.biztimes.com/article/20130111/ENEWSLETTERS02/130119949 (accessed February 7, 2013); Barrett, "Hope Persists for Golden Guernsey Plant's Future."
68. Eric Peterson, "Area Food Banks Getting Milk Products," Fox 11 News, January 16, 2013, available at: http://www.fox11online.com/news/local/green-bay/area-food-banks-getting-milk-products.
69. Barrett, "Hope Persists for Golden Guernsey Plant's Future."
70. Sarah Millard, "DOJ Files $2M Claim for Unpaid Golden Guernsey Wages," WaukeshaPatch, January 11, 2013, available at: http://waukesha.patch.com/articles/doj-files-2m-claim-for-unpaid—golden-guernsey-dairy-wages (accessed January 13, 2013).
71. Sarah Pryor, "Is There Hope for Golden Guernsey?" GMToday, Freeman, January 26, 2013, available at: www.gmtoday.com/news/local_stories/2013/01252013/01252013_golden_guernsey.asp (accessed February 5, 2013).
72. U.S. Bankruptcy Court for the District of Delaware, *In re: Golden Guernsey Dairy, LLC, Debtor, Case 13-10044 (KG), 2013.*
73. Rick Barrett, "Ohio Dairy Processor Offers $5.5 million for Golden Guernsey," *Milwaukee Journal Sentinel*, March 4, 2013.
74. U.S. Bankruptcy Court for the District of Delaware, *In re Golden Guernsey Dairy, LLC, Case No. 13-10044 (KG), "Summary of Schedules," Doc 13, January 23, 2013,* 1, 40.
75. Jeff Engel, "Illinois Firm Wins Golden Guernsey School Milk Contract," *Milwaukee Business Journal,* April 17, 2013, available at: http://www.bizjournals.com/milwaukee/news/2013/04/17/post-golden-guernsey-prairie-farms.html (accessed April 24, 2012).
76. Rick Barrett, "Golden Guernsey Dairy Plant Sold to Illinois Dairy," *Milwaukee Journal Sentinel,* May 14, 2013; Christopher Kuhagen, "Lifeway Won't Open Former Golden Guernsey Plant Until End of Year," Waukesha Now, August 27, 2013, available at: http://www.waukeshanow.com/news/221329351.html (accessed October 12, 2013).
77. "Romney Film Stretches Truth While Taking Comments Out of Context," *Bloomberg News,* January 11, 2012; PitchBook, "KB Toys Company Profile," 2012.

78. PolitiFact.com, "Video Blames Bain Capital for Demise of KB Toys," *Tampa Bay Times,* January 13, 2012, available at: http://www.politifact.com/truth-o-meter/statements/2012/jan/13/winning-our-future/video-blames-bain-capital-demise-kb-toys/(accessed October 6, 2012).
79. "KB Toys History," in *International Directory of Company Histories,* vol. 35 (St. James Press, 2001), available at: http://www.fundinguniverse.com/company-histories/kb-toys-history/ (accessed October 8, 2012).
80. Ibid.
81. Matt Taibbi, "Greed and Debt: The True Story of Mitt Romney and Bain Capital," *Rolling Stone,* August 29, 2012.
82. Ibid.
83. Hillary Chabot, "KB Toys Worker Blasts Bain for Execs' Payout," *Boston Herald,* November 17, 2009.
84. Christensen et al. (2011).

Chapter 6

1. See also chapter 8 for a fuller discussion of the asymmetries in the LP-GP relationship and the ways in which limited partners manage their fiduciary responsibilities and deal with issues of transparency, accountability, and the unequal distribution of returns.
2. Private Equity International, "Friday Letter," November 1, 2013.
3. Kaplan and Schoar (2005).
4. Braun, Jenkinson, and Stoff (2013).
5. Kaplan and Schoar (2005).
6. Ibid.
7. In September 2006, the U.S. Financial Accounting Standards Board (FASB) issued the Statement of Financial Accounting Standards (SFAS) No. 157. Paragraph 5 of SFAS No. 157 (known as ASC 820 in the updated FASB codification) requires PE funds to report portfolio companies at fair value. Funds have had to report fair value since December 2008.
8. Valuation Research Corporation, "Fair Value Rules Impact Private Equity World" (VRC alert), February 2007, available at: www.valuationresearch.com (accessed March 12, 2013); Douglas Peterson, "SEC Increases Its Scrutiny of PE Valuations," Reuters, PEHub, December 17, 2012, available at: http://www.pehub.com/177727/sec-increases-its-scrutiny-of-pe-valuations%E2%80%A8.../(accessed March 12, 2013).
9. Valuation Research Corporation, "Fair Value Rules Impact Private Equity World"; Peterson, "SEC Increases Its Scrutiny of PE Valuations." *PE Manager Weekly,* January 27, 2014.
10. John Czapla and Shane Newell, "Getting Ahead of the Curve When Valuing Illiquid Assets," Corporate Finance Review, January–February 2012: 5–16, available at: http://www.valuationresearch.com/assets/kb/Getting%20Ahead%20of%20the%20Curve.pdf (accessed March 12, 2013).
11. Jenna Gottlieb, "Establishing a Standard," *PE Manager,* June 8, 2011, available at: http://www.privateequitymanager.com/ (accessed March 6, 2013).
12. Thomas Duffell, "Communicating Value," *PE Manager 2012 Yearbook,* 2013, available at: www.privateequitymanager.com (accessed March 6, 2013).

13. Jenkinson, Sousa, and Stucke (2013).
14. Peterson, "SEC Increases Its Scrutiny of PE Valuations."
15. Dan Primack, "Term Sheet," *Fortune*, March 12, 2013; Everdeen Mason, "SEC Bars Former Oppenheimer Manager," *Wall Street Journal*, January 22, 2014.
16. Yale defines private equity to include U.S. venture capital (VC), U.S. leveraged buyout (LBO), and international VC and LBO funds. U.S. LBO funds, corresponding to our definition of private equity, yielded an annualized IRR of 22.1 percent over this period.
17. Phalippou (2011).
18. Phalippou (2008).
19. The answer to this question is called the present discounted value of the future stream of income and can be compared to the cost of the investment.
20. This section and the examples in it are drawn from Phalippou (2012a).
21. Phalippou (2008), 6.
22. Ibid., 6, 20.
23. Another commonly used investment multiple is TVPI (total value to paid-in capital). The numerator of this ratio is distributions from the PE fund to the fund's partners *plus* the (estimated) value of any companies or other investments in the PE fund's portfolio that have not yet been exited. The denominator is paid-in capital. For a fund that has been liquidated, TVPI = DPI.
24. See Phalippou (2011) or the website of any of these organizations.
25. Dan Primack, "Term Sheet," *Fortune*, October 28, 2013.
26. See Phalippou (2011) for an explanation of this counterintuitive result and examples of how a low initial NAV can raise IRR.
27. Phalippou (2008, 2011).
28. PitchBook, "Global Private Equity and Venture Capital Benchmarking and Fund Performance Report: 2Q 2013," 3.
29. Gina Edwards, "Opting for Risky and Secretive Private Equity Investments Cost Florida Pension Fund an Estimated $1 Billion on Six Deals," Watchdog City, May 6, 2013, available at: www.watchdogcity.com/getstory.asp?story=216 (accessed May 6, 2013).
30. Florida's SBA maintains that it is only required to provide data for funds that have officially closed. Because it declined to provide information to Edwards on funds that have not closed, it is not possible to draw conclusions about the overall performance of its investments in private equity.
31. Edwards, "Opting for Risky and Secretive Private Equity Investments. . . ."
32. Stock market returns in the 1980s and 1990s were not related to the size of firms; returns to large companies in the S&P 500 did not differ from returns to small and midsize companies. Thus, it did not matter which stock index was used for comparison purposes. From the mid-1990s to the mid-2000s, however, stock market returns for large companies were lower than those for companies of other sizes, and small and midsize companies outperformed large ones. See Phalippou (2012a).
33. Quoted in Dan Primack, "Term Sheet," *Fortune*, October 22, 2013.
34. Kaplan and Schoar (2005).
35. Kaplan and Schoar's (2005) analysis used the 2001 TVE data set. An analysis of PE performance using the 2003 TVE data set and including European as

well as U.S. funds found that private equity underperformed the broad stock market; see Phalippou and Gottschalg (2009). The TVE data set has since been criticized. Later in this chapter, we examine more recent analyses of PE performance that use other data sets.

36. Braun et al. (2013).
37. Saft (2010).
38. Kaplan and Schoar (2005) and Phalippou and Gottschalg (2009). Using the TVE data, these earlier studies considered a fund "liquidated" if it was officially liquidated or if it had had no activity for at least six quarters; as a result, they may have included some funds that were not actually liquidated. At the same time, the "no activity for six quarters" test excluded some funds that were liquidated, for all intents and purposes, but continued to receive dividends from prior investments. And many older funds in the data set appear to continue to hold a large volume of active investments despite their age and lack of activity.
39. Robinson and Sensoy (2011), Harris, Jenkinson, and Kaplan (2013), Jenkinson, Sousa, and Stucke (2013), Higson and Stucke (2012), and Phalippou (2012b).
40. Harris, Jenkinson, and Kaplan (2013).
41. Robinson and Sensoy (2011).
42. Jenkinson, Sousa, and Stucke (2013).
43. Higson and Stucke (2012).
44. Ibid., 3.
45. Robinson and Sensoy (2011). 9.
46. Harris, Jenkinson, and Kaplan (2013), 31, table 2.
47. Harris, Jenkinson, and Kaplan (2013).
48. Higson and Stucke (2012), 25.
49. Harris, Jenkinson, and Kaplan (2013), 27.
50. Harris, Jenkinson, and Kaplan (2013) and Kaplan and Schoar (2005).
51. These are estimates of the fair value of the companies still held in PE fund portfolios. They were made by GPs and reported to LPs in active PE funds.
52. Harris, Jenkinson, and Kaplan (2013), 14.
53. Weighted averages use the capital committed by each fund as a proportion of the total commitments for each vintage year. See ibid., 31, table 2.
54. Kaplan and Schoar (2005).
55. The Harvard Management Company, in managing Harvard University's endowment—the world's biggest endowment—sets its benchmark 4.04 percent above the stock market; see Gregory Roth, "Buyouts—Harvard's Private Equity Chief Resigns," Reuters, April 12, 2013. The Florida public workers' pension fund sets it at 3 percent above the Russell 3000; see Edwards, "Opting for Risky and Secretive Private Equity Investments. . . ."
56. Harris, Jenkinson, and Kaplan (2013), 14.
57. Ibid., 14, n. 13.
58. Ibid., 31, table 2.
59. Higson and Stucke (2012), 2, 6.
60. Ibid., 29, table II, panel B.
61. Harris, Jenkinson, and Kaplan (2013), 33, table 4.
62. Ibid., 26.

63. Robinson and Sensoy (2011) examine a number of questions related to cyclicality in PE fund performance. We summarize only the analysis related to the performance of PE funds relative to the stock market.
64. Robinson and Sensoy (2011), 8.
65. Ibid., 8.
66. Jenkins, Sousa, and Stucke (2013).
67. Ibid., 13.
68. Ibid., 14.
69. Ibid., 15.
70. Ibid., 16.
71. Robinson and Sensoy (2011), 12.
72. Ibid., 41, table 2.
73. For the full sample, the average PME is 1.19, the median PME is 1.09, the PME at the seventy-fifth percentile is 1.46, and the PME at the twenty-fifth percentile is 0.82.
74. Robinson and Sensoy (2011), 41, table 2.
75. Higson and Stucke (2012), 12.
76. Ibid., 13.
77. Ibid., 44, figure III.
78. Ibid., 32, table V.
79. Ibid., 14.
80. Jenkinson, Sousa, and Stucke (2013), 14.
81. Ibid., 15.
82. Higson and Stucke (2012) also analyze the subsample of liquidated funds. For this subsample, they find an average PME relative to the S&P 500 index of 1.18 and a median PME of 1.08.
83. Ibid., 1.
84. Ibid., 33, table VI.
85. Ibid., 25.

Chapter 7

1. The cases in this chapter focus on unionized workplaces. In chapters 3, 4, 5, and 9, we provide many case examples of the impact of private equity on the jobs, wages, and benefits of employees in non-union companies.
2. Croft (2009).
3. Gospel, Pendleton, and Vitols (2014).
4. Davis et al. (2008, 2009, 2011, and 2013).
5. Davis et al. (2013), 43, figure 3b.
6. Davis et al. (2009), 28.
7. Becker and Pollett (2008).
8. Davis et al. (2008): 52. The employment growth rate of an establishment or company over a period 't' is defined as the change in employment over that period divided by the average of employment at the beginning and the end of the period. Employment growth at PE targets is calculated in this manner. The researchers also calculated what the employment growth at targets would have been had they grown at the same rate as controls.

Aggregating and calculating the difference between these two growth rates (targets minus 'controls') yields the 'net growth rates of employment' year by year before and after the PE buyout, as well as the cumulative difference. For details, see Davis et al. (2011), pp. 15–17 and Figure 5a, p.41.

9. For the sample used in the 2011 and 2013 establishment-level analysis, the researchers examined PE transactions from 1980 to 2000 in order to track PE-acquired establishments for five years before and after the transaction. For the sample used in the company-level analysis, they included transactions from 1980 to 2003 and tracked outcomes for two years after the transaction occurred. The full matched sample of companies contained 2,265 PE-acquired companies from 1980 to 2003, accounting for 104,000 establishments (Davis et al. (2013), 21).

10. Davis et al. (2013), 18.

11. Davis et al. (2013), 3.

12. Davis et al. (2013), 36.

13. Davis et al. (2011), 39: figure 3; Davis et al. (2013), supplemental online posting, figure B.1B.

14. Davis et al. (2011) 43, figure 8; Davis et al. (2013), supplemental online posting, figure C.3.

15. Davis et al. (2013), 4.

16. This appears reasonable, although companies that disappear from the data base either because they have been acquired by other entities or because they have shut down entirely are not included in this analysis. The time period over which employment changes at firms are analyzed is limited to two years precisely because too many firms disappear from the data set to make it possible to consider what happens to employment over a longer time period.

17. Davis et al. (2013), 22.

18. Davis et al. (2013), 28.

19. Davis et al. (2011) 49, table 7, col. 1; Davis et al. (2013), supplemental online posting, table C.3, col. 1.

20. Ibid., columns 2.

21. Davis et al. (2009), 28.

22. Davis et al. (2013), 33, 50–51, tables 8 and 9.

23. Ibid., 31.

24. Kalleberg (2009).

25. Cappelli (1999), Thompson (2003).

26. Davis et al. (2013), 34–35.

27. Ibid., 35.

28. von Wachter (2013).

29. Davis et al. (2009), 34.

30. Davis et al. (2013), 36–7.

31. The Yucaipa Companies, "Managing Partner: Ron Burkle," available at: http://yucaipaco.com/managing-partner/(accessed January 15, 2013).

32. Blue Wolf Capital Partners, "What We Do Well," available at: www.bluewolf. com (accessed April 10, 2013).

33. KPS Partners, "Who We Are," available at: http://www.kpsfund.com/whoweare.asp (accessed January 15, 2013).

34. Business Wire, via The Motley Fool, "Wausau Paper Announces Definitive Agreement to Divest Specialty Paper Business," DailyFinance, May 20, 2013, available at: http://www.dailyfinance.com/2013/05/20/wausau-paper-announces-definitive-agreement-to-div/(accessed June 28, 2013); Dan Primack, "Term Sheet: The Big Deal," *Fortune,* May 21, 2013.

35. International Association of Machinists and Aerospace Workers staff, interview with the authors, December 19, 2012; Society of Professional Engineering Employees in Aerospace staff, interview with the authors, January 6, 2013.

36. The We Party, "NightmareLiner: Boeing Ignored Skeptics, Outsourced Production of 787, Put 1000s at Risk," January 17, 2013, available at: http://wepartypatriots.com/wp/2013/01/17/nightmareliner-boeing-ignored-skeptics-outsourced-production-of-the-787-and-put-thousands-of-flyers-at-risk/(accessed January 22, 2013).

37. Society of Professional Engineering Employees in Aerospace staff, interview with the authors, December 17, 2012.

38. Onex, "Spirit AeroSystems," available at: http://www.onex.com/Spirit_AeroSystems.aspx (accessed January 5, 2013).

39. PitchBook, "Spirit AeroSystems Company Profile," 2013.

40. IAM staff, interview with the authors, December 19, 2012.

41. SPEEA staff, interviews with the authors, December 17, 2012, and January 6, 2013.

42. IAM staff, interview with the authors, December 19, 2012.

43. SPEEA staff, interviews with the authors, December 17, 2012, and January 6, 2013.

44. IAM, "Big Victory at Spirit AeroSystems in North Carolina," Machinists News Network, April 5, 2012, available at: http://www.goiam.org/index.php/imail/latest/9997-big-victory-at-spirit-aerosystems-in-north-carolina (accessed January 20, 2013).

45. IAM, "IAM Wins First Contract at Spirit AeroSystems in North Carolina," Machinists News Network, January 3, 2013, available at: http://www.goiam.org/index.php/imail/latest/10903-iam-wins-first-contract-at-spirit-aerosystems-in-north-carolina (accessed January 20, 2013).

46. Onex, "Spirit AeroSystems."

47. PitchBook, "Spirit AeroSystems Company Profile," 2013; Onex, "Spirit AeroSystems."

48. PitchBook, "Spirit AeroSystems Company Profile," 2013.

49. Jon Ostrower, "Corporate News: Big Boeing Supplier Takes a Hit," *Wall Street Journal,* October 26, 2012.

50. Daniel McCoy, "Spirit AeroSystems CEO Jeff Turner Retirement Leaves Questions," *Wichita Business Journal,* November 19, 2012, available at: http://www.bizjournals.com/wichita/blog/2012/11/spirit-aerosystems-ceo-jeff-turner.html (accessed May 10, 2012).

51. Molly McMillin, "SPEEA Protests Firing of 37 Workers at Spirit AeroSystems," *Wichita Eagle,* March 19, 2013.

52. International Iron and Steel Institute, "World Steel in Figures," 2004, 19.

53. Appelbaum et al. (2000).

54. Keilin and Co., LLC, "Steel Industry Briefing: Steel Crisis, Prices, and Finances and the Future of the Industry," presented at the Basic Steel Industry Conference, Pittsburgh, December 12, 2001.

55. United Steelworkers of America, "Steel Industry Restructuring: Steel Crisis, Bankruptcies, Pension Plan Terminations, and Consolidation," presented at the USWA–IG Metall seminar, Sprockhovel, Germany, October 11–15, 2004.

56. Nicholas Stein, "Wilbur Ross Is a Man of Steel . . . and Textiles and Optical Networking and Anything Else in Deep, Deep Trouble," *Fortune*, May 26, 2003.

57. Ibid.

58. Nanette Byrnes, "Is Wilbur Ross Crazy?" *Bloomberg Businessweek*, December 22, 2003.

59. Ibid.

60. USWA, "Steel Industry Restructuring"; Daniel Gross, "The Bottom-Feeder King," *New York*, May 21, 2005.

61. USWA, "Summary: Proposed Agreement Between International Steel Group, Inc., and the United Steelworkers of America," December 12, 2002, 10–14.

62. Keilin and Co., "Steel Industry Briefing" (2001).

63. Tom Conway, USWA international vice president for administration, interview with the authors, June 1, 2012.

64. Ibid.

65. Stein, "Wilbur Ross Is a Man of Steel. . . ."

66. Conway, interview with the authors, June 1, 2012.

67. Byrnes, "Is Wilbur Ross Crazy?"; Stein, "Wilbur Ross Is a Man of Steel. . . ."

68. Conway, interview with the authors, June 1, 2012.

69. USWA, "Summary: Proposed Agreement Between International Steel Group, Inc., and the United Steelworkers of America"; USWA, "Summary: Proposed Agreement Between International Steel Group, Inc., and the United Steelworkers of America on Behalf of Former Bethlehem Steel Employees," December 12, 2003.

70. USWA, "Summary: Proposed Agreement Between International Steel Group, Inc., and the United Steelworkers of America," and "Summary: Proposed Agreement Between International Steel Group, Inc., and the United Steelworkers of America on Behalf of Former Bethlehem Steel Employees."

71. Gross, "The Bottom-Feeder King."

72. Ball, Miller, and Stenger (2009), 29.

73. PR Newswire, "Dana Corporation Announces Settlements with USW and UAW, Agreement with Centerbridge Capital Partners on Major Investment in Dana," July 6, 2007, available at: http://www.prnewswire.com/news-releases/dana-corporation-announces-settlements-with-usw-and-uaw-agreement-with-centerbridge-capital-partners-on-major-investment-in-dana-52707147.html (accessed June 11, 2012).

74. Ball et al. (2009), 35.

75. USWA staff, interview with the authors, June 1, 2012.

76. Ball et al. (2009), 34–35.

77. Ibid., 34.

78. PR Newswire, "Dana Corporation Announces Settlements with USW and UAW"; Mike Ramsey, "Dana Has Union Accord, Gets Centerbridge Investment," *Bloomberg*, July 6, 2007, available at: http://www.bloomberg.com/apps/news?pid=newsarchive&sid=aJW39ITYOyDI&refer=home (accessed June 11, 2012).

79. USWA staff, interview with the authors, June 1, 2012.

80. Marie Beaudette, "Delphi and the 'Guys in Suits,' " *Wall Street Journal*, June 10, 2009; Greg Palast, "Mitt Romney's Bailout Bonanza," *The Nation*, October 17, 2012.

81. PitchBook, "Delphi Corporation Company Profile," 2012.

82. Beaudette, "Delphi and the 'Guys in Suits.'"

83. Palast, "Mitt Romney's Bailout Bonanza"; PitchBook, "Delphi Corporation Company Profile," 2012.

84. Palast, "Mitt Romney's Bailout Bonanza."

85. Paul A. Eisenstein, "Romney Accused of Personally Profiting as 1000s of Delphi Retirees Lost Pensions," The Detroit Bureau, October 31, 2012, available at: http://www.thedetroitbureau.com/2012/10/romney-accused-of-personally-profiting-as-1000s-of-delphi-retirees-lost-pensions/ (accessed November 7, 2012); Palast, "Mitt Romney's Bailout Bonanza"; Rattner (2010); Micheline Maynard, "Bailing Out the Big Guys, Posthaste," "Books of the Times," *New York Times*, September 19, 2010.

86. Palast, "Mitt Romney's Bailout Bonanza."

87. Ibid.

88. PitchBook ("Hawker Beechcraft Company Profile," 2013) reports that the new owners put down no equity.

89. Ibid.

90. Ibid.

91. Patrick Fitzgerald, "PBGC: Hawker Can Reorganize Without 'Killing' Pensions," Dow Jones Daily Bankruptcy Review, May 11, 2012, available at: http://bankruptcynews.dowjones.com/Article?an=DJFDBR0020120511e85bp01fw (accessed December 29, 2012).

92. U.S. Bankruptcy Court for the Southern District of New York, "Disclosure Statement," *In re: Hawker Beechcraft Inc., Case 12-11873, June 30, 2012*, Docket 305, 13–14, available at: http://dm.epiq11.com/HBC/Docket#Debtors=4674&RelatedDocketId=&ds=true&maxPerPage=25&page=1 (accessed June 30, 2012).

93. Joseph Checkler, "Judge Says Hawker Beechcraft Can Tap $400 Million Loan; Hawker Beechcraft Reviewing Offers from Potential Buyers," Dow Jones Bankruptcy News, May 4, 2012, available at: http://bankruptcynews.dowjones.com/Article?an=DJFDBR0020120504e854pddl4 (accessed December 15, 2012).

94. Michael de la Merced and Peter Lattman, "Hawker Beechcraft Is Said to Be Preparing for Bankruptcy Filing," *New York Times*, DealBook, March 28, 2012.

95. AviationPros, "Hawker Beechcraft Corporation Opens Facility in Mexico," October 25, 2007, available at: http://www.aviationpros.com/press_release/10406100/hawker-beechcraft-corporation-opens-facility-in-mexico (accessed January 5, 2013).

96. IAM staff, interview with the authors, December 19, 2012.

97. Molly McMillin, "Hawker Beechcraft Files Plan with Bankruptcy Court," *Wichita Eagle,* July 2, 2012.

98. Roxana Hegeman, "Hawker Beechcraft Announces 2,300 Layoffs," Associated Press, February 3, 2009.

99. "Layoff Notices Go Out at Hawker Beechcraft," Kake News, September 25, 2009, available at: http://www.kake.com/home/headlines/61507312.html (accessed December 28, 2012).

100. U.S. Bankruptcy Court for the Southern District of New York, "Disclosure Statement," *In re: Hawker Beechcraft Inc., Case 12-11873, June 30, 2012,* Docket 305, 12.

101. Ibid., 19–21.

102. "Machinists at Hawker Beechcraft Approve 5-Year Contract," Kake News, August 6, 2011, available at: http://www.kake.com/home/headlines/Machinists_At_Hawker_Beechcraft_Voting_On_5-Year_Contract_127064828.html (accessed January 6, 2013).

103. "IAM Membership Approves New Contract with Hawker Beechcraft," Aero News Network, August 7, 2011, available at: http://www.aero-news.net/getmorefromann.cfm?do=main.textpost&id=e260a94d-ac29-4689-a583-b9db4997527d (accessed January 4, 2013); Kake News, "Machinists at Hawker Beechcraft Approve 5-Year Contract."

104. U.S. Bankruptcy Court for the Southern District of New York, "Disclosure Statement," *In re: Hawker Beechcraft Inc., Case 12-11873, June 30, 2012,* Docket 305, 18.

105. De la Merced and Lattman, "Hawker Beechcraft Is Said to Be Preparing for Bankruptcy Filing."

106. U.S. Bankruptcy Court for the Southern District of New York, "Robert S. Miller," *In re: Hawker Beechcraft Inc., Case 12-11873, May 4, 2012,* Docket 22, 2; "Disclosure Statement," *In re: Hawker Beechcraft Inc., Case 12-11873, June 30, 2012,* Docket 305, 21.

107. Joseph Checkler, "Hawker Beechcraft Reviewing Offers from Potential Buyers," Dow Jones Bankruptcy News, May 30, 2012, available at: http://bankruptcynews.dowjones.com/Article?an=DJFDBR0020120530e85ujrp07 (accessed December 15, 2012).

108. U.S. Bankruptcy Court for the Southern District of New York, "Disclosure Statement," *In re: Hawker Beechcraft Inc., Case 12-11873, June 30, 2012,* Docket 305, 18.

109. Fitzgerald, "PBGC: Hawker Can Reorganize Without 'Killing' Pensions."

110. Bill Rochelle, "Hawker Reaches Pension Settlement with Government Agency," *Bloomberg News,* December 26, 2012.

111. IAM staff, interview with the authors, December 19, 2012; Hawker Beechcraft, "Pension Filing Notice," December 21, 2012, available at: http://www.hawkerbeechcraft.com/restructuring/files/HBC-PBGC_Petition_Packet.pdf (accessed January 6, 2013).

112. Molly McMillin, "Hawker Beechcraft Gets OK to Liquidate Jet Inventory," *Wichita Eagle,* December 11, 2012; and "Analysts Speculate About Sale of Hawker Beechcraft," *Wichita Eagle,* December 20, 2012.

113. Molly McMillin, "Hawker Beechcraft to Pay Millions for Bankruptcy Services," *Wichita Eagle,* December 4, 2012.

114. Jonathan Stempel, "Bankruptcy Judge Rejects Hawker Beechcraft Exec Bonuses," Reuters, August 24, 2012.

115. IAM staff, interview with the authors, December 19, 2012.

116. De la Merced and Lattman, "Hawker Beechcraft Is Said to Be Preparing for Bankruptcy Filing."

117. PitchBook, "Company Profile: Archway & Mother's Company," 2012.

118. Julie Creswell, "Oh, No! What Happened to Archway?" *New York Times*, DealBook, May 30, 2009.

119. Ibid.; Ian Frazier, "Out of the Bronx: Private Equity and the Cookie Factory," *The New Yorker*, February 6, 2012.

120. Frazier, "Out of the Bronx."

121. John King, "Shuttered Bakery Reopens, Rehires Workers," CNN, December 24, 2008, available at: http://www.cnn.com/2008/US/12/23/cookie.factory. reopens/index.html (accessed December 16, 2012); Frazier, "Out of the Bronx."

122. Colin Leonard, "WARN Act Liability: Holding the Parent Liable for a Subsidiary's Failure to Give Notice," *New York Labor and Employment Law Report*, March 5, 2010, available at: http://www.nylaborandemployment lawreport.com/2010/03/articles/reductions-in-force/warn-act-liability-holding-the-parent-liable-for-a-subsidiarys-failure-to-give-notice/ (accessed December 15, 2012).

123. Federal Registrar, 20 C.F.R. § 639.3(a)(2).

124. Frazier, "Out of the Bronx."

125. Cezary Podkul, "Archway Joins Growing List of PE-Backed Bankruptcies: Catterton Partners–Owned Cookie Maker Archway & Mother's Is the Latest Private Equity–Backed Company to File for Bankruptcy," Private Equity International, October 13, 2008, available at: http://www.privateequityon line.com/Article.aspx?article=29267&hashID=725BC18C708EDEDF6A2113 4A569206AACEF341B9 (accessed December 16, 2012).

126. Samuel Howard, "Archway Creditors Allege Accounting Fraud," Law360, January 21, 2009, available at: http://www.law360.com/privateequity/articles/ 83981/archway-creditors-allege-accounting-fraud (accessed December 15, 2012); "Bankruptcy Tracker: Creditors Sue Private Equity Firm in Archway Cookie Bankruptcy," CreditPulse, January 28, 2009, available at: http:// www.creditpulse.com/credit-risk/bankruptcy-tracker/creditors-sue-private-equity-firm-archway-cookie-bankruptcy (accessed December 15, 2012).

127. Creswell, "Oh, No! What Happened to Archway?"

128. Frazier, "Out of the Bronx."

129. Ibid.

130. Jon Alpert and Matthew O'Neill, *No Contract, No Cookies*, HBO, 2011, available at: http://www.hbo.com/documentaries/no-contract-no-cookies-the-stella-doro-strike/index.html (accessed December 16, 2012).

131. Josh Kosman, "Not the Original Recipe," *New York Post*, May 10, 2009.

132. Sewell Chan, "Bronx Cookie Plant Is Ordered to Reinstate Striking Workers," *New York Times*, July 1, 2009.

133. Daniel Massey, "A Bittersweet Win for Former Stella D'oro Workers," Crain's New York Business, September 9, 2010, available at: http://

www.crainsnewyork.com/article/20100909/REAL_ESTATE/100909881 (accessed December 16, 2012).

134. Frazier, "Out of the Bronx."
135. Jennifer Lee, "Stella D'oro Factory to Close in October," *New York Times,* July 6, 2009.
136. Frazier, "Out of the Bronx."
137. Ibid.
138. U.S. Court of Appeals for the Second Circuit, *SDBC Holdings, Inc. v. NLRB, March 28, 2013.* Available at: http://www.ca2.uscourts.gov/decisions/isysquery/dbc7a876-dc49-4cd9-aea6-6a9e526e88cf/11/doc/10-3709_complete_opn.pdf (accessed November 3, 2013).
139. BusinessWire, "United Steelworkers Files Unfair Labor Practice Charges Against Ormet," April 18, 2005, available at: http://www.businesswire.com/news/home/20050418006052/en/News-USWA-United-Steelworkers-Files-Unfair-Labor (accessed June 13, 2012).
140. BusinessWire, "Steelworkers Embark on Weeklong New York Protest Tour," July 11, 2005, available at: http://www.businesswire.com/news/home/20050711005586/en/News-USW-Steelworkers-Embark-Weeklong-York-Protest (accessed June 13, 2012).
141. USWA staff, interview with the authors, June 1, 2012.
142. BusinessWire, "News from USW: USW Reaches Tentative Contract Agreements with Ormet for Ohio and Louisiana Facilities," June 30, 2006, available at: http://www.businesswire.com/news/home/20060630005455/en/News-USW-USW-Reaches-Tentative-Contract-Agreements (accessed June 13, 2012).
143. Aviva Gat, "Ormet Melts into Bankruptcy Again," The Deal Pipeline, February 26, 2013, available at: http://www.thedeal.com/content/restructuring/ormet-melts-into-bankruptcy-again.php (accessed June 20, 2013); PitchBook, "Ormet Company Profile," 2013; Jamie Santo, "Bankrupt Smelter Ormet Gets OK for $130M Sale to PE Firm," Law360, June 3, 2013, available at: http://www.law360.com/articles/446787/bankrupt-smelter-ormet-gets-ok-for-130m-sale-to-pe-firm (accessed June 20, 2013).
144. PitchBook, "US Foods Company Profile," 2012.
145. International Brotherhood of Teamsters (IBT) staff, interview with the authors, February 26, 2010.
146. Ibid.
147. IAM, "Arizona U.S. Foodservice Workers Win Teamster Representation," May 28, 2009, available at: http://www.teamster.org/content/arizona-us-foodservice-workers-win-teamster-representation (accessed December 18, 2011).
148. International Brotherhood of Teamsters (IBT) staff, interview with the authors, February 26, 2010.
149. Ibid.
150. Jason Hibbs, "Local US Foods Center to Close, 240 Local Jobs Gone," WPSD Local 6, November 10, 2011, available at: http://www.wpsdlocal6.com/news/local/Local-US-Foods-center-to-close-240-local-jobs-gone-133654183.html (accessed December 18, 2011).

151. Sarah Damian, "Anti-Union Retaliation at US Foods Sets Off Protests Nationwide," Food Integrity Campaign, November 4, 2011, available at: http://foodwhistleblower.org/blog/22-2011/244-anti-union-retaliation-at-us-foods-sets-off-protests-nationwide (accessed December 18, 2011); Peter Lattman, "Strike at US Foods Takes Aim at Private Equity," *New York Times,* DealBook, November 2, 2011.

152. International Brotherhood of Teamsters, "Teamsters Reach Settlement with US Foods," IBT, December 6, 2011, available at: http://www.teamster.org/content/teamsters-reach-settlement-us-foods (accessed December 18, 2011).

153. Tomoeh Murakami Tse and Krissah Williams, "Royal Ahold Sells U.S. Foodservice to Private-Equity Firms," *Washington Post,* May 3, 2007.

154. PitchBook, "US Foods Company Profile," 2012.

155. "TEXT-S&P: US Foods Inc.'s Rating Unchanged After Notes Add-on," Reuters, January 11, 2013.

156. Matt Townsend and David Carey, "SYSCO to Acquire US Foods for $3.5 Billion," December 9, 2013, available at: http://www.bloomberg.com/news/2013-12-09/sysco-to-buy-us-foods-for-3-5-billion-to-expand-food-services.html (accessed December 28, 2013).

157. Jenny Anderson and Julie Creswell, "For Buyout Kingpins, the TXU Utility Deal Gets Tricky," *Wall Street Journal,* February 28, 2010; PitchBook, "EFH Company Profile," 2012.

158. Anderson and Creswell, "For Buyout Kingpins, the TXU Utility Deal Gets Tricky."

159. Beeferman (2009), 10–11; IBEW representative, interview with the authors, November 27, 2012.

160. IBEW representative, interview with the authors, November 27, 2012.

161. "Sorting Through the Aftermath of Private Equity Deals," *New York Times,* DealBook, February 29, 2012.

162. Mary Childs and Julie Johnsson, "KKR's TXU Buyout Facing 91 Percent Odds of Default: Corporate Finance," *Bloomberg Businessweek,* January 30, 2010, available at: http://www.bloomberg.com/news/2012-01-19/kkr-s-txu-buyout-facing-91-odds-of-default-corporate-finance.html (accessed January 30, 2012).

163. Elizabeth Souder, "Moody's and S&P Downgrade Energy Future Holdings," *Dallas Morning News,* July 20, 2010.

164. PitchBook, "EFH Company Profile," 2012.

165. Nicole Bullock, "Energy Future Holdings," *Financial Times,* September 22, 2011.

166. PitchBook, "EFH Company Profile," 2012.

167. Lattman, Peter. 2012. "A Record Buyout Turns Sour for Investors." *The New York Times.* February 28. http://dealbook.nytimes.com/2012/02/28/a-record-buyout-turns-sour-for-investors/ (accessed November 22, 2012).

168. Michael Erman, "DealTalk: Long Odds for Former TXU as Gas Prices Drop," Reuters, November 22, 2011.

169. Peter Lattman, "A Record Buyout Turns Sour for Investors," *New York Times,* DealBook, February 28, 2012.

170. Childs and Johnsson, "KKR's TXU Buyout Facing 91 Percent Odds of Default."

171. Global Credit Research, "Moody's Changes Energy Future Holdings Corp's Rating Outlook to Negative from Stable," Moody's Investor Services, January 30, 2012, available at: http://www.moodys.com/research/Moodys-changes-Energy-Future-Holdings-Corps-rating-outlook-to-negative—PR_236381 (accessed January 30, 2012).

172. Ibid.

173. Richard Bravo and Mark Chediak, "Energy Future's Profitable Road to Oblivion," *Bloomberg Businessweek,* October 25, 2012, available at: http://www.businessweek.com/articles/2012-10-25/energy-futures-profitable-road-to-oblivion (accessed November 26, 2012).

174. PitchBook, "EFH Company Profile," 2012.

175. Bullock, "Energy Future Holdings"; Lattman, "A Record Buyout Turns Sour for Investors"; Childs and Johnsson, "KKR's TXU Buyout Facing 91 Percent Odds of Default"; Arleen Jacobius, "Will Giant TXU LBO Become a Distressed Debt Deal? Some Firms Champ at Bit for Energy Future Bankruptcy," *Pensions&Investments,* May 13, 2013, available at: http://www.pionline.com/article/20130513/PRINTSUB/305139968 (accessed June 17, 2013).

176. Bravo and Chediak, "Energy Future's Profitable Road to Oblivion."

177. Charles Mead and Mark Chediak, "TXU Bond Plunge Reaps $450 Million Windfall: Corporate Finance," *Bloomberg Businessweek,* December 10, 2012, available at: http://www.bloomberg.com/news/2012-12-10/txu-bond-plunge-reaps-450-million-windfall-corporate-finance.html.

178. Dan Primack, "TPG Faces a Major Fundraising Challenge," "Term Sheet," *Fortune,* November 30, 2012.

179. Jacobius, "Will Giant TXU LBO Become a Distressed Debt Deal?"

180. Beth Jinks and Mark Chediak, "Energy Future Proposes Pre-packaged Bankruptcy of Some Units," *Bloomberg News,* April 15, 2013.

181. Julie Creswell, "Battle Heats Up over Fate of Troubled Energy Buyout," *New York Times,* DealBook, April 8, 2013; Jinks and Chediak, "Energy Future Proposes Pre-packaged Bankruptcy of Some Units"; Mark Chediak, "Energy Future Holdings Returned to Profit on Hedging," *Bloomberg Businessweek,* November 1, 2013.

182. U.S. Securities and Exchange Commission, "Form S-1: Registration Statement, HCA Holdings, Inc.," Reg. 333, December 22, 2010, 1, 3, available at: http://www.sec.gov/Archives/edgar/data/860730/000095012310115879/y83802asv1.htm#101 (accessed May 22, 2011). HCA Holdings was established as the holding company of HCA, Inc., in November 2010 in order to facilitate the issuance of new debt by the firm, as we explain later in the chapter. HCA itself was formed in a series of acquisitions and restructurings, begun in the 1990s, that brought together the original Healthcare Corporation of America, Columbia Healthcare, Galen Healthcare, and HealthTrust, as well as other smaller entities.

183. "Fortune 500: Annual Ranking of America's Largest Corporations," CNNMoney, 2013, available at: http://money.cnn.com/magazines/fortune/fortune500/2013/full_list/(accessed December 28, 2013).

184. HCA webpage, hcahealthcare.com/about/ (accessed December 28, 2013).

185. Ibid., 2.

186. Carrick Mollenkamp, "HCA Pays Big Dividend to Its Owners," *Wall Street Journal,* November 10, 2010.

187. Lynn Cowan and Peter Lattman, "HCA Files for $4.6 Billion IPO," *Wall Street Journal,* May 8, 2010.
188. "HCA Files for IPO, Seeking $4.6 Billion," *New York Times,* DealBook, May 7, 2010.
189. Mollenkamp, "HCA Pays Big Dividend to Its Owners."
190. Ibid.
191. Michael Aneiro, "HCA to Sell $1.5bn in Junk Bonds to Pay Private Equity Dividend," *Financial News,* November 10, 2010.
192. Mollenkamp, "HCA Pays Big Dividend to Its Owners."
193. SEC, "Form S-1: Registration Statement, HCA Holdings, Inc.," Reg. 333, December 22, 2010, 24. "In February, April and August of 2009 and, in March of 2010, for example, HCA Inc. issued $310 million in aggregate principal amount of 97/8% second lien notes due 2017, $1.500 billion in aggregate principal amount of 81/2% first lien notes due 2019, $1.250 billion in aggregate principal amount of 77/8% first lien notes due 2020 and $1.400 billion in aggregate principal amount of 71/4% first lien notes due 2020, respectively" (ibid.).
194. "Everything You Need to Know About the HCA IPO," *Wall Street Journal,* March 9, 2011.
195. SEC, "Form S-1: Registration Statement, HCA Holdings, Inc.," Reg. 333, December 22, 2010, 176. Merrill Lynch was both a proposed underwriter of the IPO and, through its PE arm, the owner of 25.8 percent of the shares of HCA, entitling it to seats on HCA's board of directors. Underwriters also had several other conflicts with either the PE owners of HCA or lenders to the company (ibid., 176).
196. PitchBook, "HCA Company Profile," 2013.
197. Ken Terry, "Big IPO for HCA Hospital Chain, but Buyers' Remorse Remains a Distinct Possibility," Bnet, March 14, 2011, available at: http://www.bnet. com/blog/healthcare-business/big-ipo-for-hca-hospital-chain-but-buyers-8217-remorse-remains-a-distinct-possibility/2687 (accessed May 5, 2011).
198. PitchBook, "HCA Company Profile," 2013.
199. Josh Kosman, "Bain's Huge HCA IPO Gain," *New York Post,* March 11, 2011.
200. "Popular IPO Values HCA at $30–$31 a Share," Reuters, March 9, 2011.
201. U.S. District Court of Massachusetts, *Kirk Dahl vs. Bain Capital Partners, LLC, et al.,* Lead Case 1:07-cv-12388-EFH, "Fourth Amended Class Action Complaint for Violations of the Federal Antitrust Laws" (redacted document), Document 745, filed October 10, 2012, 119.
202. Ibid., 121, 141–45.
203. SEC, "Form S-1: Registration Statement, HCA Holdings, Inc.," Reg. 333, December 22, 2010, 34.
204. PitchBook, "HCA Company Profile," 2013; Luisa Beltran, "Moody's: PE Firms Took Out at Least 35 Dividend Recaps This Year, Worth More Than $11 bln," Reuters PEHub, July 12, 2012, available at: http://www.pehub. com/159048/moodys-dividend-recaps/ (accessed December 15, 2012); BusinessWire, "HCA Announces Special Dividend Of $2.00 per Share and Record and Payable Dates," The Street, December 6, 2012, available at: http://www.thestreet.com/story/11786255/1/hca-announces-special-dividend-of-200-per-share-and-record-and-payable-dates.html (accessed January 15, 2013); Jay Hawk, "HCA (HCA) Stock Slides After Company

Announces Special Dividend," Investor Guide, October 17, 2012, available at: http://www.investorguide.com/article/11173/hca-hca-stock-slides-after-company-annouces-special-dividend/(accessed January 15, 2013).

205. PitchBook, "HCA Company Profile," 2013.

206. Gregory Zuckerman, "A Windfall for HCA Investors," *Wall Street Journal,* March 4, 2011.

207. McCue and Thompson (2012).

208. SEIU, "121RN Testifies Before Calif. Senate Health Committee on RCH Ratio Violations," October 20, 2010, available at: http://www.seiu121rn.org/files/2011/05/RN-News-Dec-2010-sp.pdf

209. Linda Milazzo, "CA Nurses Strike Against Billion-Dollar Felon, HCA," December 25, 2010, available at: www.huffingtonpost.com/linda-milazzo/ca-nurses-strike-billiond_b_801204.html.

210. Linda Johnson, "Shortage of Nurses Putting Patients at Risk," Associated Press/MSNBC, March 29, 2004, available at: http://www.msnbc.msn.com/id/4587667/(accessed January 12, 2011).

211. Thomas Wood, "CA Facing Class-Action Lawsuit over Nurse Staffing," *Nashville Post,* April 11, 2006.

212. April Wortham, "HCA Sued over Meal Breaks," *Nashville Business Journal,* June 14, 2010, available at: http://www.bizjournals.com/nashville/stories/2010/06/14/daily7.html (accessed January 11, 2011).

213. Vince Galloro, "Here a Lawsuit, There a Lawsuit; HCA Sued in U.K., U.S. but Denies Wrongdoing," Modern Healthcare, October 12, 2009, available at: http://www.modernhealthcare.com/article/20091012/MAGAZINE/910099988 (accessed January 11, 2011).

214. Julie Creswell and Reed Abelson, "A Giant Hospital Chain is Blazing a Profit Trail," *New York Times,* August 12, 2012. http://www.nytimes.com/2012/08/15/business/hca-giant-hospital-chain-creates-a-windfall-for-private-equity.html?r=0.

215. Steve Early, "CNA and NUHW Join Forces Against SEIU in California," *In These Times,* January 3, 2013.

Chapter 8

1. Bain & Company, Inc., *Global Private Equity Report 2013,* 23.

2. Ibid. These include corporate pension funds, union pension funds, and voluntary employee benefit associations (VEBAs). Union pension funds defined as "multi-employer," or "Taft-Hartley" plans, were established under Section 302 of the National Labor Relations Act and require equal voting for management and labor trustees (Section 186(c)). VEBAs are funds set aside by employers that typically cover the costs of retired workers, often through negotiated agreements with unions (see chapter 7 case studies of the steel and auto parts industries for examples).

3. Baker and Smith (1998), 59.

4. Adler and Youngdahl (2010); see also Rifkin and Barber (1978).

5. Bain & Company, Inc., *Global Private Equity Report 2013,* 23.

6. Michael Corkery and Gregory Zuckerman, "Big Firms a Drag on Pension Funds," *Wall Street Journal,* September 6, 2012.

7. Authors' calculations.
8. The top ten, in order of the percentage of their allocation, are: Oregon Public Employees' Retirement System (24 percent), Oregon Investment Council (23 percent), Washington State Investment Board (22 percent), Pennsylvania Public School Employees' System (22 percent), San Bernardino County Employees' Retirement Association (19 percent), Missouri Department of Transportation (19 percent), Dallas Police and Fire Pension System (18 percent), Allegheny County Retirement System (15 percent), Houston Municipal Employees' Pension System (14 percent), and both the California State Teachers' Retirement System (CalSTRS) and the Indiana Public Retirement System (13 percent each).
9. Lydenberg (2012), 1.
10. Stout (2012).
11. Cited in Youngdahl (2012), 115.
12. Hawley, Johnson, and Waitzer (2011), 6–9; Youngdahl (2012), 115.
13. Youngdahl (2012), 116.
14. Hawley et al. (2011), 4.
15. Youngdahl (2012), 122, and n. 59.
16. Ibid., 122.
17. Hawley et al. (2011), 6.
18. Lydenberg (2012), 3–5.
19. Markowitz (1952).
20. Lydenberg (2012).
21. Bernstein (2005).
22. Lydenberg (2009), 19.
23. Lydenberg (2012), 9.
24. Youngdahl (2012), 123.
25. Hawley et al. (2011), 7.
26. EBSA (2008), 61735.
27. Ibid., 61736.
28. Ibid.
29. Brenner and Izhakian (2012).
30. Johnson and de Graff (2009), 45.
31. Lydenberg (2009), 15.
32. Markowitz (1952).
33. Waitzer (2009), 5.
34. Yermo and Severinson (2010), 8, in Hawley at al. (2011), 6.
35. Johnson and de Graff (2009), 3.
36. CFA (2006), 1.
37. Johnson and de Graff (2009), 45.
38. Waitzer (2009) and Hawley et al. (2011).
39. Waitzer (2009), 6.
40. Johnson and de Graff (2009).
41. Preqin, "Balance of Power: The Impact of Private Equity Fund Terms and Conditions," *Private Equity Spotlight* 7(7, July 2011): 3.
42. Dan Primack, "Term Sheet," *Fortune,* June 5, 2013.
43. Metrick and Yasuda (2009/2011), 29.
44. Ibid., 37.

45. Greg Roumeliotis and Bernard Vaughan, "Why Stephen Schwarzman's Payday Risks Riling Blackstone Investors." Reuters, February 17, 2012, available at: http://www.reuters.com/article/2012/02/17/us-privateequity-dividends-idUSTRE81G14Q20120217" (accessed February 13, 2014).

46. Quoted in ibid.

47. Corkery and Zuckerman, "Big Firms a Drag on Pension Funds."

48. ILPA, "Private Equity Principles," September 2009, available at: http://ilpa.org/ilpa-private-equity-principles/.

49. See the ILPA website at: http://ilpa.org/.

50. ILPA, "Private Equity Principles," September 2009, 1.

51. ILPA, "Private Equity Principles: Version 2.0," January 2011, available at: http://ilpa.org/ilpa-private-equity-principles/.

52. Ibid., 4.

53. Sagar Dalal, "Are GPs Listening? New ILPA Report Out," BiggerPockets, August 11, 2010, available at: http://www.biggerpockets.com/blogs/1193/blog_posts/8131-ilpa-guidelines (accessed May 24, 2013); Hudec (2010).

54. Breslow and Schwartz (2011).

55. ILPA, "Private Equity Principles: Version 2.0," January 2011, 4–5.

56. Dalal, "Are GPs Listening?"

57. ILPA, "Private Equity Principles: Version 2.0," January 2011, 4, appendix B.

58. Ibid., 5.

59. Hudec (2010).

60. Susan Pulliam and Jean Eaglesham, "Investor Hazard: 'Zombie Funds.'" Wall Street Journal, May 31, 2012.

61. Jennifer Bollen, "Zombie Buyout Funds Trapping $116bn of Assets," Financial News, June 14, 2013, available at: http://www.penews.com/today/index/content/4072259997/41855/restricted (accessed June 6, 2013).

62. Pulliam and Eaglesham, "Investor Hazard: 'Zombie Funds.'"

63. Ibid.

64. ILPA, "Private Equity Principles: Version 2.0," January 2011, 5.

65. Ibid.

66. Hudec (2010).

67. ILPA, "Private Equity Principles: Version 2.0," January 2011, 7–10.

68. Hudec (2010).

69. ILPA, "Private Equity Principles: Version 2.0," January 2011, appendix A.

70. Hudec (2010).

71. ILPA, "Private Equity Principles: Version 2.0," January 2011, 11–12, appendix C.

72. Hudec (2010), 1.

73. The Economic Voice, "Altius Annual Report: Ten Challenges Facing the Private Equity Sector," January 21, 2013, available at: http://www.economicvoice.com/altius-annual-report-ten-challenges-facing-the-private-equity-sector/50034330#axzz2JGn0p4Cv (accessed May 23, 2013).

74. Preqin, "Balance of Power: The Impact of Private Equity Fund Terms and Conditions," 4–5, figure 6.

75. Mercer, "2012 Global Asset Manager Fee Survey," available at: http://www.mercer.com/articles/1509180.

76. Preqin, "Balance of Power: The Impact of Private Equity Fund Terms and Conditions," 4, figure 3.

77. Dan Primack, "Term Sheet," *Fortune,* June 5, 2013.
78. Alesci, Cristina, Jason Kelly and Martin Braun. 2011. "New York City Pensions Said to Weigh $2 Billion Private-Equity Funds Sale," Bloomberg, July 19. Available at http://www.bloomberg.com/news/2011-03-02/nyc-police-pension-picks-permal-for-first-hedge-fund-of-funds.html (last accessed January 29, 2014).
79. Gregory Roth, "Wisconsin Jettisons Stakes in Blackstone, Carlyle, KKR," Reuters, August 30, 2012; Corkery and Zuckerman, "Big Firms a Drag on Pension Funds."
80. Hazel Bradford, "North Carolina Senate OKs Hike in Alternative Investments for State Pension Fund," *Pensions&Investments,* May 7, 2013, available at: http://www.pionline.com/article/20130507/DAILYREG/130509913/north-carolina-senate-oks-hike-in-alternative-investments-for-state-pension-fund (accessed June 23, 2013).
81. "How GPs Are Blocking Pension Liabilities," *PE Manager* 6(January 2013): 16.
82. Ibid.
83. Steven Davidoff, "Wall St.'s Odd Couple and Their Quest to Unlock Riches," *New York Times,* DealBook, December 13, 2011.
84. Peter Lattman, "Onex and Pension Close Year's Biggest Buyout," *New York Times,* DealBook, September 30, 2010.
85. Waitzer (2009), 5.

Chapter 9

1. Bolton, Santos, and Scheinkman (2012). In the shadow finance sector, trading takes place "in non-organized, less regulated, opaque markets. . . . In this sector, costly private information can be produced and its value can be largely appropriated by limiting its dissemination to the wider investing public." Ibid., 2.
2. Kochan et al. (2013).
3. Government Accountability Office (2008).
4. Higson (2007), 10; see also Appelbaum, Batt, and Clark (2013).
5. David Snow, "Private Equity: A Brief Overview," Private Equity International PEIMedia, 2007, 5, available at: http://www.google.com/url?sa=t&rct=j&q=&esrc=s&source=web&cd=1&ved=0CDUQFjAA&url=http%3A%2F%2Fwww.peimedia.com%2Fresources%2FPEI50%2FPEI%2520Media%2527s%2520Private%2520Equity%2520-%2520A%2520Brief%2520Overview.pdf&ei=cq8KUcjLMO6PyAHKlIDwBw&usg=AFQjCNGm-WHXihzuR9WCpKjhtdCFcrrw4w&sig2=s0kN2FS7Sk5xlvoJI390ew&bvm=bv.41642243,d.aWc.
6. "Compensation of Leading PE Managers," *Pensions&Investments,* March 27, 2013, available at: http://www.pionline.com/gallery/20130305/SLIDESHOW2/305009999/2. These figures do not include dividends received from ownership of stock in their PE firms. These cash dividend payments varied from James's $33 million to more than $100 million for Kravis and Roberts, and $204 million for Schwarzman.
7. "Comp and Circumstance," *PE Manager,* May 7, 2013, embedded in "2012 Compensation Survey Results," *PE Manager,* May 7, 2013, available at: www.privateequitymanager.com/.
8. Quoted in Coffee (2012), 1069.

9. Ibid., 1070.

10. Office of Management and Budget (2013), table S-9.

11. Peter Lattman, "Swashbucklers Transformed, and Now Much Tamer," *New York Times,* DealBook, December 11, 2012.

12. For a comprehensive analysis of the joint advantages enjoyed by LPs and GPs from this arrangement, see Sanchirico (2008).

13. "Carry May Be Ordinary Income," *PE Manager Yearbook 2012,* 30, available at: www.privateequitymanager.com/Article.aspx?article=71006 (accessed March 3, 2013).

14. Seth Hanlon and Gadi Dechter, "Congress Should Close the Carried Interest Tax Loophole," Center for American Progress, December 18, 2012, available at: http://www.americanprogress.org/issues/tax-reform/news/2012/12/18/48469/congress-should-close-the-carried-interest-loophole/ (accessed January 26, 2013).

15. Polsky (2009); Nicholas Confessore, Julie Creswell, and David Kocieniewski, "Inquiry on Tax Strategy Adds to Scrutiny of Finance Firms," *New York Times,* September 1, 2012; Floyd Norris, "A Tax Tactic That's Open to Question," *New York Times,* September 14, 2012; Victor Fleischer, "What's at Issue in the Private Equity Tax Inquiry," *New York Times,* DealBook, September 4, 2012; Mark Maremont, "IRS Examining Tax Practice Used by Private Equity Firms," *Financial News,* May 13, 2013, available at: http://www.penews.com/today/index/content/4072129617/41707/(accessed May 13, 2013).

16. For citations to academic and policy papers that make this argument, see Sanchirico (2008), note 17.

17. *What Is Carried Interest? Whiteboard Video,* Private Equity Growth Capital Council, February 6, 2013, available at: http://www.privateequityatwork.com/get-the-facts/industry-topics/(accessed February 22, 2013).

18. Sanchirico (2008), 1135.

19. For a detailed analysis of the differences between a sole proprietorship (the baker) and the GP in a PE fund, see Fleischer (2008), 32–38.

20. Sanchirico (2008).

21. See also Fleischer (2008), 10–14.

22. This tax-exempt status may entail the establishment of an offshore "blocker corporation" in a no- or low-tax jurisdiction to enable the nonprofit entity to avoid paying taxes that arise from the debt financing of investments by the PE fund.

23. For a more detailed and complete analysis of these issues, see Sanchirico (2008), 1135–45, 1151–52.

24. Rosenthal (2013).

25. A PE firm that sponsors a fund that experiences multiple bankruptcies may have difficulty raising subsequent funds. New funds, however, are typically launched at three-year intervals, before returns from the immediately preceding fund(s) may be known. Occasionally, firms with a fund that has had a particularly bad track record have not been able to raise subsequent funds. The GPs in the failing fund continue to collect management fees from LPs in these so-called zombie funds as investors wait out the contractual period of their financial commitment.

26. Nicholas Donato, "Debt Tax Shield Resurfaces in Fiscal Talks," *PE Manager,* February 26, 2013, available at: www.privateequitymanager.com/article.aspx?article=14412 (accessed February 26, 2013).

27. Nicholas Donato, "Regulators Eye Lending Standards," *PE Manager*, May 1, 2013, available at: www.privateequitymanager.com/article.aspx?article=72526 (accessed May 1, 2013).

28. AIFMD, "Directive 2011/61/EU of the European Parliament and of the Council of 8 June 2011 on Alternative Investment Fund Managers and Amending Directives 2003/41/EC and 2009/65/EC and Regulations (EC) No 1060/2009 and (EU) No 1095/2010."

29. Allen & Overy, "Analysing the Impact of the AIFM Directive," August 4, 2011, available at: www.allenovery.com/publications/en-gb/Pages/Analysing-the-Impact-of-the-AIFM-Directive.aspx (accessed March 13, 2013; updated September 6, 2013); KPMG, "Alternative Investment Fund Managers Directive: Re-shaping for the Future," KPMG, February 18, 2013, available at: http://www.kpmg.com/lu/en/issuesandinsights/articlespublications/pages/alternative-investmentfundmanagersdirective.aspx (accessed March 13, 2013).

30. Allen & Overy, "Analysing the Impact of the AIFM Directive," introduction.

31. Donna Borak, "Regulators Update Guidelines on Leveraged Lending," American Banker, March 21, 2013, available at: http://www.americanbanker.com/issues/178_56/regulators-update-guidelines-on-leveraged-lending-1057745-1.html (accessed May 1, 2013).

32. A leveraged loan is a very large commercial loan typically rated BB+ or lower (below investment grade) that carries a high rate of interest. Such loans are used in mergers and acquisitions, including, importantly, leveraged buyouts of companies by private equity funds. Other uses of leveraged loans include the recapitalization of a company's balance sheet and the refinancing of a company's debt.

33. Donato, "Regulators Eye Lending Standards"; David A. Brittenham, Christopher Rosekrans, and Satish M. Kini, "New Banking Guidance May Impact Leveraged Lending," Debevoise & Plimpton LLP, April 24, 2013, available at: http://www.lexology.com/library/detail.aspx?g=dd1d5509-db67-40ea-a0c5-6d8c5a797783 (accessed May 1, 2013); Borak, "Regulators Update Guidelines on Leveraged Lending"; "Banks Sit Out Riskier Deals," *Wall Street Journal*, Deals & Deal Makers, January 21, 2014.

34. Donato, "Regulators Eye Lending Standards"; Brittenham, Rosekrans, and Kini, "New Banking Guidance May Impact Leveraged Lending."

35. Tillman (2012).

36. Dan Primack, "Private Equity's Secret Bailout Is Ending," "Term Sheet," *Fortune*, July 28, 2013.

37. Culp and Forrester (2013) and Miller (2013).

38. GAO (2008), 52.

39. Ibid., 46. Four were U.S. commercial banks (JPMorgan Chase, Citibank, Bank of America, and Wachovia), four were U.S. investment banks or broker-dealers (Goldman Sachs, Lehman Brothers, Merrill Lynch, and Morgan Stanley), and two were foreign banks.

40. Ibid., 53.

41. Ibid., 55.

42. Culp and Forrester (2013).

43. Steven Miller, "What Is a Leveraged Loan?" LeveragedLoan.com, 2013, available at: http://www.leveragedloan.com/primer/#!refigcpbuild-outs (accessed October 18, 2013).

44. PriceWaterhouseCoopers, LLC, "The Volcker Rule Proposal: Regulators Propose Restrictions on 'Covered Funds,'" December 2011, available at: www.pwcregulatory.com (accessed January 23, 2013); *PE Manager Weekly,* January 27, 2014.

45. "Exemptions for Advisers to Venture Capital Funds, Private Fund Advisers with Less Than $150 Million in Assets Under Management, and Foreign Private Advisers," "Rules and Regulations," *Federal Register* 76(129, July 6, 2011); PriceWaterhouseCoopers, LLC, "A Closer Look: The Reporting by Private Fund Advisers on Form PF," November 2011, available at: www.pwcregulatory.com (accessed January 23, 2013); Securities and Exchange Commission, "Form PF: Frequently Asked Questions," July 2012, available at: http://www.sec.gov/divisions/investment/pfrd/pfrdfaq.shtml (accessed February 27, 2014).

46. Thompson (1991) and Presser (2003).

47. Thompson (1991) and Millon (2003).

48. Millon (2003), 25–26.

49. Ibid., 49.

50. Sale-leaseback agreements that generate cash for the business can be advantageous to a company. In the Mervyn's case, however, none of the cash generated by the sale of the chain's real estate was realized by the department store. It was the Mervyn's private equity owners that profited from the sale. Having already made a substantial return on their original investment, the inability to exit Mervyn's via an IPO or strategic acquisition did not loom large.

51. A professor of corporate law, interview with the authors, December 14, 2012.

52. Carrick Mollenkamp, "HCA Pays Owners $2 Billion," *Wall Street Journal,* November 10, 2010.

53. Pepper Hamilton & PriceWaterhouseCoopers, "Study: Majority of Private Equity Practitioners Expect Portfolio Companies to Recapitalize in the Coming Year," U.S. Newswire, March 22, 2007, available at: http://newswire.vlex.com/vid/pricewaterhousecoopers-recapitalize-193183671 (accessed March 14, 2013).

54. The tax rate on dividends and capital gains increased from 15 percent to 20 percent in 2013.

55. Cited in Arleen Jacobius, "Cheap Debt Means Private Equity Finally Pays Off," Pensions&Investments, January 7, 2013, available at: http://www.pionline.com/article/20130107/PRINTSUB/301079975/cheap-debt-means-private-equity-finally-pays-off (accessed April 4, 2013).

56. Leela Parker and Joy Ferguson, "Looming Tax Changes Drive Deals," *International Financing Review,* December 8 to 14, 2012, available at: www.ifre.com/looming-tax-changes-drive-deals/21057521.article (accessed December 16, 2012).

57. GAO (2008) and Luehrman and Scott (2007).

58. PitchBook, "Harry & David Company Profile," 2012.

59. FMag, "PE-Backed Bankruptcies," FashionMag.com, August 18, 2008, available at: http://us.fashionmag.com/news-43007-PE-backed-bankruptcies (accessed August 3, 2012).

60. Millon (2003), 43.
61. Dan Primack, "Can Europe Kill the Dividend Recap?" *Fortune,* October 31, 2012.
62. Ibid.
63. Higson (2007).
64. Jenkinson, Sousa, and Stucke (2013), 14.
65. Ibid., 15.
66. Phalippou (2012a), 15.
67. Douglas Peterson, "SEC Increases Its Scrutiny of PE Valuations," Reuters, PEHub, December 17, 2012.
68. Snow (2007), 11.
69. Jenkinson et al. (2013), 16.
70. Rick Barrett and Erin Richards, "Despite Dairy Closing, Milwaukee-Area Milk Deliveries Continue," *Milwaukee Journal Sentinel,* January 7, 2013; Jeff Engel, "Golden Guernsey Dairy Abrupt Closing Leaves Workers, State Seeking Answers," *Milwaukee Business Journal,* January 7, 2013; Jeff Engel, "Golden Guernsey Dairy Files Chapter 7 Bankruptcy," *Milwaukee Business Journal,* January 9, 2013; Thomas Content, "Waukesha Dairy Plant Golden Guernsey Suddenly Closes," *Milwaukee Journal Sentinel,* January 5, 2013; Sarah Millard, S. 2013a. "Golden Guernsey Dairy Closes Its Doors," Waukesha Patch, January 5, 2013, available at: http://waukesha.patch.com/articles/is-golden-guernsey-dairy-closed-for-good (accessed January 13, 2013); Sarah Millard, "Dairy Workers, Plant Employees Seek Answers After Golden Guernsey Closing," Muskego Patch, January 7, 2013, available at: http://muskego.patch.com/articles/dairy-workers-plant-employees-seeking-answers-after-golden-guernsey-closure (accessed January 8, 2013).
71. John J. Kalter and Tom O'Day, "New Wisconsin Law Adds Extra Requirements for Employee Notice Under Wisconsin Business Closing Law," Godfrey & Kahn Updates, January 7, 2010, available at: www.gklaw.com/news.cfin?action=pub_detail&publication_id=934 (accessed January 8, 2013); Leslie A. Sammon, "Wisconsin Business Closing and Mass Layoff Law: Wisconsin's Warn Act," Axley Attorneys, May 4, 2009, available at: http://axley.com/articles/wisconsin-warn-act-050409 (accessed January 8, 2013); Paul E. Starkman, "Responding to Economic Crises: Complying with WARN Act Obligations," paper presented at the ABA section of the Labor and Employment Law CLE Conference, Denver, September 10–13, 2008, available at: http://apps.americanbar.org/labor/lel-annualcle/08/materials/data/papers/047.pdf (accessed January 8, 2013); Jeff Engel, "Golden Guernsey Dairy Abrupt Closing Leaves Workers, State Seeking Answers," *Milwaukee Business Journal,* January 7, 2013.
72. Colin Leonard, "Warn Act Liability: Holding the Parent Liable for a Subsidiary's Failure to Give Notice," New York Labor and Employment Law Report, Bond Schoeneck & King March 5, 2010, available at: http://www.nylaborandemploymentlawreport.com/2010/03/articles/reductions-in-force/warn-act-liability-holding-the-parent-liable-for-a-subsidiarys-failure-to-give-notice/ (accessed February 27, 2014); Nathaniel R. Hull and Nicholas M. McGrath, "Warnings About the WARN Act: Catterton Partners Extension of Liability," ABI Committee News, ABI Labor and Employment

Committee, September 2010, available at: http://www.abiworld.org/committees/newsletters/employeebenefits/vol5num4/catterton.html (accessed January 8, 2013).

73. Hull and McGrath, "Warnings About the WARN Act."
74. Leonard, "Warn Act Liability."
75. Hull and McGrath, "Warnings About the WARN Act."
76. Antoine Gara, "Twinkies Defense Is Private Equity's Pension Offense: Street Whispers," The Street, November 19, 2012, available at: www.thestreet.com/story/11771361/1/twinkies-defense-is-private-equitys-pension-offense-street-whispers.html (accessed February 10, 2013).
77. U.S. District Court for the District of Massachusetts, *Sun Capital Partners III, LP et al. v. New England Teamsters and Trucking Industry Pension Fund*, Civil Action No. 10-10921-DPW, October 18, 2012, available at: http://pacer.mad.uscourts.gov/dc/opinions/woodlock/pdf/sun%20capital.pdf (accessed January 14, 2013).
78. Hazel Bradford, "Private Equity Group Backs Sun Capital Partners over Pension Liability," P&I Daily, August 15, 2013, available at: http://www.pionline.com/article/20130815/DAILYREG/130819938/private-equity-group-backs-sun-capital-partners-over-pension-liability&newsletter=daily&issue=20130815 (accessed August 18, 2013).
79. Bradford, "Private Equity Group Backs Sun Capital Partners over Pension Liability," P&I Daily, August 15, 2013, available at: http://www.pionline.com/article/20130815/DAILYREG/130819938/private-equity-group-backs-sun-capital-partners-over-pension-liability&newsletter=daily&issue=20130815 (accessed August 18, 2013).
80. U.S. District Court for the District of Massachusetts, *Sun Capital Partners III, LP et al. v. New England Teamsters and Trucking Industry Pension Fund*, 2.
81. Ibid., 3; Edwards Wildman, "Client Advisory: Potential ERISA Title IV Liabilities of Private Equity Firms—Eliminated by the Sun Capital Decision?" November 2012, available at: http://www.edwardswildman.com/files/News/fab72242-539f-496d-9456-cabc5ad7afec/Presentation/NewsAttachment/461034e0-152d-44e5-9ece-73f693dc8350/2012-CA-ERISATitleIVLiab-Nov.pdf (accessed January 14, 2013). *Metal Center News* (2007), 48.
82. U.S. District Court for the District of Massachusetts, *Sun Capital Partners III, LP et al. v. New England Teamsters and Trucking Industry Pension Fund*, 3.
83. Winston & Strawn, "District Court Limits Pension Liability Risk for Private Equity Firms," Private Equity Update, January 10, 2013, available at: www.winston.com/siteFiles/Publications/PEUpdate_January_2013.pdf (accessed March 13, 2013); Mayer Brown, "Court Rejects PBGC Position That an Investment Fund Is Part of a Controlled Group for Purposes of Pension Liabilities of a Portfolio Company," Mayer Brown Legal Update, February 8, 2013, available at: http://www.mayerbrown.com/Court-Rejects-PBGC-Position-That-an-Investment-Fund-Is-Part-of-a-Controlled-Group-for-Purposes-of-Pension-Liabilities-of-a-Portfolio-Company-02-08-2013/ (accessed March 13, 2013); Goldowitz (2003).
84. U.S. District Court for the District of Massachusetts, *Sun Capital Partners III, LP et al. v. New England Teamsters and Trucking Industry Pension Fund*, PBGC amicus curiae brief (2012).

85. Debevoise & Plimpton LLP, "Client Update: Ray of Light—Recent Decision Rejects ERISA 'Controlled Group' Liability for a Private Equity Fund," November 5, 2012, available at: http://www.debevoise.com/files/Publication/3040f740-7007-4d0f-b10a-38ee6575dfb1/Presentation/PublicationAttachment/c39c7b25-41aa-4499-a5a2-4355795fd993/Ray%20of%20Light%20—Recent%20Decision%20Rejects%20Controlled%20Group%20Liability%20for%20A%20Private%20Eq.pdf (accessed January 14, 2013).

86. Edwards Wildman, "Client Advisory: Potential ERISA Title IV Liabilities of Private Equity Firms."

87. "Commentary: How GPs Are Blocking Pension Liabilities," *PE Manager Weekly,* January 14, 2013, 1, available at: www.privateequitymanager.com/Article.aspx?aID=0&article=70316 (accessed January 14, 2013).

88. Debevoise & Plimpton, "Client Update: Ray of Light," 2.

89. Edwards Wildman, "Client Advisory: Potential ERISA Title IV Liabilities of Private Equity Firms," 2; Jack S. Levin, Alexandra Mihalas, and Jeffrey S. Quinn, "Pointers for PE Firms—Post Sun Capital ERISA Ruling," November 1, 2012, available at: http://www.kirkland.com/sitecontent.cfm?contentID=223&itemId=3222 (accessed January 21, 2013).

90. Pension Benefit Guaranty Corporation, "Brief of Amicus Curiae, Pension Benefit Guaranty Corporation, in Support of Appellant Requesting Reversal," U.S. Court of Appeals for the First Circuit, in the case of *Sun Capital Partners III, LP; Sun Capital Partners III QP, LP; Sun Capital Partners IV, LP, v. New England Teamsters & Trucking Industry Pension Fund,* December 2012.

91. Victor Fleischer, "Sun Capital Court Ruling Threatens Structure of Private Equity," *New York Times,* August 1, 2013.

92. Fleischer, "Sun Capital Court Ruling Threatens Structure of Private Equity."

93. Beth Winegarner, "Sun Capital PE Funds Count as Businesses, 1st Circ. Says," Law360, July 24, 2013, available at: http://www.law360.com/articles/459905/print?section=bankruptcy (accessed July 26, 2013).

94. Bradford, "Private Equity Group Backs Sun Capital."

95. Pension Benefit Guaranty Corporation, "Multiemployer Pension Plans: Report to Congress Required by the Pension Protection Act of 2006," January 22, 2013, available at: www.pbgc.gov/documents/pbgc-report-multiemployer-pension-plans.pdf (accessed February 1, 2013).

96. U.S. District Court for the District of Massachusetts, *Sun Capital Partners III, LP et al. v. New England Teamsters and Trucking Industry Pension Fund,* 5.

97. Josh Gotbaum, "Statement Before the ABI Commission to Study Reform of Chapter 11," Washington, D.C., March 14, 2013, available at: http://commission.abi.org/(accessed April 3, 2013).

98. J. Ronald Trost, "Another View: A New Chapter for Bankruptcies?" *New York Times,* DealBook, August 10, 2009.

99. Gotbaum, "Statement Before the ABI Commission to Study Reform of Chapter 11."

100. Ibid.

101. Alternatively, a private equity firm can buy up the secured debt of a company in danger of going bankrupt at 50 cents on the dollar. That is, it can buy $100 million of debt for $50 million. The face value of the debt will

still be $100 million even though the PE firm paid only half that amount to obtain it. This debt can then be used by the PE firm to acquire the company for one of its affiliated PE funds in what has been labeled a "loan to own" deal. Another possibility, illustrated by the Friendly's case, is a firm lending a bankrupt company funds to keep operating during bankruptcy and then using that loan to credit-bid for possession of the company.

102. Blair and Stout (1999).
103. Stout (2002), 848.
104. Shleifer and Summers (1988), 36.
105. This example builds on illustrative examples in Shleifer and Summers (1988) and Stout (2002).
106. Appelbaum et al. (2000).
107. Stone (1991), 48.
108. Wilmarth (2013), 1353.
109. Ibid., 1283–84.

═══ References ═══

Acharya, Viral V., Moritz Hahn, and Conor Kehoe. 2009. "Corporate Governance and Value Creation: Evidence from Private Equity." Available at: http://archive. nyu.edu/bitstream/2451/27878/4/Corporate%20governance%20and%20 value%20creation%20-%20viral%20acharya.pdf (accessed June 26, 2012).

Adler, John, and Jay Youngdahl. 2010. "The Odd Couple: Wall Street, Union Benefit Funds, and the Looting of the American Worker." *New Labor Forum* 19(1, Winter): 81–89.

Akerlof, George A., and Paul M. Romer. 1993. "Looting: The Economic Underworld of Bankruptcy for Profit." *Brookings Papers on Economic Activity* 24: 1–74.

Anders, George. 2002. *Merchants of Debt: KKR and the Mortgaging of American Business*. Washington, D.C.: Beard Books.

Appelbaum, Eileen, Tom Bailey, Peter Berg, and Arne Kalleberg. 2000. *Manufacturing Advantage: Why High Performance Work Systems Pay Off*. Ithaca, N.Y.: ILR Press/ Cornell University Press.

Appelbaum, Eileen, and Rosemary Batt. 2012a. "A Primer on Private Equity at Work." Working paper. Washington, D.C.: Center for Economic and Policy Research (February).

———. 2012b. "What's Wrong with Private Equity?" *Challenge* 55(5): 5–38.

Appelbaum, Eileen, Rosemary Batt, and Ian Clark. 2013. "Implications of Financial Capitalism for Employment Relations Research: Evidence from Breach of Trust and Implicit Contracts in Private Equity Buyouts." *British Journal of Industrial Relations* 51(3, September): 498–518.

Appelbaum, Eileen, Jody Hoffer Gittell, and Carrie Leana. 2011. "High Performance Work Practices and Sustainable Economic Development." Employment Policy Research Network (April 20). Available at: http://www.employmentpolicy. org/topic/23/research/high-performance-work-practices-and-sustainable-economic-growth-0 (accessed February 13, 2014).

Appelbaum, Eileen, and Ronald Schettkat. 1995. "Employment and Productivity in Industrialized Economies." *International Labor Review* 134(4–5): 605–23.

Axelson, Ulf, Tim Jenkinson, Michael Weisbach, and Per Strömberg. 2008. "Leverage and Pricing in Buyouts: An Empirical Analysis." Working paper. Stockholm: Swedish Institute for Financial Research.

Bacon, Nicolas, Mike Wright, and Natalia Demina. 2004. "Management Buyouts and Human Resource Management." *British Journal of Industrial Relations* 42(2): 325–47.

Badertscher, Brad, Sharon P. Katz, and Sonja Olhoft Rego. 2011. "The Impact of Private Equity Ownership on Portfolio Firms' Corporate Tax Avoidance." Unpublished paper. Notre Dame University, South Bend, Ind. (June).

Baker, George P., and George David Smith. 1998. *The New Financial Capitalists: Kohlberg Kravis Roberts and the Creation of Corporate Value.* New York: Cambridge University Press.

Ball, Corinne, Henry Miller, and Ted Stenger. 2009. "Liberating a Business from Its History: The Turnaround of Dana Corporation." *Journal of Private Equity* 12(3): 29–38.

Batt, Rosemary, and Eileen Appelbaum. 2012. "Mondialisation, nouveaux acteurs financiers, et changement institutionnel: Réflexions sur l'héritage du LEST" ("Globalization, New Financial Actors, and Institutional Change: Reflections on the Legacy of LEST"). In *Travail, competences, et mondialisation: Les dynamiques sociétales en question* (*Work, Skills, and Globalization: Societal Dynamics in Question*), edited by Ariel Mendez, Robert Tchobanian, and Antoine Vion. Paris: Armand Colin, Coll Recherches.

Beck, Matthias. 2010. "New Financial Elites, or Financial Dualism in Historical Perspective? An Extended Reply to Folkman, Froud, Johal and Williams." *Business History* 52(7): 1027–47.

Becker, Gary S. 1964. *Human Capital: A Theoretical and Empirical Analysis, with Special Reference to Education.* Chicago and London: University of Chicago Press.

Becker, Bo, and Josh Pollet. 2008. "The Decision to Go Private." Unpublished paper. Available at: http://goizueta.emory.edu/faculty/cai/documents/buyouts 080715.pdf (accessed January 9, 2014).

Beeferman, Larry. 2009. "Private Equity and American Labor: Multiple, Pragmatic Responses Mirroring Labor's Strengths and Weaknesses." *Journal of Industrial Relations* 51(4): 543–56.

Berger, Allen N., and Gregory F. Udell. 1998. "The Economics of Small Business Finance: The Roles of Private Equity and Debt Markets in the Financial Growth Cycle." *Journal of Banking and Finance* 22: 613–73.

———. 2002. "Small Business Credit Availability and Relationship Lending: The Importance of Bank Organizational Structure." *Economic Journal* 112(477): F32–53.

Berger, Allen N., Lawrence G. Goldberg, and Lawrence J. White. 2001. "The Effects of Dynamic Changes in Bank Competition on the Supply of Small Business Credit." *European Finance Review* 5(2): 115–39.

Berle, Adolf A., and Gardiner C. Means. 1932. *The Modern Corporation and Private Property.* New York: Harcourt, Brace, and World.

Bernstein, Peter L. 2005. *Capital Ideas: The Improbable Origins of Modern Wall Street.* Hoboken, N.J.: John Wiley & Sons, Inc.

Blair, Margaret M., and Lynn A. Stout. 1999. "A Team Production Theory of Corporate Law." *Virginia Law Review* 85: 247–328.

Bolton, Patrick, Tano Santos, and Jose A. Scheinkman. 2012. "Shadow Finance." Paper presented to the Russell Sage Foundation and Century Foundation conference "Rethinking Finance: New Perspectives on the Crisis." New York (April 13).

Braun, Reiner, Tim Jenkinson, and Ingo Stoff. 2013. "How Persistent Is Private Equity Performance? Evidence from Deal-Level Data." Working Paper (August). Available at: http://papers.ssrn.com/sol3/papers.cfm?abstract_id=2314400 (accessed October 26, 2013).

Brenner, Menachem, and Yehuda Izhakian. 2012. "Pricing Systematic Ambiguity in Capital Markets," Working paper (July). Available at: http://papers.ssrn.com/sol3/papers.cfm?abstract_id=%202119040 (accessed February 13, 2014).

Breslow, Stephanie, and Phyllis Schwartz. 2011. "Structuring Waterfall Distributions." *Practical Law Publishing Limited and Practical Law Company, Inc.* Available at: http://www.srz.com/files/News/8c5570af-2547-46e9-9bf3-79bcb2329aa8/Presentation/NewsAttachment/2c0a2ea1-0d89-4875-99de-7a7a7073ecb8/Breslow_Schwartz_Practical_Law_Journal_June_2011_Structuring_Waterfall_Provisions.pdf (accessed May 24, 2013).

Buchanan, James M. 1980. "Rent Seeking and Profit Seeking." In *Toward a Theory of the Rent-Seeking Society,* edited by James M. Buchanan, Gordon Tullock, and Robert. D. Tollison. College Station: Texas A&M University Press.

Cappelli, Peter. 1999. *The New Deal at Work: Managing the Market-Based Employment Relationship.* Boston: Harvard Business School Press.

Carey, David, and John E. Morris. 2010. *King of Capital: The Remarkable Rise, Fall, and Rise Again of Steve Schwarzman and Blackstone.* New York: Corwn Publishing Group, Random House.

Casson, Joseph E. and Julia McMillen. 2003. "Limiting Liability Through Corporate Restructuring." *Journal of Health Law,* 36(4, Fall): 577–613.

CFA Centre for Financial Market Integrity and the Business Roundtable Institute for Corporate Ethics. 2006. "Breaking the Short-Term Cycle." July. Available at: http://www.cfainstitute.org/learning/products/publications/ccb/Pages/ccb.v2006.n1.4194.aspx (accessed February 1, 2014).

Chakraborty, Atreya, Michael Weisbach, and Bin Zhou 2009. "Litigation Facing the Private Equity Industry." *Finance: Current Topics in Corporate Finance* (The Brattle Group) 1: 1–11.

Chandler, Alfred D., Jr. 1954. "Patterns of American Railroad Finance, 1830–1850." *Business History Review* 28: 248–63.

———. 1977. *The Visible Hand: The Managerial Revolution in American Business.* Cambridge, MA: Belknap Press of Harvard University Press.

———. 1994. *Scale and Scope: The Dynamism of Industrial Capitalism.* Cambridge, MA: Harvard University Press.

Christensen, Clayton M., Richard Alton, Curtis Rising, and Andrew Waldeck. 2011. "The Big Idea: The New M&A Playbook." *Harvard Business Review* 89(3): 48–57.

Clark, Ian. 2009. "Owners Not Managers: Disconnecting Managerial Capitalism? Understanding the Take Private Equity Business Model." *Work, Employment, and Society* 23(4, December): 775–86.

Coffee, John C., Jr. 2012. "The Political Economy of Dodd-Frank: Why Financial Reform Tends to Be Frustrated and Systemic Risk Perpetuated." *Cornell Law Review* 97(5): 1019–82.

Croft, Thomas. 2009. *Up From Wall Street: The Responsible Investment Alternative.* New York: Cosimo.

Culp, C. L., and J. P. Forrester. 2013. "U.S. Structured Finance Markets: Recent Recovery, Post-Crisis Developments, and Ongoing Regulatory Uncertainties." *Journal of Structured Finance* 18(1): 10–28.

Davis, Brian E., Robert Middleton, and Gregory Spitzer. 2007. "Sale-Leaseback Transactions in Today's Private Equity Environment." *Venture Capital Review* (Spring): 7–11.

Davis, Gerald F. 2009. *Managed by the Markets: How Finance Reshaped the Markets.* Oxford: Oxford University Press.

Davis, Gerald F., Kristina A. Diekmann, and Catherine H. Tinsley. 1994. "The Decline and Fall of the Conglomerate Firm in the 1980s: The De-institutionalization of an Organizational Form." *American Sociological Review* 59: 547–70.

Davis, Gerald F., and Suzanne K. Stout. 1992. "Organization Theory and the Market for Corporate Control: A Dynamic Analysis of the Characteristics of Large Takeover Targets, 1980–1990." *Administrative Science Quarterly* 37: 605–33.

Davis, Steven J., John C. Haltiwanger, Ron S. Jarmin, Josh Lerner, and Javier Miranda. 2008. "Private Equity and Employment." In *Globalization of Alternative Investments,* Working Papers, vol. 1, *Global Economic Impact of Private Equity 2009,* edited by Anuradha Gurung and Javier Lerner. New York: World Economic Forum USA. Available at: http://www3.weforum.org/docs/WEF_IV_Private Equity_Report_2008.pdf (accessed December 29, 2013).

———. 2009. "Private Equity, Jobs, and Productivity." In *Globalization of Alternative Investments,* Working Papers, vol. 2, *Global Economic Impact of Private Equity,* edited by Anuradha Gurung and Javier Lerner. New York: World Economic Forum USA. Available at: http://www.weforum.org/reports/global-economic-impact-private-equity-report-2009-globalization-alternative-investments-work (accessed December 29, 2013).

———. 2011. "Private Equity and Employment." Working Paper 17399. Cambridge, Mass.: National Bureau of Economic Research. Available at: http://www.nber.org/papers/w17399 (accessed December 22, 2011).

Davis, Steven J., John C. Haltiwanger, Kyle Handley, Ron S. Jarmin, Josh Lerner, and Javier Miranda. 2013. "Private Equity, Jobs, and Productivity." NBER Working Paper 19458. Cambridge. MA: National Bureau of Economic Research. Available at http://www.nber.org/papers/w19458 (accessed December 29, 2013).

Davis, Steven J., and Von Wachter, Till. 2011. "Recessions and the Costs of Job Loss." *Brookings Papers on Economic Activity.* November. Available at: http://www.columbia.edu/~vw2112/) (accessed January 9, 2013).

De Mooij, Ruud A. 2011. "Tax Biases to Debt Finance: Assessing the Problem, Finding Solutions." Staff Discussion Note. Washington, D.C.: International Monetary Fund (May 3).

Dodd, Merrick. 1932. "For Whom are Corporate Managers Trustees?" *Harvard Law Review,* 155 (7): 1145-1163.

Doeringer, Peter B., and Michael J. Piore. 1971. *Internal Labor Markets and Manpower Analysis.* Lexington, Mass.: Lexington Books.

Donaldson, Gordon. 1984. *Managing Corporate Wealth.* New York: Praeger.

———. 1994. *Corporate Restructuring: Managing the Change Process from Within.* Boston: Harvard Business School Press.

Employee Benefit Security Administration (EBSA). 2008. "Interpretive Bulletin Relating to Investing in Economically Targeted Investments." *Federal Register* 73(202, October 17).

Europa. 2010. "Directive on Alternative Investment Fund Managers ('AIFMD'): Frequently Asked Questions." Press Release from the Directorate General Communication of the European Commission. Brussels: European Commission. Available at: http://europa.eu/rapid/pressReleasesAction.do?reference=MEMO/10/572&format=HTML&aged=0&language=EN&guiLanguage=en (accessed February 13, 2014).

European Union. 2011. "Directive 2011/61/EU of the European Parliament and of the Council of 8 June 2011 on Alternative Investment Fund Managers and amending Directives 2003/41/EC and 2009/65/EC." Official Journal of the European Union, June. l_17420110701en00010073.pdf. Available at: http://eur-lex.europa.eu (accessed January 1, 2012).

Fama, Eugene F. and Michael C. Jensen. 1983. "Separation of Ownership and Control." *Journal of Law and Economics* 26(2): 301–25.

Fleischer, Victor. 2008. "Two and Twenty: Taxing Partnership Profits in Private Equity Funds." *New York University Law Review* 83(1, April): 1–58.

———. 2010. "Regulatory Arbitrage." *Texas Law Review* 89: 227–89.

Fligstein, Neil. 1990. *The Transformation of Corporate Control.* Cambridge, MA: Harvard University Press.

———. 2001. *The Architecture of Markets.* Princeton, N.J.: Princeton University Press.

Folkman, Peter, Julie Froud, Karel Williams, and Sukhdev Johal. 2009. "Private Equity: Levered on Capital or Labour?" *Journal of Industrial Relations* 51: 517–27.

Froud, Julie, Johal Sukhdev, Adam Leaver, and Karel Williams. 2008. "Ownership Matters: Private Equity and the Political Division of Ownership." Working paper 61. Manchester, UK: University of Manchester, Centre for Research on Socio-Cultural Change (CRESC) (December).

Froud, Julie, and Karel Williams. 2007. "Private Equity and the Culture of Value Extraction." *New Political Economy* 12(3, September): 405–20.

Goldberg, Lena, Robert Pozen, and Melissa Hammerle. 2010. *Note: Disclosure, Regulation, and Taxation of Hedge Funds versus Mutual Funds in the U.S.* 9-310-131. Cambridge, MA: Harvard Business School, August 28.

Goldowitz, I. 2003. "Special Rules for Multiemployer Plans." In *ERISA Litigation,* 3rd ed., edited by Jayne E. Zanglein and Susan J. Stabile. Arlington, Va.: Bureau of National Affairs (BNA).

Gompers, Paul A., and Andrew Metrick. 2001. "Institutional Investors and Equity Prices." *Quarterly Journal of Economics* 116(1): 229–59.

Gospel, Howard, Andrew Pendleton, and Sigurt Vitols, eds. 2014. *Financialisation, New Investment Funds, and Labour: An International Comparison.* Oxford: Oxford University Press.

Government Accountability Office (GAO). 2008. "Recent Growth in Leveraged Buyouts Exposed Risks That Warrant Continued Attention." Report 08-885. Washington: GAO (September). Available at: http://www.gao.gov/products/GAO-08-885 (accessed July 17, 2012).

———. 2009. *Hospital Emergency Departments: Crowding Continues to Occur.* Washington, D.C.: GAO (April). Available at: http://www.gao.gov/new.items/d09347.pdf (accessed July 9, 2012).

Hall, Brian J., and Jeffrey B. Liebman. 1998. "Are CEOs Really Paid Like Bureaucrats?" *Quarterly Journal of Economics* 112(3): 653–91.

Hammer, Tove H., and Robert N. Stern. 1986. "The Yo-Yo Model of Union-Management Cooperation: Union Participation in Management at the Rath Packing Company." *Industrial and Labor Relations Review* 39: 337–49.

Harner, Michelle M. 2008. "The Corporate Governance and Public Policy Implications of Activist Distressed Debt Investing." *Fordham Law Review* 77(November): 703–74.

Harris, Robert S., Tim Jenkinson, and Steven N. Kaplan. 2013. "Private Equity Performance: What Do We Know?" Working paper. Cambridge, Mass.: National Bureau of Economic Research (April). Available at: http://ssrn.com/abstract=1932316 (accessed May 20, 2013).

Hawley, James, Keith Johnson, and Ed Waitzer. 2011. "Reclaiming Fiduciary Duty Balance." *Rotman International Journal of Pension Management* 4(2, Fall): 4–16.

Hayes, Robert H., and Willliam J. Abernathy, 1980. "Managing Our Way to Economic Decline." *Harvard Business Review*, 58(4): 67–77

Higson, Chris. 2007. "The Privacy of Private Equity." Unpublished paper. London Business School, London (November). Available at: http://www.docstoc.com/docs/40312002/THE-PRIVACY-OF-PRIVATE-EQUITY (last accessed January 31, 2013).

Higson, Chris, and Rüdiger Stucke. 2012. "The Performance of Private Equity" Working Paper (March). Available at: http://ssrn.com/abstract=2009067 (accessed May 16, 2013).

Holland, Max. 1989. *When the Machine Stopped: Cautionary Tale from Industrial America.* Boston: Harvard Business School Press.

Holmstrom, Bengt, and Steven N. Kaplan. 2001. "Corporate Governance and Merger Activity in the United States: Making Sense of the 1980s and 1990s." *Journal of Economic Perspectives* 15(2): 121–44.

Hoskisson, Robert, Wei Shi, Xiwei Yi, and Jing Jin. 2013. "The Evolution and Strategic Positioning of Private Equity Firms." *Academy of Management Perspectives* 27(1): 22–38.

Hotchkiss, Edie, David C. Smith, and Per J. Strömberg. 2012. "Private Equity and the Resolution of Financial Distress." Unpublished paper (July). Available at: http://www.law.uchicago.edu/files/files/Stromberg.pdf (accessed February 13, 2014).

Hudec, Albert. 2010. "Negotiating Private Equity Fund Terms: The Shifting Balance of Power." *Business Law Today* (American Bar Association) 19(5, May-June). Available at: http://apps.americanbar.org/buslaw/blt/2010-05-06/hudec.shtml (accessed May 24, 2013).

Jarrell, Gregg A. 1983. "State Anti-Takeover Laws and the Efficient Allocation of Corporate Control: An Economic Analysis of *Edgar v. Mite Corp.*" *Supreme Court Economic Review* 2: 111–29.

Jenkinson, Tim, Miguel Sousa, and Rüdiger Stucke. 2013. "How Fair Are the Valuations of Private Equity Funds?" Working Paper (February 27). Available at: http://ssrn.com/abstract=2229547 (accessed May 4, 2013).

Jensen, Michael. 1986. "Agency Costs of Free Cash Flow, Corporate Finance, and Takeovers." *American Economic Review* 76(2): 323–29.

Jensen, Michael C., and William H. Meckling. 1976. "Theory of the Firm: Managerial Behavior, Agency Cost, and Ownership Structure." *Journal of Financial Economics* 3: 305–60.

Jensen, Michael C., and Kevin J. Murphy. 1990. "CEO Incentives—It's Not How Much You Pay But How." *Harvard Business Review* (May-June): 138–53.

Jickling, Mark, and Donald J. Marples. 2007. "Taxation of Hedge Fund and Private Equity Managers." Report RS22689. Washington: Congressional Research Service (July 5).

Johnson, Keith L., and Frank Jan de Graaf. 2009. "Modernizing Pension Fund Legal Standards for the Twenty-First Century." *Rotman International Journal of Pension Management* 2(1): 44–51.

Jung, Jiwook. 2011. "Shareholder Value and Workforce Downsizing, 1984–2006." Unpublished paper. Department of Sociology, National University of Singapore.

Jung, Jiwook, and Frank Dobbin. 2012. "Finance and Institutional Investors." In *The Oxford Handbook of the Sociology of Finance*, edited by Karen Knorr Cetina and Alex Preda. Oxford: Oxford University Press.

Kalleberg, Arne. 2009. "Precarious Work, Insecure Workers: Employment Relations in Transition." *American Sociological Review* 74(February): 1–22.

Kanter, Rosabeth M. 1989. *When Giants Learn to Dance: Mastering the Challenges of Strategy, Management, and Careers in the 1990s.* New York: Simon & Schuster.

Kaplan, Steven N. 1997. "The Evolution of U.S. Corporate Governance: We Are All Henry Kravis Now." *Journal of Private Equity* (Fall): 7–14.

———. 1989. "Management Buyouts: Evidence on Taxes as a Source of Value." *Journal of Financial Economics* 24(2): 217–54.

Kaplan, Steven N., and Antoinette Schoar. 2005. "Private Equity Performance: Returns, Persistence, and Capital Flows." *Journal of Finance* 60: 1791–1823.

Kaplan, Steven N., and Per Strömberg. 2009. "Leveraged Buyouts and Private Equity." *Journal of Economic Perspectives* 23(1): 121–46.

Katz, Harry. 1995. "The Decentralization of Collective Bargaining." *Industrial and Labor Relations Review* 47(1): 3–23.

Kaufman, Allen, and Ernest J. Englander. 1993. "Kohlberg Kravis Roberts & Co. and the Restructuring of American Capitalism." *Business History Review* 67(1): 52–97.

Kochan, Thomas, Eileen Appelbaum, Carrie Leana, and Jody Hoffer Gittell. 2013. "The Human Capital Dimensions of Sustainable Investment." Paper presented to the Sustainable Investment Research Initiative Sustainability and Finance Symposium. University of California, Davis (June 7). Available at: http://www.cepr.net/index.php/publications/reports/human-capital-dimensions-of-sustainable-investment (accessed March 13, 2013).

Kochan, Thomas, Harry Katz, and Robert McKersie. 1986. *The Transformation of American Industrial Relations.* New York: Basic Books.

Lazonick, William. 1992. "Controlling the Market for Corporate Control: The Historical Significance of Managerial Capitalism." *Industrial and Corporate Change* 1(3): 445–88.

———. 2011. "Reforming the Financialized Business Corporation." Unpublished paper. University of Massachusetts, Lowell (January).

Lazonick, William, and Mary O'Sullivan. 2000. "Maximizing Shareholder Value: A New Ideology for Corporate Governance." *Economy and Society* 29(1): 13–35.

Loomis, Carol J. 2005. "KKR: The Sequel: Older and Wiser, the Former Buyout Kings Are Still in the Thick of the Wall Street Action." *Fortune,* June 13.

Lowenstein, Roger. 2004. *Origins of the Crash: The Great Bubble and Its Undoing.* London: Penguin.

Luehrman, Timothy A., and Douglas C. Scott. 2007. "The Hertz Corporation (A)." Harvard Business School Case. Boston: Harvard Business School (October). Available at: http://www.hbs.edu/faculty/Pages/item.aspx?num=35057 (accessed February 13, 2014).

Lydenberg, Steve. 2009. "Beyond Risk: Notes Toward Responsible Alternatives for Investment Theory." Working Paper (October 13).

———. 2012. "Reason, Rationality, and Fiduciary Duty." Top paper. New York: Investor Responsibility Research Center (IRRC) (February 21).

Markowitz, Harry. 1952. "Portfolio Selection." *Journal of Finance* 7(1): 77–91.

Marples, Donald J. 2008. "Taxation of Private Equity and Hedge Fund Partnerships: Characterization of Carried Interest." Report RS22717. Washington: Congressional Research Service (July 8).

McCue, Michael, and Jon Thompson. 2012. "The Impact of HCS's 2006 Leveraged Buyout on Hospital Performance." *Journal of Healthcare Management* 57(5): 342–56.

Metal Center News. 2007. "Scott Brass Acquired by Sun Capital Partners." *Metal Center News* 47(3, March 2007).

Metrick, Andrew, and Ayako Yasuda. 2009/2011. "The Economics of Private Equity Funds." Paper presented to the Swedish Institute for Financial Research Conference. Stockholm, June 9, 2009. Available at: http://ssrn.com/abstract=996334 (page numbers refer to this paper). Subsequently published in *Review of Financial Studies* 23 (2011): 2303–41.

———. 2010. "Venture Capital and Other Private Equity." Working paper. New Haven, Conn.: Yale University School of Management (December).

Millon, David. 2003. "Piercing the Corporate Veil, Financial Responsibility, and the Limits of Limited Liability." Public Law and Legal Theory Research Paper Series. Working Paper 03-13. Lexington City, Va.: Washington & Lee University (September).

Mitchell, Mark L., and J. Harold Mulherin. 1996. "The Impact of Industry Shocks on Takeover and Restructuring Activity." *Journal of Financial Economics* 41(2): 193–229.

Office of Management and Budget (OMB). 2013. "Summary Tables." In *Budget of the United States Government, Fiscal Year 2014.* Washington, D.C.: OMB (April 10). Available at: http://www.whitehouse.gov/omb/budget/Overview (accessed April 10, 2013).

Oi, Walter. 1962. "Labor as a Quasi-Fixed Factor." *Journal of Political Economy* 70(6): 538–55.

Osterman, Paul. 1984. *Internal Labor Markets.* Cambridge, Mass: MIT Press.

Paglia, John K., and Maretno A. Harjoto. 2012. "Did They Build That? The Role of Private Equity and Venture Capital in Small and Medium-Sized Businesses." Unpublished paper. Pepperdine University, Graziadio School of Business and Management, Malibu, Calif. (November 16). Available at: http://bschool.pepperdine.edu/newsroom/wp-content/uploads/2012/12/Paglia-Harjoto-PE-VC-11.29.2012-IEGC.pdf (accessed January 25, 2013).

Palley, Thomas. 2007. "Financialization: What It Is and Why It Matters." Working Paper 525. Annandale-on-Hudson, NY: Bard College, Levy Economics Institute.

Phalippou, Ludovic. 2008. "The Hazards of Using IRR to Measure Performance: The Case of Private Equity." Working paper. Amsterdam: University of Amsterdam. Available at: http://ssrn.com/abstract=1111796 (accessed March 20, 2013).

———. 2011. "Why Is the Evidence on Private Equity Performance So Confusing?" Working Paper (September). Available at: http://ssrn.com/abstract=1864503 (accessed August 18, 2012).

———. 2012a. "A Comment on Recent Evidence on Private Equity Performance." Working Paper. Oxford: University of Oxford, Oxford-Man Institute (November). Available at: http://papers.ssrn.com/abstract=1969101 (accessed March 14, 2013).

———. 2012b. "Performance of Buyout Funds Revisited?" Working Paper. Oxford: University of Oxford, Said Business School (June). Available at: http://ssrn.com/abstract=1969101 (accessed March 20, 2013).

Phalippou, Ludovic, and Oliver Gottschalg. 2009. "The Performance of Private Equity Funds." *Review of Financial Studies* 22(4): 1747–76.

Platt, Harlan D. 2009. "The Private Equity Myth." *Journal of Business Valuation and Economic Loss Analysis* 4: 1–17.

Polsky, Gregg D. 2009. "Private Equity Management Fee Conversions." *Tax Notes* 122(7). Available at: http://papers.ssrn.com/sol3/papers.cfm?abstract_id=1342030## (accessed October 18, 2013).

Prahalad, C. K., and Gary Hamel. 1990. "The Core Competencies of the Corporation." *Harvard Business Review* 68(3): 79–91.

Presser, Stephen B. 2003. *Piercing the Corporate Veil.* Eagan, Minn.: West Publications.

Private Equity Growth Capital Council (PEGCC). 2007. *Public Value: A Primer on Private Equity.* Washington, D.C.: PEGCC. Available at: http://www.pegcc.org/research/private-equity-and-economic-white-papers-from-the-pegcc/ (accessed May 16, 2013).

Rattner, Steven. 2010. *Overhaul: An Insider's Account of the Obama Administration's Emergency Rescue of the Auto Industry.* New York: Houghton Mifflin Harcourt.

Rifkin, Jeremy, and Randy Barber. 1978. *The North Will Rise Again: Pensions, Politics, and Power in the 1980s.* Boston: Beacon Press.

Robinson, David T., and Berk A. Sensoy. 2011. "Cyclicality, Performance Measurement, and Cash Flow Liquidity in Private Equity." Working paper 2010-021. Columbus: Ohio State University, Charles A. Dice Center (September). Available at: www.ssrn.com/abstract=1731603 (accessed May 6, 2013).

Rosenthal, Steven M. 2013. "Taxing Private Equity Funds as Corporate 'Developers.'" Washington, D.C.: Tax Policy Center of the Urban Institute and Brookings Institution (January 21). Available at: http://www.urban.org/publications/901552.html (accessed February 21, 2013).

Sanchirico, Chris William. 2008. "The Tax Advantage to Paying Private Equity Fund Managers with Profit Shares: What Is It? Why Is It Bad?" *University of Chicago Law Review* 75: 1071–53.

Senbet, Lemma W., and Tracy Yue Wang. 2012. "Corporate Financial Distress and Bankruptcy: A Survey." April. Available at: www.papers.ssrn.com/sol3/papers.cfm?abstract_id=2034646 (accessed June 10, 2012).

Shleifer, Andrei, and Lawrence H. Summers. 1988. "Breach of Trust in Hostile Takeovers." In *Corporate Takeovers: Causes and Consequences,* edited by Alan J. Auerbach. Cambridge, Mass.: National Bureau of Economic Research.

Singh, Kavaljit. 2008. *Taking It Private: The Global Consequences of Private Equity.* Dorset, UK: The Corner House.

Snow, D. 2007. *Private Equity: A Brief Overview*, Private Equity International PEIMedia. Available at: http://www.peimedia.com/resources/PEI50/PEI Media's Private Equity-A Brief Overview.pdf (accessed February 13, 2014).

Stone, Katherine van Wezel. 1991. "Employees as Stakeholders Under State Non-shareholder Constituency Statues." *Stetson Law Review* 21: 45–72.

Stout, Lynn A. 2002. "Do Antitakeover Defenses Decrease Shareholder Wealth? The Ex Post/Ex Ante Valuation Problem." *Stanford Law Review* 55: 845–61.

———. 2012. *The Shareholder Value Myth: How Putting Shareholders First Harms Investors, Corporations and the Public.* San Francisco: Berrett-Koehler.

Strömberg, Per. 2008. "The New Demography of Private Equity." The Globalization of Alternative Investments Working Papers, vol. 1, *The Global Economic Impact of Private Equity Report 2008.* New York and Geneva: World Economic Forum (January).

Strömberg, Per, Edie S. Hotchkiss, and David C. Smith. 2011. "Private Equity and the Resolution of Financial Distress." ECGI-Finance Working Paper 331/2012. Available at: http://ssrn.com/abstract=1787446 (accessed May 8, 2012).

Temple, Peter. 1999. *Private Equity: Examining the New Conglomerates of European Business.* New York: Wiley.

Thompson, Paul. 2003. "Disconnected Capitalism: Or Why Employers Can't Keep Their Side of the Bargain." *Work, Employment, and Society* 17(2): 359–78.

Thompson, Robert B. 1991. "Piercing the Corporate Veil: An Empirical Study." *Cornell Law Review* 76: 1036–74.

Tillman, Joseph A. 2012. "Beyond the Crisis: Dodd-Frank and Private Equity." *New York University Law Review* 87: 1602–40.

Useem, Michael. 1996. *Investor Capitalism: How Money Managers Are Changing the Face of Corporate America.* New York: Basic Books.

Wagner, Alan. 2013. "Secondary Buyouts Make 3Q Comeback, PitchBook Data Show." PitchBook Blog. September 30, 2013. http://blog.pitchbook.com/secondary-buyouts-make-comeback-in-3q-new-pitchbook-data-show-2/ (accessed December 23, 2013).

Waitzer, Ed. 2009. "Defeating Short-Termism: Why Pension Funds Must Lead." *Rotman International Journal of Pension Management* 2(2): 4–8.

Watt, Chad Eric. 2008. "Gaining Insight While Most Are Pulling Back." *Dallas Business Journal,* November 7–13.

Wilmarth, Arthur E., Jr. 2013. "Turning a Blind Eye: Why Washington Keeps Giving In to Wall Street," *University of Cincinnati Law Review* 81: 1283–1446.

Wood, Geoffrey, and Mike Wright. 2010. "Wayward Agents, Dominant Elite, or Reflection of Internal Diversity? A Critique of Folkman, Froud, Johal and Williams on Financialization and Financial Intermediaries." *Business History* 52(7): 1048–67.

Wright, Mike. 2013. "Symposium: Private Equity: Managerial and Policy Implications." *Academy of Management Perspectives* 27(1): 1–6.

Yermo, Juan, and Clara Severinson. 2010. *The Impact of the Financial Crisis on Defined Benefit Plans and the Need for Counter-Cyclical Funding Regulations.* Paris: OECD Publishing.

Youngdahl, Jay. 2012. "The Time Has Come for a Sustainable Theory of Fiduciary Duty of Investment." *Hofstra Labor and Employment Law Journal* 29(115): 115–39.

Zorn, Dirk M. 2004. "Here a Chief, There a Chief: The Rise of the CFO in the American Firm." *American Sociological Review* 69(June): 345–64.

Zorn, Dirk, Frank Dobbin, Julian Dierkes, and Man-Shan Kwok. 2005. "Managing Investors: How Financial Markets Reshaped the American Firm." In *The Sociology of Financial Markets*, edited by Karen Knorr-Cetina and Alex Preda. Oxford: Oxford University Press.

Zuckerman, Ezra W. 2000. "Focusing the Corporate Product: Securities Analysts and De-diversification." *Administrative Science Quarterly* 45: 591–619.

═ Index ═

Boldface numbers refer to figures and tables.